D1601436

Thinking Past a Problem

Thinking Past a Problem

Essays on the History of Ideas

PRESTON KING

D
16.9
.K53
2000
West

FRANK CASS
LONDON • PORTLAND, OR

First published in 2000 in Great Britain by
FRANK CASS PUBLISHERS
Newbury House, 900 Eastern Avenue
London, IG2 7HH

and in the United States of America by
FRANK CASS PUBLISHERS
c/o ISBS, 5804 N.E. Hassalo Street
Portland, Oregon, 97213-3644

Website: www.frankcass.com

Copyright © 2000 Preston King

British Library Cataloguing in Publication Data

King, Preston, 1936–
Thinking past a problem: essays on the history of ideas
1. Idea (Philosophy) 2. Idea (Philosophy) – History 3. History
– Philosophy
I. Title
121.4

ISBN 0-7146-4980-5 (cloth)
ISBN 0-7146-8042-7 (paper)

Library of Congress Cataloging-in-Publication Data

King, Preston, 1936–
Thinking past a problem: essays on the history of ideas / Preston
King
    p. cm.
Includes bibliographical references and index.
ISBN 0–7146–4980–5 (cloth). — ISBN 0–7146–8042–7 (pbk.)
1. History – Philosophy. 2. Idea (Philosophy) I. Title.
D.16.9.K53 1999
901–dc21   99-29124
                                                                   CIP

*All rights reserved. No part of this publication may be reproduced, stored in
or introduced into a retrieval system or transmitted in any form or by any
means, electronic, mechanical, photocopying, recording or otherwise, without
the prior written permission of the publisher of this book.*

Typeset by Vitaset, Paddock Wood, Kent
Printed in Great Britain by
The Book Company, Ipswich, Suffolk

In memory of Michael Oakeshott

Contents

Acknowledgements

Chapters 2, 3, 4 and 5 are all slightly modified versions of Chapters 1, 2, 4 and 12 of my 1983 *The History of Ideas: An Introduction to Method* (Croom Helm), though not in that order. Chapter 6 first appeared as the Introduction, Vol. 1, to my 1993 *Thomas Hobbes: Critical Assessments* (Routledge). Chapter 7 first appeared in 1995 in *History of European Ideas* (21:2, 209–33). Chapter 8 was first published in 1996 in *Politics* (16:3, 187–98). Chapter 9 was earlier published in 1990 in *British Society for the History of Philosophy Newsletter* (Spring, 24–42). Chapter 10 was written at the invitation of *The History of Political Thought*, but was never published there. Chapter 11 was first published in 1968 in *Politics and Experience* (Cambridge University Press). Chapter 12 was first published in *Political Quarterly*, 1976.

1

Introduction

1

This volume brings together several essays which have mostly appeared elsewhere. They attend to a cluster of problems from divergent and overlapping angles. The treatment is not as systematic as I had wished; indeed, there have been obstacles enough to getting as far as this. But I hope that the core question is caught by the title of the book, taken from the opening essay. This invokes the embeddedness of the past in, and the sly complexity of, what we may call – too summarily and unblinkingly – 'the present'. The concern is not to supply or to defend or to attack some particular historical account (such as may be found in the Book of Genesis or Marx or Toynbee), nor a history of ideas (as by George Sabine or Sheldon Wolin or Iain Hampsher-Monk), nor really a history of the history of ideas (despite the limited account along these lines offered in Chapter 3 and the relevant section in Chapter 11). The focus, rather, is more upon philosophies of history and, *a fortiori*, upon philosophies of the history of *ideas*. The thrust of my book *The History of Ideas: An Introduction to Method* (King, 1983) was to do with noting and debating the merits of key figures and theories widely recognized to constitute that book's subject. The object here, by contrast, is to assemble only my own essays in this area, published before, in and after my book in 1983. The present collection has at least the merit of convenience, while the reader may be left to judge the true merits of the convenience.

I work from the assumption that all history is, broadly, some form of history of ideas, and that the initial problem is to identify the distinct type of idea which one's history may be to do with. Any matter of concern to us, on the assumption that it has duration, may be approached in principle from an historical angle. The subject can be concrete, like 'Gladstone'; it may be abstract, like 'progress'. It can be grand and deal with the rise and fall of a vast empire (Gibbon), or with the rise and fall of entire civilizations (von der Muhl), or so grand as to extend even to the 'History of the Concept of Time' (Heidegger). But history equally focuses upon somewhat narrower terrain, such as serfdom in Saxony in the fourteenth century, or *El Consejo supremo* in Aragon under Felipe II, or Samuel Parker and the Church of England of yesteryear. I find it notoriously difficult to see what history cannot embrace: infancy, 'prehistory'; biology, astronomy; marriage, disease, war; politics, physics, philosophy. Philosophy is axiomatically implicated in most of what we term 'the history of ideas', 'the history of thought', whether political, economic, social, scientific or other.

I take it that thinking is a form of action, as where one solves a puzzle or composes an essay or tries to defuse some larger difficulty, though it will not do to claim that action in turn necessarily involves thinking. The thinking and writing of history proceed from positing some concern or concept, answering questions regarding it, but within a clearly temporal framework, and not as Eternity. As to the *scale* of the enterprise, who is to say what this must be? It may be as broad or narrow as is allowed by the nature of the question, plus the evidence bearing on it. It is not tenable to suppose that history is *only* to do with the god of small things, with gradual or piecemeal or evolutionary transformation, nor that exploration *ought* only to extend to the garden and never reach for the stars. Arguably, Russia in 1917 was no less radically and suddenly transformed than was the Soviet Union in December 1991. Arguably, it was desirable for Uncle Sam to withdraw or be expelled from Vietnam more speedily than he entered.

As to *change*, who is entitled to insist that history be exclusively to do with this? Change is only to be accounted for in relation to that which endures. As well as change, history also supplies and depends on some account of *duration*. We may see this even in so simple a circumstance as where the reporter records the suspect immobility of the dead rhino, an immobility that persists from the point that Tito shoots the animal to the moment, finally, where the old Marshall sets foot on his trophy's head. History, then, is marked as much by duration as by change, and no sense can be made of the one except in relation to the other. We have not said enough if we say that history is *all* about change, since history involves something more. And since history involves something more, to say it is only about change is less than accurate. To maintain that history is only about change is a selective claim. It is not the selectiveness that makes the claim false, but rather the business of passing off the selective claim 'History is only about change' as a comprehensive statement of the truth about the nature of history.

The historical account is a selective account. 'Selective' is not the same as 'distorted'. Were that the case, then all history would be 'distorted'. The range of claims that may be advanced about duration and alteration are infinite. The run of claims that might in theory be made could not all be uttered. An historical account, looking out upon an infinity of options, directions and minutiae, must attend to some and lay others aside. It must pick and choose. The objectivity of the undertaking, far from being undermined by selectivity, rather presupposes it. We cannot pretend from the outset to be objective, except in the knowledge of the principle which guides our selection. It is not the mixing but the matching that is the problem. One must unlock the closet in which lurks the *principle* that directs and governs what is being executed. So the historian, of whatever sort, must first ask: What am I about? What thread am I following? What principle, hypothesis or intuition am I exploring? The historian, fully aware that everything cannot be done, must put the question to self, with all the severity the circumstance demands: What, in sum, is my brief? A history, to be coherent, viz. rational, requires a guiding principle, value, orientation or focus, which serves as a criterion of relevance in the action of ego upon data. History, including any history of ideas, cannot avoid taking a bearing. There is always the risk of dogmatism in this. But it is not an avoidable risk; so much borders (almost) on the commonplace. What seems less banal is the insistence that this intrusion of ego – of the present, of the hypothesis, of the imagination – holds *whatever* the scale of the history, and whatever the balance it strikes between change–persistence, alteration–duration, and without the certainty that some particular scale or balance is safer *in se* than another.

There is no History as such. There is this history or that. No history covers everything, is everything. A history that assumes the contrary, loses its head; it surrenders the fundamental ground of its rationality, which is the recognition by history of its selective structure, and thus its acceptance of the need to elicit, at least to seek to elicit, the criterion by which selection (here or there, now or then) proceeds. Any history unavoidably 'sins' by omission. There has to be a focus on some End. Otherwise, there is no end. Focus is our means of covering the gaps. Full of presumption as focus may be, there is no forward movement without it. Ego can make out no path by fixing solely on the data underfoot, never looking to the horizon. A degree of imagination, of looking ahead, trading on instinct and the uncertainty of experience, is essential if ego is to accomplish any object. Ego is present; to grasp the past requires incorporating it into the present. Ego operates upon the past with the gloves, mask and scalpel of a present perspective. Such paraphernalia does not 'corrupt' the past, but opens a way into it.

One of the most important functions of the present is simply to accommodate the past. To know about the past is to know about it in the present, as a part of the present, from a present perspective; otherwise we cannot know it at all. There can be no such thing as the pure past, if 'pure' means untouched, 'untainted' by present concerns. Of course we must distinguish past from present in some way, but it is rather more like distinguishing 'apple' from 'fruit', than 'to be' from 'not to be'. The distinction, in short, is nothing like so stark as some think or wish. There are distinct varieties of past and present. And most types of 'present' absorb some complementary type of 'past' (see Chapter 2). The commitment to keeping the past out of the present is based on nothing so much as a confused appreciation of the delicate logic of this interrelation.

Those who think the past is corrupted by the present tend to view the whole object of history, whether of politics or philosophy, as enabling us to escape the present, as we would measles or chickenpox. This fear of contamination is understandable, but like the panic that often overcomes drowning persons, its only effect is to make the work of rescue more difficult. This dread that the present will infect the past, as real as the problem may be, is too radical a formulation and the implicit remedy is too destructive, leaving aside the absurdity involved. What has to be refused is the very idea that 'the present' is the source of infection, and that the best remedy is amputation.

We may see that a change of time or place may readily enough alter the force or application of a claim whose meaning otherwise is clear and unaffected. Take the argument about the appropriate assessment of the work of a criminologist like Fred Imbau (1962) whose *Criminal Interrogation and Confessions* became famous as a textbook promoting 'dodgy' psychological techniques for securing confessions from accused persons. What Imbau promoted was clear enough; the question was whether what he promoted was morally acceptable. One latter-day argument would be that Imbau was wrong to encourage police in the interrogation process to lie (by falsely sympathizing with the motives of a suspected murderer) in order to draw the suspect out. An opposed argument would be that, in his day, Imbau was right to promote such tactics, since these supplied the police with a non-violent alternative to beating confessions out of suspects. The point, however, is that the Imbau-type case, regarding the propriety of moral assessment, is less a matter of a difference between an earlier and a later time than a matter of understanding the alternatives present in the mind of an actor at the moment that a particular course is entertained. The difference in *time*, in short, is subsidiary to the difference in moral *circumstance*, which is clearly as much a matter of outlook, setting, options or place as of time *per se*.

The remedy appropriate for anachronism can be woefully misconceived and unhappily mis-stated. Suppose Russell Banks (1998) supplies a lengthy Tolstoyan and highly factual novel (*Cloudsplitter*) that seeks to reconstruct the psychology of John Brown (who seized Harper's Ferry in 1859 in an effort to free the slaves). Suppose Banks goes as far as the available data allows in trying to fill the inevitable gaps, but in the end, consciously or not, somehow falls back upon experience of his own father, an honest but implacable man, to make the psycho-history of Brown coherent. Criticism of Banks for anachronism will be well-judged should he conflate *his* experience with that of his subject in the face of available evidence which shows, or allows the inference, that Brown's experience was quite different. But the criticism will not work if based on the automatic, dogmatic assumption that Banks' experience, in the relevant respects, is simply and *necessarily* different to that of his subject. The assumption that the past is automatically distinct from the present is the key component of an encompassing particularism, and it exacerbates rather than overcomes the problem posed by anachronism.

We have come by now far enough to see that the proposal, *per impossibile*, that we remove ourselves from the present to enter the past is self-defeating. We should be content to think that the past is corrupted by a present perspective only if the latter violates the *truth* of the past. We should see, moreover, where a present perspective does violate the truth of the past, that it is not the present perspective we can be urged to shed, but rather the content we have been able to identify as 'distorted'. We should accept, finally, that past truth is violated not only by making the past falsely *identical* with what is now, but also by making it falsely *different* from what is now. If we are alarmed by *anachronism* (falsely asserting an identity or continuity with the past), then we should equally be alarmed by *particularism* (falsely asserting a difference from the past, thus claiming an otherness that does not obtain). The chief and the distinctive feature of my analysis in what follows is a more sustained and consistent insistence upon this outcome: first, that the past is known only by incorporation into the present (Chapter 2), and second, that particularism (Chapter 4), and the contextualist variations on this (especially in Chapters 5, 7 and 8), constitute an irrelevant defence against anachronism.

It will be claimed by some that particularism and contextualism are worlds apart. But if they differ, in the way that one domestic cat differs from another, they are the same, in the way that any two cats are equally members of *felis catus*. Contextualism is a contemporary methodological claim that valid history is only secured via the approximately complete reconstruction of 'the context'. The inspiration of this claim has to be that we can make no present assumptions that are valid for the past, that the past is marked by a chronic alterity, that our chief obligation, in the pursuit of what Oakeshott called 'the historical past', is to escape the present. This aim, to reconstruct the context of the past, is implicitly burdened by a concern to escape the anachronistic tyranny of the present. The point is not that there is no genuine problem sparking contextualism, or that it is burdened by all gross absurdity. The claim, 'I am 20', will at some time have been valid, but no longer is, given the march of time. The truth of the claim may depend upon who says it and when. It may even be true that there is *no* claim whose sense is not somehow affected by its context. But assuming this is so, it would only mean that in the pursuit of truth we are always inevitably operating 'contextually', in the way that Molière's hero is amazed by the recognition that he has always been speaking prose. It does not mean that one will or can know better by resolving to unravel 'the context'. In short, historical contextualism supplies a strikingly inadequate solution to the problem of distinguishing true from false and better from worse in history.

First, the contextualist project makes no sense except on the assumption that the past is automatically and necessarily different from the present, or else why bother exhaustively to reconstitute it, as contextualism requires? Second, one cannot in any event reconstruct the context of the past except by entry through the portals of the present, raising the question how it would be possible to guarantee that reconstituting (contextualizing) the past was not just another form of inference from the present. If the context of the past hinges upon the perspective of the present, how, if at all, may we exclude the possibility that the one is not the creature of the other? Third, the past, even the very narrowest tranche we seek to reconstitute, can never be completely reconstituted, so that the bald recommendation that we contextualize it always shuffles between ambiguity and impossibility. My concern, accordingly, is less to impose upon the historian an obligation of some particular stripe, but more to remove some of the false obstructions that have been trundled into place by others. I do not argue for the historian's liberty in any terribly abstract way, but only for the removal of that particular type of repressive constraint that requires the avoidance of anything grand, of any ambition, of any conjecture that chances to surmount conformity and stonewalling.

For good or ill, some of these reflections on history carry over into the analysis of ideology. The notion of ideology is in large part one summary way of attending to history. Where we speak of anarchism or socialism or liberalism or capitalism, all viewed as ideologies, what we face are large swathes of history made coherent, not always persuasively, by reference to some given rubric. These notions are so large as historical constructs, and contain so many divergent lines, philosophically speaking, that I am tempted to keep a certain distance from them. This is only to say that in many histories, the project being executed wavers precisely because the rubric – the theme or principle – is not precisely or consistently articulated. Ideologies persist as forms of historical engagement all the same, and are an important part of the repertoire, for better and worse, of what we call 'the history of ideas'.

I have, like Napoleon, Marx and Oakeshott, been inclined to portray 'ideology' as negative. But by 'negative', I do not mean that histories of what may be called 'ideologies' cannot be written or should not be written or that there is no significant difference between them in quality. Anthony Arblaster, Barbara Goodwin, Andrew Heywood and Andrew Vincent, are some of those who execute this sort of historical task, even when they do not refer to what they are doing as history, and they do it well enough. In saying that I view ideologies as 'negative', nor do I mean that they are simply imprecise, fuzzy overviews of divergent developments which are educationally and mnemonically valuable, especially to the uninitiated. Inasfar as they are so, that is just a good reason for viewing them as the starting point, not the repudiation, of serious argument.

My view of ideology as negative starts sympathetically from much the same premise as does Oakeshott's, which was reason enough for my essay on ideology (reprinted here as Chapter 11) to appear originally in the Oakeshott *Festschrift* (King and Parekh, 1968). If my essay on ideology started from Oakeshott's problem, it diverged somewhat in attempting to get round it; for Oakeshott's orientation was conservative, my own, socialist. As for the problem itself, it reflects a connection between the parallel challenges of historical reconstruction and moral direction. And I think that Oakeshott's formulation of the difficulty has been distinctly undervalued.

First, Oakeshott's concern to rescue history from the obsessions of the present is clearly inspired by a commitment to get the account of the past right; if his solution does not work, the objective remains admirable. Second, Oakeshott's antipathy to what he calls 'rationalism' is plainly inspired by the belief that we can never say altogether self-consciously what the appropriate moral principles are by which we should be guided; if he risks in this falling into subjectivism, he has still put his finger on the key social *aporia* of modernity. As Oakeshott (1962) writes:

> Every admirable ideal has its opposite, no less admirable. Liberty or order, justice or charity, spontaneity or deliberateness, principle or circumstance, self or others, these are ... always confronting us, making

us see double by directing our attention away to abstract extremes, none of which is wholly desirable (p. 69).

I do not see that this problem has been taken nearly seriously enough by figures like Rawls, Nozick, Barry, Pettit and many others, especially in relation to the arid revival of contractualism in the 1960s.

I believed then that Oakeshott had a good grip on the problem, but an inadequate solution to it. The reason given by Oakeshott for objecting to ideology is that it 'abbreviates' the fullness of the historical tradition, and that it is the abbreviation which, in effect, secures the distortion. By contrast, my view was that, however awkward rational abstraction might prove, there could be no viable alternative to it; all understanding requires abstraction, imagination, leaps of understanding and Popperian conjecture. Oakeshott objected to the possibility of 'rational conduct', understood as the deployment of an abstract principle to guide concrete activity, a crucial problem to which I return in other contexts. The trouble was that he veered into the path of a parallel piece of misdirection in supposing that one can locate right behaviour by adhering to *traditional* knowledge, or to *habits* of good behaviour. For Oakeshott did not take seriously enough the idea that tradition is itself merely one of the more characteristic of modern *ideologies* (starting from Burke), and that habits, however automatic we may make them, are always *learned*. My idea of ideology as negative thus had nothing to do with its (inevitable) abbreviation of, or abstraction from, the infinity of past time. How I set this out is best gleaned from Chapter 11.

I shall end this part of the discussion by saying that ideology is important for me here precisely because of its potential or actual historical character. To take the matter further would be inappropriate, since the resulting discussion would lead too far afield. In formulating what I referred to as 'an ideological fallacy', it is as well to note that I was clumsily concerned with a species of 'situational logic'. It is partly because of my commitment to 'the logic of the situation', in morality and in history, because this commitment is unnervingly shadowed by 'historical contextualism', and most especially because I find the latter morally and intellectually misconceived to a degree, that more space has been allocated to contextualism than might be viewed as warranted.

2

It seems appropriate, in this section, that I account, as best I can, for the evolution of my ideas on history. My early education was in the American South. From 16 I studied history in the university that W.E.B. Dubois had attended. I was taught mainly by a garrulous, chain-smoking Yankee, Theodore Currier, who had also taught the unflappable John Hope Franklin. One of my classmates and good friends, David Lewis, has written well and *in extenso* on Dubois, though not yet, I think, on Franklin. The region (Nashville and the South generally) was a-bubble along a time-line of conquest, extermination, expropriation, enslavement, civil war, reconstruction, Jim Crow, discrimination and civil disobedience, all tumbling into the delirium of the Blues, Jazz, Soul on one side and into the depressive twang of Country and Western on the other. The region was and (no doubt) remains burdened by its history. I state this in order to say that I was and no doubt remain similarly burdened. In part, the reader may blame me on my education, not so much the university learning, but the sense of being which may be imposed by the space and time in which one grows up.

Unhappily perhaps, I had not the detachment to perceive history as 'another country', as 'dead and buried', as a scented chamber obscurely inaccessible. It was not a force which you just left alone, or which you might gently overtake, undetected and untroubled, and least of all a force that was likely to leave you alone. I had the impression of a past that was deeply rooted, arbitrarily ordered, often starkly threatening. One sought to make sense of the cacophony, even as one's ears overflowed with the sound of music and laughter. The persistence of the past seemed too solid a legacy for any amount of chain-pulling to flush away.

This view of the past as present, seems to have forced itself upon me in a bizarre way. I am happy to put it to myself, philosophically, that this cannot be. But the impression sadly persists, if not exactly of being born with this outlook, then at least of having been unconsciously conditioned by it. If somehow a given, this burden (as it remains) was of the order of an analytical *insight*, as distinct from a gospel of *engagement*. It was no more a matter to be excited by, to enter the lists for, to have faith in or to die for, than the claim that 'minus 1 plus 1 = nothing'. My sense, in short, was and is that history is never over and done with, unless or until we have entirely forgotten it, .apart from the fact that forgetting history is a world away from terminating it. So I for a long time, for good or ill, had a visceral sense of the past as always part of the present, and of history as just a (sometimes) sophisticated way of articulating that inter-penetration.

When I reached the London School of Economics (LSE) at 20 years old for postgraduate work, I had leave from my father, principally to rummage about in the philosophical archives of the nineteenth and twentieth centuries, prior to doing something more 'practical', i.e. law. My fascination with the logical and philosophical character of history remained in play. Only one person at LSE appeared to me to have any real interest in or grip on this kind of subject: Michael Oakeshott. Of course, Karl Popper raised questions of a genuinely interesting historical sort in *The Open Society and Its Enemies* (1945), some of these ideas being more fully developed in *The Poverty of Historicism* (1960 [1957]). There can be no question but that I was deeply appreciative of Popper. He was mentally tough, refreshingly so, a world removed from the assumption that seminars are a venue for polite exchanges among *cognoscenti*. More than this, he was very helpful to me. Indeed, he probably protected me (despite my clear opposition to American policy in various areas), at least up until the publication of *Toleration* (1976). For this book failed, alas, to endorse four-square the perspicuity of Popper's falsifiability criterion in science.

As much as I was taken with *The Open Society* and deeply impressed by *The Logic of Scientific Discovery* (1959b), which Popper smilingly signed and generously gave to me on the day it first appeared, and though I was more committed to Popper's seminars than to any others at the LSE, I confess to having found *Historicism* a touch arid, apart from the key attack on claims to predict 'the future course of human history'. By contrast, Oakeshott on history, as in *Experience and Its Modes* (1933), I found unqualifiedly absorbing. If Oakeshott's politics could not magnetize me, Oakeshott the man was delightfully civil, generous with his time and self-deprecating. I was led through Oakeshott to Collingwood's *The Idea of History* (1946), and these two seemed to me to supply the best of then contemporary writing on the nature or logic of history and the history of ideas.

I broadly agreed with Oakeshott in his opposition to speculative theories asserting 'laws' of history. I agreed, that is, in so far as I could not see that any of the theories of that sort, with which I was familiar, actually worked – or worked well enough to satisfy me. Oakeshott's target was basically Marx, even as, paradoxically, he saw much to admire in Hegel. Marx's history is thin and, at points, naive; it remains that it is insightful and important, as G.A. Cohen (1978) has shown in an original and sympathetic way in *Karl Marx's Theory of History*. Grand speculative theories litter the course of religious and philosophical reflection, as in St. Augustine, Condorcet, Comte, Buckle, Spengler and Toynbee. That Marx's history (like these others) is selective and partial goes without saying, but that is not enough to rule it out as a *type* of history.

The problem with Oakeshott, as I saw it (and indeed with Berlin and Popper too) was that he wanted to prove too much, namely, that grand, speculative history was as such intellectually impossible and untenable. I could not see that because I did *not* have any valid or perfectly satisfactory criterion of truth or of justice that this could prevent the aptness of belief in truth or justice, nor could I see that because I did *not* have any valid grand narrative that this entitled me to infer that it was improper for a Marx or Spengler or Toynbee to attempt such a construction. All of these attempts at grand history fall short. None which claims inevitability seems genuinely persuasive in this. Yet it seems unlikely that any history, however restricted in scope, will satisfy all the people all the time and so escape the fate of the palimpsest. I could see no way of categorically excluding existential claims to inevitability. If one could prove that historical determinism does not work, then presumably one could also prove that determinism as such does not work – and we have been given no satisfaction in that regard. How would one prove a negative in such matters? Was it worth trying? It seemed very like trying to prove the non-existence of God.

I supposed that it is impossible to conceive, categorically, that there *is* a past, without some at least tacit notion of the sorts of patterns or trends that this past did or might form. Moreover, to see history as marked by a pattern or patterns need not require that we see the latter as ineluctable, whether retrogressive, circular or progressive. The key question would seem to be if and how these patterns hold, *as tested against available evidence*. Of course we may distinguish between grand patterns and those less ambitious, favouring the latter. But if the grand pattern merits being treated cautiously, then so do the less grand types. And this is so, if only in recognition of the consideration that only a fraction of the evidence can ever be in, whether as what we know *versus* what might be known, or as the present *versus* an infinity of future time. We are right to warn against the risks involved in grand historical designs, but the risk in flying does not dictate that you must not fly. My fledgling position was that entertaining design, grand or mean, explicit or not, was unavoidable, and however false the design entertained in any given case, one was not in a position to extract from this a demonstration of the categorial illogic of design as such, even grand design, in history.

Oakeshott, Berlin and Popper all basically stood as one man in

opposition to attempts at the grand and the ineluctable in historical
design. There seemed a kiss-swapping consensus in those days; even
when they strongly diverged these men simply did not argue with one
another, or did not appear to. Bernard Crick may have mounted a
testy assault on Oakeshott in the journal *Encounter*, but this was from
exile, so to speak. The dispute between Popper and Wittgenstein may
have been fiery, certainly famous, underscoring the Popperian position
that it was reality, not language, that mattered. Yet Wittgenstein
(d. 1951) had departed the scene as much as five years before I ever
set foot in London. Engaged in putting together the Oakeshott
Festschrift (King and Parekh, 1968) in the 1960s, I invited Ernest
Gellner's comments on the enterprise, and he waved me off with a
laconic: 'I'm agin him!'. I said then, in effect, and in print later, that
we came not to praise Oakeshott, but to be 'critically attentive' to those
problems which absorbed him. I was quite prepared to argue around
Oakeshott, without repudiating him, as also to promote him, given that
uncritical appreciation seemed a fundamental contradiction in terms.

All the same, one could glean from Gellner's *Words and Things*
(1959) that, if he did oppose Oakeshott, he never openly traded blows
with him, by contrast with the Oxford linguistic philosophers, whom
he took such delight in cudgelling. What Gellner, like Popper, was
most determined to oppose was any empty play of language. Linguistic paraphernalia, after all, were just not Oakeshott's meat. He may
not have been sure about how one locates reality, but there was
no mistaking his assumption that it was this, rather than linguistic
abstractions, that mattered. Despite a certain distance, an apparent
diffidence, and a definite eccentricity, Oakeshott was cemented into
the real world, even more so Popper and Berlin. For if Berlin loved
words, he kept his grip on one issue, at least, liberty, which Popper,
too, embraced with a fierce religiosity. So there seemed to settle upon
the land a consensus, at least as between Oakeshott, Popper and
Berlin, relating to history, broadly, as indeterministic, unpredictable
and particularistic.

This apparent fear of historical determinism, of grand historical
designs, on the grounds that this was the chief source of modern
tyranny, seemed to me a little overdone. I emerged from a region, at
a time, where history seemed to have a great impact on the present,
without too much being made of a grand design, unless this was a
doctrine (maybe it was only a psychology) of progress, which we all
seemed still in 1950 to embrace to some degree. Few where I came
from read Marx, or were caught doing so, or in any way pretended to
take him seriously if they did. The Second World War, on the other hand,
was promoted as a crusade for democracy against the realization

of an unhappy Nazi future. Strangely, many of us who believed ourselves on the side of the angels and of the future seemed not to have considered for a moment (certainly I did not) that such a leap of faith into the depths of historical inevitability would or could further enslave us. I emerged from Georgia, a very young fellow, from the most elemental of racial despotisms, without much of an impression that this despotism was caused by a metaphysical inclination to subsume the past under the present, or by any distinctive commitment (on the part of the despots) to historical grandeur, nor by anyone's fervent espousal of doctrines of historical inevitability, while being myself committed, more and less consciously, to the fact and likelihood of further progress. So though I was fascinated by history, by its bizarre twists and turns, and though I believed it could be turned and redirected if the will were strong enough and the circumstances right, I was not sure that the apparent consensus on history that seemed to exist between London and Oxford was altogether tenable.

I first heard Berlin lay into historical inevitability at a seminar at the LSE in late 1956 or early 1957. I found it very entertaining but, as I argued from the back of the crowded room, obviously flawed. After some discussion, Berlin asked me, perhaps a touch petulantly, what positive account I would put in place of his argument, given that I thought his argument did not work. And I could only say, unexcitingly but honestly, and as he may have expected, that I had nothing to put in the place of his overview, while being persuaded of the illogic of his case. I was indulged with a drink at the pub when the proceedings were concluded.

Popper's (1960 [1957]) case against historical prediction (in the Preface to *The Poverty of Historicism*) was, by contrast, concise, elegant and persuasive. But what it demonstrated, important as this might be, was that there was no distinguishing between science and history in terms of predictability and unpredictability. Popper's approach to history, in the light of his implacable opposition to both Hegel and Marx, seemed to neuter it, an approach oddly contrary to his imaginative redesign of scientific method. My conclusion, years later, was basically that Popper had made the mistake of not extending his philosophy of science, or at least his principle of testability, to history itself, though his later embrace of a type of philosophical evolutionism would have been consistent with some such modification. My thinking here was that, as science needs an hypothesis (a conjecture), so history needs a theme, which serves as a guide through relevant data, no matter how grand or mean the scheme, the important focus being the *testability* (in principle) of the historical claim, not its scope.

Where Berlin's emphasis was upon the nonsense of historical inevitability, and Popper's upon the impossibility of historical prediction, Oakeshott's was upon the particularity, the unique character, of historical events. The three orientations were different, but pretty compatible all the same, and were happy to lie about in a roughly triangular fashion in the same bed, the odd arm or leg of argument hanging out to this side or that. Where I always believed that Berlin's campaign against historical inevitability was flawed (though I too opposed historical determinism), and that Popper's point was sound but evasive in relation to the question of the distinctiveness (or not) of historical method, and that Oakeshott's promotion of uniqueness was logically self-defeating, it remains that I found Oakeshott's treatment of history by far the most interesting of the three. I was eventually prompted to think it worth elaborating a view of history which construed the past as always contained within the present, but which would go much further than Oakeshott, so that it should simply cease to make sense to construe the past as in any way *alien* to the present *per se*.

In any event, taking Popper, Berlin and Oakeshott, powers in the land when I was a new boy at the LSE, my fear, which grew prodigiously over time, was that their fear might (least of all with Popper, most of all with Oakeshott) push working historians, especially in the history of ideas, to the conclusion that the only worthy type of history would consist in a scrawny, mangy, Namierite form, challenging nothing except zest, producing little of interest, pulling the curtain down on relevance and delight. The case is overstated, of course. But it was in this that I always found common cause with Bernard Crick. My sense, doubtless explained in part by my conditioning, was that history could not or should not be neutered, against the apparent inclination of three key figures whom I owed great respect, and whose work I found in this particular so unsettling. I would come and have stuck to the conclusion that grand history, *any* history, always needs a theme or organizing principle, more self-conscious than not (despite the danger of dogmatism this runs) just to qualify as a candidate for coherence. A fairly concrete illustration of this type of concern is supplied in Chapter 10.

Oakeshott's work on history then was of particular interest to me, not as any piece of substantive history, nor as an argument against such history, but as a set of critical reflections on the nature or *logic* of history. Oakeshott's critical reflections were of course influenced by such antecedents as Rickert and Dilthey in Germany and by Croce in Italy. But he had a way of coming at the matter, which was entirely new to me. I found the Oakeshott presentation impressive. What I was most taken with was his beginning, which focused upon the inevitable embeddedness of the past *in* the present. For Oakeshott, it was impossible directly to experience the past, precisely because it is *past*, the upshot being that the past must always reduce to 'a certain reading of the present', which struck me as genuinely illuminating.

I was all the more puzzled by the sophisticated way in which Oakeshott's argument looped back over his own premise and effectively garrotted it. Love of the past became, for Oakeshott, a matter of necromancy, if not necrophilia. In the end there seemed too great a tension between the characterization of (1) all experience as present, and (2) past experience as independent of the present. Thus, enthused as I was by Oakeshott on history, I proved unable to endorse his uncongenial construction of the past as autonomous, as dead, as *necessarily* unlike the present. If the past was in all senses unlike the present then, I inferred, there could be no way in which we could approach it from the present. On this reading, I concluded that Oakeshott's treatment of the past must render it inaccessible, despite his analytical opening which subsumes past under present. Approaching Collingwood, I could at least secure a better grasp of Oakeshott's 'problematic': the concern to get away from a spuriously 'scientific' history, to understand history in terms of the motives of the agents making it, to enter the past and to understand it through 're-enactment' – echoes of which would be found in the later work of figures like William Dray and Hayden White.

Difficulties remained all the same. The key problems I struggled with were two. First, to articulate more elaborately the logical *lapsus* caught up in Oakeshott's characterization of the past; second, to explain to myself why he should fall into a crevasse of such depth, so clearly lit. I say no more here about the first. As to the second, it seemed that Oakeshott somehow managed to confuse some notion of the integrity of the past with the rather different (and more incoherent) notion of the independence of past from present. This led into a 'particularism', which reconfigured past events as 'unique'. This move seemed intended to defeat any possible admission of historical 'laws' ('iron' or not) of determinism, 'scientism', of thoroughly predictive futures, and thus (presumably) loss of human agency. The reasons for this embrace of uniqueness I found understandable, but, equally, untenable. Oakeshott's refusal of 'scientism', which should have reinforced the role of agency or morality in history, paradoxically stripped it out, by slippage into relativism and amoralism, into the suspension of comparison and judgement. Oakeshott's concern to protect the independence or autonomy of history circled back, again and again, to the fixation on the avoidance of anachronism: the

business of 'reading history backwards'. There is the justifiable implication in Oakeshott that anachronism may feed into notions of teleological, religious or scientific determinism, since to see everything that
is happening now as identical with what happened before, admits no
gap between behaviours past and present, facilitating unreliable
generalizations from what we now know to what may have been (where
the content of 'now' may differ sharply from that 'then').

Oakeshott's analysis, in the concern to escape historical anachronism, and a closely affiliated determinism, came to focus upon locating
'a historical past' that was genuinely and logically distinct from the
present. My elemental objection was that, though there were distinct
types of past, there was no such thing as an 'historical' past *per se*.
The past might be multiple and it could be retrieved and recounted
accurately or inaccurately, distortedly or fairly, dully or imaginatively;
but the past, at the limit, could never be abstracted from the present
as such, and it could certainly not prove intelligible thus abstracted.
My position in all this was straightforward, but the position at the
outset was most deftly articulated (if not in the end consistently) by
Oakeshott himself.

That the past is submerged in the present seemed to be the key.
That there is an 'historical past', as distinct from a 'practical past',
seemed a bubble of muddied water. The problem was not to distinguish the 'historical' from the 'practical', but the historically reliable
from the historically unreliable. If every reconstruction of a past is
(1) selective, (2) occurs at a moment that is chronologically present,
and (3) reflects some actually current perspective or commitment,
then every 'historical' past is, in these senses, 'practical'. 'Practical'
and 'distorted' (or 'false') are not of course equivalents. The burden
of historical writing must be overwhelmingly to exclude the distorted
and the false, not the relevant, nor necessarily the practical. The
invention in the nineteenth century of what we are disposed to call
'historical' thinking seemed to me in the end to have really rather little
to do with inventing some distinctive sort of past, as opposed to
signalling the need to evade an especially banal sort of mistake. And
this is the mistake encapsulated in anachronism, in the unreflective
assumption that past thought, action, fashion, etc., are *necessarily*
identical with present thought, behaviours and the like.

The best way to deal with the analytical relationship between past
and present came to seem to me to lie in the articulation of distinct
species of present, distinguishing the *chronological* from the *substantive* present, subsequently identifying subtypes of each of these. My
procedure was essentially to align distinct and incompatible types of
present with their counterpart pasts. I thought I could show that all

types of substantive present, and all but one type of chronological present – what I called the *instantaneous* present – incorporate some form of past. The upshot would be that we can conceive of no *accessible* past that is not incorporated analytically into some construct of the present. Thus to construe the past as categorially distinct from the present seemed a piece of dramatic misdirection, which diverged from my conditioning, intuitions and reasoning. Though we may well conceive of a past that is 'dead', we can only do so on the implicit understanding that we can say nothing about it. My assumption was that, from this point, the analysis must shift to better and worse ways of studying the past, and away from emphasis upon a past so autonomous that it can only be accessed (if at all) by seers and mystics.

I am no more than a shadow of Oakeshott in the matter of his opposition to anachronism. My complaint, rather, was that one could not meaningfully oppose anachronism on the grounds that it incorporates a 'present' perspective. In 1983, Oakeshott quite rightly, invited the reader to agree (in *On History and Other Essays*) that, for example, Gibbon's understanding of contemporary despots informed Gibbon's portrait of the Emperor Marcus Aurelius. Oakeshott claimed, perfectly reasonably, that the universal beliefs about human nature entertained by Hume, and current in the eighteenth century, informed Hume's wider understanding of the past. But Oakeshott exceeded himself in going on to claim that this business of being mired in the present, 'attributed to Gibbon and other historians, is neither inevitable nor a virtue but a likely defect which every genuine historian consciously seeks to avoid' (p. 69). It is clear enough in a way what he means: the lens which you wear, and which is worn by all or most of your contemporaries, may be a distorting lens, when you train it on the past. But what Oakeshott did not see was that the difficulty lay not in the presentness or contemporaneity of the view taken, but rather in the aptness or ineptness of that view.

A 'present' view could mean a variety of things, such as a view that is taken by a given person (outlook), or a view that reflects something distinctive about the present (novelty), or a view that is shared by a majority of contemporaries (fashionable), or even indeed a view that is correct (soundness). Were we to take a present view perhaps to mean no more than the view now taken by a given person (outlook), then the fact of this view being limitedly, chronologically 'present' (in the way of reflecting someone's current outlook), can in no way ensure that this present view is not also a 'past' view, in the sense perhaps of being an outlook that others held *previously*, or in the sense of representing a currently held fashion that is *old-fashioned*, or in the sense of equating with a view that was and continues to be *sound*.

It then becomes important to detach the formulation of 'anachron-ism' as ineptness from its formulation as immersion in the present. The formulation of anachronism as ineptness might be framed in the following way: what the agent, A, believes or does now, at time t_2, is no necessary evidence for what A or others believed or did at the antecedent time t_1. The outlook of A, at the close of the twentieth century, may be materialistic. The outlook of A's antecedents, at the opening of the twentieth century, may have been theological or animistic. It will not do then for A to suppose that what A thinks or does is necessarily what A's antecedents thought or did. It will not do to suppose that, because A entertains some given set of ideas, that A's antecedents equally entertained such ideas. Thus, A is guilty of anachronism, wherever A supposes, naively, that ideas current for A were also necessarily current for A's antecedents. Anachronism simply consists in the mistaken inference from 'I or we think or do p', to 'p was always or was earlier thought or done'. There is no necessary con-nection. In this sense, anachronistic inference is similar to inductive inference. Inductive failure runs to the effect that: 'One cannot infer, from the repeated occurrence of x, that x will recur in future'. Anachronistic failure runs to the effect that: 'One cannot infer, from the thinking or doing of p now, that p was done always or earlier'. This mistaken inference, this anachronism, is what we are entitled to call 'reading the past backwards'.

What lies at the core of what is sometimes called 'historical' understanding is this crucial and justifiable aversion to anachronism. Anachronism is to do with the simple sort of logical difficulty already indicated, and nothing more. As with induction, however, there is a limit to what one can do about it. It is one thing to suppose that present behaviours and outlooks are *not* necessarily like those of the past. (This is the corrective to anachronism.) It is quite another matter to suppose that the behaviours and outlooks of the past are *necessarily* unlike those of the present. (This is the error committed by particu-larists like Oakeshott and contextualists like Skinner.) The point is that there is both continuity and discontinuity between past and present, and that there can be no intelligible focus upon discontinuity without referring to or assuming persistence. If your train leaves the station, and the station leaves with your train, you will not be well placed to detect that your train is moving. Change is a function of constancy. Change is the gift of constancy. To note change is always to note how what changes varies with respect to that which does not.

Constancy, over the short term and substantively, would always appear more likely than change. What is validly registered in the complaint against anachronism is that the past is not *necessarily* like the present. By the same token, the past is not necessarily *unlike* the present. We are usually justified enough in assuming the persistence of the past. But it must depend on what part and what type of past we are attending to. It is difficult to think that we can avoid, overall, some assumption regarding the persistence of the past, in the way we assume 'tomorrow is another day', that 'the sun also rises', tomorrow and tomorrow. Change in modernity has accelerated, often grotesquely, and too often far more than many can or ought to bear. But it remains that the preponderant weight of argument lies with constancy, even if this constancy can only be assumed, and even if the assumption will often enough be defeated – whether tomorrow or next week, or next month or next year.

Any grasp of the past forms a part of some present understanding. This is not to say that one's present understanding is correct, or that one has got one's history right. The point is that it is wise never to confound 'getting history right' with 'abandoning the present'. History is not dead, inasfar as we know it. And it makes little sense to think of it as consisting exclusively of 'unique' events, since exclusively unique events are unknowable. One writer whose position seemed at key points quite close to my own was Ernest Nagel (1961), whose *The Structure of Science* was acutely perspicuous on history, indeed a breath of fresh air, though I only read him (after 1983) when it was much too late to make best use of him. Oakeshott's particularist approach and the later contextualism closely associated with it – both influenced by Wittgenstein and J.L. Austin – placed a notable emphasis upon leaving nothing out of the account, avoiding generalization, never rising above the level of the local and the limited. Oakeshott especially was overly disposed to qualify any 'abbreviation' of the past, of tradition, as mere 'ideology'. But Nagel (1961) ruled otherwise: 'however detailed a historical discourse may be it is never an exhaustive account of what actually happened'. Nagel observed that historians are 'greatly troubled by the circumstance that they cannot hope to render the "full reality" of what has transpired or to state the total set of causal conditions for what has happened' (p. 576). In this connection, Nagel cited Charles A. Beard, who, struck by the impossibility of coming to terms with the 'millions, billions of historical facts [that constitute the] all-embracing totality called history', was reduced to regarding historical explanation as either dogmatic or subjective (p. 577).

It is an exaggeration to think that knowledge of a subject is identical with reproducing that subject as such. Nagel (1961) correctly thumped the common historical assumption that knowledge about the past must be 'inadequate merely because it is not about everything in the past'. He rejected the notion that 'we cannot have competent knowledge of anything unless we know everything'. Indeed, were that so, then 'every [history would be] a necessarily mutilated version of what actually happened'. Nagel (1961) even produced my favourite example of a map (p. 577) as 'abbreviated' knowledge, though it was only much later that I learned he had beaten me to so happy an example. For a map is useful precisely because it *is* an abbreviation. A map which reproduced every possible natural feature of a landscape might be useful for secret training, but it would not serve the normal purpose of a map. Cartography facilitates understanding of and movement over a space, and this purpose would be defeated by the simple full-scale replication of the space one requires to see mapped. Nagel took the view that history cannot be unique, complete and discrete. Rather, it hangs from limited determinate questions; it abstracts; it is and must be selective.

Despite the pleasure of recognition derived from my delayed encounter with Nagel, the difficulty remained that he was only able to perceive the social sciences, including history, as an imperfect approximation to the natural sciences. So much is clearly reflected in his claim that 'the goal of scientific explanation is sometimes defined as the discovery of the necessary and sufficient conditions for the occurrence of phenomena [and historical enquiry is] farther removed from it than are the physical and biological sciences' (1961, p. 582). Nagel went much too far in attempting to assimilate history to science, and was unfortunately almost entirely eclipsed by Thomas Kuhn's (1970 [1962]) popular reverse move to assimilate science to history (*The Structure of Scientific Revolutions*).

The relationship between history (as a sort of social science) and the natural sciences is not a matter properly entered into in the essays that follow. But, despite the contention that surrounds the question and, however glancing and premature the following remarks, it would only be honest to admit, with regard to 'man as a subject of science' (in Ayer's phrase), that I consider such a subject, if science it is, to differ significantly from such sciences as are concerned with non-reflexive matter, such as the 'mass in motion' of Hobbes. History strikes me as the subject of self-reflexive agents, not non-reflexive matter. It is a discipline in which the subject studies, less an external object, than self. One can of course externalize the self, as for example when one speaks, by an incongruous extension, of 'self-mastery'. (This is bizarre, because ego is defined as 'master' in relation to an alter defined as 'slave'; and it is curious to think of a person being enslaved to self in anything like the sense in which one person enslaves another.) But one most importantly externalizes the self by projecting a rule and then sticking relentlessly to it. How may one best make sense of the resulting regularities (of Kant appearing and disappearing so predictably that one sets one's clock by him)? Surely not by the external facticity of the event, the mechanical cuckoo winding and unwinding, but rather by taking account of the motives or principles by which human conduct is directed. And this would be the key point where I should have to part company with such figures as Nagel and Ayer, leaning rather more towards figures like Collingwood, MacIntyre and Oakeshott himself. For Oakeshott deftly locates the heart of the matter in *On Human Conduct* (1975b), where he makes the capital distinction between 'the wink' and 'the blink'.

Roughly, I would view an area of study or a science as constituted not just by its supposed procedure or method but equally by its object or subject. If we constitute science by reference to method, I suspect we may equally do so by subject. Palaeontology cannot quite proceed in the same way as chemistry, nor history in the same way as physics, and this without prejudice to the 'objectivity' of the one *vis-à-vis* the other. Both planetary bodies and human brains (objects and subjects) have a material dimension; both demonstrate behaviours which one may appropriately attempt to predict. It remains that subjects are not distinctively objects, game theory is not chemistry, humans are rather more than widgets. One seems, indeed, to understand reflexive and self-directive human behaviour more distinctively in terms of *decisions* than *forces*. When we attempt to predict human behaviour, which we may do in a sense, and to learn from past performance, we seem to do so in the light of, and by reference to, those norms which the agents involved have adopted and internalized, leaving to one side the contested position of gorillas, elephants, dolphins, dugongs and other non-humans.

There would appear to be a key difference between subjects and objects of study. A subject reflects upon itself, understands descriptive rules applied to itself, can break those rules, can create for and impose upon itself its own rules. A subject is not to be confused with an object, like a hurricane or a volcano or a ripening avocado, which does none of these things. We are as concerned to foresee how Russia will evolve, as to predict the path that hurricane Hache will follow. But where Russia takes decisions, Hache does not. This need not mean that Russia is quite unpredictable or that Hache's moves can be foreseen in every way. But to understand Russia we must not only have a purchase on her resources, conditions and environment, but equally on her laws, norms, cultures, 'mind' – in sum, her decisional procedures. To understand decisions is not quite the same as to understand forces.

We cannot assume, like those guilty of anachronism, that past and future behaviours will necessarily align with those of the present. Nor shall we assume, like those guilty of particularism and contextualism, that past and future behaviours will necessarily diverge from those of the present. The relation between future, present and past is in principle always a matter for investigation, even as we recognize that we do not move nakedly through the universe, shorn of all idiomatic presuppositions about change or stasis. Inasfar as we assume both, there arises the question of how we may explain or account for the alteration or for the persistence.

In inspecting human societies, historically, in regard to both change and stasis, I take it that crucial elements in what concerns us are not just the externalities of change, the causes, but the reasons for change and the justifications. Thus we understand social change as a function of the ideational change that supplies its impulse. Societies of course may be changed externally, as when swept away by wind or flood or decimated by famine. But more often we seek to understand human history via outlooks, justifications, impulses and ideas, which must include technological ideas. Human societies, collectively, in changing or maintaining effective ideas and norms, equally change or maintain the course of history. So we understand current society by grasping its rules, its norms. And we understand future society either by reference to the persistence of current rules and norms, or by reference to projected changes in these rules and norms. The point is not so much that we cannot predict the future because we cannot know the rules by which we shall operate in that future. The point is rather that where we try to predict the direction of future society, and assuming that such society operates on the basis of newly developing principles and impulses, then 'prediction' implies foretelling or imagining changes in these principles and impulses. To state the logical requirement of prediction, however, is not necessarily to say that the requirement cannot be met.

Any supposed ability to predict the direction of social movement must depend upon seizing the degree to which and the ways in which the internal rules that fuel such motion themselves change. It is difficult enough, however, to grasp the rules and norms that we do follow, let alone to predict those that it may be assumed we are going to follow, in advance of following them. It is hard to think that one can predict what is going to happen socially, historically, in future, while standing outside the logic of the decisional procedures that will drive this future. The imagination, of course, is a powerful solvent to obstacles of this sort. Yet the reality in most ways is likely to be immensely more complex than the imagination that seeks to master it. For myself, I should be happy enough to think that I understood where we actually are, and how we actually function. There is always a future in this, even if it has no long horizon. The rules and norms that to some extent propel us form and change as a function of argument *pro et contra*. It is this process that establishes direction and change of direction. As much as rules may direct, changes in them emerge from the bending of these directions, where they collide with the cases they may be intended to adjudicate. I suspect that one cannot actually come to grips with rules without somehow interacting with them, bridging the gap between 'knowing' them and 'knowing how' to use them.

I assume that history is made sense of by the ideas, rules, norms, intuitions and impulses which chaotically direct it. Thus a history of 'ideas' is an especially important type of history. My assumption is that one does not penetrate to the core of things, if ever one does, except by entering into the life of the mind which determines, through argument and public deliberation, the path that comes to be followed. Because the unfolding of history is an interaction between knowing what and knowing how, to understand it involves both such skills. It is in this sense that to understand history constitutes and requires a form of practical engagement. I take it that understanding history is (or may be) objective, but that its prospective objectivity cannot be viewed as identical with the objectivity suitable to, say, physics.

Though humans may be governed more by self-reflexive decisions than by impersonal forces, it remains that they may still, metaphysically, be determined by forces which stretch beyond the will. And if so, we should have no way of attending to that. Otherwise, what would seem to matter is this: to understand what individuals are doing, or are likely to do, or have done, is significantly (not exclusively) to understand how they think, both in the matter of logic and of morals. If agents do what they do because (on balance) they think that this is the right or apt thing to do, then it is important to be able to make sense of this process of reasoning. Yet to make sense of this process of reasoning is really, distinctively, to do it, and to be able to do it, for oneself. One does not penetrate the causes of a bridge's collapse by asking what it thought it was doing at the time. One may well ask what the engineers thought they were doing, but not what the *bridge* thought. To understand how others thought, at some more remote time, is, however, inevitably neither more nor less than to be able to think, and indeed to be thinking, just like them, only now. To be able to understand how others think is to be able now to do the thinking oneself, and for oneself; it is presently to enter into the mind, not to peek from afar at the brain. What the Southern Confederacy (in firing on Fort Sumter) or Nazi Germany (sending its tanks into Poland) 'thought they were doing' is intimately linked to assessing the morality or immorality of what was done. If the past is so different from the present as to prohibit our doing this, then we can equally have no expectation of coming to grips, in any meaningful sense, with that past.

It will be obvious that the position I present in this Introduction is sketchy and preliminary. I feel obliged to supply it, however, not because it approximates to a carefully honed argument, but only because I believe I owe it to the reader to furnish a brusque overview into which the detailed arguments supplied in the chapters that follow can be seen roughly to fit.

2

Thinking Past a Problem

1. History and the past

When we say of any item or event, including thought, that it 'exists', we attribute to it duration. We attribute duration, we *assume* it; it is not a matter for proof. It is in order for any existing item, at any point in its existence, to be attributed a past, present and future, none of which three is necessarily to be regarded as unending. A large part of any existence, not necessarily the largest, must be that which we call its 'past'.

'History' means many things. But one of the most conventional of its meanings involves an equation with 'the past'. On this reading, if anything that exists (including any idea) has a past, then every idea, by implication, must have a history. A history of any phenomenon or institution or idea is less to be accounted a *body* of knowledge than a *way* of (or approach to) embodying knowledge. There is no difficulty in accepting history to be a discipline, as long as we accept it to be such by reference to perspective, and not any distinctive subject-matter.

So what is this historical perspective? It is, as already suggested, duration: to do with persistence, change, growth, evolution, etc. History is not merely to do with change, since everything which endures need not change. History is not merely to do with difference, since identities also endure. History is never beyond the reach of morality, since it cannot be engaged except as an exercise in selection, which is to say choice, as between better and worse, between what fits and what will not. History is not exclusively to do with the unique; were there nothing humdrum in the past, the very concept of uniqueness would collapse for want of opposition, and history (thus defined) with it. History is never subject to total reconstruction, since our evidence is always partial and our formulae about the evidence, again, are selective.

The problem is, that if history is only to do with the past, and we can only comprehend it in the present, indeed only by making it a part of the present, how can we ever really know it as past – as it was (or 'is')? It would seem that, if we genuinely know history in the present, then it can no longer be past; that if we only apprehend it as present thinking, we cannot seize it as genuine history; that if we know it only by present excogitation, then perhaps it is not really the past (*wie es eigentlich gewesen*) that we are excogitating at all. Here we have what has been called a paradox, certainly a problem. This is a present problem; it was also a past problem, one which existed before, and our present job, in relation to this past and present difficulty, is to try to think our way past it. In thinking past this problem (if ever we succeed), the trouble is to avoid restating it in a new way. The solution must lie somehow in the interpenetration of past and present. It must lie in some notion of a 'thinking past' or even perhaps a 'living history', hopefully without blurring the necessary contrast between 'then' and 'now'.

2. Past and present

Let us take it that whatever we do or think now is done or thought in *the* present. We may take it too that whatever we do or think at any time is done or thought in *a* present. Since the idea of the present, or of a present, can in this way seem so all-encompassing, we may be led to believe that there is no past. We may be led to believe at least that we, alive now only in the present, cannot let slip our chains and directly escape into the past. But we may equally conclude – it appears so compelling a conclusion – that there *is* a past, and that the great difficulty is to find our way to it by escaping the present, slipping past the present, by tacking for what is different, other, not of the here and now. Both conclusions, (1) that the present is all-enveloping, and (2) that to understand history we must escape from the present, are based upon a certain confusion as regards what we may mean by 'present' and, *a fortiori*, 'past'.

If we think of ideas, we can distinguish between them as new and old. A notion like 'tolerance', where we understand 'the inhibition of negative action against a person or item to whom or which we object', represents for our species a relatively new ideal. A notion like 'vengeance', as expressed for example in Mérimée's *Colomba*, represents a much older and far more common aspiration. Such ideas, indeed virtually any ideas, may be attributed 'body', i.e. a history, a certain temporal depth or extension. An idea which one excogitates or reviews now is indisputably a present idea. And because one knows it only in a present, one may conclude that it has no past. Yet we reflect that a text first published in 1651 or 1690 or 1748 or 1762 or 1859 or 1867 must indubitably contain past ideas. And the conclusion may somehow prompt us to imagine that to get a purchase on those ideas, we must escape the present; that to understand the past, we must necessarily perceive it as different. Both conclusions – (1) that any thought presently traipsing through a mind is an exclusively present thought, and (2) that any genuinely past thought must be different – derive from a certain confusion about what we mean by 'present' and 'past'.

Past and present are correlative notions. We conceive of the one as excluding the other. If an item is past, we are tempted to view it as dead and gone. If it is present, we have a bird in the hand. We often find it difficult to conceive of a past idea being alive in the present, since so blessed an event hints that this idea's day is not done, i.e. that it is really present, not past at all. Anyone in 2051 reading a book originally published in 1651 may release a sigh of agreement. The reader, astonished to discover such congruence after a lapse of so many centuries, may be tempted to speak of 'universal' or of 'trans-historical' ideas or values; and yet there remains the suspicion that what is going on in a given mind today, given that it *is* going on now, cannot quite be what was occurring then.

To begin to sort out this difficulty, what we must reconsider are some of the various meanings that are attributed to the 'present', in which, as we hypothesize, everything takes place. These different senses of the 'present' will marry in a mutually exclusive way with correlative senses of the 'past'. What we shall discover of course is that some senses of the present actually incorporate (perfectly legitimately) non-correlative senses of the past. For example, if one speaks of the present as an unfolding event, perhaps a war (in its last stages, but which could extend backwards for Six Days or Thirty Years), this sense of the present automatically incorporates some sense of a past, in this case of all past time traversed by the event up to a time-marker, which we may dub the instantaneous 'Now!'. In this sort of circumstance, it will be plain that an event in some sense held to be 'present' will coherently incorporate a non-correlative sense of the 'past'. In short, although correlative senses of past and present are mutually exclusive, it does not follow that non-correlative senses are so.

It will now be in order to inspect more closely some of the senses of the 'present'. What we discover is that in every case but one, history is never understood as necessarily excluding the present. Nor is the past, in any general and encompassing sense, understood as being divorced from the present. Nor do all languages consecrate the past–present–future distinction as ours does. Swahili, for example, distinguishes between past, present and future via the tense prefixes *li–na–ta*. But there are two other such prefixes, at par with these, which precisely signal continuity and duration, i.e. the *a* tense and the *me* tense, as, for example, in *ndege waruka* (birds fly), as opposed to *ndege wanaruka* (birds *are* flying) or as in *amefika* (he is coming and is now here) as opposed to *anafika* (he is arriving), to use textbook examples.

3. Chronology: the instantaneous present

In general, our notions of time have two distinct aspects. On the one hand, we consider time as pure temporal sequence, as 'passing time', rather than in terms of what may occur within whatever sequence we demarcate. We may call this *chronological time*.

We may also consider time as an eventful sequence, as an occurrence or phenomenon which takes place, which fills up the time and which governs chronology – rather than an abstract chronology which governs the event. We may call this *substantive time*.

Present time, then, has its chronological and substantive aspects. We shall begin with two types of chronological present. We shall then proceed to consider two types of substantive present. The first of the two types of chronological present may be called the *instantaneous* present.

The commonest and most stringent means of distinguishing between past and present is achieved as follows. First, we stipulate time to be represented by a three-point sequence of past, present and future; second, we represent the present as the middle point in this sequence; and finally, we represent this middle point as instantaneous, as what occurs ... now. If we locate the present as that which we read or hear or say (etc.) ... *now*, then whatever transpired or was recounted earlier in this paragraph, in this essay, in this day (and so on), is already past, is already final, is already history, including the 'now' last cited, together with the 'present' allusion to it (as soon at least as we move to consider the present parenthetical clause).

One may write a history, at least some part of a history, *in* the instantaneous present, but it is impossible simultaneously to write a history *of* it. Theoretically, the history of an instant might be written. In practice, the thing has never been done. But not even theoretically can we conceive that we may instantly record the history of the same instant through which we now live. As soon as we put pen to paper, the subject of our concern has vanished, is past.

If we write about the present, it cannot be the instantaneous present that we write about. It is none the less the case that, in the instantaneous present, we continue to write, to act, to reflect. There is then no bar to our 'doing' history in such a present. But as this history cannot, within the instant, be of itself, it must entertain as an object something other, i.e. a past.

If we wish to write a history of the present, then this sort of history we cannot write where we mean the 'present' to be instantaneous. This present is such that whatever is written or recorded within it is necessarily historical. At least this is so where we intend 'history' to signal the study of the past. In the instantaneous present, *every* object of study is 'historical'. One has no choice. The historian may well entertain an interest in past events for their own sake. He may well feel disposed to loosen the tie between past and present, but it really cannot matter. In the instantaneous present, logically speaking, nothing remains open to reflection and reconstruction except the past.

If any subject that we would write about, at the point of our writing, is necessarily already past, and thus a part of history, then no event, which it is open to us to write about, can possibly be denied to us as a subject on the ground that to write about it will prove unhistorical. If we construe all events, at the point that we reflect on them, as historical, then we are left with no basis on which to designate some accounts as historical and others as 'unhistorical'. To enjoin writers of history to seek to be historical can only prove redundant, at least where we take the present to be instantaneous, on which reading no possible event about which we might write could prove to be other than 'past'.

If we start from the distinction between past and present which renders the latter 'instantaneous', we see that the conclusion which follows is that it is only possible ever to write about 'the past'. Accordingly, to suggest in any way that the historian *should* write about it, is superfluous.

It may of course be argued that the present, however instantaneous, remains the time-point we occupy when inspecting what we choose to call 'the past'. This would imply that the ideas we form of the past, since they only exist for us in the present, are not (properly speaking) past. But this conclusion is based upon a confusion. The ideas we *now* have of the past only exist for us in *the* present. But we have had ideas before, which existed in *a* present, a present which no longer is, and which therefore now forms a part of the past. In other words, the ideas we now have are present ideas, but inasfar as they existed or were expressed before, they are properly to be called past ideas.

The reason why we are not, in this, confronted either with paradox or contradiction is that we entertain not just one framework concept of the present, but at least two, neither of which we have so far mentioned. The first of these notions encompasses all actual consciousness, awareness, reflection, whether new or old, repeated or not, as long as it remains *actual*. This, indeed, is the most encompassing framework sense of the present we employ and it will be useful to call it 'P'. By contrast, the second of these framework concepts, simultaneously the more common and the less encompassing, is that which assumes a three-point sequence of past–present–future, in which, whatever its duration, the 'present' occupies the middle point. It will be convenient to call this less encompassing framework concept of the present 'p'. Accordingly, if we speak of the 'present', but meaning P, and not p, then it will be clear that P deliberately ignores distinctions between past, present and future. It is precisely in this sense that we speak, without qualification, of 'Eternity'. But if we speak of the 'present', now meaning p, and not P, then of course we shall confuse matters in suggesting that p also incorporates the 'past'.

If we say, 'whatever happens, happens in the present', then presumably we intend by 'present', P, if, that is, we seek to be consistent. Our trouble starts with the temporal ambiguity associated with an expression like 'whatever happens', since it may imply the specific time-marker 'now', but may equally imply an infinitive function indifferent to tense. A world leader, in his situation room, who says (just having assumed office): 'what happens here decides the fate of the world', may be talking as much about what has been the case as about what he expects to occur in future. This framework sense of the present, of a tenseless present, to be represented as P, is perfectly coherent. But it must become paradoxical where we understand it as p.

When we spoke earlier of 'present time' (p. 28), what was intended was p, not P. The instantaneous present, therefore, constitutes one sub-variety of p, i.e. p_1. The other sub-varieties of p shall accordingly be labelled p_2, p_3, p_4 and p_n.

4. Chronology: the extended present

That view of the present which locates it as the middle point on a time-scale which begins with 'past' and ends with 'future' is p. On that view of the present, already discussed, where p is construed as p_1, the present is regarded as an instantaneous middle point, such that it becomes impossible for present experience, so understood, instantly and simultaneously to be written about. On the instantaneous view, what is written about always occurs *earlier* in time than the business of writing about it; thus one only writes *in* the present, but necessarily and always *about* the past.

This view of the present as instantaneous, however, is only one view. Beside it we may set another, which is perhaps quite as persuasive, and in any event a very widely held notion. This is a view which we may hold of the present as extended. The instantaneous present is the merest fraction of time and no sooner are we aware of it than it has quite slipped past us, beyond any possibility of our seizing it, save in retrospect, as something that has already happened. By contrast, the *extended* present is a concept of the present as an episode which, if not 'enduring', at least persists; it is a process in which we may be engaged at the same time as we reflect upon and even produce accounts of it. The instantaneous present appears to defy the prospect of duration or persistence; the extended present does not. The extended present has 'body'. There is something about it we can hold onto and account for. This indeed becomes its defining characteristic: a display of body sufficient to enable one to 'seize' it, to provide an account simultaneous with one's experience of it. The longer the present, so conceived, is permitted to 'endure', the more there is to reflect upon and to write about, and the more of an account can be provided. Conversely, the shorter the duration, the less there is to seize and to account for. This extended present we shall summarily label p_2.

Where we conceive ourselves to be at work within the extended present, we may posit as present virtually any period of time whatever, as long as we do not slip from the constraints of p (which keep us boxed in between some past and future) into the eternity of P (which, by contrast, makes us entirely tense free). We may conceive ourselves to be locked within an extended present by reference to a great variety of chronological criteria, such as a daily or weekly or monthly or yearly or millennial, etc., cycle.

Any p_2 is coextensive with the daily or weekly or other unit of duration stipulated for it. The New Year, which has as its correlative the Old Year, may serve as one such unit. The Old Year is conceived as 'present', even if one is down to its last hour. The New Year is conceived as 'present', even if one is only into its first hour. The Old Year, even into its last hour, remains present as a p_2 extending mostly backwards. The New Year, even in its first second, becomes present as a p_2 extending mostly forward, in this case for in excess of 364 days. The extended present, then, is just a fixed period of time; within that period, all earlier and later times, whether spent or prospective, become 'present' simply by virtue of remaining within the period stipulated. Thus, when one rings in the New Year, or rings out the old, one does so by grace and favour, in this case of p_2. This extended present allows us to say 'now' to more than a moment and for longer than an instant, as when we speak of 'the present year', or of 'the present century' and sometimes of groups, reduced to a temporal measure, such as 'our generation'. The crucial consideration about p_2 is that we are able to contemplate and recount it at the same time as remaining within it.

The concept of 'the present' has, as we see, significantly different senses. It is because of these differences that we are entitled, without paradox, to say for example that 'most of the *present* year, alas, is *past*' or that 'the *present* century has only just begun and our future success [within it] is already assured'. Strictly speaking, of course, the '*present* year', taken as a case of p_2, cannot also be '*past*'. Except that the speaker here does not intend the *year* as 'past', but rather that part of the year which antedates the present conceived as instantaneous. Thus p_1 and p_2 are here being employed at the same time, without setting up (in this sort of case) the faintest ripple of confusion. But the potential for confusion is evident enough.

The present as p_2 both includes the 'past' and excludes 'it'. But it is not the same past that is both included and excluded. Where p_2 is read as 'the New Year', then the correlative past of p_2 is 'the Old Year': p_2 (the New Year) can never include its own correlative past, the Old Year. What p_2 presumably may include is a non-correlative past, such as that which correlates with p_1. In p_1, the instantaneous present, the correlative past is all or any previous time up to the present instant. Although the meaning of p_1 cannot include this past (because it is correlative to p_1), p_2 can be said to include it (precisely because it is non-correlative to p_2). Thus only is one able intelligibly to say things such as 'most of the *present* year, alas, is *past*'.

The instantaneous present does not *contain* any past. We know that it cannot have itself as its object. And this leads us to think that its *object* can only be the past. But the inescapable evanescence of p_1 makes it difficult to say anything further about its content at all.

The extended present, however, does contain a past. It is not merely that it takes some past as an object of attention, but also that it contains some past as a part of its present (p_2) content or meaning. It is then in this sense, for a start, that the past, certainly *a* past, can be said to exist in the 'present'. One only has to be clear about the type of present one envisages, and also that the correlative past to this particular sense of the present is excluded.

The upper and lower limits which we may fix for this extended present are almost arbitrary. A p_2 can be understood as one year or less or as a thousand years or more. There are no purely chronological reasons which argue for making it one or the other.

If, however, one makes p_2 too long, one risks conflating it with P. If one makes it too short, one risks conflating it with p_1. One difficulty with any instant is, of course, its shallowness of depth; its eerie evanescence is too elusive to come to grips with. And this is one of the problems with the instantaneous present: as instant, it can have no object but the past; but by the same token, it can constitute no object of itself.

The extended present, despite its apparently arbitrary limits, can at least be the object of its own study. And that is the utility of the concept. In attempting to understand any present, we must presumably give it 'body', which is some degree of temporal depth. When we speak of 'the' present, or of 'this' present, what we refer to, if it is to be understood, cannot simply evaporate as soon as cited. Where we slap the label 'present' upon a length of time, it must have something to stick to. The chronological present, conceived as p, must be extended if we are to grasp it – hence p_2.

The problem (with regard to the extended present) is to determine by how much the present must minimally be made to stretch beyond an instant in order to become comprehensible. Despite the difficulties we confront in attempting to seize it, even an instant has duration, i.e. upper and lower temporal limits. The extended present cannot have arbitrary limits, since if it did there would be nothing to stop it merging with the instantaneous present. This is the question we must now address, even as we pass over (safely enough, I think) the question how far back in time the extended present may reach, at least as long as we do not confound p_2 with eternity.

To curtail discussion of the appropriate cut-off point for the nearer limit of p_2 – this could in principle be reduced to a year, a quarter, a month, a week, a day, an hour, a minute, *seriatim*, until we approach an instant – I propose that we simply apply the simultaneity criterion. The thrust of this criterion is that p_2 must at least extend sufficiently far over time to enable any observer, whether historian, experimenter or other, to provide an account of p_2 (e.g. the Old Year) while remaining within it. On this criterion, the dimensions of p_2 will necessarily vary. The only thing to be avoided is a time-unit which is insufficiently extended (taking account of available and relevant recording techniques and equipment, such as shorthand and cameras) to accommodate both an experience and an intelligible record of it. Any other conclusion that one draws on the practical level will prove falsely tidy. I think it worthwhile none the less to risk the falseness in the tidy by plumping for a commonsensical circadian cycle, consistent with the keeping of diaries, to represent for most purposes the lower limit of p_2.

We may say, correctly enough, that we commonly attribute to our concept of a present some body or duration, and thus conventionally allow ourselves to dilate upon this 'present' as 'history'. But having said as much, it must be clearly understood that the 'simultaneity' involved is of a kind which still in no way excludes *sequence*: the record, fashioned at a later time, has always as its object some activity located earlier in time.

When we advance to project a concept of the present as extended, it in no way implies that we have overcome the notion of temporal sequence. We can and do extend the present beyond the form it assumes as an instant; so extended we are perfectly well able to experience and to record it – 'simultaneously'. We do not in this deny that the record, in the process of being recorded, always follows in time that which it is its object to record. It does not follow that, in p_2, the 'simultaneity' of the present (as experience) and of history (as a record of experience) is to be regarded as unreal. In the extended present, 'simultaneity' must be defined in terms of the time-unit (the day or month or year) constituting the p_2. In p_2, accordingly, we are less to do with experience and the recording of experience being enacted *at the same instant*, than with experience and the recording of experience occurring within *the same time-span*.

The heart of the matter turns round what time-span is designated as 'present' for any given purpose. If it is an hour that we take to be 'present', then we may be later in the hour or earlier in the hour. But as it is 'the hour' which constitutes the content of the present, then whatever happens within it, happens *in* the same time, and, in this sense, *at* the same time.

Time present, taken as p, may be a day, it may be a second. We are aware that, within the day, each hour succeeds the next: here is sequence. But each fraction of a second also succeeds the next: here too is sequence. It all depends upon the fineness of our measure. The 'instant', chronologically speaking, cannot represent an absolute. Time, taken as a whole, must in principle be infinitely divisible. Time present (p) may be represented as a fraction of time ($^p/.$), of which p_2, no less than p_1, is equally fractional and infinitely divisible. It does not therefore matter that the day is longer than the second. If it is only the *day* (as a whole) that we are talking about, as when it is only the second (as a whole) that we are talking about, then (from this perspective) everything that happens in the day or in the second happens *at the same time*.

The extended present, although it enables us, for example, to write 'current affairs' or 'contemporary history', does not for all that enable us to dispense with temporal sequence. It merely designates the duration of the units which are taken to enter into, or to constitute, any such sequence. If we take 'today' to be 'the present', and then set about counting off the passing hours, we have merely shifted from the day as the unit of succession, to the hour as that unit. And in this case it is the hour that becomes the 'present'.

Any record or reflection can always be perceived as involving activity at a later time adverting to activity (of some sort) at an earlier time. This is so, at least, if the unit of time chosen is small enough. For much activity which can be so construed, i.e. as later/earlier, can also be seen, as in the case of p_2, as simultaneous. If we take a piece of writing or reflection, for example, to occur at time t, we shall conclude that the subject (the writing or reflection) cannot take itself as its own object at t. But this is only so if $t = p_1$. For a piece of writing or reflection occurring at t may well take itself as its own object at that time if $t = p_2$. In short, p_2 allows for simultaneity of reflection and experience; p_1 does not. But one can always reduce a given time-span from a larger p_2 to a smaller, and from this to a p_1, either of which steps may eliminate simultaneity for the unit chosen and readmit sequence.

If we are dealing with an instantaneous present, it is superfluous to recommend that historians not write about it. A present that is instantaneous can be written *in* but not *about*. In p_2, the present can be written about while lived in. Sequence in time depends upon movement across the present from past to future. If the unit of present time is a second, then the transition is instantly made. If it is a full year, then the simultaneity that was at first impossible suddenly becomes manageable. Of course, when writing about this year, what is being written about always precedes in time the process of writing about it. But we can only say this where we have ceased to focus upon the year as the governing unit of present time, contracting it to some far smaller measure, such as a minute or second.

It remains, however, when writing about the present conceived as extended, and despite the simultaneity criterion, that it is never possible to write about it *fully* while still caught up in it. One may well write about some of the events of 1999, for example, while still alive in 1999. But to cover the *entire* time-span represented by 1999, it will be necessary to enter a time-span designated 2000 or later. Accordingly, one cannot fully write about 1999 while still alive in 1999. It is not intended by 'fully' anything impossible, but only to traverse the entire temporal range of the unit designated as 'present', which in this case is '1999'. Thus, even with the extended present, an account of any p_2 which is to cover it fully can only be completed where the agent providing it stands wholly outside the time-unit designated as present, where, in short, the present, for the historian recording it, has been turned into the past.

The point at which present becomes past is, of course, determined by the extent of the duration assigned to the former. The extended present, taking account of its duration, is necessarily confined within variable limits. Thus, if it is recommended that historians do not dilate upon the present, and this is understood as the extended present, it must remain unclear as to the precise period about which they are enjoined not to pronounce. The extended present, constituting an arbitrarily (and so variably) stipulated duration, is characterized by a peculiar problem where it is sought in some general way that historians should not write about it.

When we are told that historians *do* not write, or *should* not write, about the (extended) present, this might mean that they do not or ought not to provide an account of any of the developments of the last quarter or year or decade or century or millennium or whatever. As a general description of what historians actually do or omit, it is confused and does not help us. As a general recommendation, it is neither good nor bad, merely inapplicable. Not knowing the duration intended to be covered by such a recommendation, we could never be clear precisely as to the relevant point at which to bring it into force. On the face of it, there is no more reason why the present should be restricted to a year than to a decade, or to a decade instead of a century. If, after establishing a vague circadian minimum, we can only *arbitrarily* stipulate the duration of the extended present, then any recommendation that the historian should not write about it must prove equally arbitrary. Although our concept of p_2 is more helpful than that of p_1, it still does not carry us nearly as far as we require to go, and largely because of its purely chronological character. A more substantive concept is needed.

5. Substance: the unfolding present

We now approach a third concept of the present, p_3. This I shall refer to as the *unfolding* present. It should be clear, once attention is drawn to it, that we do not necessarily, nor perhaps usually, delineate the limits of the present purely chronologically. We are not compelled simply to dream up time-sequences, such as a week or fortnight or quarter or triennium or quinquennium, and accordingly to conceive of the duration of this 'present' as restricted in the implied degree. Where we do, the sort of present with which we are concerned is either an 'instantaneous' or an 'extended' present. But time, including present time, may be fixed by reference to criteria which are not themselves temporal.

In order to determine the duration of the 'present' or 'past', we may establish criteria which exclude the priority of time, or any fixed unit of time, and substitute for this some pre-selected set of circumstances conceived as unfolding over time. Take, for example, a footrace. It might be devised in at least two distinct ways. First, a winner might be declared to be that competitor who is ahead after the lapse of a specified period. What would control such a race as this is the notion of the expiry of an agreed temporal sequence. Alternatively the race (as normally happens) may be devised such that the winner is the one who first covers a circuit or reaches a specified terminus. What basically controls this second (and customary) sort of race is the notion of describing or completing a spatial trajectory in front of competitors, not (as in our hypothetical first race) being ahead after a specified lapse of time. Where the concern is with being first to reach the finish, however long this takes, then the governing criterion involved cannot in any significant way be temporal. This race – which is present, in being, in process, taking place – must take place *over* time, but is at no point itself directly governed *by* time.

The non-temporal criteria governing the unfolding present are highly variable. We have taken note of a species of race in which the chief governing criterion is the traverse of a determinate spatial field. But one could as readily have instanced an embrace, a quarrel, a discussion, trial, concert, tennis match; perhaps a protracted set of negotiations, a lifelong rivalry, a great depression, a world war, an attempt to control world population growth, or to develop energy resources alternative to fossil fuels. Any one of these cases presents us with an example of the unfolding present. Each one implies different (but always non-temporal) criteria for the determination of the duration of this present.

The present may be considered to evolve for so long as the embrace, match, negotiations, depression, war or whatever lasts. Since each of these cases must be governed by distinct criteria, it is neither useful nor even possible to touch upon them individually. We only require to note what it is that they have in common. What they all reflect is an attitude towards the present which characterizes or delimits it by reference to some specific event or activity which is evolving, developing or unfolding. While we conceive the event as unfolding (match, depression, war), we demarcate the time as present. But when we conceive the evolution of the event as completed, we consign the spent time which enfolds it (no matter how recent) to the past. It is in this sense that we speak of an activity or arrangement, when ended, as being 'over and done with'; and it is only in this sense that we may properly speak of the past as 'dead'. The content of the unfolding present is only transmogrified into a past when the evolutionary sequence attributed to (or assumed for) it is regarded as having reached its term. Thus, for the evolving present, the past is 'dead', but only in the sense that some action or process is seen to be completed. However, it is always essential to retain that any one process, even if completed, must always be assumed to contain others, which are not.

When we think of the present, which we frequently do, as an evolving or unfolding present, time itself (chronology alone) is expressly
excluded as the criterion by reference to which we demarcate its
boundaries, which are boundaries of contemporaneity. It is with
reference to the event only, and not some otherwise arbitrarily determined quantum of time, that we say in this case what is 'present'.
When we fix the present in this way, we presuppose for it a beginning,
middle and end. This concept of the unfolding present presupposes
that we can fairly clearly demarcate a specific time as a beginning.
But nothing more need be assumed, to determine the beginning of
the unfolding present, than an understanding and recognition of
those characteristics which mark the event itself. The determination
of the completion of the occurrence (together with its initiation) is
derived only from the agreed characteristics of the occurrence, not
from any abstractly postulated temporal sequence. In this way, one
may conceive of the present as congruent, perhaps, with one's lifetime,
or with the triumph of republicanism in France, or with the global
proliferation of nuclear technology, or with the continuing desiccation
of the Sahara or even with the projected burning out of the sun. In
none of these cases is the present conceived as an instant, nor as an
extended (and already agreed) chronological sequence. The unfolding
present is, of course, subject to chronological measurement, but its
duration is determined only by the time it takes some specific event
(which is its essence) to unfold.

Any given case of chronological time or substantive time may
naturally coincide with the other. We may instance a second, minute,
hour, day, week, fortnight, month, year, decade, century, etc., as purely
temporal or chronological sequences. But whereas seconds, minutes,
weeks, fortnights, decades, centuries, etc., have not much to be said
for them, except as perfectly abstract chronological markers, the same
is not quite true for the day, the month and the year, the day roughly
correlating with the turning of the earth upon its axis, the month with
the waxing of the moon, and the year with the earth's circuit round
the sun. In such cases as these (the day, the month, the year) we have
examples of 'time' which may be intended merely chronologically
('After a year, we shall take legal measures') or by contrast substantively ('If winter comes, can spring be far behind?'). Though we may
merge these senses of time, it is only important to retain that they are
always in principle separable – the one recording the abstract passage
of time, and the other being riveted upon an unfolding drama.

Like p_2, and unlike p_1, p_3 contains a past within itself. Obviously,
the past which p_3 contains cannot be that which is correlative to its
present. The past correlative to p_3, is the same specific event designated

for p_3, where p_3 is conceived as terminated. It is also any *other* event which can be conceived as terminated by an agent located within p_3. The specific event designated as the content of p_3 cannot at the same time be terminated, although termination may be projected for it as a future possibility: this 'projected past' cannot be an *actual* past for p_3. Any other event than that specifically designated as constituting p_3 and conceived as terminated cannot with certainty be supposed to have *no* continuing effect; it remains, after all, located within p_3. In other words, an unfolding situation, upon which a variety of apparently alien ideas or models may impinge, cannot with certainty ever be said entirely to escape the influence of such ideas and models (which is not the same as saying that all are equally 'relevant'). With p_3, accordingly, although in principle it must be held to exclude its correlative past, it is difficult to locate any *actual* 'past' that is entirely excluded. An unfolding event cannot itself be past. And any other correlative 'past', however remote, as long as it can be conceived of in p_3, cannot be reliably excluded as entirely devoid of effect upon p_3, nor therefore in this sense as 'past' or 'dead'.

Any event, which we specify as the specific content of p_3 on a given occasion (call it ap_3), must be attributed a beginning. But, under pressure, this position will yield one more moderate, agreeing the possibility of an unlimited trace on influences: these can be chased as far back as the evidence will allow. The event ap_3 (let us call it the Falklands War) must also be attributed an end. Under pressure, however, this position, too, will yield somewhat, here to the consideration that no element in any event can ever be said entirely and definitively to have run its course. A beginning and end are implicit in the very idea of an event. But we may trace the causes of the 1982 Falklands War between Britain and Argentina as far back at least as 1833; and presumably its consequences – in bitterness, estrangement, destruction and unrecuperated minefields – will reach indefinitely far into the future. These causes and consequences precede and follow the specific event, ap_3, but also form some part of it. In p_3, then, a past, in this perfectly coherent sense, always penetrates the present.

The correlative past of the unfolding present cannot speak to us and we have no access to it. The correlative past of this p_3 is strictly dead and is thus a past about which we can know absolutely nothing. It is a past which, in p_3, cannot even be formulated. In p_3, one may posit antecedents and consequents, not the simple and unquestioned 'death' of any factor of which we remain aware. In p_3 one may posit earlier or later, and also much or little relevance, but not the complete irrelevance of one to the other. Although the correlative past of p_3 is not available in p_3, other pasts are. The correlative pasts of p_1 and p_2 *are* available; they are alive and form a necessary part of the meaning of an unfolding present. An event or phenomenon, like learning from one's mistakes (and successes) only emerges as a possibility because of the interpenetration of the present and its non-correlative pasts. For p_3, only a non-correlative past is dead, not any other, and not the past as such. In p_3, the past, in several of its senses, relates to, connects with and influences the present. Tennis players and military strategists are constantly engaged in the study of earlier games or wars, with a view to learning what went wrong, or right. What they study may be earlier, even 'over', but not past *tout court*. Past laboratory experiments may be 'over', but they would be regarded as pointless were it concluded that nothing was presently to be learned from them. How indeed is it to be imagined that there should ever be any improvement in the arts or sciences, or even survival for the species as a whole, were the past as such (here we address particularly the non-correlative pasts of p_3) really closed to us, and in this stripped of any instructive effect?

There must in principle remain many more senses than four of 'the' present. Enough has been said, all the same, to suggest something of the complexity of our ideas about present time, whether as P or p. Virtually any statement about the present must carry certain implications about the past and about the complex way in which we conceive the past. Certainly every statement about the past must presuppose 'the' present, first in the sense that a 'past' assumes *opposition* to some present, second, in the sense that it assumes incorporation into some other, non-correlative present, and third, in the sense that, generally, 'knowledge' of the past (ordinarily we call such knowledge 'history') is only a present knowing, grounded in presently available evidence, reasoning and conjecture. In this analysis there lies some suggestion, even demonstration, of the necessary and non-paradoxical ways in which the past penetrates, and coheres with, the present. Given that the past is, in so many ways, a necessary part of 'the' present, perhaps (in fully recognizing this) we shall be less tempted than before to expect or demand that these two should in any indiscriminate sense be kept apart. Analytical, political, social or economic theory is assumed to have its past; it certainly has its history; from the point that a past is assumed, histories are sure to follow. Familiarity with history helps, in turn, to keep the *analysis* relevant. It is precisely when we cease to perceive the past as in many senses present, when we conceive it as comprehensible only in its differentia, when we cease altogether to conceive it as enduring, as germane, as a source of enrichment, that we are likely to render analysis sterile.

6. Substance: the neoteric present

So far we have discussed three concepts of the 'present' (p): as instantaneous (p_1), as extended (p_2) and as unfolding (p_3). Among further senses of p that might be disengaged, there is only one (p_4) of which, I believe, we require to take account. Incurring some apparent pleonastic risk, we may call p_4 the *neoteric present*.

When we say, perhaps of a fashion, that it is contemporary, we may mean not only that it is something which may be observed *in* the present, but also that it is distinctively characteristic *of* the present. But often, as in the case of fashion, we wish to distinguish what merely *happens* in the present, which in various ways may be 'ancient', 'hackneyed', 'conventional', 'traditional', etc., from that which is 'novel', 'innovative' and 'modern'. This contrast is constantly at work within the present. A play now being staged may be modern or ancient. A form of speech may be up to date, or obsolescent. A constitutional procedure may be traditional in the sense of having 'withstood the test of time'; alternatively it may be markedly innovative, having withstood little more than the experimental twists and turns of a few legal minds.

The neoteric present, then, assumes a distinction within the substantive, behavioural content of the present, as between what is new and what is recurrent, often as between present forms of behaviour alternately labelled 'modern' and 'primitive'. The notion of a 'neoteric' present fastens upon the present not first and foremost as a unit of time, whether as instantaneous or extended chronological sequence, or as the unfolding of some specified event.

In all concepts of the 'present' as p, p's assumed intermediacy between past and future is held constant. Beyond that, there is considerable variation between the different sub-varieties of p. The neoteric present, as suggested, is not an instant; it represents an extended period of time. Unlike p_1 or p_2, its limits (or duration) are determined by non-chronological criteria. Unlike p_3, the criterion of 'presentness' in p_4 is not just an event, but some more complex and recurrent pattern of behaviour. An event may be human (war) or natural (flood); a pattern of behaviour, by contrast, if not exclusively human, is at least only animal. An event is fairly easily singled out for attention, with its obvious and predetermined rules, traits and features; a pattern of behaviour is a more involuted way of doing things, which may be revealed repeatedly over a great number and range of specific happenings.

The neoteric present registers a concern less with any specific event, than with a complex and recurrent pattern of behaviour. It is this notion which is reflected in the inclination to perceive the present in terms of specific behaviours, fashions, outlooks, commitments or orientations; or characteristic institutions, technologies and so on. Periodization – dividing history into periods – is of course characteristic of the extended present (and of its correlative or counterpart past) where the concern is to divide time by reference to quite arbitrary temporal criteria, whence the 'quinquennium', 'decade', 'century', 'millennium' and so on. But periodization is even more characteristic of the neoteric present, where the determining criteria are less arbitrary, and are intricately behavioural. The neoteric present (and its counterpart past) are constituted of a characterization of a particular temporal sequence by reference to the recurrent, but historically distinctive, behaviours which are (or appear to be) displayed within it. Where we speak of a 'stone' or 'iron' age, of the 'middle' ages, of a 'steam' age, 'nuclear' age, a 'revolutionary age'; of a 'time of troubles', of the *Mfecane*, of the age of the '*Renaissance*', of the 'Reformation'; of an age of slavery or tyranny or independence or democracy or whatever, what we are in each case referring to is a set of behaviours or practices taken (sometimes mistakenly) to be distinctively characteristic of a given temporal sequence. And this is as readily done for the chronological present as for the chronological past.

If the present is but an instant, then it is never possible to write about anything other than the past. If the present is protracted, then we can write about it while remaining within it, but only insofar as we recognize that when we write, we are always writing later about something which has already occurred earlier. Also, where the present is attributed duration, there is not one, compelling, non-arbitrary criterion we may impose for determining the degree of its duration. Accordingly, the limits of the present may be fixed by perfectly arbitrary chronological criteria (the 'extended' present), or by developmental criteria (the 'unfolding' present), or by behavioural criteria (the 'neoteric' present). In the last two cases, we are confronted with substantive, non-chronological (or non-temporal) criteria for demarcating the present. Where we demarcate the present by reference to an unfolding event, or by reference to a set of recurrent behaviours (which are regarded as distinctively contemporaneous), we are not so much measuring activity by time, but time by activity. We are not imposing a chronological sequence upon activity, and taking chronology as master of the measure; we are imposing activity upon chronology, and taking activity as arbiter of duration, and, in this case, of the duration of present time.

Where we invoke a non-chronological criterion of the present (as in the 'unfolding' or 'neoteric' present), the whole concept is built upon some assumption of the persistence of action through an infinitely divisible series of temporal loci. Earlier and later points in time are assimilated to one another by reference to some selected activity, which is assumed to persist across these points. If we take a *specific event* such as a tennis match, a test match, a baseball World Series, a depression, a war, what we are dealing with is activity spread out over time. The time involved (its duration) may stretch from a day to a week to a decade and more. If we take *recurrent* (but contemporaneously distinctive) *behaviours*, we are again confronted with activity spread out over time, and probably (on average) over greater periods of time. (It is to be assumed that alterations of outlook, institutions, technologies and the like normally persist for rather longer than determinate events.) But whether we take specific events or the persistence of recurrent behaviour as the measure of present time, it is clear that such notions of the present refer to activities which occur or unfold across an infinitely divisible sequence of points in time.

Where we are dealing with concepts of the present which establish its duration by reference to an unfolding event or a recurrent pattern of behaviour, what we are automatically assuming is that distinct points in time, or indeed periods of history, are not (and cannot be) unique simply by virtue of representing such distinct points or periods. The distinctions between these points in time or periods in history follow only, as in the neoteric present, from the positing of a unity of action or behaviour across distinct temporal loci. A neoteric or unfolding present is posited only where the persistence of coherent behaviour across time is assumed; it is only this assumed persistence which generates the delimitation of distinct points in time, temporal sequences or periodization.

Of course, it is normally assumed that every 'period' is distinct from every other, perhaps 'unique' *par rapport* with every other. It is a claim, moreover, which we must sympathetically consider. But what is often ignored are the criteria we are permitted to entertain for establishing the bounds of a 'period'. Certainly, if the criterion is substantive or non-chronological, as in the neoteric present, the omission is monumental. For if the duration of the period, present or other, is determined by reference, for example, to the persistence of a pattern of behaviour, then such a period, if 'unique', is from the start unique only on the basis of a comparison between behaviours spread out over a vast number of (different) points in time. The uniqueness of a distinct period in short – following non-chronological concepts of 'present' and 'past' – does not spring from the fact that it is located at some distinct point in *time* (for it is, in fact, spread over an *infinity* of points in time), but from the fact that it betrays distinct and divergent *activities* or *behaviours* (which, incidentally as it were, are restricted to some roughly determinate duration). Any periodization thus come by represents a duration far more substantial than an instant; the determinant of the duration is the activity, not any abstract notion of time itself. And such periodization necessarily pre-supposes comparison and thus continuity across a lengthy sequence of distinct temporal points.

The prejudice which supports the notion of historical uniqueness is, it would appear, basically that: *prejudice*. But the prejudice is understandable, insofar as the skeleton of supportive argument can be detected. That is to say, it seems plainly true that what happens at an earlier point in time cannot be quite the same as what happens at a later point in time, for these two points in time are themselves (and necessarily) different. If a part of the character of an event is the time at which it occurs, then the conclusion for uniqueness is dramatically demonstrated.

This then is valid enough. What happens at time t_1 can never be exactly the same as what transpires at t_2 for the simple reason that t_1 and t_2 are different. It is only important to see, however, that the force of this argument is purely temporal or chronological. Any event which occurs at an earlier time *will* necessarily differ from any which supervenes later, but the only necessary difference is chronology itself, nothing else. It cannot be maintained that a difference in temporal location *necessarily* matters in other respects. We cannot maintain that any given difference in time creates an exactly proportionate difference in activity or behaviour. There is no such correlation. It is perfectly meaningful to say, for example, that fishing techniques for a given people are exactly the same at t_1 as at t_2. (The interval covered by those points may be 1 year or 100 years.) If we select for such techniques and engage in periodization on the basis of these, we shall not necessarily discover that changes in behaviour strictly coincide with some fixed chronological progression.

It is said of a subsistence people of the Andaman Islands, the Onges, that they have no tomorrow, nor any means of measuring time. Probably this is not quite so. All peoples measure time minimally by the rising and setting of the sun, or by the waning and waxing of the moon, or by the changing of seasons, a phenomenon apparent under every latitude. It is none the less so that no individual is ever always involved in the business of counting time; there are times when everyone 'marks' time; and this is only to say that on occasion (at least) one takes no notice of it. There are at least two ways of ignoring time. The first is when one is lost in reverie. The other is when one 'measures' time only by reference to what happens within it. This covers both the unfolding present and the neoteric present. But to measure time only by reference to the activity that fills it is none the less to have a concept of time, one which ignores mere chronology. Suppose us to encounter a people who have little or no sense of *pure* chronological progression; who are not governed by clocks; who characterize past and present essentially (which is in no way historically uncommon) by reference to the distinct occurrences or behaviours which are regarded as differentiating them, but who, moreover, do not imagine earlier times to have been very different from their own and who earlier in time did not in fact instance activity or behaviour very different from their contemporary activity and behaviour. In these circumstances, there will be no marked contrast entertained by such a people between past and present. The reason will be that, measured by substantive behavioural criteria, the contrast is not in fact very great.

One might speak of such a people as entertaining an enveloping view of the present. If so, they reflect a no less enveloping view of the past. The persistence of standard behaviours and practices makes it difficult, on any substantive criteria, to establish a marked difference. It is misleading to speak of such a people as devoid of 'a sense of history'. Less theatrically and more precisely, their chronological history is marked less by substantive change than by continuity. Whether substantive continuity is to be viewed as good or bad is subject to endless dispute. But if one chooses to think it bad, one cannot hold by way of explanation to the misplaced notion that no 'sense of history' is as yet in place. All that matters is that one avoid reducing the notion of 'little or no substantive change over a given chronological trajectory' to the notion either of 'having no history' or of 'having no *sense* of history'.

The past, then, may be, and often is, distinguished from the present not by reference to chronology ('the passage of time'), but by reference to significant and substantive changes in behaviour and activity. Where there is great substantive change, the duration of the chronological 'present' may be severely circumscribed. Where there is little substantive change, the 'present' may assume more encompassing chronological dimensions. What is clear is that the assertion of persistent, substantive, behavioural identity over distinct temporal zones is perfectly intelligible. At least it is so in principle. It cannot follow that any particular assertion of persistence will necessarily be correct. But it is equally apparent that it will not necessarily be incorrect. To recognize that different historical periods are only necessarily different in time, does not convert the 'uniqueness' principle into a mistake. It only highlights its triviality. The notion of the uniqueness of the past is most impressive where it suggests that the substantive *behaviour* of the past (by virtue of being chronologically past) is consequently and necessarily unique. But such a conclusion, as indicated, is false. A progression in time necessarily means that any later event is later *in time*. But it cannot mean that it is necessarily different *in substance*. In expressing approval of a performance, audiences today, as hundreds of years ago in many places, may still clap loudly with their hands. The passage of time does not of itself necessarily alter the behavioural content of the act. One's manner of hunting, fishing, speaking, rearing and so on may remain much the same, whether over a year or a thousand years. Substantive procedures or norms may persist in a very similar fashion over considerable stretches of time. On the other hand, they may change radically and swiftly. This latter condition, as A.N. Whitehead observed at Harvard in 1925, has been peculiarly characteristic of the West since the nineteenth century.

We cannot merely assume that every period *is* (non-trivially) different from every other, most especially where we are dealing with a neoteric present (with its counterpart past). Periods necessarily differ in temporal location, but not necessarily in activity or behaviour. Where there is little change (as we are disposed to say) 'time stands still'. Of course, if we circumscribe a period by reference to the activity or behaviour which is thought to differentiate it from earlier periods, it automatically follows that one period will (necessarily) differ from another. But in such a case, the criterion for periodic differentiation is activity or behaviour, not time. Thus the determination of the duration of a 'period' often or usually follows on from the determination of the persistence or lapse of some specified activity or behaviour. The 'period' is automatically assumed to cover a vast number of points in time. In making of these a temporally coherent unit, i.e. a 'period', we assert either a continuation or similarity of activity or behaviour or outlook or style or ideas for the duration stipulated.

7. The past: identity and comparison

It is not possible to maintain that 'history is a world from which identity has been excluded' nor that 'the institution of comparisons and the elaboration of analogies are activities which the historian must avoid if he is to remain an historian' (Oakeshott, 1933: 167–8). Suppose we take a view of the present as 'unfolding' or as 'neoteric', together with counterpart (or corresponding) views of the past. A view of the past as 'unfolding' must clock certain developments (a match, a blockade, a war) up to the point where they end. A counterpart view of the 'neoteric' present, call it the '*démodé* past', must recount certain behaviours (e.g. a leadership style or battle formation) perhaps up to the point where (from a present perspective) they become obsolete or inoperative. On either of these views of the past, it has duration. The duration which it has is circumscribed (and so determined) not by the mere passage of time, nor by mere chronological 'pastness', but by the sum of points in time required for a particular process to draw to a close or to be superseded by some other. The condition for being an historian in such a case as this must consist in being able to compare activities or behaviours over distinct temporal periods. If the past is held to be characterized by behaviours that are no longer present, this can only meaningfully be maintained on the basis of some explicit or implicit comparison with behaviours which are present. If the comparison disengages a difference, then we have in this a substantive distinction between past and present. But just to be able to compare always assumes, at some more fundamental level, a continuity, and even – if one likes – an 'identity'. Where the chief criteria for distinguishing between past and present – as when we employ concepts of an unfolding or neoteric present, together with their counterpart pasts – become not the dreary ticking of a clock, nor the bare succession of second upon second, but rather altered activity, behaviour or institutions, then the entire exercise, the establishment of this great divide between periods, can be seen to consist in an irremediably comparative exercise, the upshot of which is mutual and unavoidable hinging of past upon present. We may well insist upon the past as entirely alien, but then this is a past that we can never know nor comment upon in any way whatsoever. The past that we do know, which is aptly styled 'history', is only conceivable on the basis of comparison and interpenetration with the present: no bounds could be set to it without such comparison.

We may well insist upon the unique, the distinctive and the incomparable character of the past. But the 'past', while always suggesting a point in time anterior to some 'present', is distinguished from the present according to different (and inconsistent) criteria. If the present is 'instantaneous', then its counterpart past is all antecedent time. On this view, we are always forced back upon the past, and can never talk about the present, in such a way as to compare it to the past. The consequence must be that it is pointless and inconsequential for us to view this past as 'unique', 'incomparable' or whatever. If the past that absorbs us is the counterpart to the instantaneous present, it is effectively all in all: far too encompassing to be captured by such feeble phrases.

If, by contrast, the present is 'extended', and is assigned duration by reference to purely arbitrary chronological criteria, as for a week, fortnight, quarter, semester, triennium, decade, century and so on, then there will be an illimitable profusion of past times (such as the 'sixteenth' century or the 'seventeenth'). A history of nineteenth-century philosophy covers a period that endures *chronologically* for a time equal and thus identical and thus comparable to any similar operation performed on 'the twentieth century'. On this most elementary of levels there is comparability. Every specific concept imposes a framework and creates a basis for comparison. Any given assumption of continuity may of course be misplaced. We may find that assumptions of periodic uniqueness are equally misplaced. Simply because periods are chronologically differentiated, it does not follow (as already indicated) that they are substantively or behaviourally different, or that such differences accord with the chronological units designated.

If the present is evolving, then the counterpart past has 'evolved'. If the present is 'in process', then the past is a process that is spent. On this view, the present is present by reference to some activity that is unfolding, and the past is past by reference to some activity that is terminated. But on this view of the 'present', one will almost unavoidably and simultaneously occupy more 'presents' than one. Suppose the unfolding present is identified with reference to both a depression and a war, but where the depression is 'bottoming out' and the martial indulgence is just beginning to 'hot up'. The end of one case of an unfolding present would, in this circumstance, overlap with the beginning of another. These two constitutive elements of the unfolding present (there will simultaneously be very many more) overlap and are not congruent. This must mean that the unfolding present, if defined simultaneously in terms of more than one evolutionary process, which is what we would expect, can have no single pair of temporal bounds, but a plurality of these. And if this is so for the unfolding present, it must equally apply to its counterpart past. In these circumstances, the overall criterion for demarcating past from present will never be entirely clear. Suppose Stalin, perhaps, simultaneously to have identified the unfolding present with the invention of writing and with the triumph of communism. The one criterion would take the present back by as much as 6,000 years, the other only 60.

The present, to be understood at all, must have body. The corollary to this notion is (broadly put) that any 'past', if it is to be seized, must enter the present in at least one of its different senses. What occurred in the past is trivially, i.e. temporally, non-identical with what is occurring now. But if the past is conceived as *wholly* different from the present, then we are left with no means of presently making sense of it. If the 'war', 'famine', 'pestilence', 'depression', 'civil war', 'inflation' and so on, of a past cannot be captured by concepts presently intelligible, then this 'past' is quite closed to us; it must, beyond doubt, remain beyond understanding. The condition for there being a past to which we can attest consists in the latter (1) being, in principle, assimilable – not strictly speaking to *the* present – but to *a* present, and (2) in this past being non-correlative to the present through which it surfaces.

8. History as past and present

History, where conceived of as some particular species of reflection, some given set of ideas, is always present reflection, always some present set of ideas. Thus, historians, where we take them to be reflecting upon the past, are naturally and always reflecting in the present – or at least in a time zone which is 'present' for them. History, or what we know to be history, is always part of some present. History, of course, always adverts to the 'past', but this in turn can only constitute a particular ordering of present ideas. The history that we know is not and cannot be past experience itself. Such experience is by definition 'past', out of reach. It can, equally naturally, be said that we *do* know past experience, but only in the sense that this part of what we presently know we choose, for reasons however good or bad, to call 'past'.

To say that historical study or writing, at the time it transpires, is a present activity, is to talk – unless we are talking about Eternity – in such a way as automatically to presuppose a chronological dimension, the category of time. The reflection involved in historical study or writing may well be present, but to say as much straightaway implies a distinction between this 'present', on the one hand, and a 'past' and 'future', on the other. This tripartite distinction corresponds well enough to what we know, or to what we think we know, based upon our experience of such phenomena as night and day, the succession of the seasons and daily traffic jams. The only difficulty, if indeed it is a difficulty, is that we never actually occupy a past or future; we only occupy different varieties of present time: and so, however much we move about within and agitate it, whether as toddlers or nonagenarians, we do not escape the present.

It is in the above sense that history, taken as something we do or think about, is always a present activity. But it does not follow, given the chronological presuppositions from which we cannot escape, that that is all that history is about. It is always present insofar as we are

thinking about it, or writing it (now). But this very activity, overwhelmingly present as it is, necessarily posits something else as the
object of its concern. What historical reflection presupposes, as
present activity, is past activity both similar to and different from
itself. History is always present, then, but only in the sense that
historical reflection is always reflection *in* the (or a) present. What
does not follow is that the supposed *object* of this reflection is also
present. It is, of course, present in the elementary sense that evidence
for it is now *available* at the point of being reflected upon. But this is
not to say that presently available evidence for a past event is the same
thing as the past event itself. Of course we are never able to seize a
past event 'itself', or past thought 'itself'. We may offer opinions,
press arguments and present evidence. But such activity is at best
approximate, hypothetical. We may well believe that A murdered B,
and have good reason for it. But the 'reason' is always that, and is
never to be construed as amounting to more than, a present reading
of available evidence. History is not *simply* the present. If it were, we
should not call it history. History is seized, grasped, intuited, understood *in* the present. But it is present reflection whose object is to
portray and explain the past, a past which by definition cannot be re-
entered chronologically. The past as such we have no evidence for;
we never seize nor know the 'past' itself as such. The past, strictly
speaking, is never seen, but only assumed, and such evidence as we
have in the present may be set out in accordance with this assumption.

Reading and writing about history are, as they take place, 'present'
events. History itself, despite the fact that it projects the past as its
object, is a present event. 'History' can never be equated with the
actual 'past'; it is only a 'record' or 'evidence' of, or an hypothesis
about, the past. History is certainly written in and by the present; thus
there must inescapably be some reflection of the present, if only a
perspective, in what is written about the past. But the claim that the
past *is* the present will not quite do, no more than will the claim that
what *is* true is what we *think* to be true.

The sort of problem which one has to cope with in all this is none
the less understandable enough. No problem comparable to time
displacement arises, for example, in spatial displacement. We may live
in Atlanta and doubt the existence of Vladivostok. Yet it is at least
possible (in principle) to make our way from the one to the other, and
à vue d'oeil (so to speak), surrender our doubts to that heaven to which
troubled thoughts ascend. But however much we move from Atlanta
to Vladivostok, we are never conceived to move out of the present,
whether into a past or future. However sure I may be that I travelled
to the other city, however much evidence I may tender in the form of

tickets, stickers and stories, however numerous may be those witnesses who will vouch for my departure, exposure and return, there remains one thing that I cannot do, which is directly (chronologically) to journey back to the event, or bring it forward into the chronological present. The indifferent observer cannot attend me while I rerun the experience and thus finds it impossible – in the most direct of senses – to *see* that what I say is true. There is, in short, no way of directly salvaging what we experience as the past, whether to bring it forward to us, or project ourselves backwards into it.

Danto (1965: 81–2, 84) seems to imply that scepticism about the existence of the past (or duration) is exactly parallel to that about space (or extension). By the example I provide, it will be clear that I take a different view. Certainly existence implies both duration and extension. Of course the tenability of duration and/or extension can be challenged – but not convincingly. None the less, it does not appear that the problem of defending against scepticism in the one case provides an exact parallel to the problem which obtains in the other. When one says one did something at an earlier point in time, it may well be possible to establish that what one says is true, although never by literally reconstructing and, as it were, re-entering the event itself. But when one declares that one building or one city is at some given remove from another, one's interlocutor does not in principle require either testimony or witnesses to decide whether what one says is true. He need only pace off or otherwise measure the distance for himself.

When we talk or read or think about the past, we take the concept of a past and the implied notion of duration for granted. We have no choice. It is never a particular account of the past that we must take on trust, but the concept of a past *per se*. Any particular account will be subject to the rules of evidence which must apply in distinguishing between true and false assertions about the past. Such accounts, within these evidential limits, are always subject to dispute. And the historian has no specially privileged access, he is neither oracle nor deity, and he is no better able, in the strict sense, to re-enter the past than his readers. His advantage, in principle, lies only in a greater command of the evidence (not of the *past* as such) and perhaps greater skill (or fuller briefing) in arguing his case. The vital point is that the positing of a past, where this involves some notion of duration, and irrespective of whether we assume change or constancy, is not to be avoided. We cannot posit a past without assuming a present. We cannot assume past or present, change or constancy, without assuming duration. And indeed, without some assumption of duration, we cannot posit any species of existence. Existence implies duration, as does any form whatever of causal explanation. Thus although we only

have evidence *for* a past (being one thing or another), and can never
directly test assertions about it (as we can in principle with assertions
about spatial extension), it is not possible for us to speak sensibly and
intelligently about existence or causality without positing some such
notion. In this sense, historical knowledge is a crucial component of
any knowledge. But given that it projects a non-recuperable temporal
dimension, it is proved doubly conjectural.

The past is only to be understood through the present; but, *in* the
present, we can have no *direct* experience now of what is chronologically past. We shall have *memories* of what we take it to have been
and *evidence* for what we suppose it was, but nothing more. Memory
and evidence exist in the present. But memory becomes unintelligible
if taken severely as memory of itself; present evidence becomes absurd
where exclusively construed as evidence *for* the present. Memory is
to be conceived as memory of a past; present evidence is consistent
with the supposition of a past. Memory serves as an equivalence, not
for what *is* taking place, but as a present account of what may have
occurred. We must recognize historical reflection always to be present
at the point engaged in. We must recognize too that in retrojecting
the object of such reflection into the past, we simultaneously accept
that we are forever denied direct access to it. This is not the same
as to say that we have no idea about it as past. For if we had *no*
idea, there could equally be no problem. We have memories, we have
documents, we have various evidences. But evidence for an event is
not itself the event. And so there must always abide a discrepancy
between the past that we assume, and the evidence – as currently
available – which we display in support of it.

In as far as we have any knowledge of the past, the past must be
rendered present. This rendering is what we call 'history', and because
it supplies only a part of the past, and because the chronological past
cannot in any event be directly re-entered, historical knowledge is
always perforce conjectural. History – taken as record, chronicle or
conjecture – is always present.

The present, accordingly, must not be conceived as barring access
to the past, except chronologically. Otherwise, without the present,
we are necessarily denied access of any kind, even of the conjectural
variety presently available, conjecture which we are too often embol-
dened to equate with certifiable knowledge of the past *per se*. No
'reconstruction' of the past, after all, is ever literally that; it involves
no reversal of chronology; it is an essay in the formulation of a truth.
The impediment to be removed is not a present perspective, which is
literally inescapable, but a false or inappropriate perspective, whether
assignable to the past or present.

9. Chronology and substance

Every writer, even when immersed in fiction, is also something of an historian. Every being who entertains any notion of personal or corporate identity incorporates into that identity an historical dimension, a concept of duration. Since we must face the *general* inescapability of history, we must recognize, too, that it cannot, in any *general* sense, prove irrelevant. This is especially true in regard to that view of history which conceives it to be to do with the counterpart past to the instantaneous present. Any actual event which we may recount, allude to or reflect upon, is, at the point that we do these things, already an historical phenomenon. The central consideration is that recounting, alluding to or reflecting, at the point it actually takes place, is present, not past. An agent must decide at that point how it will be done, indulged or pursued. For the agent, decision, orientation and commitment cannot be recycled and revivified as something which they are not – namely, as the past, an action completed or a thing *done*, as opposed to a potential presenting itself as something *that has to be done*. Past and present are continuous, as are fact and value, history and philosophy, but in each case the one is not to be reduced to, or explained by, the other.

If every actual event we write about is necessarily past (as in the instantaneous present, and its counterpart, call it the 'enveloping' past), then the concern to keep the present out of the past, or to have historians *qua* historians isolate themselves from the present, is necessarily misplaced. The recommendation is not one that can be acted upon. Insofar as historians write about actual events, they *can only* write about events that have already occurred, that are instantly located within the past. They may, on this view, write *in* the present, but not *of* it; for when they turn their hand to this, the present about which they would write is already past. If we distinguish between past and present as, respectively, instantaneous and enveloping, then we shall see that it cannot be that there was ever a history of actual events written which could possibly have failed to be *historical*.

We have indicated that some contemporary writers are much concerned that historical writing should remain historical, intending that it is improper for the present to impinge upon the past. But we have also suggested, invoking one set of matching notions of present and past, that the sort of miscegenation feared cannot occur anyway.

If the past does not begin ... *now*, marching backwards, unendingly, then where does it begin? We might say, as do governments in respect to delimiting access to archival materials, that the past does not begin from *now*, but from 100 or 50 or 20 or 5 years ago, or indeed begins at whatever point in time that takes the fancy (or suits the interests) of those who decide these matters. And depending upon the decision taken at a given time, or in a given country, historians will be presented with deeds of title to appropriate stretches of the 'past'. This concept of the past we might call 'extended', by contrast with the first, which we called 'enveloping'. Both are purely chronological. We use different concepts of the past of course on different occasions and to serve different purposes. The enveloping past is one both recent and distant. The extended past is one that may be either recent or distant, as when we refer to the 1970s on the one hand or the fifth century BC on the other. The past where defined as recent or distant can only be so defined according to the tastes of those involved, which is to say by reference to their canons of relevance.

The past, like the present, has both chronological and substantive dimensions. The purely *chronological* perspective mechanically locates some events closer to us *in time* than others, as when we say that Christ was born about 2,000 years ago or that Magna Carta was devised approximately 800 years ago. The *substantive* perspective, by contrast, operates in terms of persistence, duration, influence, causality, recurrence and even injunction, as when it is claimed that the Divinity (of 2,000 years ago) should be worshipped (now) or that political rights (of some kind, retrojected to an origin 800 years back) should be defended or extended (now). We may see that what is reckoned to be chronologically distant may prove substantively close. A present awareness of historical events, or the contemporary operationalization of hoary maxims and practices, without taking these matters out of the chronological past, does insert them into the substantive present. And the implication of this must be that the substantive past does not positively correlate with the chronological past. Thus an event which we adjudge to have transpired some time ago is not necessarily to be accorded less substantive relevance or contemporaneity than last year's drought in Australia or the outcome of yesterday's footrace in Athens, Ohio. What happened a chronological century ago will not necessarily, today, belong exclusively to 'another age'. Difficulties constantly arise regarding how deeply buried the 'past' really is, or (alternatively) how inextricably embedded it is in the present. What is certain is that the substantive and chronological pasts do not coincide and are not to be conceived as correspondingly distant from the present.

We have suggested, on the one hand, that there is nothing easier to do than disentangle past from present, since a precise criterion is ever available to serve this purpose. But we have also suggested that the influence of the past is suffused throughout the present, pointing to the contrary conclusion that distinguishing between them cannot really be so easily accomplished. Both positions are correct. And this can only mean that they are not really 'contrary'. The past is chronologically everything which accumulates backwards from the now. But the influence of the past, the substantive past, necessarily survives into the present. This substantive past is not uniform as between all societies, nor between the different components of the same society. The past is not present. But no present is entirely divorced from or uninfluenced by the past. The past is not *chronologically* present. But there is no escaping the fact that much of it is *substantively* so. It is only from the substantive perspective that one may remark that the past remains alive in the present. There are vast stretches of the chronological past which remain dead for us (whether forever or not is a different matter) simply because we have no consciousness of them. But the saint, politico, executive or writer at work in the present is nothing without a memory, even if only a memory of linguistic conventions, and memory is but a record of past activity or reflection or conclusions. It is therefore the substantive, not the chronological, past which is necessarily suffused throughout the present.

From the perspective of the instantaneous present, there is no actual event we can recollect or write about which is not historical (in the chronological past). From the same perspective, there is no historical event which we can recollect or write about other than in the present. The condition for writing about any aspect of the past is that we survive into the present. The present, 'the now', may as easily be filled by reflecting upon the Book of Genesis, by bathing in the waters of the Pacific or by landing on the Moon. 'Now' is logically and necessarily distinct from 'then' in chronology only. 'Now' is only accidentally distinct from 'then' in content or substance. In the chronological present, we may fill our minds with different concerns. What we fill our minds with will depend upon an interplay between personality and opportunity (perhaps an opportunity represented by fields filled with rattlesnakes, or libraries lined with books). The doing of anything requires perspective, while serious and sustained 'thinking' is in this respect perhaps the most demanding of all 'doings'. Historians certainly require perspective, but it is important to see that they are only one species of thinker, while no thinker, serious or otherwise, can do what they do if cut off from the substantive past. It is only by being mired in the chronological present that one can revel in the substantive past. And the substantive past is almost everything one might think about or puzzle over or work upon in the present. Indeed, it is and has to be present. We can only put it down as 'past' by counting off its chronological distance from the present, or by assessing its degree of irrelevance (*qua* style, tradition, behaviour, etc.) *vis-à-vis* contemporary concerns, interests or commitments.

There can be no perception of the past as past other than in and from time present. The content or substance of the 'past' is nothing more than the content or substance of the present, but (1) rearranged in terms of a time-chart or (2) ordered by reference to some imputed degree of irrelevance or insignificance, and usually both. The *conditio sine qua non* of an awareness of the past as past is the existence of the present. The present is not only a condition for the perception of the past, but an eternal opportunity, too, for seizing and appraising it in novel ways. The chronological past can never be reproduced. But with the substantive past, there is never anything else one can do. Whether or not new factual components surface, new ways of assembling these components are always on offer, and the historian, along with the rest of us, cannot refuse. The present will continually disgorge new ways of viewing the past, further factual components to be incorporated into it, and new techniques (like carbon-dating and computerization) to aid and abet those whose professional purpose it is to 'recapture' the infinity of past time in its substantive aspect. The present can never be denied the potential for harbouring additional evidence or new methods of investigation or simply new perspectives on both evidence and methods.

There can be no complete or finished or definitive history. Such history as is written can only be partial, incomplete, even tentative. No study even of a limited period can actually exhaust that period. The writer, consciously or otherwise, is always governed by an inadequacy and usually, too, of course by a *sense* of that inadequacy. Historians do not attempt to study 'the past' as such. They only concern themselves with those stretches of it – and from such perspectives – that interest them. They may have consciously formulated reasons for their interest, because they think the period really important or merely because it is a manageable subject for which research funds happen to be available. It is equally possible that they may be quite unable to formulate any reasons for their interest at all. But in the degree that no coherent perspective is imposed upon historical data, we may suppose it will prove incoherent in proportionate degree. In short, historical writing is always selective. Were it not, it would merely prove unintelligible. The past then neither is nor can be presented 'pure'. It is not only mediated through present perspectives but is also embodied in them.

The past is never exclusively past, and the historian cannot in part avoid the 'anachronism' of assimilating past to present. One must of course concede the obvious, which is that the chronological past cannot but be past, that the actual sequence of events is unalterable and that time is non-reversible. But we must also concede what may be less obvious, which is that the past cannot be inspected at all except through some lens (there are many) of the present, that present perspectives are not optional in historical writing, and that they impose upon the past something (an orientation) which is not necessarily *in* the past. A writer, for example, who wishes to show that John Locke was governed by hidden assumptions wholly alien to contemporary exegetes, in this rivets upon the historical figure in question a characteristically contemporary orientation. That is to say, they draw attention to those facets of Locke's work which render the latter least relevant to certain contemporary concerns, from which approach is abstracted the more general principle that such a procedure is the most fruitful to be applied in the history of ideas.

It is perfectly in order that we should deplore so narrow, parochial and even at times self-righteous an orientation. But it would never be right to deplore it on the grounds that it is 'anachronistic' or 'unhistorical'. No writers who aim to speak to the future, which is to say (almost literally) beyond the grave, can logically expect to be judged by standards peculiar only to their own time.

10. The history of ideas

We may assume that history is somehow to do with the 'past'. And when we speak of history alternatively as governed by laws or by accident, as instancing universals or particulars, as consisting of unique or recurrent events, as being like or unlike science, as being displayed in encompassing narrative or brittle factuality (and so on), it is always understood that we are somehow making assertions about the 'past'.

We may, of course, have histories of anything – including history itself. Not least important, we may have histories of ideas. Just as we may have histories of politics, so we may have histories of ideas about politics. If questions may be raised about the appropriate method or methods to be adopted in the writing of political, economic, military, scientific and other forms of institutional history, it will be clear that such questions may be raised with equal or greater force in relation to the history of philosophy. And any history of ideas, in its most significant dimensions, is effectively reducible to a history of some branch or aspect of the history of philosophy. As regards the history of philosophy, observers may urge us to direct attention essentially to the great texts, or alternatively to reconstruct the intricate contexts out of which these texts emerge. We may be advised to be faithful only to the past, or alternatively to seek after those contemporary lessons which the past may teach. Perhaps we shall be urged to make sense of the way in which we have come to think as we now do, even to pursue solutions to contemporary difficulties. Such approaches as these may be combined in virtually illimitable ways.

Much of what is said about the writing of history, and particularly the history of ideas, assumes a concept, the 'past', which requires closer inspection. Otherwise, any recommended method for writing about 'it' will not only begin, but also end, in confusion. One might begin by inspecting directly different concepts of the past. This task I am content to leave to others. For present purposes, it must suffice basically to draw attention, as has been done, to different varieties of 'present' time. In any event, all concepts of 'the past' are drawn in opposition to some one or more concepts of present time while equally being conceived as integral to non-correlative senses of the present. Thus an unfolding war, a case of p_3, has depth, or duration, and, accordingly, earlier and later phases. Any earlier phase is 'past', and yet remains a part of this unfolding present, but only because the sense in which it is past is non-correlative to the concept of present time (p_3) here being instanced.

The problem of reconstructing past arguments is an enduring one. We have already observed that the substantive past cannot be entirely divorced from the present, and thus that a methodology which would recommend this must be misconceived. At the same time, the perception of what happened in one mind, or time, may be distorted by confounding it with what happened in some other mind, or at another time. It is only important to see that eliminating this sort of distortion in no way depends upon erecting a massive logical breakwater between the substantive past and the present. The basic problems involved in historical distortion are not exclusively to do with confounding past and present, nor with chronological reversals ('reading history backwards'), but mostly with an inadequate grasp of a particular occasion, and its corollary, which is the confusion of distinct occasions.

In seizing a particular event, or a particular proposition, one may easily misapprehend it in a variety of ways. One may mistranslate and misinterpret, as has been observed. When we attempt to assess a philosophical argument, the fact that it has already been argued automatically renders it an historical phenomenon. Conceived as a philosophical phenomenon, the proposition may be assessed in terms of logical cogency. Conceived of as an historical phenomenon, it may be assessed in terms of the circumstances in which, and the reasons for which, it was enunciated. If we seek to reconstruct the event or the proposition in terms of its meaning, then 'meaning' is potentially ambiguous, since it may be construed to refer either to the matter of cogency, or to the matter of circumstantial reasons for uttering it, or to both. It is true that a proposition (by itself) is open to variable interpretation and that to understand it, as an historical event, is in part to reconstruct the concrete social presuppositions upon which it rests. But it is also true that such reconstruction, taken *au pied de la lettre*, cannot fail to sink into infinite regress.

There can be nothing wrong, of course, with attempting to secure a better purchase on a writer's meaning by exploring her circumstances, psychology and the like. In mining any vein, it is difficult to know when one will strike it rich, so to say. But there can equally be nothing wrong with attempting to recapture this meaning by exploring the logic of the author's formulae. I suspect that it is the latter orientation which should take priority. There is always the risk, in exploring an author's reasoning, that we may simply confound it with our own. But there is no reason to be unduly fearful of such an outcome. For it is clear, in view of the impossibility of our ever placing a limit on the regressive inspection of context and circumstance, that we are never able to put ourselves in a position where we can claim, without cavil, that we really have completely and entirely reliably recovered the given author's actual 'historical' meaning.

It is reasonable enough to suppose that thinkers address themselves to audiences. It is doubtful as to how much can be learned by insisting that these audiences are of some specific and limited kind, unless this is somehow (and plainly) revealed by the thinker involved. Social thinkers are almost always concerned to recommend that some specific action be undertaken. Where they become major figures in the history of ideas, however, they are normally far more concerned to *explain* the logic of concepts and the character of social activity. Where the thinker makes a singular and specific recommendation, such as to overthrow or preserve a particular government, much is presupposed about a local situation which the exegete of a successor generation must lay bare. But where the thinker is concerned, by contrast, with the logic of a concept or with understanding social activity or some aspect of it, the need is usually less pressing. The problem is that too many observers appear disposed to think that social thought, such as political theory, is merely to do with recommending behaviour. Some of it always has to do with this. But it may be that such recommendations are of least interest to later students precisely because they are so time-bound. The methodological recommendation that we exhaust ourselves reconstructing the context, conceived somehow to lie outside the simple text, is probably inspired by the thought that we should only inspect a theory from the perspective of the (usually limited) discrete recommendations that may be unobtrusively embedded within it, rather than from the perspective of methodology, logical analysis and powers of descriptive generalization, which normally constitute its most important historical elements.

It has been observed that (some) words over time change their meanings, and thus that one had best be careful not to suppose that they always mean the same thing. This is true enough. But we may equally observe that (some) words over time also preserve their meanings, and thus that one had best be careful not to imagine that there is not or cannot be continuity. Words may change their meaning over time, but they may equally change their meaning over space. The word '*entrée*' in France means 'main course', but, in Australia, it means 'first course'. And just as the meaning of words may change over time and space, so they may *persist* over the same continua. The reference to geography is only intended to emphasize a small but significant point: that change of meaning is not exclusively or even most importantly a function of chronological time.

Without any reference to time at all, we may safely state that words are often used differently (*tout court*). This is no more exclusively a problem for historical than for any other species of analysis. When the Anglican minister from the pulpit urges that we 'love' our neighbour, it is obvious that he means something different from what is intended when on honeymoon in the bridal chamber, lights extinguished, he solicits the 'love' of his spouse. Words *are* used in different ways. But that is a general problem, not an exclusively historical problem, and context is the crutch of understanding which any text, however limitedly, will itself hold out to us.

A connected argument in part creates its own context, or better, it in part constitutes its own context. No serious historical argument takes place *sui generis*. The fact that it is serious suggests that it refers to other events, assumptions or points of view which are, all the same, not actually and fully and directly stated in the text itself. Nor does any serious analysis of such a text presuppose that it is *sui generis* entirely detached from its environment, such that it is possible that one can, let alone should, simply focus on the text itself. To focus on the text itself is in any event and necessarily to focus upon all that to which it adverts and relates. To focus first and foremost upon a text, where it is primarily the text which is to be understood, cannot possibly therefore involve the error of ignoring the 'context'. The text is not enough. But the very fact that it can to some degree be understood implies reference to a common fund of understanding which is in the text but which also points beyond (or beneath) it. We do not begin to grasp the meaning of an argument by first looking over our shoulders at other considerations, which at best are only other arguments anyway. If a text expresses an argument, and it is this we seek to understand, then we seek first to capture the meaning of the argument within its own textual confines. The fact that an individual can write an essay or a book must mean that she is dealing with a social system, a set of practices, of which the book-writing only constitutes a more connected element. The fact that such a text points beyond itself is not merely commonplace but universal. This can in no way imply that the text may be ignored, or relegated to some secondary level of importance. Insofar as the intention is to understand *it*, it is important to focus upon it. Only when the text appears anomalous, inconsistent, incomprehensible or laughably false, have we genuine cause to look beyond to see whether other, external evidence may not better help to establish its sense.

There may be distortion where historians of ideas suppose that their subject of study has something to say about each topic normally treated in the discipline. It of course is one thing to suppose that all great thinkers have something to say about every significant topic, and another to satisfy a curiosity as to whether they actually do, and if so, what it is. There is nothing any more misconceived about tracing the origins of an idea (this is a research programme) than about trying to demonstrate that some particular thinker was advancing a moral or a message relevant only to their own epoch (yet another research programme). In the one case, the writer rightly assumes that beliefs and practices established today have evolved (and will continue to evolve) over time, and that there must be some *connection*, possibly up to and including identity, between the substantive content of past and present. In the other case, the writer rightly assumes that practices established today, having evolved, *are not totally identical* with those of any earlier time, and thus may choose to spy out these differences. In the case of either programme, the execution may be admirable or poor. But it is difficult to suppose that there are convincing arguments that either researcher might advance to demonstrate that the other's programme was wholly absurd.

There may be distortion where the historian of ideas presupposes that the subject of study has enunciated a doctrine that is more coherent than it is, the danger being that one may read into the original text arguments that are not actually there. There is indeed always such a risk. But it would appear that there is a notable difference between, on the one hand, assessing the degree of coherence in a philosophical position (which presupposes that coherence of some kind was actually sought) and, on the other, falsely interpolating arguments, with the result that a spurious coherence is imposed. The fact that past thinkers, who are substantively present as subjects of study, may be less coherent than many exegetes have supposed, cannot of course be taken as an argument either against summarizing their work (how else could we discuss anything?) or for providing textbooks in the history of ideas. A textbook does summarize and select, but these exercises do not necessarily convey distortion, no more than a road-map, through compression, misleads. The only error is for the naive or the overeducated to misread a decent and self-confessed summary as constituting something more than it would ever likely pretend to be. Imagine a motorist travelling through highland Kenya and complaining that the splendour which envelops him or her is not properly recorded on the mean little Shell map obtained at a Nairobi petrol station.

Some students have objected that it is conceptually impossible to write the history of an 'idea'. The basic reason for this objection appears to stem from the consideration that the words which give expression to an idea change their meaning, that words are used (even in the same time–space continuum) in different and conflicting ways, from which it appears to be concluded that a single history cannot be written of all these divergent meanings. All of this is sound. And who would wish to write a history of an indiscriminate heap of topics, even should this prove possible? It still does not follow, from words being accorded different meanings, that one cannot focus, even concentrate, on them. The fact that words mean different things is a commonplace. But it does not and cannot bring meaningful and fruitful trading in them to a halt. Even so simple and indispensable a word as 'the' has a wide range of distinct meanings and usages (as in 'the wife' where it means *my* or as in 'the lion' where it refers to a particular species of animal). We can live comfortably with the fact that different words will mean different things, that is, as long as we have a reasonable idea of what the particular meaning is on any particular occasion. Without such knowledge, there is confusion. But it is never variability of usage as such which creates the confusion. Where we are confronted with a piece of writing, the ideas it expresses are perforce expressed in words. Assuming that we can seize in particular sentences the particular meanings of these words, and assuming that the sentences together convey some coherent meaning (much that is written *is* confused, *is* gibberish) then we are in a position to seize the sense of an idea through the words that express it. Were we not able to do this, then the bulk of human communication, as known to persons reading these lines, would simply collapse. Insofar as it is possible to convey ideas through words, so is it possible to reconstruct a history of ideas through the study of words. Ideas may of course be expressed other than in words; there is always art and architecture, and dance and mime. But the bulk of the ideas which those who read this will have imbibed are the gift of words. Without these, it is difficult to imagine our ideas being other than confused or elementary, and if both, then possibly moronic. Words can convey an idea. They can do so over time. It would seem plain, accordingly, that an idea in this sense may have a genealogy, a history. And it must in principle be possible to write a history of an idea if the latter has a past.

It should be obvious that words, certainly, have a history. Otherwise, it would be difficult to suppose that etymology could constitute a possible subject of study. It is perhaps less obvious that ideas have a history. A word, although only a mere sign or symbol, is none the less some sort of thing. As 'things' have a certain materiality about them, they endure over time, and through that endurance reflect a historical dimension. Ideas, by contrast, although expressed through words, cannot be exhausted by some one fixed form of words. There are many different words and combinations of words which will express the same idea, whether in one language, or as in translations between different languages. Whereas words normally correspond exclusively to fixed symbols, ideas never correspond exclusively to particular words or arrangements of words. Further, ideas often correspond to nothing that actually exists at all: take the famous case of *phlogiston*. As ideas cannot be expressed exclusively through some one form of words, and as they often correspond to nothing real anyway, one can readily understand the inclination of many to conceive of them as immaterial (in more than one sense) and following on that to conclude that they do not have a history or (at the least) that no history of them can be written.

The problem is that if it is impossible to write a history of ideas, it is impossible to write a history of anything at all. For it is inevitably the case that any history is also a history of ideas. The subject of any history is always in some degree arbitrarily designated. Suppose it to be said that we can write a history (a biography) of a person, like Napoleon, Attila or Chaka. It is plain that none of these figures at 40 years of age was the same as at four. If we take the simple matter of physical continuity in relation to cell regeneration, it will be clear that there will not be a single cell which will have endured or survived in its original form over such a period of time. So that in the most physical of senses there will be no one Napoleon, Attila or Chaka to write about. What holds for them will hold for any other figure at all.

Similarly with the thinking of individuals: the intellectual difference between Einstein at six and Einstein at 60 is so great as to enable one to say, in respect of such differences, that the two minds are not the same. Yet neither the fact of total physical change nor of a spectacular and comprehensive intellectual development would warrant the conclusion that to write a biography of such a figure must prove an absurd or impossible undertaking. Biographies are written. But in order to do so, we must work from the assumption, the *idea*, of personal identity as borne by distinct individuals. If we assert a personal and continuing identity for Marx, despite the possibility of a radical divide between the younger and the older Marx, then we shall not be persuaded that we cannot provide, or that there is something illegitimate about providing, an account of Marx's intellectual life as a whole.

Suppose it to be said that we can write a history of a state (like the United Kingdom or France) or of some institution within the state (like Parliament). Whatever may be remarked of a history of 'ideas', it is not normally suggested that histories of this (supposedly more concrete) type are impossible or illegitimate. And yet similar problems arise. The United Kingdom covers so many different ideas that it would appear impossible to write a single history of the whole. There is much of art, music, drama, culture, style, politics, technology and so on. The 'idea' of the United Kingdom is in itself entirely geographical. But the geographical 'logic' of the unit referred to is in no way self-evident. This unit consists of one large island, the northern tip of another and a miscellany of tiny islands nearby, together with a variety of colonial possessions in the Caribbean, South Atlantic, South Pacific and Indian Oceans. It could be argued that the geographical 'idea' of the United Kingdom is so incoherent that it could not repay study. But one may be thankful that few historians would allow themselves to be distracted by such fatuous declamations. Of course, one way in which a geographical unit like the United Kingdom might be conceived and studied more coherently is by battening upon its *political* rationale. But that too is largely arbitrary. The emphasis upon political unity may be more than offset by class, cultural, ethnic and other disunities. In any event, the political unit is grossly unstable. At one time it included perhaps half of Africa, plus India, Pakistan and Sri Lanka, Australia, New Zealand, North America, etc. At an earlier time it included no part of Ireland; earlier still it included no part of Scotland; and we may well argue that, yet earlier, it equally excluded all of Wales and much even of what we now call England. (The Normans of course are identified as the initiators of the present political system which, interestingly, is commonly styled 'English'.) If we wished to argue in this way we could conclude that it is not 'possible' even to write a political history of the United Kingdom. But those engaged to write such histories will no doubt reply to such arguments with the silence they deserve.

If we look at an institution like Parliament, we are presumably not thinking of a particular building or timepiece that may adorn it. We are presumably thinking of a set of practices. These practices could be described in different words, in different combinations of words and naturally in different languages. But let us say that the object of our concern was the notion of 'representative government', which may fairly be thought to have something to do with 'democracy', 'liberty', 'rights' or 'habeas corpus', but also with 'power' and 'authority' and other notions besides. It would appear, at the least, unavailing to urge that a history of 'representative' or 'parliamentary' government in the Island(s) could not be written; certainly it is known to have been done. But to write such a book is most assuredly to write the history of an 'idea'. Histories may be well or badly written, and so with histories of 'ideas'. But the major problem will stem from assuming that ideas are necessarily distinct from practices. We have already remarked that an idea may very well refer or correspond to nothing that really exists, but even here a history may be written. (It is perfectly possible, for example, to provide a history of theories of spontaneous generation, astrology, demonology and so on). We cannot study a practice, a behaviour, a phenomenon or whatever without conceptually divorcing it from its environment. Thus to study something in particular, whether historical or otherwise, is to impose upon it, or to make of it, an idea. It is only with such an idea that we select for relevance. And without that idea, being unable to select, we can write no history whatever. Thus to suggest that a history can ever be written such that it in no way contains or reflects a 'history of ideas' is a serious (but dull) mistake. History may not be reducible to mere ideas. But there can be no history without them, nor any history which is not also 'of ideas'.

There are of course different levels of abstraction, and some ideas, like 'representative government', are arguably less abstract than others, like 'justice'. On the other hand, it may be that the problem with what we more restrictively call histories of 'ideas', may have less to do, strictly speaking, with their being 'abstract', than with the possibility of their being executed in some manageable way. One of the first criteria of manageability is that the idea being investigated should somehow correspond to a determinate practice. If we wish to write a history of 'equality' where this is intended to mean 'treating everybody in every way precisely and exactly the same', then presumably there is no actual practice of which one can provide an account. We would do better perhaps to analyse the logic of the concept or possibly subject it to various forms of ethical investigation. But if, by contrast, 'equality' is taken to mean 'all adults are entitled to vote', then the evolution of the idea *qua* practice can certainly constitute a subject of historical inquiry, and so with 'liberty', 'toleration', 'justice' and related notions. Abstraction is not a bar; unmanageability is, and the two are not the same.

It is pointless to advise either historians or philosophers not to concentrate exclusively upon a particular idea or a particular text 'in itself'. That is all that may interest them or all they may have time for. It is impossible to show that there is some one best way of seizing the meanings of ideas or texts. Approaches differ and doubtless always will do. In any event, to the extent that texts have meanings, the meanings refer to events which extend beyond the texts themselves. Thus no one who studies a text, to the extent that the text makes any sense, is studying that alone. For the text implicates a reality which lies beyond itself. Similarly with ideas: ideas are not texts, but may be expressed through them. To the extent that they are focused upon and the focus betrays a meaning, which is other than circular, then the idea is not a 'mere' idea, but something which extends beyond itself into the so-called 'real' world. By focusing upon an 'idea', one is not focusing upon 'nothing'. And any suggestion that there is some one best way of comprehending an idea as 'something' can scarcely fail to prove spurious.

It does not follow that to understand an idea requires that we understand all of the different ways in which it has been formulated, any more than understanding a country (like the United Kingdom) requires a knowledge of every conceivable thing about it. To argue otherwise is all very well, but such an argument can only, at best, constitute a counsel of perfection. To say that understanding an idea literally involves understanding '*all* the occasions and activities in which a given agent might have used the *relevant* form of words' is only to say that one can never possibly understand any idea whatever. The occasions on which one *might* use (or have used) a particular form of words surely cannot be numbered. And indeed we can never be sure that we have ever tabulated all *possible* usages, if for no other reason than that these possible usages must be regarded as infinite.

11. Conclusion

It is appropriate now to draw the discussion to a close. To write any history, one might have an 'idea', and select for it. Although one may distinguish between institutional and philosophical history, between the history of a system and that, more broadly, of a practice, the engagement remains selective and is no more fatuous in the one case than in the other. It is not so much that the writing of history requires that its object should have endured, as that the substantive matter dilated upon be arranged in such a way as to assume duration. In writing history, the idea that we select for, such as 'the state', must be attributed some degree of duration. The substantive criteria that we entertain for such a notion may be plucked from a time that is chronologically very distant. But whatever these ideas, whatever their origins, to the extent that they take on some coherent meaning in our minds in the present, it can be said that they are alive in this present. They are, at the least, alive for us. This does not *prove* that they are 'transhistorical', 'timeless' or 'eternal'. It is not possible, in the nature of things, to prove matters of this kind. But what is clear is that, if these ideas, whether as institutions, practices or philosophies, ever existed in the past, we shall only know them as ideas present in our minds. If we hold the past to be 'dead' then we also hold that we have no access to it. If we claim, as we do, that we 'know' the past, then we only know it as a part of the present. We must understand this tyranny, in order to reconcile to it our 'knowledge' of the past. The past we know, or that we claim to know, is known only because it is somehow in and of the present. Once we inspect more closely the different notions that we entertain of the present, we are well positioned to begin to discern the different notions we entertain of the past. As this work of understanding proceeds, particularly as regards the interpenetration of non-correlative senses of past and present, we may expect to discover that this interpenetration, if complex, is not in the least paradoxical.

The Twentieth Century: A History of the History of Ideas

1

A major problem confronted in the history of ideas has to do with whether we can be said to know the past. It might be contended, for example, that all knowledge is exclusively present. The contention can be viewed under two aspects.

First, if the ideas which we *hypothesize* to belong to the past are now actually being thought in the present, then the hypothesis must appear baseless, since all we have demonstrable evidence for is present thinking.

Second, if the ideas we know ourselves now to be thinking in the present are attributed to the past, then we cannot ever know the attribution to be valid, since we cannot actually think these present ideas in the past. Essentially, what we here confront is a case for all knowledge being present knowledge.

However, a rather different kind of case could be made, namely for the proposition that all knowledge is past knowledge. Any idea which we claim to be present must be assumed in some fashion to have evolved. Any idea that we formulate on paper or speak aloud is expressed in language, which is a social convention, and to which may be attributed existence and therefore duration. Thus, if we take any current doctrine, we are entitled to assume that it, too, as with any word moreover, has a past and a history. We need not look beyond this very argument where we seek to justify placing a trace on genesis, opening an eye to chains of influence, anchoring what is apparently present in the past. Any idea or doctrine that we at least do not concoct, given that the point at which it was formulated or recorded must precede the point at which we receive and assess it, must be a *past* idea or doctrine. Further, given that very few of our ideas are *our* ideas and that even the novelties we devise are pieced together from the ready-made components of communal life, it becomes difficult to conclude that there can be a present which is not past.

These two positions – that all knowledge is of the present, and alternatively that it is all of the past – take on the appearance of plain contradictories. On the one hand, to understand past ideas, we are enjoined to think them through for ourselves, to bring them to life, perhaps to 'enact' or 're-enact' them. On the other hand, such understanding, we are told, may only be achieved by ceasing to think as we do now, by shedding present outlooks, by removing ourselves to remote times, by appreciating how different *our* thought is from *theirs*, by reconstructing their contexts rather than assume any constancy or continuity between earlier and contemporary ways of thinking.

A great deal of the contestation involved in the contemporary debate over the logical status of the history of ideas is in some measure attributable to a failure to provide a clearer and fuller analysis of the interlocking concepts of 'past' and 'present'. The purpose of Chapter 2, which is not intended to be exhaustive, is to provide some minimal assistance in this direction. In this chapter, I seek only to review some of the more important figures who have recently written on or around this subject.

2

Michael Oakeshott (1901–91) who succeeded H.J. Laski as Professor of Political Science in the London School of Economics (1951–69) was one of the most influential students of the history of ideas in the English-speaking world. His social philosophy is anchored more in a commitment to historical, rather than to sociological or psychological, method. History, science, ethics and aesthetics are all for Oakeshott so many different ways or 'modes' of seizing experience. These 'arrests' of experience 'modify' it, render it abstract, taking away from the concreteness and totality of experience as such. Oakeshott perceives history to be only one possible, and not a necessary, form of experience. But it none the less remains of prime importance to him. Central to Oakeshott's analysis of history is his view of its character as paradoxical – positing a concern with the past, but a concern which can only be displayed in the present, and by reference to present evidence. Oakeshott's analysis is both sweeping and perceptive. In 1933, in *Experience and Its Modes*, it is expressed in one form. In 1955, in an essay entitled 'The Activity of Being an Historian', it is expressed in a somewhat modified form. Oakeshott's (1983) *On History and Other Essays* extends somewhat the same vein of argument.

A great deal has been written about Oakeshott, but not very much relating to Oakeshott on history. Oakeshott has been variably referred to, in most instances on his own initiative, as conservative,

traditionalist, historicist and so on. Much of the secondary literature
on him has been critical. For example, Rotenstreich (1976) comments:

> Just as Marx made man a function of his social circumstances, so
> Oakeshott makes man a function of his historical circumstances as
> embodied in tradition – and this is a strange affinity. [T]here is as little
> justification for Marx's ... historicism as there is for Oakeshott's.
> (p. 131)

The assessment of Oakeshott supplied in Chapter 4 is also critical,
being narrowly set in counterpoint to what it characterizes as
Oakeshott's 'historical particularism'. Whatever else Chapter 4 may
do, it reflects considerable unease regarding the supposed paradox to
which Oakeshott draws attention – that which portrays history as to
do with a dead past, but a past apprehended in and only in the evidence
of a living present. In the case of the history of ideas, again, the
problem set is: How, in what intelligible sense, can ideas be construed
as quite cut off from us, as populating a dead past, and simultaneously
prove fully intelligible and accessible by virtue of being incorporated
into present experience?

3

R.G. Collingwood (1889–1943) was elected to the Waynflete Chair of
Metaphysical Philosophy at Oxford University in 1935. After his early
retirement in 1941, Gilbert Ryle was elected to succeed him. In his
Autobiography (1939), Collingwood characterized his academic objective overall as basically consisting in bringing about 'a *rapprochement*
between philosophy and history'. Indeed, in his earliest book *Religion
and Philosophy* (1916), Collingwood went so far as to claim that these
disciplines were 'the same thing'. By contrast, in *An Essay on
Philosophical Method* (1933), he referred to philosophy as 'a distinct
and living form of thought' and not as 'a part of history'. While maintaining a very tight fit between history and philosophy, the *Essay*
clearly suggests that some philosophical systems are truer than others
and that the object of philosophical, as distinct from historical
enquiry, consists precisely in the assessment of such truth. It is agreed
that Collingwood changed his philosophical views at the latest between
1936 and 1938. Knox (1946) in support of a marked historicist
development in Collingwood's thought, quotes from notes written
by the latter early in 1939: 'philosophy as a separate discipline is
liquidated by being converted into history' (p. x). Donagan (1962)
agrees that 'Collingwood radically changed his mind' between 1926

and 1938 'about the relation of philosophy to history' (p. 12). Colling-wood, indeed, in a rather uncompromising mood, in the *Autobiography* (1939) denies 'the permanence of philosophical problems' and accordingly concludes 'that the alleged distinction between the historical question and the philosophical must be false'. Donagan espies in Collingwood a marginally greater coherence than does Knox, but the sense of disarray persists.

The paradox enunciated by Oakeshott is reformulated by Collingwood, but without the same deliberate, intentional and concentrated effect. To begin, Collingwood held Oakeshott in high regard and believed that the latter had developed 'a brilliant and penetrating account of the aims of historical thought' (Collingwood, 1946, p. 153). In fact, Collingwood regarded Oakeshott as representing the 'high-water mark of English thought upon history' (1946, p. 159), where it is understood that the period indicated is that prior to the emergence of Collingwood himself. Anticipatory positions parallel to Oakeshott's were accorded to Wilhelm Dilthey in Germany and to Benedetto Croce in Italy.

While Collingwood believed that Oakeshott's work represented 'a new and valuable achievement for English thought' and that it entirely vindicated 'the autonomy of historical thought', its independence *qua* science, he also believed Oakeshott's work to be hobbled by a crucial failure. This failure, he thought, derived from the fact that Oakeshott did not or could not show history to be 'a necessary ... element in experience as such', and so did not or could not show why there should be any such discipline 'as history at all'. Collingwood viewed himself as moving off in a significantly different direction. Oakeshott, on Collingwood's estimate, would have been right to travel with him, but proved unable to hurdle the view that history was 'either past or present, but not both'. Collingwood believed that Oakeshott should have, even on his own analysis, perceived history as 'a living past, a past which, because it was thought and not mere natural event, can be re-enacted in the present and in that re-enactment known as past'.

There is no doubt but that Oakeshott has a problem, yet it is not quite the problem which Collingwood took it to be. Collingwood understood Oakeshott to be firmly distinguishing between past and present. This is true enough, unless we place emphasis upon 'firmly'. Because while Oakeshott emphasizes the distinction, he equally intimates the impossibility of ever really making it. History, writes Oakeshott (1933), 'is the continuous assertion of a past which is not past and of a present which is not present' (p. 111). This is much the same as saying that, in history, the past is in the present, and that the present is in the past. Thus, while Oakeshott conceives past and

present to be distinct, he also conceives them, somehow, to be simultaneous and in a manner by no means entirely alien to Collingwood's
preferred solution except that Oakeshott warms to the idea of 'a dead
past' while Collingwood fancies the idea of 'a living past'.

Collingwood set out then to destroy the distinction between past
and present, a distinction attributed to Oakeshott. However, Oakeshott
accepts some notion of the simultaneity of past and present, but
frankly regards the idea as paradoxical and only commits himself
to simultaneity (this Collingwood apparently appreciated) as part of
his strategy for somehow keeping the past to itself, i.e. in the past.
Collingwood (1946) therefore, in his concern to show that the 'fact
that [historical experience] is also present does not prevent it from
being past', basically presented as a solution what Oakeshott (1933)
had styled a 'paradox'. When Collingwood's work is taken as a whole,
at least in regard to the question of the logical status of history, what
confronts us is a brilliant, a genuinely illuminating, piece of tergiver-
sation. Historical and philosophical thinking are alternately displayed
as identical, as distinct and again as identical. Collingwood is not the
simple historicist which a selective reading of his work, especially the
Autobiography, might be assumed to reveal. But he clearly 'oscillates'
between the acceptance and rejection of historicism, despite his own
resolve to push beyond this impasse. I agree with the conclusion of
Rotenstreich (1976) that Collingwood's valuable contribution never
achieves any valid synthesis; this, if it is to be achieved, must be
built upon a more direct and coherent 'analysis of historical time'
(p. 68). It is with this that Chapter 2 of this volume was designed to
assist.

Collingwood's *Autobiography*, according to R.B. McCallum (1943),
was 'regretted by most of his [Collingwood's] Oxford friends' because
of the sudden and unargued change of outlook which it supposedly
reflected (p. 467). All the same, the book's line of argument is on the
whole clear and firm. It also represents Collingwood's last major
statement on historical method. Further, it develops most fully and
interestingly the historicist component in Collingwood's thinking.
There is much counter-argument available on Collingwood. The
criticism by Leo Strauss, in the *Review of Metaphysics* ('On Collingwood's Philosophy of History', 5:4 (June): 559–86), is primarily
addressed to Collingwood's *Idea of History*. But Strauss essentially
singles out for attack what he regards as Collingwood's historicism.
Strauss argues that a sense of history and familiarity with the history
of ideas are valuable because they defend against parochialism in an
anachronistic guise. But he concludes that what is politically true and
right, generally or universally, is to be emphatically distinguished from

the separate question regarding how such views have come to be formed.

4

A.O. Lovejoy (1873–1962) has, in one place, been called 'the chief inspirer of the history of ideas'. It is a large claim, which effectively reduces, perhaps, to the fact that he was the most eminent of the founders of the *Journal of the History of Ideas*, which first appeared in January of 1940. In brief, Lovejoy's argument was that we understand ourselves better by understanding the ways in which we have evolved, which largely means to understand the manner in which we have come, over time, to hold the ideas that we do. Lovejoy wrote a great deal, as will be evident from any moderately detailed bibliography, including that supplied at the close of this volume. Four of Lovejoy's essays, however, are of particular relevance. The first is his 'Introduction: The Study of the History of Ideas', which constituted the opening chapter of his book, *The Great Chain of Being* (1936). The second essay is 'The Historiography of Ideas', first published in 1938 and subsequently incorporated in 1948 into one of Lovejoy's several volumes of essays. The third is 'Present Standpoints and Past History', originally published in 1939, and reprinted in 1959 in Meyerhoff. Finally, there is Lovejoy's 'Reflections on the History of Ideas' (1940), with which, in effect, the *Journal of the History of Ideas* was launched. These four essays are all marginally distinct from one another; none the less, if we make exception of the third, they cover much the same ground.

Lovejoy was much concerned with tracing intellectual influences. In the process, he opposed not so much the exploration of detail but rather an excess of specialization. Lovejoy's concern, in his words (1936), was to put 'gates through fences' – these fences being the boundaries of the various academic disciplines. He had reservations about literary and philosophical specialization within the limits, for example, of nation and language, on the grounds that such boundaries too often obscure the actual flow of influences across them. Lovejoy (1938) put his case in the following terms: 'the more you press in towards the heart of a narrowly bounded historical problem, the more likely you are to encounter in the problem itself a pressure which drives you outward beyond those bounds' (p. 6). He adverted to the need to understand some astronomy, and not a little of Aristotle, for example, to be able to provide any adequate exegesis of Milton's meaning in various passages of *Paradise Lost*. Lovejoy (1936) warned against any undue concern with major writers, where one seeks to elicit the actual thought of a period, since minor writers, as he wrote, may serve the purpose better, by revealing more that is characteristic of the time. Lovejoy, then, avowed no particular partiality towards writers major or minor, nor more of a commitment to text than context, but essentially committed himself to pursuing historical truth across whatever disciplines and epochs enquiry might dictate. Lovejoy's historical approach was unquestionably interdisciplinary (1938), on the assumption, it would appear, that historical research should be more problem-oriented than period-oriented, as well as on the assumption that the more narrow and detailed one's focus upon a particular subject or period, the less effective one may prove, for that very reason, in achieving any proper understanding of it. Lovejoy placed considerable emphasis upon sweep, upon comprehensiveness, a concern governed by the hope of getting the analysis 'right' – in relation at least to the problem set. Lovejoy (1939) conceived of the past as firmly distinct from the present, as unquestionably objective, but also as equally firmly relevant to the present, and thus as not in any way dead. Lovejoy (1940) believed that historical inquiry should in some degree prove 'instructive', and indeed 'provide material towards possible general conclusions – conclusions which do not relate merely to ... past and particular events' (p. 8).

In sum, Lovejoy regarded history as vast both in scope and detail, its substance only subject to arrest where the manacles of a specific problem or question are locked round some discrete part of it. He accepted that new problems do arise, but regarded them as rare, and concluded that the best means of coping with the history of ideas consists in (1) breaking down the more encompassing, compound doctrines that emerge (e.g. romanticism, rationalism, primitivism and pragmatism) into analytically smaller units, which he refers to as 'unit-ideas' and (2) in tracing the evolution of those 'unit-ideas' over time.

Lovejoy (1936) was, by his own account, much prejudiced in favour of 'distinguishing and analysing the major ideas which appear again and again'. It is, of course, a view for which he has been severely criticized in much of the later literature. However openly Lovejoy (1939) accepted the thesis that historical study is a selective undertaking anchored in the present, he energetically rejected the subjectivist implications often attributed to or associated with it.

5

Maurice Mandelbaum, in his critical assessment of Lovejoy's programme, argues that it may (1) disguise or distort the central intent
or motive of an author's work and (2) 'minimize the independence
of an author's thought' by suggesting connections or influences
which are doubtful or non-existent (Mandelbaum, 1965, section 1).
But Mandelbaum's concern is not to say that these difficulties, following Lovejoy's approach, *must* arise, only that they may do and by
implication are to be guarded against. Mandelbaum had earlier
written (1948) an appreciative notice which argued that Lovejoy's
approach represented a 'fruitful conception of history'. He viewed
this approach as consistent with a pluralism which excludes any 'single
all-pervasive pattern', accommodating not only clearly discernible
continuities and limited generalizations, but equally clearly discernible discontinuities, since 'no continuity perseveres unmodified and
unbroken' (1948, p. 423).

Mandelbaum (1948) writes of Lovejoy's pluralism as though the
views of the latter were essentially identical with those formulated by
Mandelbaum himself when a doctoral candidate. In his *Problem of
Historical Knowledge* (the doctorate in published form), Mandelbaum
(1938) seeks to argue for the objectivity of historical knowledge, to
counter the relativism of figures like Benedetto Croce, Wilhelm
Dilthey and Karl Mannheim, and to do this in a manner consistent
with a 'historical pluralism'. Like so many writers of recent times (e.g.
Collingwood, Oakeshott, Popper, Berlin), Mandelbaum argues that
there is no one single pattern, purpose, predictable denouement or
inevitability about history. No formulation or representation, says
Mandelbaum, is 'able to render justice to the pluralist nature of the
historical process as a whole' (p. 288). He contends that any 'attempt
to decipher the message which is contained in "the historical process
as a whole" is futile' (p. 306). Mandelbaum (1971) returns to this theme
much later in his attack on 'historicism', although most of what he
has to say on this head is formulated more rigorously by Popper and
Berlin.

In sum, Mandelbaum perceives a great deal in common between
himself and Lovejoy. He reveals a basic sympathy for Lovejoy's aims.
Accordingly, he is not unduly ambitious (1965) in his criticism. In his
book (Mandelbaum, 1971) on (or 'in') nineteenth-century thought,
where he sets himself the task of 'sifting ... presuppositions which
were held in common by a diverse group of thinkers whose antecedents and whose aims often had little in common' (p. ix), Mandelbaum in part exemplifies Lovejoy's approach. He readily employs

(what Lovejoy would have called) 'unit-ideas' like 'historicism', 'development', 'geneticism', 'organicism' and so on, to organize his material. Mandelbaum (1971) explicitly accepts Lovejoy's 'great-chain-of-being' concept as applicable to the work of figures like Lamarck and Darwin (pp. 79, 396, n.4).

It remains that Mandelbaum flinches from loose talk about 'an overriding spirit of the age' (a disposition he detects for example in Greene, 1957). He thinks it important to be able to trace influences over time, but that it is vital to avoid any suggestion of a monistic and ineluctable causal flow in the process. He feels it important to be clear about this in a way perhaps that Lovejoy was not. Hence his emphasis upon the manifold 'strands' that make up any era or epoch, upon both continuity and discontinuity in temporal sequence, upon the lack of fit between all of these elements, and upon the fact that any historical period is only such in certain respects and not in all (Mandelbaum, 1965, 1977).

While Mandelbaum fleshes out the diversity of types of historical inquiry, he never abandons a basic commitment to some concept of historical unity and coherence. While committed (1938) to some notion of historical particularism, to the view that 'the historian deals with specific events' (p. 3) by contrast with the scientist who, in effect, formulates universal laws (i.e. 'judgements regarding "typical" occurrences'), Mandelbaum (1938) accepts all the same that 'the complete separation of the historical method and the method of the physical sciences is impossible', that the two procedures are 'opposed to each other only in ideal cases', and that 'in the practice of the physical sciences they are often blurred' (p. 4). While disposed to define 'the historical enterprise' in terms of 'understanding every event in the light of its actual historical context' (p. 8), Mandelbaum (1938) none the less rejects as unfortunate 'the sharp division which is often made between "research historians" and "great" or "synthetic" historians' (p. 293), on the grounds that 'historical understanding tolerates no bifurcation between fact-finding and synthesis' (p. 294).

Mandelbaum (1965, part II) is very much concerned to avoid the holistic and in part historicist view, as expressed by figures like Comte, Hegel, Marx, Spengler and Toynbee, that to understand any particular historical period, or any aspect of such a period, one must understand the whole of history as such. He is concerned to avoid the notion, especially in the history of philosophy, that each stage somehow leads inexorably and connectedly to the next, so that this supposed movement can be easily read backwards from the present. Although he entertains an overarching view of history, he also is concerned to reveal its variability, especially by means of the distinction he establishes between histories that are either 'general' or 'special'.

Mandelbaum (1965) means by *special histories* those which 'seek to establish how a particular form of human activity, such as art, or religion or science, has developed over time, rather than attempting to trace how it has contributed to this or that particular society' (p. 45). Mandelbaum appears to mean by *general histories* those which provide descriptions or accounts of the process of change as this occurs within a specific society or institution (e.g. a nation, army, university or church). He regards general histories as reflecting a broader, more encompassing perspective; by contrast, 'the focus of interest of special histories is narrower' (p. 46); general histories, he suggests, rely upon special histories to convey 'the social context which governed the life of men at a particular time and place' (p. 45).

For Mandelbaum, general histories, histories of institutions, because of their organized character, which allows them to persist over time, must be continuous. By contrast, special histories, as of philosophy, although they *may* be continuous, are not necessarily so, since influences may leap across historical periods without following any strictly temporal sequence. These special histories then, though not necessarily continuous from an institutional perspective, may be so in other respects. As Mandelbaum (1965) puts it: 'a temporally discontinuous series of events may legitimately be viewed as having a measure of unity and continuity, such that it constitutes a proper subject-matter for historical inquiry' (p. 54). One obvious implication in all this is that one may hold a history of philosophy, for example, to be perfectly legitimate, without necessarily supposing that the pattern of change displayed can be regarded as ineluctable, desirable, progressive or 'developmental'.

Despite Mandelbaum's qualifications, many contemporary critics consider that such an approach to philosophical history, or to the history of ideas – putting it both more broadly and loosely – must none the less fail. To link together different thinkers across different periods may be held to distort their ideas, perhaps because it is really only *our* ideas that we are reviewing, or because we have been unable to reconstruct *their* context (as blurred by undue immersion in our own), or because the limited evidence we select from these thinkers is just unrepresentative of their thought. For example, G.A. Kelly (1975), in his review of Mandelbaum (1971), rounds on him in precisely these ways. Kelly (1975) charges that Mandelbaum's 'linkage of "otherwise divergent thinkers" in "almost identical" contexts' often overlooks their actual purposes, and the variety of these 'and tends to create a pastiche of theory independent of the theorists themselves'.

The charge is also frequently levelled that, in a philosophical history of this kind, we may never be quite clear as to whether the purpose of the writer is genuinely to reconstruct the way in which a set of ideas has actually evolved or merely to employ these ideas as a stalking horse for the author's own philosophy (which he should formulate for himself, it may be thought, both more briefly and more lucidly).

6

Leo Strauss (1899–1973) worked from 1925 for seven years in the Academy of Jewish Research in Berlin. He left Germany for France in 1932, and later moved to England. He finally settled in America in 1938. He joined the university in exile of the New School for Social Research in New York, where he remained for ten years. He moved to the University of Chicago in 1949 and served there for 18 years, the last eight of these (from 1959) as Robert M. Hutchins Distinguished Service Professor of Political Science.

Strauss was one of America's most eminent and productive champions of political philosophy. Strauss's chief academic medium was history, but he attacked historicism and positivism – this last not only in the form of contemporary social science behaviouralism – with notable acerbity. His assumption was that the gap between past and present could and must be bridged, although not in any absurdly literal way, hence his intense interest in 'pre-modern rationalism, especially Jewish-medieval rationalism and its classical (Aristotelian and Platonic) foundation' (Strauss, 1965, p. 31). Strauss's interest was in rationalism, but it was an interest which he usually approached in an approximately revelatory manner, through the almost occult interpretation of texts.

Strauss believed modern rationalism – dating most notably from first, Machiavelli and Hobbes, second, Rousseau and third from Nietzsche – to be engaged in an inevitable process of self-destruction. It reflected a shift from the concern with contemplation and self-understanding (philosophy) to a concern with power and control over nature (science). It also reflected a shift from a condition of moral certainty to that of a certain amorality, principally that of an historicist relativism where a value is held to be valid depending upon the era in which it is uttered. Before Strauss took his leave of England (this was in 1937), Oakeshott, while taking issue with him on important points of interpretation, correctly wrote of Strauss's *Political Philosophy of Hobbes* as 'the most original book on Hobbes which has appeared for many years' (Oakeshott, 1975a, p. 133).

Strauss *qua* exegete was nothing if not 'original' – in ways which have engendered reactions ranging from fervent adulation to acid rebuke. And all of it is understandable: Strauss was no sceptic or relativist. Although he displayed considerable respect for his texts, conjoined with an uncannily exhaustive, perhaps rabbinical, control of them, his sense of outrage could whip him up to and over the lip of invective and parallel misjudgement. In his analysis of Machiavelli, Strauss moves back and forth across the textual minefield of *The Prince* and *The Discourses* with remarkable ease and adroitness; to Strauss's readers are revealed even the hidden meanings and connections between Machiavelli's chapter numbers. It is all too cabalistic to be true, and is yet engaging. Besides, every decent reader wants somehow to round on Machiavelli; Strauss provides the means. The crude scissors of his morality are brought to bear upon the literary corpus of the quick-witted Florentine with a gratifying finality.

Yet, one can never quite surrender oneself to Strauss's judgement. His coarseness occasions a wariness equal to the delight excited by his mastery of detail. For Strauss (1958), Machiavelli becomes a 'teacher of evil', an 'evil man' (p. 9), 'immoral and irreligious'. Those scholars who 'do not see the evil character of his thought' fail in this respect, following Strauss, 'because they ... have been corrupted by Machiavelli' (p. 13). The attack is pure *ad hominem*, and it is not an entirely occasional lapse. In one breath, as it were, Strauss would hold the 'indispensable condition of "scientific" analysis' to be 'moral obtuseness' (p. 11); in the next, with no less a display of 'moral obtuseness' (in the manner indeed of an obliging refugee who must praise his protectors) Strauss celebrates 'the foundation of the United States' – by contrast with all the governments of Europe – as an edifice unqualifiedly 'laid in freedom and justice' (p. 13). The breadth of interest, the marvellously heady analysis, the leaden and moralistic misjudgement, the repetitiveness, the excruciatingly partisan commitment; these disparate elements are all wrapped up in one large package. The reader may attend to whichever items he likes; it is excusable, in any reading of Strauss, that one should be fascinated or repelled or both.

The exegesis provided by Strauss of classical philosophy, specifically Plato, Aristotle and Xenophon, was not that of an antiquarian. The past which he manipulated was not conceived as dead. His justification for these excursions was not to relax as a tourist but to train for present or future action: 'the questions raised by the political philosophers of the past are alive in our own society' (Strauss and Cropsey, 1963). The seriousness with which Strauss analysed past thought stemmed from his appreciation of the past as somehow present. And this is basically what Strauss (1949) meant when arguing that 'political philosophy is not a historical discipline'. A sense of history, to be sure, defends one (Strauss maintained) against anachronism, and accordingly proves valuable. But it is not, for all that, 'an integral part' of philosophy itself. A history of philosophy is useful in that it may make one familiar with the way in which characteristic philosophies have come to be formed. But for Strauss there always remained the distinction between how a philosophical view evolves and whether that view proves valid.

In effect, Strauss was concerned with the study of the moderns in order to determine how (what he called) 'the crisis of Political Philosophy' came about. He studied the ancients by contrast because he believed theirs represented a perennial philosophy. A 'simple continuation of the tradition of classical political philosophy [was] no longer possible' (Strauss, 1964a). This impossibility was attributable to 'the crisis of our time' in the West, represented at the one extreme by a loss of internal purpose (e.g. liberalism, anarchism, nihilism) and externally by the threat of Soviet communism ('the most extreme form of Soviet despotism'). The 'return to classical political philosophy', then, though 'necessary', must also prove adaptive or 'experimental'. In Strauss's words: 'Only we living today can possibly find a solution to the problems of today. But an adequate understanding of the principles as elaborated by the classics may be an indispensable starting point' (p. 11).

For Strauss, in fact, the classics *were* the indispensable starting point. And he offered his services as an indispensable guide. He seemed burdened with a superlative reverence for the past. He was not disposed to present himself as harbinger of things new, but rather as the astute sage who would initiate readers and students into the mysteries of a living heritage and help to deploy these mysteries in the defence or construction of a happier present – 'happiness' being understood in the Aristotelian sense of 'virtuous'. Although virtually all of Strauss's work involves an exercise in the history of ideas, it none the less proceeds from the postulate that there are historical problems and philosophical truths which are 'transhistorical', 'perennial', 'enduring' and 'fundamental'. His immediate concern was to understand the past, but his ultimate object was simply to attain a genuine philosophical understanding *per se*, independent of historical accident. As Strauss (1952c) wrote in the Preface to his book on Hobbes, 'I assumed that political philosophy as a quest for the final truth regarding the political fundamentals is possible and necessary.'

It is precisely because past thought *is* alive, following Strauss, that one may hope to 'understand the great thinkers of the past as *they understand* themselves' (my italics). Strauss understood the 'enduring questions', those which interpenetrate past and present, to relate to freedom and government, constitutionalism or regime type, tyranny and virtue. In commenting upon Machiavelli, Strauss (1958) observed that many 'contemporaries are of the opinion that there are no permanent problems and hence no permanent alternatives' and that it is precisely Machiavelli, given the supposed novelty of his problem, who best stated their case. Strauss conceded some weight to the argument, but characteristically concludes ('stated baldly') that this 'proves merely that the permanent problems are not as easily accessible as some people believe' (p. 14). Strauss proposed to take the student beyond surface appearances to seize the true nature of historical problems, to know them, not as dead, but alive, a current irresistibly rippling through the present.

For all its intricacy and also lack of grace, as one must confess, there can be no mistaking the challenge with which Strauss confronts the relativist outlook in the history of philosophy. Strauss (1953) insists that 'history' has meant 'throughout the ages primarily political history' and accordingly that 'what is called the "discovery" of history is the work, not of philosophy in general, but of political philosophy' (p. 34). Historicism was accordingly regarded by Strauss as more a problem for political and social philosophy than for any other disciplines, although the work of Thomas Kuhn (1970 [1962], p. 138) would suggest that Strauss in this may have been unduly restrictive. In any event, Strauss's inclination was not numbly to defend his position, but to leap across the trenches to exploit the vulnerability of his enemy. Strauss provides less a direct defence of his approach, than an assault, as he sees it, upon the crucial logical weakness of historicism.

'Historicism', wrote Strauss (1953), 'asserts that all human thoughts or beliefs are historical, and hence deservedly destined to perish; but historicism itself is a human thought; hence historicism can be of only temporary validity, or it [simply] cannot be true'. And Strauss was perfectly entitled in this to insist upon consistent self-application as one of the first tests of the coherence of a principle. If a doctrine or method is only true for its time, then to conceive this as a doctrine or method and apply it to itself must yield an incoherence. If a philosophy or method is only true in its own context, then this very contextual observation in turn will only prove true in its own context, which would imply that it cannot always be true. Strauss was inclined to believe that the proponents of historicism always adjudged their doctrine to be true – which must involve the projection of a moral and methodological universal. Hence the difficulty involved in simultaneously embracing the moral and methodological scepticism and relativism which is implicit in notions

82   *Thinking Past a Problem*

of epochal uniqueness and historical particularism. In sum, for
Strauss, 'this historicist thesis is self-contradictory', since one cannot
assert 'the historical character of "all" thought ... without transcending history, without grasping something transhistorical' (1953, p. 25).

It is in the manner indicated that Strauss (1953) came to draw the
following conclusion:

> if historicism cannot be taken for granted, the question becomes
> inevitable whether what was hailed in the nineteenth century as a
> discovery was not, in fact, an invention, that is, an arbitrary inter-
> pretation of phenomena which had always been known and which had
> been interpreted much more adequately prior to the emergence of the
> historical consciousness than afterward. We have to raise the question
> whether what is called the 'discovery' of history is not, in fact, an
> artificial and makeshift solution to a problem that could arise only on
> the basis of very questionable premises. (p. 33)

More than any other recent academic thinker, Strauss became
identified as the founder of a 'school'. The commitment to the
formal need for a 'transhistorical' ethic and epistemology, however
variable its content for any particular spokesman, was emphatic. In
the *Festschrift* published on the occasion of Strauss's retirement
(Cropsey, 1964), one is provided in cameo with some hint of Strauss's
influence upon American letters. Strauss represented a virtually neon-
lit target. The resulting fusillade has been as one might expect. A
careful and summary article by J.G. Gunnell (1978), which raises
gently the question of the tenability of Strauss's enterprise, is best
interpreted as the marksman's anticipatory clearing of the throat.

7

The work of figures like Oakeshott and Collingwood is now the object
of considerable and supportive academic attention. The work of
figures like Lovejoy and Strauss, by contrast, is less well received. The
centre of support for the former two is, naturally enough, located in
Britain and the Commonwealth. Support for the latter two is concentrated in the United States. Quentin Skinner betrays considerable
hostility to the methodologies espoused by Lovejoy and Strauss. The
chains of influence which they insist upon, he takes to be more nearly
mythological, due to the great difficulty, perhaps impossibility, of
actually demonstrating them. Skinner is concerned, moreover, that
to trace a history of ideas must require that we actually impose these
ideas upon history. It is dangerous, he claims, 'for the historian of
ideas to approach his material with preconceived paradigms'.

Skinner has published a large number of essays, as one may see from the Bibliography. Most of these may readily be fitted into one of two categories. The first relates, broadly, to appropriate (and inappropriate) methods for writing the history of ideas (most importantly Skinner 1966b, 1969a, 1970, 1971, 1972b, 1972c and 1974). The second relates basically to the historical reconstruction of what Skinner calls Hobbes's 'ideological' context (most importantly Skinner 1964, 1965a, 1966a, 1966c, 1969b, 1972a and 1972d).

Skinner's essays deal, first, with the general question of valid methodology. Second, they concern the application of this methodology to a specific social philosopher of the seventeenth century. Skinner's *Foundations* (1978a) provides another, specific test of the general methodology, but in this case as applied to a period rather than to an individual philosopher. A great deal of comment has been generated on Skinner's general programme, as in Parekh and Berki (1973) and Gunnell (1982) and in an issue of *Political Theory* (August 1974) devoted entirely to Skinner's work. Less has been written about the execution of that programme (although numerous reviews of Skinner, 1978a have appeared, as for example, Shklar, 1979; Holmes, 1979; Kelley, 1979; Mulligan, 1979; Boucher, 1980 and Black, 1980). In Chapter 5 of this volume, an attempt is made to say something both about Skinner's programme and about a specific test of it, but the question taken to be of prior interest is Skinner's application of his general theory to the work of Thomas Hobbes. There is further discussions of the contextualist project in Chapters 6, 7 and 8.

8

There is a great deal of literature on the problems associated with writing histories of ideas. It would still be desirable, in this connection, for Skinner to bring together his various methodological essays, and to compress and to publish them as a connected statement. Also, selections from some more recent writers (there are quite a number of them, for example, Leslie, 1970; Haddock, 1974; Ashcraft, 1975; Kvastad, 1977; Lockyer, 1979 and Femia, 1979) could be usefully brought together to ease the problems of access which hobble readers interested in these matters. The edited collection by James Tully (1988), *Meaning and Context: Quentin Skinner and His Critics*, is a useful step in this direction.

4

Michael Oakeshott and Historical Particularism

1

History occupies a central position in the political theory of Michael Oakeshott. In 1934, reviewing *Experience and Its Modes*, R.G. Collingwood (1970) described 'the chapter on history' as 'the real nucleus' of the book, and characterized the account overall as 'the most penetrating analysis of historical thought that has ever been written'. There is the risk, of course, when drawing near to such evidence as this, that those in whom we repose our trust may themselves be snared in a circle of mutual admiration. I have in mind Oakeshott's later reception of Collingwood's *Principles of Art* (1938a). In his review, Oakeshott wrote (1970): 'I can do no better than state at once that it is the most profound and stimulating discussion I have ever read of the question'. But no matter. To chasten those disposed to regard Collingwood's testimony as suspect, we may recall E.H. Carr's verdict. Carr (1964) declared Collingwood to be 'the only British thinker in the present century who has made a serious contribution to the philosophy of history', despite the fact that Carr had severe strictures to lay both upon Collingwood and Oakeshott.

The view that history is central to Oakeshott's *oeuvre* is in fact widely accepted. J.L. Auspitz, contributing to the most elaborate recent symposium on Oakeshott's work and discussing Oakeshott's *On Human Conduct* (1975b), addresses this point. Auspitz (1976), occupying somewhat neutral ground, writes: 'History is the understanding of events as contingently related, and Oakeshott sketches the outline of a case, to be elaborated elsewhere, for the irreducibility of contingent relations to the causal or probabilistic relations which are paradigmatic in the social sciences'. Kenneth Minogue, who is close to Oakeshott, and in this sense occupies the government front bench, also understands Oakeshott to perceive 'human conduct' as 'essentially contingent' and therefore as incapable of being 'understood in terms of systems and processes'. Minogue's conclusion: The fundamental "logic" of human explanation is that of history' (1975).

As for the loyal opposition, the perception of the centrality of history in Oakeshott persists. A.H. Birch (1969) for example, in arguing with Oakeshott, none the less identifies the latter's view of history as the chief question to be disputed. Birch contends that political scientists are given to understand by Oakeshott 'first, that the nature of political activity makes historical explanation the only appropriate mode, and second, that the nature of historical explanation prevents them from seeking answers to many of the questions which are normally regarded as central to their subject' (p. 222). Birch perceives Oakeshott's retreat into a particularly restrictive concept of history unrealistically to exclude the prospect of identifying 'regularities, tendencies, types and typical sequences' (p. 225), all such, for Birch, constituting 'sociological explanation'. Birch, while effectively arguing against what one might call Oakeshott's 'particularist' concept of history and arguing for what Birch himself calls 'sociological explanation', none the less hints that the latter need only be viewed as an addition to Oakeshott's other modes of experience. The important consideration in all this is the proper emphasis that must be placed upon Oakeshott's commitment to historical explanation as that most appropriate to the understanding of human conduct. Oakeshott is sometimes little disposed to say clearly that which is susceptible to more ambiguous formulation. What Minogue more boldly asserts, Oakeshott (1975b) formulates less robustly: 'The theoretical understanding of a substantive action or utterance is, then, in principle, a "historical" understanding' (p. 107). Where we turn directly to the subject of our concern, we find that the veil is never quite torn from the face of this argument.

2

It will be clear as to the centrality of history for Oakeshott. But history may be conceived in different ways. The most extreme contrast is that in which it is regarded, on the one side, as governed by laws and thus predictable, and, on the other, as governed by no laws and so as unpredictable. It is most uncomfortable to be made to divide a large cake in two, and then to choose which of the two it is better to eat. This would prove an uncomfortable challenge, but not one, all the same, from which every brave man will withdraw. Oakeshott, certainly, is less timorous than most. As a part of this, naturally, one cannot but applaud his 'deep respect for the individual action', his 'eye for shades of difference between plausible likenesses', indeed his 'ear for echoes and the imagination' (1975b, p. 106). But one fears that the emphasis upon history as non-recurrence, difference, individuality, context, contingency, circumstance, uniqueness and the like, must often ultimately collapse into self-enclosure and the unintelligibility associated with a great profusion of private worlds. It does not matter that the concept of history as physics, as determinism or materialism or predictability should sin in some rather different way.

Oakeshott's assertions about the nature of history may be construed as constituting a defence of historical 'particularism'. In the face of this construction, we may encounter the rebuttal that Oakeshott is as much concerned with generality as with particularity. There are indeed statements which may be extracted from Oakeshott's most recent work which are consistent with this rebuttal. For example: 'A specific engagement to understand begins in a "going-on" abstracted from all that may be going on and understood in terms of an ideal character specified as a composition of characteristics, a unity of particularity and genericity' (1975b, p. 12). Or again: 'there can be no relationship save between identities, and all identities are unities of particularity and genericity' (p. 102). And most forcefully: 'particularity is neither intelligible nor capable of inviting investigation' (p. 12).

Despite these quotations, it remains that Oakeshott suggests an identity between 'particularity' and 'uniqueness'. This is done in *On Human Conduct* (p. 102). There are similar suggestions in *Experience and Its Modes* (1933). And were we to say that Oakeshott's arguments constitute a defence of historical 'uniqueness', there could not subsist any possible grounds for complaint. The point is not that, in Oakeshott, 'history is made up of details'. Everything is. There is no more a need to defend Oakeshott than Gangesa or Democritus against so tepid a charge. The point rather is that, for Oakeshott, history is experience perceived as 'unique events'. It will be true of course that particular events, as with particular facts, cannot be seized other than in relation to other events and facts – and on the basis of an infinite range of assumptions. But a distinction is to be made between a particular as merely a unit in a series (e.g. one copy of *Leviathan* among tens of thousands) and a particular more singularly as the only one of a kind (such as the last Tasmanian tiger or Mauritian dodo – should either chance to be out and about somewhere). It is this second type of particularity which Oakeshott projects upon history, and characterizes as unique. What Oakeshott is arguing against, albeit in an almost exclusively definitional manner, is the idea of history as science, of 'unique events' being governed by 'universal laws', of 'practice' (the wink) being explained in terms of 'process' (the blink).

3

The doctrine of historical particularism – the notion that historical events are unique – is in no way peculiar to Oakeshott. It is a view for which we are all disposed to evince some degree of sympathy. Nor is it necessarily a conservative view. It could in part be anarchistic (as with Kropotkin) or Marxist or Darwinian or Popperian. Nor is it patently absurd, for the reason that every unit in a set or integer in a series or member of a group is, in some stipulable sense, 'unique'. Peter, like John, was one of 12 disciples, and thus not singular; but to the extent that it was him and no other who was denominated father of the church, his position was unique. Any event, historical or other, may be regarded, depending entirely upon one's perspective, as either particular or general, as either unique or commonplace (and therefore as both). All that matters is to say, and with good reason in any given case, whether and in what respects the event or phenomenon inspected is either one or the other. To call history unique is to commit a category mistake; it is to confound what is common and recurrent with what is not. But we shall return to critical considerations of this sort later.

The categorization of history by Oakeshott as a plenum of unique events is intended to exclude the notion of there being universal or inexorable laws at work within it. If one took a static or cyclical view of history (as with the Book of Ecclesiastes in the one case or Vico in the other), one would in either case assume a form of determinism which would somehow imply the existence of such laws. The odd thing about the nineteenth-century 'discovery' – or rediscovery – of history as something other than theological or scientific determinism, is that it posited epochal and periodic differentiation or uniqueness married to an overarching and rational dynamic. Hegel assumed that the free individual was the agent of history and that through him/her there laboured 'the cunning of reason', so that what was 'accidental' or 'incidental' was controlled by a higher (or deeper) rationale or purpose which the individual as such could not know. Hegel was struck by the way in which the obvious and fundamental truths of one era become the equally obvious absurdities of another. Marx, of course, like Hegel, sought to retain the appreciation of historical particularity while insisting none the less upon an underlying rationale, in this case of 'historical materialism' or, as Plekhanov later put it, of 'dialectical materialism'. Darwin, though he assumed every species was unique, managed to unlearn the notion that each species represented a special single instantaneous act of creation, and instead of this perceived indeed a 'process', of what he called 'natural selection'. In all of these cases, there is joined some notion of historical periodicity, individuality or uniqueness, with historical rationality, causality and sometimes predictability.

Oakeshott is certainly reacting against Hegel and Marx while none the less being much subject to the influence of the former. The chief difference for our purposes is that Oakeshott's historical particularism attempts to break away most decisively from the notion of causality in history, as accepted by his nineteenth-century predecessors. But even in this respect, Oakeshott does not stand alone. Even Karl Popper, in *The Poverty of Historicism* (1960), takes a position which is in some respects similar. Popper, however, is much more careful, and his judgement more rounded. He distinguishes, for example, between 'trends' and 'laws', arguing that history at least displays the former if not the latter. Furthermore, Popper does not maintain that *all* historical hypotheses are singular statements about one or more individual events (p. 107), but only that they are so 'as a rule', which is to say in some (possibly even most) but not in all cases. Finally, Popper insists that one of the major tasks of history must remain 'the disentanglement of causal threads' and does not merely or exclusively involve 'the description of the "accidental" manner in which these threads are interwoven' (p. 147). Popper, then, asserts with Oakeshott that history involves 'the appreciation of the unique'. But unlike Oakeshott, he does not repudiate what he calls 'causal explanation' in history.

Overall, Oakeshott perceives history as a sequence of unique events, events which have no purpose or end, events which are dead, beyond hope of modification, beyond the applause or catcalls of moral praise or blame, events which are none the less inferred from present evidence, and present evidence only. This is an odd, interesting, bewildering, in part contradictory and no doubt 'unique' set of ideas. And they, again in part, have set up their resonances. One might even say that they have, if not started, then accentuated, a 'trend' in Popper's sense. The trend is against making moral judgements in historical analysis, against treating the ideas of the past as though they were present (even though paradoxically, they are), against confusing one period with another, and towards differentiating every period (however impossible the task) from every other, towards placing the emphasis upon discontinuity rather than continuity, and upon the uniqueness and irrelevance of the past despite its inevitable apperception in and only in the present.

Oakeshott believes that human conduct is to be understood 'in terms of contingent relations' and that such understanding 'is contextual' (1975b, p. 105). If historical events are unique, then each, for Oakeshott, must be assimilated on its own terms, for its own sake and as a whole. This differentiation between diverse historical moments is nothing other than periodization, with its commitment to contextual analysis in the history of ideas. The discussion has by now been pushed much beyond Oakeshott. But Oakeshott's self-enclosed definitionalism, with its recommendatory import, has encouraged many scholars to further differentiate themselves, and to place a stress upon what is limited and local, on the comfortable assumption that it could not, in any event, ever legitimately prove much more than this. On the other hand, one suspects that it would prove out of place to blame such a writer as Oakeshott for an orientation which may merely prove symptomatic of the brittleness of an age.

One of the most celebrated proponents of contextual analysis in our own time is of course Quentin Skinner. Skinner (1969a) does not argue, with respect to the history of ideas, that the context determines what a given writer says, but only that it places a negative limit upon what that writer could have meant. It is clear that, to grasp the meaning of any communication, we must in some degree be familiar with the conventions which qualify what is conveyed as a communication. It remains that, at any point where we think that we have grasped what was intended, we may be mistaken. But we only think our grasp is secure where we think we understand the conventions. And a convention, like a tradition, as Oakeshott has observed, is a tricky thing to get to know. And how, one may ask, is it ever possible to be sure? Skinner suggests that we may undertake 'the study of all the facts about the social context of a given text'. Oakeshott, in parallel, characterizes the historian as totally immersed in the past, suffering no lacuna, in search of the whole.

The obvious question is whether any programme which enjoins the study of *all* the facts is in any way feasible. The answer will be obvious. Now we never know in itself when something has been communicated. From the point that we think we know even that much, quite apart from the substance of any communication, it is already to be presumed that we have some familiarity with the conventions involved. The problem is to determine how much of a contextual understanding we require in order to be able to grasp what an author has to say. One may easily sink into an infinite regress of putting thoughts in context without any clear criterion to stipulate what would constitute an adequate level of such attainment. In sinking beneath the waves of such 'contextual' analysis, the original author's 'intentions' may directly escape recovery. This, for the reason that psychological *intentions* are never entirely to be divorced from the logic of one's formulae and their associated *implications*. In this way, too, a philosopher who takes the logic of his own argument seriously may easily be led to embrace implications which are demonstrated by another to follow from his premises, even where those logical implications are inconsistent with some psychological or moral intentions which the author may originally and explicitly have embraced. Inasfar as a past thinker displays a logic, he also proffers it as a handle, one by which his meaning may be relevantly gripped in future, and in relation to the concerns of that future.

John Dunn (1969), for example, is one of those who sinks into a bog of 'contextual' analysis in the attempt to recapture 'Locke's *own* meaning'. In his 'excavation', Dunn eschews the notion that he should provide 'a critique of [Locke's] argument'. Dunn will not argue with Locke apparently on the assumption that the one in the present and the other in the past cannot possibly share any relevant common ground. 'I simply cannot conceive of constructing an analysis of any issue in contemporary political theory around the affirmation or negation of anything which Locke says about political matters' (p. 2). Dunn then commits himself to historical periodization, to an unequivocal divorce between past and present, and to the idea that no moral should be abstracted from the one and applied to the other. Only Dunn's sort of account of Locke is characterized as 'historical', i.e. as valid, not such accounts as those provided by Alan Ryan or C.B. Macpherson or Leo Strauss or Richard Cox or Raymond Polin.

Dunn, given the commitment to a radical divorce between past and present, appears disposed to want to deny us the possibility of fitting Locke into a tradition (that of 'English empiricism'). The danger for the particularist is clear. If we stipulate the nature of the tradition, that stipulation is a contemporary exercise and its consequence must be to shape the way in which we see past events building up to and influencing the present. And if the past, in this way, does influence the present, then of course it is also somehow a part of the present, and in this sense requires to be contended with, even argued with. Of course it will be true that it could not have been Locke's 'own ambition', in the seventeenth century, to espouse Marxist and liberal views which only became current from the nineteenth century. But it has never been the case that contributing to an outcome necessarily requires a psychological intention or commitment to do so. There can be no question that the Newtonian theory of gravity contributed to the Einsteinian theory of relativity. But to say that Newton had this influence does not require us to add that he knew Einstein's theory or intended to contribute to it. It is always probable that a great thinker will somehow spark or inspire the emergence of new ideas with which he could not possibly be familiar in their evolved form. And this is because the logic of a position, although it may correlate with a writer's meaning, is never reducible to the 'psychology' of his mind.

In attempting to explain Locke's ideas, Dunn feels compelled to fall back upon his 'psychology', and his 'biography'. Dunn identifies in Locke two incompatible concepts of 'substantive morality'. He conceives of Locke as torn between the disposition to concoct an ethic built upon obedience to God and one built upon an increasing individual pursuit of power. In Dunn's own words, 'one of these [Lockeian commitments] is purely secular', the terrestrial utilitarian object being 'to maximize the influence and power of the individual'. The other commitment is religious and is 'concerned with individual salvation'. Dunn's (1969) conclusion is that Locke joins these two moralities, but (*contra* Macpherson) makes the power motive subsidiary to the religious object of achieving salvation (pp. 257–8). The 'highly conjectural explanation which [is] implicit throughout [Dunn's] account' (p. 256) is that Locke never surrendered himself to pleasure, never became 'a gay and careless libertine' (p. 258), never threw off the restraints imposed by his religious morality – because Locke 'was brought up in a Calvinist family' (p. 259); lacked 'assurance' and 'confidence'; 'suffered to much anxiety'; was 'distinctly ill physically'; was 'too anxious', 'very neurotic' and characterized by 'personal weakness'. All of this is intended to explain the priority system attributed by Dunn to Locke's ethics – to explain why Locke *thought* as he did. We must concur with Dunn in the view that the account is 'crude' and even 'vulgar', but not on the grounds that to admit an offence is necessarily exculpatory. In this example one may detect something of the difficulty associated with attempting to comprehend some aspect of the past, in this case systems of thought, by reference to contextual readings which so often reduce to vulgar biography. Dunn, in his 'historical account' of Locke's politics, attempts to cut himself off from the present to secure a firmer grip on the past. His success consists merely in using some Lockeian part of the past to support one of the sides in a contemporary debate over the possibility or impossibility of neutralizing history *vis-à-vis* present concerns and commitments. To the extent that he succeeds, to that extent does he demonstrate a larger failure.

Dunn (1969) is surely correct in saying that Locke, given his seventeenth-century English context, most probably could not even imagine the possibility of an egalitarian social revolution and that it might prove inappropriate to judge him morally in relation to such a (for Locke non-existent) possibility. 'A Locke confronted by the possibility of achieved social revolution is no longer the Locke on whose attitudes we have the evidence to pronounce' (p. 240). What is important to recognize is that this stricture cuts two ways. Dunn and those of like views are only concerned with one of these ways. The principle the particularist stipulates is this: do not transfer a writer from an earlier period to a later and assume that one can say anything whatever about what such a writer, in altered circumstances, would have thought. The principle the particularist overlooks, however, is that one must be equally obliged, logically, not to transfer a later period to an earlier and to make a pronouncement on behalf of an earlier writer regarding what he would *not* have thought. In this respect, the complaints levelled against Macpherson by Dunn can equally well be levelled against Dunn himself, as where the latter confidently assures us that Locke's 'deepest social and moral assumptions ... would probably have placed him among the defenders of the Ancien Régime' a century later. How could one possibly say, psychologically, *what* Locke would, even probably, have done? Of course, one can make the *type* of statement made by Macpherson or Dunn about what a past writer, in a future at some remove from him, would or would not have done, on the assumption of a continuity between past and present, and of the relevance of one to the other. What one cannot do is to deny the continuity and relevance and then proceed to hypothesize about what past figures would not (even probably) have thought at some later time.

But the object here is not again to enter directly into a discussion of the status of historical contexts and of traditions of ideas. It is merely to say that what Oakeshott offers us is associated with an important stream of contemporary thought to do with historiography and the study of society. In doing this, it is not necessary to exaggerate the substantive achievement, as with Kenneth Minogue, where the latter declares Oakeshott's *On Human Conduct* to be 'worthy to stand beside ... *Leviathan*' (1975).

4

The similarity or congruence of (1) Oakeshott's argument and (2) much present practice is such as to suggest the utility of reviewing the tenability of the second by reference to the more elaborate arguments of the first. Certainly Oakeshott's argument can be reasonably construed as constituting a defence – perhaps the defence – of an approach which we may label historical particularism. But we are not required to insist that all of those who appear ideologically addicted to historical particularism have necessarily read Oakeshott.

The most important statements in Oakeshott's philosophy of history are contained in *Experience and Its Modes* (1933) and in the essay entitled 'The Activity of Being an Historian (1955).[1] The latter amplifies the former in certain important respects, although W.H. Greenleaf (1966) has recorded the view that 'The Activity of Being an Historian' succeeded in adding 'little to the earlier analysis'. In my judgement, *On Human Conduct* (Oakeshott, 1975b) adds little of significance to the discussion. For Oakeshott, experience may be construed in four different ways: contemplatively (or poetically), practically, scientifically and historically. In the first case,[2] we 'regard the world in a manner which does not allow us to consider anything but what is immediately before our eyes and does not provoke us to any conclusions'. (This *contemplative* perspective is that 'of the artist and the poet'.) In the second case, we recognize the play of cause and effect in events, but our concern is only with the effect upon ourselves, only with the (good or evil) consequences which these events have for us. (This practical response 'is the response of a partisan'.) In the third case, we still consider events in terms of their causal relationships, but independently of any impact upon ourselves. (This theoretical response is the achievement of the scientist.)

The world through which we move is, for Oakeshott, a single and unitary world of experience. All of the events which populate it, to be perceived at all, must be *present* to the mind (as much as any study of the *past*). The difference between the fourth case – the historical response – and all the others, is that these never relinquish experience as present, while history only perceives experience as past. The historical perspective, in short, is one which envisages no use or application of the past; it is one which accepts the past as it is, and 'for its own sake'. Oakeshott states that 'what the historian is interested in is a dead past; a past unlike the present'.

We shall not, for the moment, concern ourselves with the question of how or in what way Oakeshott differentiates between history and the other modes of experience which he identifies. We need only emphasize here the fact that Oakeshott establishes a rigid distinction between these various modes. This is not the same as saying that Oakeshott intends that there can be no other modes than those he identifies ('the choice ... must, to some extent, be arbitrary'). It is only to say that he affirms that each of the modes which he identifies is 'wholly and absolutely independent of any other' (1933, p 75). Oakeshott insists upon this separation: 'No one of these modes of experience is, in any sense whatever, based upon or dependent upon any other; no one is derived from any other, and none directly related to any other' (p. 76). These modes, he says, these worlds of experience, 'are wholly irrelevant to one another' (p. 327).

Of course, we shall confront a problem if Oakeshott's modes of

experience are held to be 'wholly and absolutely independent' of one
another and if, at the same time, they are held to represent distinctions
which are admittedly arbitrary. Oakeshott makes both claims. If these
modes are admittedly arbitrary, but still legitimate, then presumably
their experiential content must be equally legitimately divisible in
other ways. If that is so, then it becomes difficult to understand how
the 'attempt to pass in argument from one world [mode] of ideas
to another' should constitute, following Oakeshott, a 'case of irrelevance', of 'error', of 'confusion'. In this argument, we confront a
preliminary difficulty. Granted, the notion of 'passing' is imprecise.
But it is not clear, for example, how one could be or why one should
be categorically denied the possibility of writing 'history' while
making scientific or 'practical' (i.e. moral) judgements in the course
of doing so. Political history would appear to necessitate 'practical'
judgements. It may be an important part of the explanation of Zulu
imperialism that Chaka was ruthless, or of European imperialism that
figures like Francis Drake (as Captain of *The Golden Hind*) or Cecil
Rhodes (as head of the British South Africa Company) were driven
by greed, the ethic of unlimited material accumulation. Attributions
of motives and characteristics such as 'ruthlessness', 'greed' and
'fairness' do after all serve an explanatory purpose, while constituting
none the less substantive moral ('practical') judgements. To begin to
be able to deny the possibility of such a connection as this between
historical and practical modes must at least require that the distinction
between them prove more than merely arbitrary.

5

Oakeshott wishes to distinguish between events in terms of perspectives on them which are contemplative or scientific or practical or
historical. He assumes that all experience is present experience. He
assumes that we can enjoy no direct experience of anything that is
past, due to the fact that it is *past*. We can only perceive what is present.
As we live only in the present, we cannot simultaneously live in (what
we may take to be) the past. We have only present evidence for the
past whether in the form of documents, letters, monuments or whatever. It is such evidence as this which permits us to infer that a past
did exist, without permitting us directly to enter into and to inhabit
it. Thus an *historical* perspective, for Oakeshott, is still by implication
a *present* perspective. (As Oakeshott puts it, 'the past ... is a certain
sort of reading of the present'.)
    Since, for Oakeshott, all experience is present experience, the
crucial consideration is the distinction between historical and other

responses to experience, and the tenability of this distinction. As a part of this, it is necessary to provide some connotative stipulation about the content of history. It is inescapable that Oakeshott should oblige us in this matter. But we shall discover that Oakeshott imparts to history and to the historian an equivocal character. But let us begin with the first aspect of the historian's identity, where he is recommended to us as 'one who understands the events of the world before him as evidence for events that have already taken place'.

This statement, although only one of two which Oakeshott offers us (the second is taken up in section 7), is sufficient to permit us to consider the tenability of history conceived as a distinct mode of experience. The basic question must be whether all other modes of experience contain within them any historical dimension, actual or potential. If, of course, the three other 'modes of experience' either explicitly or implicitly understand present events as 'evidence for events that have already taken place', then there can be no clear distinction between 'history' (so understood) and these other non-historical modes.

Oakeshott observes that the attitude of the poet, as distinct from that of the historian, is one of wonder. And yet, we may rightly interject, the poet may wonder at something which he takes to be *past*. For Oakeshott, the attitude of the practical man is that of a partisan. But we may insist that, even as a partisan makes the past serve a present purpose – he may be a patriot or a zealot – this very orientation presupposes that this 'practical man' *qua* 'practical man' has some distinct sense of a *past*. The attitude of Oakeshott's scientist reveals a sense of timelessness. But will be clear to us that the assumption of a causal process assumes sequence, and thus there is also implicit in 'science' some sense of a *past*. The historian, it must follow from all this, cannot be alone in regarding 'present events as evidence for events that have already taken place' (1962, p. 150). In this understanding of present events as evidence for events that have already taken place, we have, accordingly, no clear criterion for distinguishing between the historian on the one hand, and the practical man, poet or scientist on the other.

It is possible for the universe to be tidily packed into four or more small self-contained boxes, such as those Oakeshott passes round. The merely taxonomic business of dividing the intelligible world into so many distinct realms of discourse is perfectly acceptable at least in as far as (1) the classification is intended to be exhaustive, (2) the same material cannot be organized more satisfactorily in other ways, and (3) the purpose of and criteria for the classification are clear and coherent. Oakeshott is placed in a difficult position straightaway where he accepts that his categories or modes are not exhaustive (i.e. the three or four are not the only ones) and yet holds that the differences between them are 'absolute'. If his categories or modes are not exhaustive, so as to cover all experience relevant to them, then there can be no guarantee that some different experience, whether genuinely new or merely overlooked, will fit into the established categories or modes, will not overlap them and require them to be restructured. A classificatory scheme which is not exhaustive can never claim that its component parts are in any way mutually exclusive, or absolute. It is indeed for this reason that Birch (1969) is perfectly entitled to support his claims for 'the possibility of sociological explanation' by quoting against Oakeshott (1933) the latter's own formula that 'there can be no limit to the number of possible modifications in experience'. A vital part of the difficulty for Oakeshott's own argument lies in the non-exhaustive character of his modes.

In any event, the only new category or 'mode' for which Oakeshott makes a case is 'history'. The others – roughly, 'poetry' for aesthetics, 'practice' for 'ethics' and 'science' for itself – are conventional, although again not exhaustive. But history, as has been hinted, is not a category (as Oakeshott first defines it) which we can separate out from any experience whatever. If we say our experience is present, and that it can be read or reconstructed in such a way as to yield some sense of a past, then this will be true for all experience. This is no more than to say that we have some concept of duration, or of temporal 'extension'. Inasfar as we have a sense of the present – and Oakeshott insists (wrongly) that all experience is present – it is clear that such a concept is logically meshed with some notion of a past. If we mean by *history*, 'understanding the past' (as Oakeshott sometimes does) it will be clear that every present understanding contains within itself some past dimension. If all experience is present (never mind if it is not) and if we can have no sense of a present divorced from some assumption of a past and if (as Oakeshott suggests) history merely consists in inferring or intuiting or reconstructing a past from the present, then no experience is non-historical. If no experience is non-historical, then 'history' cannot be said to constitute an absolutely or otherwise distinct mode of experience.

In fact, there is no subject of study – whether philosophy or physics, whist or history itself – which has not a history. We may well say that history is somehow distinct. But we may as readily maintain that it is indistinct. For if history, taken as duration, may project as its object all of experience, or any subsidiary study or aspect of experience, then it is always married to such studies and aspects, and in such a way as to make any notion of a categorical divorce between it and them logically unacceptable. In this sense, history is less a subject of study than a way to study a subject. History most certainly is not – again taken as duration – a specific method or methodology, since there are many different methods compatible with it. But as we shall see later, Oakeshott is disposed to confound his preferred historical methodology with 'history' *per se*.

In sum, Oakeshott wishes to distinguish between history and other parallel activities; but he leaves us in the end with at least two different notions of what 'history' is. The first of these, as we have seen, characterizes history as a past which we infer from present evidence. Given this general criterion, however, it must follow that anyone, whether a poet, moralist, politician or scientist, who makes such an inference is *pro tanto* enveloped in history. It is difficult to imagine, moreover, that any agent could avoid making such an inference. Were Oakeshott to accept, however, that the other modes – poetry, practice and science – also assume a 'historical' character, then his original attempt to distinguish between them (certainly in any categorical sense) must fail.

6

Although Oakeshott has occasion to insist that the modes he stipulates are 'wholly irrelevant to one another', 'wholly and absolutely independent', etc., he eventually equivocates over the tenability of this absolute independence and mutual irrelevance. Oakeshott proceeds to change the rules. The first rule he advances requires us to regard history and the other modes stipulated as wholly distinct. But a second rule quickly permits us to enjoy 'pasts' which are contemplative, practical, scientific *and* historical.

Oakeshott's concept of history, taken as a wholly distinct category or mode of experience, fails to maintain a distinction between itself and the other modes. What is revoked is less Oakeshott's direct *characterization* of history than his stipulation regarding its *independence* as a mode. This retrenchment is explicit in *Experience and Its Modes*, but its implications are never directly addressed by the author. Oakeshott (1933) comes to write that '[h]istory is certainly a form of experience in which what is experienced is, in some sense, past'. He continues, 'But the past in history is not the only past, and a clear view of the character of the past in history involves the distinction of this past from that in other forms of experience' (p. 102). What this implies is that 'other forms of experience' also and self-consciously enjoy a past (inferred from present experience). Hence the author's reference to the contemplative past ('poetry'), the practical past, the scientific past and the 'historical' past.

The nature of the reversal which Oakeshott hereby achieves is of interest and warrants fuller attention (as under 1, 2 and 3 below). But the most salient feature of the analysis is that it quite contradicts the position earlier stipulated. What he says, inasfar as the concern is to maintain that (the study of) science, poetry, ethics and history all have a history, or that they all have a past, is perfectly sound. But we encounter problems to the extent that the concern is to maintain that the 'pasts' attributed to these subject areas have no genuinely 'historical' dimension. This unfortunately is the road which Oakeshott seeks to have us travel. All four modes, he suggests, reveal a 'past', only one of which he thinks historical. Poetry yields a 'contemplative past' (the reality) but is not genuinely historical, is 'specious'. Practice yields a practical past (the reality) but it is history front to back, is 'unhistorical'. Science yields a scientific past (the reality) but the timelessness of its propositions undermines their historicity.

(1) Oakeshott says little directly about contemplation as a perspective on history. The important thing about it, however, is that it does not locate history in the past, which is the only place where history is 'history'. The contemplative response is no more concerned to moralize about the past than it is concerned to unearth the causes or consequences of historical events. The attitude it strikes is one of wonder. But, for Oakeshott, such an attitude has nothing to do with 'history'. For any object of contemplation, in the course of being contemplated, is automatically ensnared by, and assimilated to, the present. Indeed, although Oakeshott refers to contemplation as a 'response' to 'the past', his object is to deny it any genuinely 'historical' status at all. Thus Oakeshott qualifies contemplative history as 'specious'. He suggests that the historical novel, for example, is fiction, not history. The contemplative past is present imagination flooding the broken plains of past record. Thus overwhelmed, the past loses its distinctiveness as past; it and the present are merged together in a uniform offering which, for Oakeshott, is simply 'unhistorical'.

(2) Oakeshott has far more to say about the 'practical' past. But the central observation is the same: namely that it is 'unhistorical'. The 'practical' man is accused of 'reading the past backwards', only recognizing those past events which can be related to present activity. In the 'practical' past, Oakeshott suggests, history is only assimilated in terms of its present or future effects, whether desirable or abhorrent. Such sounds and signals which touch neither of these poles remain unperceived and inexistent in the 'practical' past; here there is no equipment available to receive such effectively weak emissions. In such circumstances, the past, for Oakeshott, cannot exist on its own or for itself; it only exists as a part of the present and indeed in order to

serve present purposes. The 'practical' perspective, then, suffers from the fact that it obliterates from view a 'past' that is distinctly past; it makes it impossible to come to grips with the past as such. The practical response 'is the response of a partisan', converting 'past' into 'present', and so altering its character as history. Like the 'contemplative' past, therefore, Oakeshott denies the 'practical' past a distinctly 'historical' status.

(3) Oakeshott thinks of the scientific past as providing a more 'objective' perspective, which assimilates events in terms of cause and effect, without reference to whether they harm or hurt us, or serve any practical purpose. The scientific perspective thus perceives the past, if not on its own terms, at least 'for its own sake'. For Oakeshott, however, this is still insufficient. For a scientific view of (or response to) an historical event may convert the actual event into a hypothetical situation. The result of this can only be that such an event, although detached from the present, is also wrenched out of the past. It becomes conjectural and merely serves as an instance of a general law, which has no specifically historical character at all. The conclusion must be that the scientific response to the past, being 'timeless', for that very reason cannot possibly be 'historical'.

To put the matter summarily, Oakeshott makes history, poetry, science and practice absolutely distinct. Next, he gives each of these an 'historical' dimension, thus apparently destroying the absolute distinction at first established. He then appears to halt in this train of reflection before the consideration that to have a 'past' and to have an 'historical past' are not quite the same. (Thus, for example, Oakeshott does not attempt to show that the sense of a 'past' involved in 'practice' is not a sense of a 'past' – but that it is somehow not an 'historical' past that is involved. The patriot and the zealot have a sense of a past, it is implied, but not an 'historical' sense, insofar as they seek to employ 'past' evidence for present purposes.) Oakeshott, in short, admits that each of his modes is penetrated by some sense of a past. Rather than accept the implication that would follow from such an admission – that science, practice and poetry all have an historical dimension – Oakeshott assumes a new but unargued distinction between having a sense of past on the one hand, and having an historical sense on the other.

This raises for us the question of the connection between the notions 'past' and 'historical'. We must note, to begin, that 'past' is a noun and 'historical' an adjective. The 'past' will refer to any former moment of time or to all such moments. 'History' as the parallel noun will generally refer to the more momentous of such moments. Oakeshott employs 'past' in the first sense, but not 'history' in the second sense. He asserts that history is distinguished by the activity of 'reading present evidence as evidence for events that have already taken place'. We may take it that this is much the same as 'understanding the past'. In any event, unqualified reference to history as what has 'already taken place' must imply that 'its object is an all-encompassing past', not some more restricted past to do merely, say, with great men and great deeds. In these circumstances, Oakeshott provides no distinction, clear or otherwise, between 'the past' and 'history'.

Oakeshott tells us that we may infer the past from the present, which is to say that we cannot attest to the existence of a past in itself. He also tells us that history consists in such inferences. But if the past does not exist in itself, and if history provides us with (or consists of) such inferences, then the past (for us) can only be understood as history. If this is so, it will not appear to matter greatly whether we speak of a contemplative, practical, scientific and 'historical' *history*, or of a contemplative, practical, scientific and 'historical' *past*. And it will not appear to matter greatly whether this last is called a historical history, a past past, a past history or 'the historical past'.

Where 'the past', as conventionally, is taken to signify any or all former time, and 'history' to signify important aspects of this, the two notions overlap without being identical, in the sense that 'the past' need not imply 'history', while 'history' does assume 'the past'. There is no evidence to suggest that Oakeshott contemplates such a distinction. If this had been the intention, he would perhaps have been more disposed to speak of an 'historic past' than of an 'historical past'.

Of course 'the past', as above, may be taken to cover prior moments of time, while 'history', not as above, may allude to the selective *study* of some of these. In this case, too, the two notions overlap, in that 'history', so understood, assumes 'the past', but not vice versa. Indeed, such a distinction, like the first, assumes that 'the past' may stand outside 'history'. What is important here is that Oakeshott's analysis formally excludes such a possibility. For him, there is no past which is not an object of study, which in any way stands outside evidence present to the mind of an ever-contemporaneous beholder. The 'past' is merely a contemporary construct through which we order experience, and cannot intelligibly be said to 'exist' beyond our perception of it in present evidence. Nor can it impliedly be known apart from some form of study of it. Here we are not concerned with a failure (in the form of an omission) to distinguish between 'the past' and 'history', but rather with a *decision* to conflate them. Insofar as this is so, there is, for Oakeshott, no past to which we can humanly attest which is not history, as well as no history which is not to do with the past.

Of course, it may be said that what Oakeshott intends in referring to an 'historical past' is 'an historical perspective on the past'. It is clear that the poet–author of *The Waste Land* or the political writer of *Mein Kampf* or the geneticist discoverer of the double helix is not primarily concerned to offer lessons in history. The question is whether one can say anything very much more precise than this. Is it true that the scientist is concerned with 'timelessness'? His concern may be to elaborate a theory of evolution. Is it the case that the patriot is 'unhistorical'? His report on the past may of course be mistaken or biased or distorted; he may even have deliberately 'cooked the books', but in none of these respects can he be absolutely and categorically distinguished from the common-or-garden variety of historian, nor even from the most exceptional of these, for we shall find none above mistakes, bias, the occasional distortion and sometimes worse. Is it so that the poet's sense of wonder, that his desire to experience and to communicate delight, renders his sense of the past 'specious'? The delight he wears about him may be the savoury jacket of a tale or of a theory. Witness Swift:

> So, naturalists observe a flea
> Hath smaller fleas that on him prey;
> And these have smaller fleas to bite 'em
> And so proceed *ad infinitum.*

It may even be that Oakeshott seeks to distinguish between historians and the rest by reference to an attitude, as in the form of a commitment to the past. But such an attitude could never be established on any other basis than that of degree. We all in part share the commitment to the past. Indeed, without it we could have no present. We shall make the sort of distinctions Oakeshott advances between history and science and so on and there will be no harm in this – as long as the necessary elasticity of these terms is not destroyed. In the end, it cannot greatly matter how we distinguish between, say, history and science. (We might say, for example, that statements of the first sort are usually singular and that scientific statements are generally universal, but neither characterization could itself be universalized.) The important question, in the end, should be whether statements of either sort are correct, or at least testable. The trouble is that we may manipulate definitions such that an individual, normally (and loosely) regarded as a 'scientist', is denied the title where they make the sort of statement or conduct the sort of investigation normally regarded

as the province of one whom we loosely characterize as an 'historian'
– and vice versa. We may do the same with political scientists, political
philosophers, moral philosophers, and so on. But we shall not thereby
make the concrete statements they advance one whit the more
intelligible or unintelligible or the more true or false. These labels for
human performances, where transmuted into rigid barriers, whether
between intellectual 'fields' or experiential 'modes', do little to
advance our understanding.

The past is implicit in all intellectual and other endeavour. We have
located no way of studying it which we can agree upon as categorically
better than every other. It is not unusual to encounter distinctions
between the 'past' and 'history'. Some of these may prove helpful, but
none in any notable degree. One aspect of Oakeshott's argument
denies the distinction, since 'history/the past' is taken to be no more
than a reading of present data as evidence for events that have already
taken place, and because all experience, even at the point where it
has expressly become practical or scientific, may be so read. Another
aspect of Oakeshott's argument affirms the distinction, which is
instanced where he speaks of the 'historical past', in this qualifying
'history' as a particular type of 'past'. But he nowhere demonstrates
what sort of distinctive past history could be, other than in terms,
perhaps, of an attitude: the historian's commitment to or immersion
in his craft. In any event, one cannot implicitly deny and then
expressly affirm the distinction. The point is not that the distinction
cannot be made. E.H. Carr (1964), for example, writes: 'excellent
books can be written about the past which are not history' (p. 48).
The distinction is of a trivial kind, but Carr is at least explicit about
his purpose, which is to reserve the word 'history' to cover *man's* past.

7

We now turn to Oakeshott's second formulation (for the first, see
section 5) where he stipulates that the historian does not merely read
the present as evidence for the past – as originally argued – but,
instead, that s/he 'never does anything else'. As Oakeshott puts it, the
historian's 'attitude to the present is one in which the past *always*
appears'. And Oakeshott, at various points, remarks that it is this
which makes the historian 'different' or 'supreme' or 'unique' and so
on. What is to be remarked about this second formulation is that it
involves a divergence from the first. In the first, the difference is not
quantified, and in this sense represents a difference of *kind*. In the
second, it is quantified and in this sense represents a difference of

degree. The historian, on this second stipulation, is not an historian by virtue of her/his present and *categorical* concern with the past, but by virtue of the fact that s/he is aggregatively more concerned with the past than is the poet or practical man or scientist. There is not a great deal in such a formula. Oakeshott, perhaps made uncomfortable by the prospect and wishing to avoid the difficulty, reveals an inclination towards escalation. Hence the desire to say, not that the historian is merely *more* concerned, but that s/he is *only* and *exclusively* concerned, with the past.

The assertion that the historian is *only* concerned with the past proves trivial on one understanding of 'past'. That is to say, if we make a distinction between past, present and future, and insist upon the present as a severe and instantaneous line of demarcation between past and future, then the historian has little option in the business of concentrating her/his entire attention upon the past. For the future, after all, since it is not yet at hand, must remain forever inaccessible, and the present, as soon as one seeks to write about it, is of course (conceived of as an instant) already past.

There is a second problem. This relates more directly to the distinction between the historical and other modes of experience. On the above view – of the present constituting an instantaneous line of demarcation between past and future – not only is the historian always forced back upon her/his past, but so are the poet, practical man and scientist. The poet may dream her dreams, as do we all, but at the point where she wishes to communicate these to us, she must make of them some sort of record, and in the course of doing this she must recall her thoughts, and remember, too – perhaps in ways almost too subtle to record – the sort of understanding which we have been educated to give to the various signs and symbols that will be paraded before us as language. The position of the practical man and scientist will not prove notably different. The practising lawyer in search of a precedent, the ethologist reviewing data (recorded an hour, day, month or year before) are directly at work *upon* a past, if not *within* a past, and a past moreover that is conceived as such. For them, there can be no magical access to a future, and the present may be too evanescent to warrant considering. It is redundant now to say, but perhaps necessary to emphasize, that for the 'scientist' of our dreams, one concerned with universals, and enveloped (as we may think) in the 'timelessness' of these, there is equally no escape. The universal can never be known as such, although it may be hypothesized. It can never be known for the reason that the *total* accumulation of such data as might prove it remains a prisoner of the future, and is thus again inaccessible. Accordingly, where we argue that the historian is *only* concerned with the past, it should be clear that a similar case can be made for the 'practical' or 'scientific' man. This is only so, of course, on that reading of the 'past' to which we have drawn attention. The object is merely to suggest that, on one significant rendering of 'past', there is no reflective experience which can possibly focus upon anything else.

There is finally a third problem, of which Oakeshott is aware. It is tied to the second. As we have already seen, if it is possible to conceive of the historian being *wholly* wedded to the past, then an equally convincing case can be made for the poet, practical man or scientist as being wholly committed to the past. But one may put a slightly different question: How would it be possible for any contemporary or *present* activity to be concerned *exclusively* with the *past*? The question applies to historical, as well as to any other, activity. And the answer, presumably, is that such exclusive commitment to the past – in the present – is not a feasible programme. If we make a distinction between past and present, and make this distinction as narrowly severe now as before, and identify the historian as operating in the present, and identify her/his commitment to the past as a *present* commitment, then this commitment to (or immersion or involvement in) the past cannot be *exclusively* (if at all) to the past. This 'exclusive' commitment to the past is not properly speaking exclusive. It is a commitment to a certain type of engagement in the present. And since one can *only* now be engaged in the present, the historian's can be seen to be a present engagement, and indeed as a certain type of commitment *to* the present. (Even if the commitment is only to the effect that the present should emulate or celebrate the past.)

Just as it may be difficult to imagine any poet, practical man or scientist being concerned with the past only, and exclusively for its own sake, so with the historian. The disinterested observer, therefore, may well be provoked to enquire and to doubt whether it is possible that any historian could ever actually be concerned with the past only and exclusively 'for its own sake'. There is obviously a serious logical difficulty associated with the prospect of achieving such detachment. More modestly, one might be moved to ask whether any actual historian was ever motivated to do so. The answer to this is probably affirmative. But motivation and execution remain two quite distinct spheres of concern. And we return to the problem of the non-existence of any concrete historian whose work could accurately be said to be (or to have been) concerned exclusively with the past.

If the historian is an historian, in the end, by reference to a degree of immersion – which for Oakeshott is *total* immersion – in the past, we must ask where we shall find such an historian. Oakeshott, for example, has much praise for Tocqueville and Maitland as historians. But they certainly cannot qualify on the grounds which Oakeshott stipulates. Take Tocqueville: in the study of America he was much absorbed by what France might likely become; while in the study of the *ancien régime* he was clearly motivated by a desire to determine how France had come to be what she was, particularly by reference to the centralizing tendencies which he detected and feared in his own time. Tocqueville, Maitland, Ranke, Carr, Toynbee and Trevor-Roper are of course only examples. But *à travers* these and similar examples, one remains unaware of any historians who, as historians, are or were wholly and exclusively immersed in the past other perhaps than in some quite trivial sense (such as that every event on which one might reflect is past, with the consequence that any form of sustained reflection may imply 'total' immersion in the past).

One anonymous critic goes further, to maintain that studying the past within its own intellectual horizons is not to study it at all. It is observed, for example, that the contemporaries of Socrates had no perception of him as the great figure we see in him. To attempt to comprehend him merely from their perspective is automatically to overlook his genuine importance, which cannot certifiably exist in itself. The moral is that, without perspective (another sense of the present providing access to the past), there can be no just appreciation of the value of the past. And this is valid enough. But the central logical consideration is what matters. And this is that, inasfar as one can only gain access to the past through the present, there can be no understanding of the past which is not also an understanding of the present; nor can there be any commitment to the past which is not also a commitment in the present, and therefore a (variant) present commitment.

We must assume that the historian – the student of history, whether s/he writes or not – is influenced by the past. Inasfar as this is so, then we have an example of the past influencing the present. The example is ever present and inescapable. For this reason, it does not matter that the historian does, or does not, wish to influence the present. S/he is part of the present. And s/he is influenced by the past of which s/he has become aware. S/he may imagine that there is nothing to be learned, or by contrast that s/he serves as an oracle in transmitting the truth which has been vouchsafed to her/him. But in the degree that s/he speaks to her/his contemporaries, s/he seeks – and selectively by necessity – to pass on what s/he thinks s/he has learned, whether it is of little moment or great. All that is ruled out is the idea of the past existing in and for itself. For if it did, we could not know it to exist at all.

8

In the end, Oakeshott is not so much concerned to tell us what history
is. For all experience, not just history, projects and presupposes some
sense of a past. Nor is he obsessed with the historian where conceived
as an agent wholly immersed in the past. For no contemporary agent,
including the historian, can be wholly immersed in the past. If indeed
we insist on reading Oakeshott merely descriptively, or merely analytically, which is the way he consciously seeks to be read, then we collide
straightaway with an impossibility. For Oakeshott is really less
concerned to advise us as to what history *is* or as to what historians
do than to tell us what the methods of history *ought* to be and how
historians *ought* to proceed. In other words, Oakeshott is providing
us, in a highly disguised fashion, with an historical methodology for
the humanities and social sciences.

   Some elaboration on this is in order. The first point to stress is that,
somewhat contrary to Greenleaf, Oakeshott's views on the identity
or character of the 'historian' evolved and changed between 1933 and
1955. In his 1955 essay, Oakeshott attempts to correct some of the
ineptness of the earlier analysis. In 1933, Oakeshott quite confidently
wrote of *the historian*, as much as to suggest that he knew him
well, and how he performed. In *Experience and Its Modes* (1933), he
revealed little interest in what some one or random group of historians
might *think*. He was concerned rather with what he took them to be
doing. 'Our business', he declared, '... is to discuss all that the historian
merely assumes, to consider what he merely postulates'. He remarked
that his view of history 'may differ considerably' from that of the
practising historian; he was not concerned to say how history had
been or should be written; he was only concerned 'with history itself'
(p. 88) – whatever (as he puts it) 'the historian may think' (p. 91).
Oakeshott had occasion to refer to the historian who may take a
different view as 'the unreflective historian'. 'The historian's business',
he declared, 'is not to discover, to recapture, or even to interpret; it is
to create ...' (p. 93). In the early work, in short, Oakeshott was not
really concerned with what any actual historian might *think* he was
doing. Oakeshott was only concerned with what he, Oakeshott, took
the historian actually to be doing, whatever else the historian might
mistakenly imagine. There is of course just a touch of arrogance –
perhaps misplaced – in this procedure. But what is clear is that, after
22 years, most of it disappears.

   By 1955, Oakeshott is compelled to drop the categorical statements
of 1933 relating to what the historian, consciously or otherwise,
actually does. No longer do we attest to these firm and dogmatic

references to *the historian*, but only to the 'historian' (tidily packaged in inverted commas). No longer are we advised so uncompromisingly of the *business* of the historian. Our attention is drawn, more diffidently, to 'the *activity* of being an historian'. Oakeshott is no longer discussing 'history' (as it is) or historians (as they are) but an 'activity' which may somehow differ from both. Thus in 1955 Oakeshott believed that he could concede what in 1933 he could not conceive: 'if we go to writers who have been labelled "historians" ... and ask, what kind of statement are they accustomed to make about the past, we shall find a great preponderance of practical and contemplative statements'. In other words, and more explicitly than heretofore, Oakeshott (1962, p. 151) comes to the conclusion that history is not just what historians do. Thus we open the door to the question as to whether it is not something they *ought* to do.

In 1933, Oakeshott had maintained that the historian was one who never did anything else but reflect on the past. In 1955, this position is entirely abandoned, since it is admitted that the 'preponderance' of statements made by practising historians are of an 'unhistorical' kind. In 1933, Oakeshott insists that the historian is an 'historian' by virtue of the fact that, professionally, he always and only reads the present as evidence for the past. In 1955, he, like we, can identify no *actual* historian who performs in this way.

Oakeshott then divorces 'the activity of being an historian' from (what he earlier took to be) the actual historian. Oakeshott no longer believes, as it would appear, in the 'historian', but he does believe that one may glean from the latter, corrupt as his art may be, intimations of truly historical writing. His revised view appears to run to the effect that most of those whom one might earlier have called 'historians', do not consistently reveal an 'historical' attitude, but that where this attitude is (intermittently) found, it 'is, generally speaking, found *only* in the writings of those whom we are now accustomed to recognize as "historians"'. Accordingly, for the later Oakeshott (1962, p. 153) someone whom we are accustomed to call a historian, may be devoid of an attitude which would qualify him as being engaged in the activity of being an 'historian'. By implication, one may no longer start from an individual or body of these as concerned with history. One may only start with some prior criterion of historicity by which to measure the degree of historical commitment of any such person or body. Oakeshott, as it happens, strains to avoid this explicit methodological denouement. He does not wish to be caught telling the historian in any way what to do. But Oakeshott's failure to oblige in this respect only generates an unavailing circularity.

Let us then review the itinerary of this Oakeshottian Odyssey.

Oakeshott came to settle upon a characteristic which would distinguish the historian from other specialists. This characteristic, in effect,
was that of total immersion in the past for its own sake. To apply this
Oakeshottian criterion of an absolute or exclusive commitment to the
past for its own sake, however, creates the immediate and striking
difficulty of eliminating any actual historian, alive or dead, as an
'historian', since it becomes plain that no practising historian is ever
(and perhaps in principle never can be) immersed in or committed to
the past in the degree Oakeshott requires. Oakeshott, in short, finding
it impossible to locate an actual historian who conforms to his
criterion of an 'historian', is inclined to withdraw his somewhat awkward concept of the historian conceived as an *agent* and to substitute
for it a more accommodating view of history conceived as an *activity*
in which the historian may be said to be engaged. To do this makes
it easier for him to advance an abstract assertion about what the
historian *qua* historian 'does', without being so readily committed to
the notion that any concrete historian actually and necessarily does
these things. Although this change of emphasis makes it easier for
Oakeshott to dispose of the practising historian as irrelevant, it
equally makes it easier to see how fundamentally definitional Oakeshott's basic approach is. For if it is not the historian to whom we
look to disengage the character of historical writing, then there must
be some prior criterion which we must posit by which to judge the
degree of the historian's historicity. But the chief abstract criteria
advanced by Oakeshott relate, in effect, to immersion in the past,
whether in some unquantified degree or totally. Since everyone is in
some degree immersed in the past, and since no historian is *totally*
immersed in the past, Oakeshott leaves us with no means of determining precisely and distinctly what 'the activity of being an historian'
can be.

Oakeshott accordingly entertains us with a digression about the
progress of historical writing. He begins by suggesting that the
attitude of total immersion in the past, which is what properly
characterizes the activity of being an historian, is 'an activity which
(like many others) has emerged gradually'. His argument continues
roughly as follows. Historians, in the past, were not as professionally
accomplished as some historians of today. There have been significant
technical improvements in the writing of history. Thus a real difference exists as between some contemporary and all earlier historical
writing. The latter was not genuinely historical, nor is the former
entirely so. But one may observe the evolution from a less to a more
'historical' mode of writing, even if no particular historian embodies
that mode perfectly (1962, pp. 151–3).

Oakeshott, of course, has a heuristic. But he is notable for the lengths to which he will go to obscure this. Even in 1955, he presents his view of history as an evolutionary fact, not as a preferred way of writing history, but this is all that it is. As description, what he has to say about what historians actually do is obviously untenable. The fairest option must be to restructure his description of historical activity as a methodology for the writing of history. In *Experience and Its Modes* (1933), accordingly, we should not interpret Oakeshott as portraying what historians do. Where he tells us what history *is* or what the historian *does* we do better to interpret him to mean that this is what it *ought* to be and what he *should* do. As here:

> History is the past for the sake of the past. What the historian is interested in is a dead past; a past unlike the present. The *differentia* of the historical past lies in its very disparity from what is contemporary. The historian does not set out to discover a past where the same beliefs, the same actions, the same intentions obtain as those which occupy his own world. His business is to elucidate a past independent of the present, and he is never (as an historian) tempted to subsume past events under general rules. He is concerned with a particular past ... with the detailed dissimilarity of past and present ... with the past as past ... with each moment ... insofar as it is unlike any other ... . (p. 106)

Again, what Oakeshott says, in the above, cannot begin to work as a reliable statement about what historians actually *do*. We need not even suppose that he intends it so; certainly not all historians yield their assent. E.H. Carr (1964), for example, writing as an historian, sketches a sharply opposed view of what historians do: 'We can view the past, and achieve our understanding of the past, only through the eyes of the present'. He continues: 'the historian is of his own age ... The very words he uses ... have current connotations from which he cannot divorce them'. Thus: 'The historian belongs not to the past but to the present.' And he concludes: 'the function of the historian is ... to master [the past] as the key to the understanding of the present' (pp. 24–6).

What Oakeshott and Carr and so many others are saying in this sort of way is not first and foremost related to what the historian is doing but to what they think he ought to be doing and how he ought to look upon his role. The one may emphasize detachment from, the other commitment to, the present. But the emphasis is, all the same, a methodological recommendation. This is not to say, abstractly, that any statement about what historians do can be translated into a matching statement about what they ought to do. The point, rather, is that in these and similar cases the argument will often only make sense when restructured as a recommended procedural formula.

Oakeshott's attempted distinctions between 'history' and other 'modes of experience' as well as between four different types of past are of no great moment. What is plainly communicated is less these distinctions than the writer's opposition to certain ways of writing about the past, most especially ways (1) which involve the continual interjection of moral judgements and quite other ways, (2) which would portray historical sequence as an instance of some one or several iron laws of change. Of course, there are many other writers who have advanced quite direct and straightforward arguments against the vice of moralizing in history, as well as against the pernicious tendency to regard everything that happens in history as inevitable (as an instance of a scientific law). Significant attention has been directed by Isaiah Berlin and Karl Popper, for example, to the latter position. Popper's argument is particularly helpful, especially that part directed against historical prediction. Of course, to the extent that he argues that science is not really predictive either, we have less of a case for non-predictive history than for the non-predictive character of knowledge in general. What matters, however, is that such arguments should be directly and unambiguously addressed to the specific methodologies that are proposed for the writing of history. Oakeshott has enjoyed some influence among historians of ideas, and yet he displays virtually no direct argument whatever of the sort alluded to. His case against the 'practical' or 'scientific' past is less an argument than a simple statement of distinctions (within the 'past') which, in a merely definitional manner, is intended to 'persuade' us of the sole legitimacy of the 'historical past'.

9

Oakeshott's distinction between a sense of the past in general and an *historical* sense of the past in fact serves to draw a line between such writing (about the past) as he favours (which supposedly betrays no moral commitments and serves no broader purpose) and that to which he is antipathetic. When Oakeshott argues against, say, the concept of a practical past or of a scientific past as history, he is leaning upon a logical distinction between a commitment to contemporary purposes (the scientist or patriot, for example, may *use* the past but does not really *believe* in it) and a commitment to the past *per se*. (Even on Oakeshott's own understanding of the matter, however, there cannot be a commitment to the past *per se* or otherwise which is not *a fortiori* a *present* commitment.)

Oakeshott never satisfactorily resolves the question of the relationship between 'past' and 'present', where the study of the past is
simultaneously projected as a *present* world of experience and an
experience which is none the less *past*. 'The historical past', he
observes, '... because it cannot be mere past, is present; but it is not
merely present' (1933, p. 110). 'The historical past is always present;
and yet historical experience is always in the form of the past' (p. 111).
'History ... is present ...; but ... it is the continuous assertion of a
past which is not past and of a present which is not present' (p. 111).
'It is not merely that the past must survive into the present ... the past
must *be* the present ... (p. 109). In none of this is there any clear
indication as to how history can be both past and present, at the same
time. In fact, Oakeshott regards this relationship as paradoxical (i.e.
as a genuine contradiction which cannot be logically resolved): 'we
appear', he writes, 'to be faced with a paradox' (my italics, p. 109).
The appearance becomes certainty a few pages on, where we are
advised, with reference to historical experience being simultaneously
past and present, that 'this contradiction must remain unresolved so
long as we remain in the world of historical ideas' (p. 111). Oakeshott
clearly appreciates that to characterize the historical mode as simultaneously 'past' and 'present' is awkward. But he cannot help us to
move beyond this elementary recognition. He appears even to imagine
that he does not have to. But this difficulty, left unresolved, undermines his analysis. Oakeshott leaps deftly into the adjoining argument
just as the timbers of the first can be heard to creak. In fact, a remark
which he applies to Weldon's *Vocabulary of Politics* applies with
particular force to parts of *Experience and Its Modes*. 'Reading this
book', Oakeshott wrote, 'is rather like listening to somebody who
talks very fast; speed of utterance sometimes carries us over awkward
points.'

Oakeshott's paradox is not, in fact, a paradox. If we say that 'all
experience is present', this must imply that the past is something we
infer from present evidence. This need not imply either that there is
no past or that we cannot have access to it. Where we infer past from
present, this must suggest both that it existed and that we are not
denied knowledge of it. Otherwise, we could not infer it. Where we
identify an experience as past, present or future, we fix it from the
perspective of time, or duration. Inasfar as we have no sight, sound,
smell, taste or touch of time, neither have we any direct *experience* of
time, where 'experience' is projected as 'sensation'. Thus our direct
experience is of experience. It is not of past, present or future time.
Time, together with its three non-sentient tenses, is not so much a part
of experience as a means by which we may structure experience. This

will bring us back to the beginning, now to deny that '*all* experience is present'. For some experience *was* present. Experience is *in* the present. But assuming that the past is as real as the present, there must also have been past experience – experience *in* the past. Therefore there *was* experience in the past, just as there *is* experience in the present. But since experience is assigned both to past and present, it cannot *all* be in the present.

The point is that there can no more be direct experience of the present (as abstract time) than of the past (as abstract time). There is merely experience which we order by reference to time. By our canons of time, there can be no present study of past events which does not unfold in present time. Not even the scientist knows timelessness, nor can the historian ever cut himself adrift in times unqualifiedly past. The past is studied in our present, just as it was in our past. Such present study involves not so much a commitment in the past as a commitment (in the present) *to* the past. But any commitment in the present is also a present commitment. It most certainly is not a past commitment. Thus a present study of the past is not even a present commitment to the past but a present commitment to the present *study* of the past. Any present commitment, supposedly 'to the past', is normally only intended to refer to a present emulation or adoration of some past event, style or process. But present emulation unfolds in present time. Hence the elimination of the 'paradox'; there can be no commitment in the present *to the past* but only *to its present study* or emulation. And that commitment can only serve a present or future – it cannot now serve a past – purpose. Obviously, it does not follow that a present purpose such as serving the truth must prove to be partisan because it is not past.

10

Oakeshott's argument, as it bears upon the distinctiveness of history, fails. The argument for a distinctly 'historical past' also fails. The relation between 'past' and 'present' is not well conceived. The methodological premises of the engagement are disguised. If Oakeshott's view of history were frankly marshalled as a methodology, then it could be directly argued for and against in these terms. But he strenuously resists such a move by enveloping his prescriptivism in an evolutionary version of the *Zeitgeist*. He invites us to view history, and the manner of writing it as conveniently evolving to meet some criteria which he has rather more hinted at than stated. Consequently, Oakeshott never directly seeks to persuade us that the criteria which he *prefers* are actually preferable.

Consider Oakeshott's promotion of detail. In writing history, he maintains, one supplies detail, fully, completely, without lacunae, avoiding generalization, always explaining more by detailing more:

> the only explanation of change relevant or possible in history is simply a complete account of change. History accounts *for* change by means of a full account *of* change. The relation *between* events is always other events ... The conception of cause is thus replaced by the exhibition of a world of events intrinsically related to one another in which no *lacuna* is tolerated ... History, then, ... is the narration of a course of events which ... explains itself ... And the method of the historian is never to explain by means of generalization but always by means of greater and more complete detail. (1933, p. 143)

This can be taken as a statement about what historians do or ought to do or both. It will not quite convey what they do; there are always lacunae, events never explain themselves. One does not explain the Great Depression by merely piling on more and more detail to do with the characters feasting on (or conjured up within) Steinbeck's *Grapes of Wrath*. Time is short and history, perforce, is selective and is thus compelled to seek out those facts which are somehow regarded as significant. But neither is Oakeshott's programme sufficiently elaborate to be able to persuade us that this is something that historians should do, were doing it genuinely possible. Facts are infinite, life is not; all gaps can never be filled.

In summary, the salient features of Oakeshott's philosophy of history are as follows. There is first and foremost the notion of history being *entirely* committed to the past (even if this is a commitment in and of – and implicitly to – some present activity). There is conjoined with this some notion of such commitment being ethically neutral even if it is never clearly explained how the notion of complete commitment to a present pursuit can entirely escape some moral colour or evaluative overtone. There is, too, the suggestion that any understanding of the past can only be achieved through the pursuit of the unique, not the typical; that we must place our emphasis upon differences, not similarities.

One may conveniently label Oakeshott an historical particularist, where this is meant to suggest that he 'paradoxically' insists upon a commitment to the past rather than the present, assumes that comparison between 'different' periods is vicious or impossible, seeks to exclude generalization from past to present and vice versa, assumes that avoiding contemporary issues is much the same as being objective, and demands (more or less in the manner of traditional empiricists) the accumulation of sheer detail as a means of reaching up to the heaven of historical truth. All of this is permeated by the assumption that to understand an historical event is to penetrate its context, to see it as distinct, to regard it as unique.

We may now return to a criticism adumbrated at the start. To say of any event, '*This* is what happened', cannot automatically pre-suppose that that event is unique. For having remarked upon its occurrence, evolving circumstances may entitle or require that one note a recurrence: 'It is happening *again*'. We are only entitled to remark of an historical event that it is unique where we seek to contrast it with other events which are not so singular. Where we render every historical moment, era or circumstance unique, it may be presumed that, in this, we advert to the principle of time, and to the logical consideration that each moment is its own and no other and is always formally distinguishable from the rest. As that is likely so, it will not prove inappropriate to note that precisely the same obser-vation may be made of space, or extension. Indeed, every square inch of matter (whether of wool or gelignite or pig iron) is uniquely itself and no other; its spatial locus alone guarantees as much. It remains, all the same, that the atoms of this or that mass of iron or the 'events' of this or that stretch of time will prove much the same as those of some like mass or time. It is important that we do not speak of history as such as a repository of unique events, since in doing this we remove all hope of contrasting the exceptional with the unexceptional.

It has been said often enough that it is right to regard history as a field of action, replete with unique events, where nothing repeats itself and where no event is to be regarded as subject to general laws, as perhaps in science. And it is true that so complex a notion is not on the face of it absurd. None the less, if history is so understood, it must be the case either that (1) each historical event (every moment of the past) is unique or that (2) only some are. Let us take it that (2) at least is true. One of the things we mean when holding an event to be unique is that it is exceptional, one of a kind, somehow unusual, even extra-ordinary. There is always room for such observations. And one reason why we shall feel compelled to exclude consideration of (1) is because it commits us in advance to excluding (2) and because the evidence suggests the idea to be nonsensical.

When characterizing an event as unique, besides intending that it is unusual, we may mean further that it is beyond explaining, much as Hobbes suggests that in describing an event as magical we merely signify that we find it incomprehensible. If that is so, then again we shall accept that only some historical events are in this sense unique, not that all are. Further, if historical events are described as unique, in the sense of being incomprehensible, it cannot be consistent to suggest that the historian enjoys any form of privileged access to the understanding of these events. A great deal may be made of the difference between science and history by reference to the fact that the historical event to be explained cannot be recaptured, by contrast with the laboratory experiment, which one is able (in principle) to repeat. The object of the observation may be to suggest both that the historical event is somehow ineffable and that the determination of it is permitted only to the few. But too much may be made of the distinction. Let us indeed accept that history is not events-in-themselves, out there, beyond our grasp, but that it is a reconstruction of a past on the basis of evidence presently available. The event does not repeat itself, of course. But neither does the evidence simply disappear. The event-in-itself, if we are allowed to conceive of it thus, may not be re-enacted, but the evidence, apart from parts of it being added or subtracted, can still be rerun. And that is what happens every time the student of history assesses it.

In the sense indicated, historical assertions are in principle as testable (by reference to the surviving record) as are scientific assertions (by reference to repeatable experiments). What one seeks to establish in either case are the grounds, and the soundness of these, for drawing some given conclusion. If the scientist does this on the basis of an experiment, it is vital that the experiment be replicable. If the historian does this on the basis of the surviving record, it is only necessary that this evidence should remain intact. A successful experiment does not guarantee the truth of a scientific conclusion, but it may check the subversion of the conclusion. A proper immersion in the historical record does not guarantee the validity of an historical reconstruction, but it will prove essential, even if the reconstruction is only to prove plausible. If then it is accepted that the writing of history depends on a great range of causal generalizations, it only remains to establish the nature of the distinction that obtains between the nature of historical and scientific explanation.

I suspect that most observers would be content to follow Popper (1960) where he records that 'history is characterized by its interest in actual, singular, or specific events, rather than in laws or generalizations' (p. 30). Popper is assuming a distinction between singular, general and universal statements, and that most scholars denominated 'historians' are primarily concerned with the first, while those denominated 'scientists' are primarily concerned with the second and third. Popper's position is only satisfactory, however, if we treat it as being itself a descriptive, historical *generalization*. It is typical of so very many generalizations that can be and have been made about the past. It can be tested against the record of the past, and be tucked into our expectations for the future. What is clear is that Popper's is not a merely singular statement, that it does not contradict the fact that many historians (like Arnold Toynbee) and myriad social scientists perceive history as a sociological or generalizing 'science' or 'subject', and that one can only exclude the concept of history as a 'generalizing' venture by definitional fiat.

I shall conclude by suggesting that it is of no use whatever to seek to characterize historical events as unique. If it is merely intended that only some of them are unique, then the conclusion is so obvious as scarcely to require saying. If it is intended that all historical events are unique, then we confront an absurdity in the attendant implication that none is commonplace. Where historical events are viewed as unique, then none, each being one of a kind, can be related or compared to any other (there is no understanding without comparing). Each unique event must prove as inaccessible as every other. If history is unique, it is beyond understanding. If it is beyond understanding, to call it unique will not improve our understanding. Because we do not perceive history to be governed by universal laws, it does not follow that we can demonstrate that there are no such laws. If Moses or Vico or Hegel or Marx or Toynbee insists upon these laws, it will behove us to check their proposals for concrete historical flaws, rather than seek to prove, quite beyond our possibilities, that such thinkers are mistaken 'by definition'.

Oakeshott is by no means the only contemporary figure to adopt a particularist position, with its emphasis upon periodization, the distinctiveness of each intellectual identity in the past, and the uniqueness of both period and identity. It is a view advocated, albeit in marginally different ways, by many, if not most, practising historians. G.R. Elton (1969), for example declares that 'the unique event is a freak' but insists that historical events 'must be ... particular' (p. 23). History, he declares, 'is "idiographic", that is, it particularizes, and not "nomothetic", that is, designed to establish general laws' (p. 41). He defines history as consisting of all human developments of which we have some record: 'it deals with them from the point of view of happening, change, and the particular' (p. 24).

Historians of course are frequently disposed to think that any of their number who paints on too broad a canvas is not an 'historian' (e.g. Spengler, Toynbee, Sorokin). Just as philosophers are disposed to think that any one of them who writes too extensively is a 'journalist' (e.g. Bertrand Russell or Jean-Paul Sartre). Although Elton does not insist upon a strict historical uniqueness, it is clear that his emphasis is very much upon the particular. Indeed, there is no good reason why it should not be. He clearly prefers to work to a smaller scale, and that is as well. But his mistake consists in generalizing from this particular preference so as to turn it into a universal: 'unfortunately', he advises us (and it is a delightful turn of phrase), 'bird's-eye views are strictly for the birds' (1969, p. 94). But of course the conclusion is false. Were it true, then we should all be transmogrified into birds. We all have overviews, and can discover no way of working without them; the more we look at our subject in detail, the more extensively modified will our overview become; but to modify an overview is not to eliminate it; this is no less evident in Elton's own excellent work on the Reformation.

The late Pieter Geyl (1962), in raining blows upon the limp *oeuvre* of the late Arnold Toynbee, reveals a disposition akin to that of Elton's: 'Every historical fact', he comments, 'is unique and therefore incomparable with other historical facts'. It is clearly impossible for so sensible and attractive a writer as Geyl to adhere rigidly to such a view, but he will emphasize that, 'in a certain sense, no historical fact is detachable from its circumstances, and in the elimination of the latter violence is done to history' (p. 123). It is a point he frequently makes in different places: parallels in history may well be indispensable and even instructive but generally they 'are never wholly satisfactory' because 'each phenomenon' is distinct, 'never to be repeated' (p. 150). Comparisons are permissible, 'but there are peculiar dangers attached to them' (p. 157). 'The circumstances may be similar; they will never be the same.' Factors 'may belong to one ... class', but each 'always [has] ... something exclusively its own' (p. 184).

There is no valid reason for us to complain too loudly about such an orientation. The eternal struggle engaged as between the general and the particular is enacted here, as it were, before our eyes, in the arena of history. Geyl stresses the particular. But there is instanced here, too, the inclination to go further, and to extend the particular preference into some species of universal injunction. It is a bit like the tired idea – real as it may be – of every comedian aspiring to be tragedian. We may imagine the particularist, working away, and very well too, in his sacred and sacrosanct abode; we need him, we cannot work without him; but this genial and modest being, at some point finds his ambition suddenly transformed; his hopes rocket into the heavens; and the message of his ascent is that *he* is the message, there is no other.

Geyl, like Elton, is not simply concerned to act out his particularism; he must profess it; he must convert it – inconsistently – into a universalism. 'The historian', for Geyl, is basically the particularist. And anyone who does not fit the description cannot, impliedly, be an historian. The historian, he tells us (in coming down rigorously against Sorokin) is one who 'has his attention primed for the endless variety of reality, for the particularity or singularity of each country, of each age, and, more than that, of each incident or phenomenon within these larger frameworks' (p. 158). Well, yes. That is *one* type of historian. But we are surely not compelled to say that such is the character of *the* historian. Geyl has a firmly fixed notion of what the historian is, and once he begins to compare or to generalize (however necessary these activities may prove) he ceases to be a historian. For Geyl, writers like Toynbee are not historians, they are prophets. And historians, he declares, 'feel that the best traditions of their profession are insulted when the prophet poses as an historian' (p. 203).

Elton (1969) proceeds in much the same way. He pours cauldrons of molten contempt upon the heads of 'the great system-makers, such as A.J. Toynbee'. These 'system-makers' are characterized by the fact that they select their facts following 'some principle of choice implicit in the question' asked. (I am not clear that it is possible, if that is implied, to select one's facts *without* following a principle somehow implied in the question one asks.) Elton, too, has a firmly fixed idea of what an historian is. And where he asks some such question as who it is that will slip through the eye of the needle, and into the historical promised land of genuine historical writing, it is clear that scholars with prophetic humps on their backs, will (by Geyl) be attributed unpleasant lumps of nonsense in their heads and they will not get through.

Oakeshott, then, expresses a view commonly held among historians themselves. But he is certainly one of the earliest and most accomplished philosophical advocates of such an orientation. To insist upon the limitations of Oakeshott's philosophy of history is not to say that he has nothing to teach us. Oakeshott's 'conservatism' (his own expression), like Burke's, is one of the very few examples of such an outlook which one has cause to enjoy and admire. Oakeshott expresses his aversions, whether to 'ideology' or 'rationalism' or 'liberalism', in a manner that is more than impressive and one that always bears the stamp of a thinker who is very much his own man. Thus does one maverick pay homage to another. This judgement may not prove salutary, but neither is it solitary (see, for example, Himmelfarb, 1975). It remains that Oakeshott's philosophy of history is denied the coherence that might be wished for it. It does not follow that other like-minded advocates cannot sustain a case. But one may infer that the closer their position(s) approximate to Oakeshott's, the more likely are they to encounter the range of problems to which I have sought to draw attention.

NOTES

1 Reprinted in *Rationalism in Politics* (1962).
2 This 'mode', which is aesthetic, is not considered in *Experience and Its Modes*. It is taken up in the *Voice of Poetry in the Conversation of Mankind* (1959), which is reprinted in *Rationalism in Politics* (1962).

Skinner: The Theory of Context and the Case of Hobbes

1. Austin and Skinner

Quentin Skinner, like many contemporaries of similar views, may be said to have fallen under the spell of J.L. Austin. This dependence upon Austin is in part acknowledged, but is also transparent to a degree which obviates any need for acknowledgement. Some of the crucial difficulties found in Skinner are in fact traceable to Austin. It is important, accordingly, to preface any review of the former with some at least fleeting, and perhaps more than fleeting, reference to the latter.

One might say that a chief concern of Austin's (1961) was to eliminate altogether the notion of 'universals', were it not for his disarming claim that 'I do not know what they are'. As so often with philosophers, Austin quickly reverses himself thus: 'Universal *means* ... that x which is present, one and identical, in the different sensa which we call the same name'. For Austin, 'universal', taken as a word, has a meaning, but no 'universal', taken as an entity, exists. Thus he maintains that an argument, such as that, 'there are universals', is 'wrong', on the view that universals will likely be mistakenly projected as 'objects of thought' or of 'contemplation', so inducing us to 'embark on mythologies' and the invention of 'myths'.

Basically, the moral of the tale, for Austin (1961), is to keep one's distance from universals; 'there is remarkably little', he confides, 'to be said in favour of "universals", even as an admitted logical construction'. Austin is impressed by the particularity of existence, and would impress upon us the fact, and the legitimacy of the fact, that identical words signify different things. As he puts it: '"grey" and "grey" are *not* the same'. By implication, one's experience, for Austin, is particular: one's experience of 'grey' involves sensing a specific greyness; one has no sense or experience of 'grey' in the abstract or universally (pp. 1–9).

What is of immediate importance, in the context of the present discussion, is not whether 'there *are* universals', but whether saying this may not be (or have been) mistaken for saying, even by Austin himself, that 'universal "statements"' are somehow systematically misleading. Austin seems to take this position in a peculiar, but significant, way. In his aversion to universals, Austin at points seeks to reduce them to mere generalizations, to past experience, to what is already known. Let us see how he does this. According to Austin (1962), if one claims that 'All swans are white', one can still be right, despite the presence of black swans in Australia. How is this possible? Because one may have made this claim prior to the discovery of Australia – more relevantly prior to one's knowledge of the existence of black swans in Australia. So that when confronted with the Australian counter-example, one is entitled to claim, according to Austin, that one was not really talking about *all* swans, about swans *everywhere*, and especially not about swans *in Australia*, or 'on Mars', etc. Such an approach may, for good reason, be considered perverse. But Austin could only resort to it because of his implicit aversion to universal statements.

'Reference', Austin insists, 'depends on knowledge at the time of utterance'. This is itself a universal statement which is simply false. We refer all the time to things of which, 'at the time of utterance', we simply do not have knowledge, 'knowledge' in the sense of 'enjoying direct sense experience of' whatever it is we are said to know. If one says 'All swans', one is entitled to be taken to mean '*All* swans'. Of course, one may always interpose qualifications, as when one says, 'All swans [but only in America and Europe and only in 1776] are white'. Without such qualifications, however, the discovery of a non-white swan simply refutes one's otherwise unqualified universal. Even quite vague generalizations, in the realm of practical experience, will justifiably be read as universals. The prospective traveller who is told that Sydney's hottest or Nairobi's fairest or London's bleakest months are December/January, will justifiably read any such assertion as a stipulation regarding the sort of weather to expect in these places in future at the time of year indicated (perhaps 'until further notice'). It may well be that we say what we say as far as we can on the basis of what we know, i.e. have experienced or learned. What is certainly true is that whatever we do say is commonly anticipatory or future-oriented or universal in character and is directed as a claim upon experiences which we cannot in fact have had. It is obvious that we cannot enjoy direct sense experience of future events or circumstances, given that they have not yet occurred. But this in no way prohibits us from making *reference* to them. Such is the work of universals. And a future conceived of as total novelty would simply terrify us; it would be a future upon which we could make *no* anticipatory claims.

We do not necessarily require any such formula as 'universals *exist*'.

The relevant point is that we do and must utilize universal statements all the same; that these are in various ways future-oriented and infinitely extensive; and did we anticipate the immediate future to differ so radically from the present, if we expected that *all* our present anticipations must fail to lead us in any way through future time, then the only thing we should perhaps be left to anticipate would be some form of large-scale psychological disintegration. Austin's claim about reference depending on knowledge at 'the time of utterance' is really quite remarkable. For in saying this he implicitly rules out universals as viable types of statement. Worse, he implies that such universals as one does formulate batten upon and depend on or derive only from past experience (reflecting a primitive inductivism). But worst of all, he implies that we are always allowed, in regard to the universals we do formulate, to insure ourselves against error in formulating them, by abandoning logical responsibility for all statements made about what we have not yet experienced (which, from one perspective, of course is all of future time). Austin's contention, then, that 'the reference' in effect of all universal 'statements … is limited to the known' (1962, p. 143) is untenable.

Austin was not only concerned to play down 'universals'. He was also committed generally to drawing away some of the attention customarily accorded to questions of truth and falsity in philosophical discourse. 'It was for too long', claimed Austin (1962), 'the assumption of philosophers that the business of a "statement" can only be to "describe" some state of affairs, or to "state some fact", which it must do either truly or falsely' (p. 1). Still earlier, in his 1950 essay on 'Truth', Austin (1961) had written: 'The principle of Logic, that "Every proposition must be true or false", has too long operated as the simplest, most persuasive and most pervasive form of the descriptive fallacy' (p. 99). One of the considerations which obviously troubled Austin was the fact that descriptions, which we assess as true or false, are selective, and are often enough uttered to serve some purpose other than the attainment of truth (p. 144). When, for example, we speak of descriptions as being 'balanced' or 'unbalanced', as 'germane' or 'relevant', and so on, it is clear that we are not just eliciting their truth-value. And to concentrate only upon the truth-value of what is said may distort the actual thrust or 'force' of the utterance. Austin (1961) was concerned to urge 'that what we have to study is *not* the sentence but the issuing of an utterance in a speech situation' (p. 138). Austin regarded it as unsafe merely to inspect 'statements', only to focus upon the question of their truth or falsity. Hence his concern to broaden interest in speech as an 'act' and as a whole. 'The total speech act', he wrote, 'in the total situation is the *only actual* phenomenon which, in the last resort, we are engaged in elucidating' (1961, p. 147).

Austin's strategy was to detail the variety of things that one can do 'in' and 'by' speech, and to shift the focus away from any exclusive concern with making true and false statements. 'Utterances' are of course of different kinds and legitimately serve different purposes. A question ('Who goes there?') or exclamation ('Whew!') or order ('Take over!') may be 'good'/'bad', 'apt'/'inept', etc., but it will not relevantly be assessed as 'true' or 'false' ('relevantly' in the sense of taking account of its primary thrust). Austin was 'right' in claiming that we cannot pigeonhole *all* utterances as simply 'true' or 'false'; much that we say and declare will not be assessed most 'happily' with respect to a putative truth-value. This broad conclusion, of course, is not new; historically, philosophers at least have been as much committed to the pursuit of 'good' and 'evil' as to that of the 'true' and the 'false'. But this need not matter unduly. If to distinguish between the true and the false has not exclusively absorbed philosophical attention, it has certainly taken up a good deal of philosophical time. And there is no particular reason why Austin (or anyone else) should not inspect some other question, inasfar as there *is* some other question, and assuming it to be worthy of inspection.

Austin's assumption was that to focus merely upon the truth or falsity of a proposition was to narrow, and thus to distort, the object of the concern. He declared an interest instead in the 'total speech act', in the 'total speech situation', as 'the *only actual* phenomenon' to be explained. Austin betrays an attitude indeed almost scornful: 'I admit to an inclination', he tells us, 'to play old Harry with ... (1) the true/false fetish, (2) the value/fact fetish' (p. 150). But Austin appears to regard the true/false distinction as a fetish, a dichotomy irrationally reverenced, for the reason that focus upon it cannot elucidate the 'total speech act'. But the question one is entitled to ask is whether the 'total speech act', *qua* totality, can ever be elucidated anyway.

If the 'total' speech act, or 'total' speech situation, actually exists, it is difficult to suppose that we shall ever know it as such. Basically, what we shall have are descriptions of it. But, as we know, these descriptions can never be exhaustive. This means that they are selective. Any given utterance will and can only cover a limited part of all that might be uttered. It is not only descriptions said to be true or false that are selective and that are uttered for a purpose; all propositions or statements or utterances, broadly conceived, just by being the particulars they are, reveal themselves to be selective, and hence serve a purpose. If every judgement, every assessment, every 'speech act' *is* selective, then equally so is every judgement of a

124 *Thinking Past a Problem*

judgement, every assessment of an assessment, and every speech act about a speech act. Every speech act that we know is known as a selective perception attended by an infinite range of assumption, implication, entailment, application, atmosphere, motive, intention and consequence (intended and unintended). If we must speak about a 'total speech act' and 'a total speech situation' then we must take all of these things together. To do this is to speak about everything – the entire world, the whole of reality – at once. And this we cannot do.

This is not to say that Austin is without interest or relevance. His analysis of 'performatives' is acute and helpful and is widely recognized to be such. Austin correctly observed that statements serve other purposes than that of asserting truth and falsity, as where they are employed to express commands, wishes, exclamations and questions. In the case of 'performatives', the utterance, Austin argues, serves less as the description of behaviour than as the performance of an act. Austin provides the example of an individual who declares: 'I take this woman to be my lawfully wedded wife'. The statement is less to be read as a formula to be adjudged true or false, than as a significant part of an engagement, i.e. marriage, upon which one embarks.

While it may be useful to draw attention to this category of 'performatives', it would be seriously misleading to suppose that the analysis of a philosophical text in terms of its performative effect could itself serve as a serious piece of philosophical investigation. If one sought, for example, to decipher Hobbes's *Leviathan* in terms of its author, Hobbes, promising or allowing or commanding something we should have overlooked in this a more immediate concern with the logic of the book's argument. And it is principally this logic, particularly in relation to the question of political obligation, that has attracted the attention and often admiration of later readers (for example, of Warrender, Watkins, Gauthier, McNeilly and others).

It would be most surprising to discover that philosophers were ever relevantly and importantly concerned with issuing verdicts, orders, permission and a variety of social signals as opposed to their 'traditional' and 'fetishistic' concern with 'expounding' or 'exposing' or 'expositing' both the true and false and the good and bad. The ethical and political and metaphysical philosophers who are customarily accorded greatness have, as with their less highly touted predecessors and successors and associates, never been spared the local trials, troubles, indeed turmoil elsewhere and elsewhen. But the fact of their local entrapment is not normally regarded as a respectable reason for ceasing to study them *philosophically*. There is a limit on the extent to which a detailed philosophical understanding of Hobbes will provide an equally detailed historical understanding of seventeenth-century England. Inversely, as we shall see, a detailed historical appreciation of Hobbes's period will not, in fact, make it much easier for the student to grasp the logical structure of Hobbes's argument. No more than a firm and detailed purchase on Newton's *context* will significantly facilitate the non-mathematically endowed student's grasp of Newtonian principles, as much as one may value for the novice this grasp of circumstantial data.

2. Text and context

Skinner (1969a) proposes to attack two views. The first is that 'it is the *context* "of religious, political, and economic factors" which determines the meaning of any given text, and so must provide "the ultimate framework" for any attempt to understand it'. The second view attacked is claimed to be one which 'insists on the autonomy of the *text* itself as the sole necessary key to its own meaning, and so dismisses any attempt to reconstitute the "total context" as "gratuitous, and worse"' (p. 3). Skinner's conclusion is that 'neither approach seems a sufficient or even appropriate means of achieving a proper understanding of any given literary or philosophical work' (p. 4). But let us take the first of these views.

No one of note, as far as I am aware, has ever maintained that the context alone 'determines the meaning of any given text'. The author, F.W. Bateson (1953), from whom Skinner quotes in formulating this 'orthodoxy', is simply misinterpreted. Bateson nowhere says, and plainly does not intend, that it is the *context*, whether alone or for the most part, which determines the meaning of any given text. What Bateson actually urges upon his readers, in his words, is 'a philosophy of critical balance' (p. 26), an 'equilibrium between literary meaning in the ordinary sense and the social context in which meaning alone acquires value' (p. 25).

We are not required to insist that Bateson's distinction between 'literary meaning in the ordinary sense', on the one hand, and 'the social context', on the other, is entirely clear. It is not. And it is here that Bateson may have muddled Skinner. It remains that the distinction *is* made. When Bateson complains about critics like William Empson, his grievance is that parts of poems, or parts of novels, are wrenched out of context, and so misread – but only out of the literary context *of the poem or novel as a whole* (i.e. of the text). Similarly, when Bateson complains about critics like Lionel Trilling, his objection is that such exegetes, burdened by too exclusively sociological an orientation, 'in such a hurry to get to the implicit ideas and social attitudes', end up *skimming* 'the literature instead of reading it' (1953, p. 25). So far then from Bateson maintaining that the religious, political and social context *determines* the meaning of any given context, he is really negating such a position. He does this by distinguishing between 'a literary context', which is the poem or novel taken as a whole, and 'a literary background' such as the 'author's biography, the social history of his age', earlier criticism, etc., all of which Bateson regards as 'background topics' which have only 'extrinsic' interest and are of 'limited critical relevance' (1953, p. 14).

For Bateson, then, the text constitutes its own context, at least at what he called 'the *verbal* and *literary* levels'. The 'social context' is regarded by him less as a final determinant of meaning, than as a fourth level of explanation (after the 'intellectual') 'of which the critical reader of literature', he suggests, 'must retain an *awareness*' (1953, p. 16, my italics). So Bateson's is an argument for balance, not at all for the exclusive virtues of 'the *context* of religious, political and economic factors', as Skinner puts it.

A part of the difficulty with Bateson is that he does not emphatically distinguish (as Skinner does) between text and context. In his advocacy, a part of what he means by 'context' is in fact the *text* of a work of literature taken as a whole, not some isolated line or phrase 'taken out of context'. He also, however, makes a case, as we have seen, for an *awareness* of the intellectual and social contexts, as distinct from the immediate context (or simply text) of the work of literature itself.

It will clearly be difficult to find anyone of weight who maintains that the socio-economic context somehow itself alone determines the meaning of any given text. To argue that the social context provides an 'ultimate framework' for understanding, is not the same as maintaining that this framework 'determines the meaning'. If a framework 'determined' the meaning of a text, it could by implication serve as a substitute for it. If the framework cannot substitute for the text, then neither can it fully or exclusively determine its meaning.

If the argument for understanding the social context merely presupposes that it may facilitate our understanding of a text, then the position is not a contentious one. The position may be elaborated as follows. Any writer, in fashioning a text, makes assumptions which reach beyond it. One must be familiar with at least some of these to make sense of what is written. Another way of putting this is that not everything which a writer means will be directly formulated in the text, so that to pay attention only to the text (where it represents a fairly alien experience) may lead readers astray, or (more precisely) leave them astray. The way in which a writer writes may be governed by rules of grammar, without the writer enunciating those rules. A writer may be governed by social assumptions, an etiquette, an outlook, without actually articulating these things. A writer may be prompted by a paradigm, without ever pinpointing that model which alone makes sense of the words. (The nineteenth-century historian who wrote of a declining house that it was 'running out of steam' said something which, to a medieval monk, would presumably have been wholly unintelligible; the paradigm assumed by the writer, but not explained, could not have formed any part of the furniture of that more distant reader's mind, and may well become alien in a future far less remote.) There is, then, a case, as Bateson contends, for the awareness of social context. The question is: How much of a case?

The second view which Skinner attacks is said to insist 'on the autonomy of the *text* itself as the sole necessary key to its own meaning'. Skinner appears to attribute such a view to F.R. Leavis. But this attribution, like his attribution to Bateson, is not altogether reliable. (It does not quite matter that Leavis, nettled as he was by the man, should himself have failed to get right Bateson's position.) Although Leavis (1953) did dismiss 'any attempt to reconstitute the "total context" as "gratuitous, and worse"', he did not argue for the *text* as 'the sole necessary key to its own meaning'. At the very outset, Leavis concedes (it is 'freely granted' and 'will not be disputed'), in regard to 'the observations from which Mr Bateson starts', that 'some scholarly knowledge may be necessary' in order to be able 'to judge' a text, in this case, 'a poem' (p. 162). Leavis regards it as a 'commonplace observation that a poem is in some way related to the world in which it is written'. To repeat *commonplace*, but not false (p. 173). Leavis goes on to deny that he would like 'to insulate literature for study, in some pure realm of "literary values"', affirming that 'I do indeed (as I have explained in detail elsewhere) think that the study of literature should be associated with extra-literary studies' (p. 174).

Leavis is not enamoured of 'the way in which scholarship is set over against criticism' and clearly believes that the former must be associated with the latter. What he would have us aim for is 'accuracy', and is pleased to accept 'scholarship' insofar as it does not distract us from the 'matter of relevance'. The 'insistence on an immense apparatus of scholarship before one can read intelligently is characteristic', he writes, of 'the academic overemphasis on scholarly' – meaning extra-textual – 'knowledge'. The problem, for Leavis, is to avoid misdirection, overemphasis and irrelevance. He assumes it a mistake, for a start, to begin with the assumption that 'the necessary scholarly knowledge' is only to be found outside the texts which one proposes to explore. He contends that 'some' – not all – 'of the most essential [scholarly knowledge] can be got only through much intelligent reading' or 'practical criticism' of the texts themselves. He believes that these, so often, if 'duly pondered', cannot fail to leave the reader (as for example of seventeenth-century poetry) 'aware of period peculiarities of idiom, linguistic usage, convention, and so on' (1953, p. 163). Leavis then contends that much of the social context can be inferred from a careful reading of a piece of literature, and that the critic's primary, but not necessarily exclusive, emphasis should be upon the text itself. To have it the other way round, Leavis insists, must 'stultify' literary criticism, for the reason that the 'context', or the prior commitment to understanding it, by contrast with the 'text', is infinitely regressive, 'expands indeterminately' (p. 174), and cannot ultimately be wrestled to the ground.

If the argument for understanding a text is that to do this, one must concentrate first and foremost upon that text itself, then all undue insistence upon the contrary may appear odd. A text is what it is and no other. Assuming identical initial conditions, which is to say a given historical time-frame, and the emplacement of many different writers at work within it, we normally regard it as impossible, before the fact, to project that some specific work of genius, say *Leviathan*, will emerge. Such an *oeuvre*, we only celebrate after, not before, the event. Thus at any point that we call a text 'original', which is what we may presume a work of genius to be (among other things), we also imply that it, specifically, cannot have been inferred merely from the broad social context out of which it emerged. If we cannot infer a specific text from its context in advance of its emergence, then neither presumably can any subsequent exploration of the context on its own provide a distinctive and authoritative account of the character of that text. The conclusion is that where the aim is to understand a text, there can be no substitute for textual analysis, whether we say 'in the first place' or *per contra* 'in the end', as long as the focus is specifically upon that which we seek to know. And this is consistent, of course with Leavis's position, to the effect that, if we do not control the study of 'social context' with regard to relevance, immersion in it can take us an illimitably long way from our textual beginning, with no certain hope of ever being led back to it at all.

In sum, both Bateson and Leavis are misread by Skinner. (Perhaps one should observe that the heat between the first two was sufficiently intense to explain the mutual unintelligibility which attended their clash.) It is not the case that Bateson argues for exclusive resort to context and Leavis for the text as 'the sole necessary key to its own meaning'. Rather, both men argue for a certain emphasis. With Bateson, the emphasis is upon a balance between the 'verbal', 'literary', 'intellectual' and 'social' texts and contexts, with a call for greater stress upon these last contexts than previously. With Leavis, some concession is made to context, accompanied by the objection that too great an obsession therewith may lead one away from *accurate* criticism focused directly upon the literature itself. These contrasting positions are not to be seen as either clear and/or absolutely firm oppositions. The commonsensical position would seem to be the right one: to understand a text, one may require some knowledge, independently gleaned, of social and other contexts; at the same time, one cannot expect to grow familiar with a text by spending the bulk of one's time ignoring *it* and attending instead to its context. The question is whether one may expect to be able to say much more than this.

It is a part of Skinner's contention that to 'focus simply on the texts themselves ... must necessarily remain a wholly inadequate methodology for the conduct of the history of ideas' (1969a, p. 31). This is both true and false. It is true in the sense that any text, as suggested earlier, presupposes conventions of various kinds which cannot be made explicit in the text. It is false in the sense that one does not *necessarily* have 'to adopt an interpretation on the strength of evidence quite outside the texts themselves' (p. 35). (For example, a moderately well-educated Briton cannot be thought to require any special education to grasp the import of G. Lowes Dickenson's *A Modern Symposium*, 1905.)

A part of the difficulty stems from the fundamental consideration that no text, if in any way intelligible at all, can ever possibly be regarded as completely detached from its environment anyway. Just as assumptions and outlooks characteristic of the social setting may prepare the ground for the interpretation of a text, so will the text, by its assumptions, implications and applications, lead one back into the social environment. Anyone therefore who argues for the text alone (although such a proponent is really a straw man) contradicts what he must assume, since the text, in the basic sense suggested, never *is* alone. But, also, anyone who argues that there can be no adequate interpretation of texts without reference to 'evidence quite outside the texts themselves' equally contradicts himself. If the evidence in question really is 'quite outside the texts themselves', then such evidence cannot literally be necessary to the understanding of these texts. Suppose, for example, 'outside evidence' for the reading of a text is taken to be the views of the writer's contemporaries regarding what that writer was up to. It is essential to keep it in mind that contemporaries are, alas, often enough mistaken: imagine Richard Nixon providing a reliable account of Herbert Marcuse's *intentions*.

(We shall later see that Skinner himself was mistaken in embracing seventeenth-century views about Hobbes on ethics.)

3. From text to context

It seems fair to say that Skinner has expended a great proportion of his energies attacking the difficulties associated, mostly, with textual analysis (as in the work of Lovejoy, Strauss and others of like views). He has tried to work out his own variety of contextual analysis while blunting its implications (i.e. by refusing to *reduce* any author's meaning to an understanding of his context).

Skinner holds to be mistaken 'the fundamental assumption of the contextual methodology [namely] that the ideas of a given text should be understood *in terms of* its social context' (1969a, p. 43). Skinner apparently intends that one understands a text 'in terms of' its context where one seeks to clear up 'puzzles about actions ... simply by stating the conditions of their occurrence' (p. 44). The idea here seems to be that a philosophical work might be regarded as 'caused' by certain antecedent conditions; for example, a chaotic civil war might be regarded as somehow having 'caused' or induced Hobbes to write *Leviathan*; or corrupt, aristocratic rule might be held to have somehow 'caused' Rousseau to write the *Origin of Inequality* and *Emile*. It might be implied in this that a complete reconstruction of the context would necessarily yield up the text – treating the latter as the textual effect of the contextual cause. Contexts then cannot be said, not in any tight sense, to 'produce' or 'cause' the writing of texts, although they may, resorting to a looser terminology, 'occasion' them. Skinner is right to seek to lay the ghost of a clumsy reductionism. How to do it is another matter.

Skinner sets about the task in a complicated way. He conceives of texts as statements, which are governed less by causes than by intentions, and intentions of two quite distinct sorts: in the first case 'an intention to have' stated whatever one stated, 'but also an intention in doing it, which cannot be a cause, but which must be grasped if the action itself is to be correctly ... understood' (1969a, p. 45). Skinner distinguishes in short between 'an intention to do x' and 'an intention in doing x', where the former refers to those reasons entertained by a writer and which effectively prompt his statement, while the latter refers to 'the *point* of the action for the agent who performed it' (p. 44).

In the course of his argument, Skinner takes it that 'meaning' and 'understanding' are not 'strictly correlative terms' and cites J.L. Austin's *How To Do Things With Words* (1962) to support the conclusion. The effect of this would be that 'even if the study of the social context of texts could serve to *explain* them, this would not amount to the same as providing the means to *understand* them' (1969a, p. 46). Skinner's contention here, following Austin, is that every 'given utterance' has both a meaning and 'an intended illocutionary force'.

For Skinner (1969a) the object of the history of ideas is to enable us to recover 'the actual intention of the given writer' as writers to whom we direct attention (p. 49). Skinner excludes the possibility of 'the *text* itself' being the 'sole necessary key to its own meaning' (p. 3). He equally excludes the possibility of the context *determining* this meaning. If we exclude, as with Skinner, examination of both the text and the context as a means of establishing meaning, unless we intend that text and context should somehow be taken together, it is difficult to know which way to turn. If we look at Skinner's practice, what we note is either an evasion or a turning away from textual analysis. We also notice, despite formal protestations, a reliance upon contextual reconstruction. For while Skinner does not perceive the context as determining an author's meaning, he does see it as providing 'an ultimate framework for helping to decide what conventionally recognizable meanings ... it might in principle have been possible for someone to have intended to communicate' (p. 49).

It is not so much that Skinner is opposed to 'contextualist argument', as that he does not wish such argument to become fully reductionist. The ideological context of any thinker is plainly of great importance to Skinner. The difference is that he thinks to employ this contextual material merely negatively, not itself directly to establish the meaning of any text. The borderline between negative and positive readings may not prove so easy to establish. If we fall back, for example, upon Hobbes's 'ideological context' to rule out contemporary deontological views as apposite, we are simultaneously, as it happens, merely confirming views consistent with those held by many of Hobbes's contemporaries, and our own, which conceive Hobbes's morality to be dictated at best by prudential concerns.

If we take together the, in effect, very limited objection which Skinner opposes to contextualist argument, with the marked displeasure directed by him to textual criticism, then the nature of Skinner's penchant appears somewhat clearer. Cautiously, but briskly, he directs us back through time to Collingwood, at the height of the latter's historicist phase. Skinner 'to revive Collingwood's way of putting it' skeletally indicates that 'there simply are no perennial problems in philosophy', 'no universal truths', and that to believe otherwise is 'foolishly and needlessly naive'. For Skinner, 'the classic texts cannot be concerned with our questions and answers, but only with their own'. For him, 'any statement ... is inescapably the embodiment of a particular intention, on a particular occasion, addressed to the solution of a particular problem'. For Skinner, accordingly, the classic texts 'help to reveal ... not the essential sameness, but rather the essential variety of viable moral assumptions and political commitments' (1969a, p. 52). It is Skinner's assumption that we may 'discover from the history of thought' that there are no such timeless concepts, that universal truths do not exist, and it appears that this discovery itself constitutes for him a timeless or universal or transhistorical truth (an inconsistency which Strauss insisted it was impossible for the historicist to avoid). In short, to discover that there are 'no timeless concepts' nor any 'universal truths' is, for Skinner, 'to discover a general truth not merely about the past but about ourselves as well' (p. 53).

Obviously enough, to advise that there are no perennially valid answers and no universal truths, while simultaneously holding out for at least one such perennially valid answer and at least one such universal truth, is at least infelicitous. It is a difficulty often enough pointed out; we may none the less allow that 'Skinner has implicitly disavowed at least some forms of relativism' (Schochet, 1974, n.17). But we must also note that the disavowal (Skinner, 1972c, p. 152) is exiguous, indirect and several years late. Besides, any thinker taken for a relativist must also be assumed to regard his relativism, at least, as non-relative. This form of non-relativism seems to be quite as much as one can honestly elicit from what Skinner actually writes.

Skinner (1966b) disarmingly allows that 'to insist upon the uniqueness' or particularity of every idea or event *could* make it impossible to explain everything (p. 200). But the problem is far more serious: to accede to such a view must imply that explanation *is* impossible. Given this particularist commitment, Skinner appears virtually compelled to exclude the possibility of a later writer being influenced by any predecessor. If, Skinner maintains, the historian asserts such a connection, he may be mistaken. If the historian bases his assertion directly on the claim of the later writer, the latter may be mistaken, perhaps even 'lying about his intellectual connections' (p. 206). Even if a later writer genuinely thinks he *has* been influenced by an antecedent, we only have valid evidence that he *thinks* this, not evidence that he is *correct* in thinking this. The later writer, most importantly, may simply be reading his own thoughts back into the writings of the earlier figure. And even if an earlier and a later writer actually seem to be saying substantively the same thing, it remains that these 'correlations' may be random, and not based upon a 'necessary inner connection' of influence at all (p. 208). For Skinner, accordingly, 'the attempt to trace influences must be irreducibly arbitrary'. Hence valid evidence for even a single case of influence is 'impossible to recover' (p. 210). Three years later, Skinner (1969a) waters down his position, regarding the tracing of intellectual influences, less now as 'impossible' than as 'extremely elusive' (p. 25). But he does not tell us why, that is for what *reasons*, he shifts in this way. The effect is to leave his argument standing. And what it stands on and draws its strength from is the rich harvest of detail, and the contextual reconstruction upon which this tightly and unendingly depends.

As Skinner (1966b) puts it, the 'appropriate strategy must then be not to begin by abstracting leading ideas or events, but rather by describing as fully as possible the ... matrix within which the idea or event to be explained can be most meaningfully located' (p. 213). For Skinner, in a manner similar to Oakeshott's, 'the only approach to an understanding "of historical influence" must be to construct a complete account of the historical situation'; not 'to explain, but only in the fullest detail to describe'; to lay out 'a total historical context'; to examine and describe 'the context itself in the greatest detail' (p. 214).

To describe 'the context ... in the greatest detail' can of course prove a highly absorbing endeavour. It is also in principle unending. It is as important, in understanding a writer, to seize the 'problem' as much as the 'solution'. But these are normally to be expected to be revealed by the text itself, if at least it is perspicuous enough. The 'intention' of the writer, and the 'occasion' of the writing, however, are different matters. We must normally go beyond the text to appreciate what is involved. And the trouble is that we can go *so* much further, that the question of deciding what to pay prior attention to – text or context – should not be looked upon as a subject which it is in any way profitable for the bystander to advise upon.

In this connection, let us cite a statement cited by Skinner, from Machiavelli, to the effect that, 'a prince must learn not to be virtuous' (call it APriM). But we shall use it to make a divergent point. The meaning of APriM (i.e. its sense and reference) is clear enough, even if it is not clear whether in its time, it was a mere commonplace, or by contrast strikingly new. It is useful to decide between these possibilities, since to do so enables us to determine whether Machiavelli intended to introduce a novelty or to lend his weight to an item of traditional morality. What we must first accept, however, is that Machiavelli's formula is either new or not, that no direct answer is easily to be found in Machiavelli, and thus that we must seek for an

answer elsewhere. The problem is: where? The more obvious answer
would be: in the social or intellectual context.

Now any such statement as APriM, assuming that its meaning is
plain, will qualify for assessment as true/false or correct/incorrect or
good/bad, etc. Whatever the actual assessment, it remains that the
statement itself reposes on a bed of bottomless assumption. One of
these assumptions, as held by the propounder of the statement, may
be that APriM is either novel or traditional. If we wish to know *fully*
what M, the propounder of APriM, meant, we must elicit what he
said and what he *implied*, and also what he *assumed*. Such concerns,
including the last, are not external to 'APriM'; they are in fact a part
of it; thus what was assumed by M (if we can ever recover it) in stating
APriM, will directly relate to the meaning of this statement. If we are
primarily concerned to establish what M said, or what he implied, we
shall inspect, first and foremost, his text. If we are primarily concerned
with what M *assumed*, then we shall have to look beyond his text. The
first and least difficulty lies in deciphering what a text says; second
and more awkwardly, there is the problem of deciphering its logic; if
we are dealing with a descriptive statement, then the question of its
factual accuracy may prove equally troublesome, but finally and most
vexing, there is the problem of unearthing assumptions.

The trouble with assumptions is that they are not necessarily
entailed by or implied in statements. The 1964 Warren Commission
Report, for example, concluded that President Kennedy was assas-
sinated by Lee Harvey Oswald acting alone. This conclusion *implies*
that there was no conspiracy, an implication 'contained', as it must
be, in the initial statement. What the conclusion *assumes* cannot be
so clear. It may have been assumed that there really was no second
gunman in an upper-storey window of the Texas Book Depository
in Dallas; it may have been assumed that it was simply inconvenient,
publicly disquieting, to think there was a conspiracy; it may have been
assumed, taken on faith, that the investigation actually was exhaustive. The assumptions that may have been made can have no limit.
Nor can we clarify what was assumed merely by inspecting the text
of the *Report*, unless we simply reduce 'assumption' to 'implication'.
The authors may have made any one of these assumptions, and indeed
assumptions of a quite different sort from any of those enumerated,
and any one of these could affect the way in which we understand the
conclusion to which they came about Oswald having acted alone.

Similarly with the statement by M that APriM. The logic of what
is said is clear enough. But the actual skein of assumptions underlying
it is not at all transparent. The chief question cannot be whether the
statement APriM was somehow in wide circulation at the time M

made it. The question rather would have to be: did M *think* it current then? M might have conceived APriM to be widely current among rulers but not scribes; or among scribes but not rulers; or to be the unconscious practice of rulers, formulated by no one; or formulated by everyone, but not openly admitted by anyone; or to be recognized and opposed by most, and secretly avowed by only a few, etc. If we address what M was doing, by reference to what he assumed, then no evidence will directly tell us what this was; not what *he* said, but not what his contemporaries said either. To determine, if we can, what M's contemporaries thought about APriM, or simply whether, before M's sally, they even conceived it, would not directly tell us what M himself assumed, and what *he* therefore fully intended. It is of course impossible that we should ever elicit fully what any writer fully intended, however much evidence we have on hand, since such evidence is never complete. And to attempt forlornly to elicit it is unlikely ever to prove highly rewarding. But no matter. To fully unearth M's assumptions, we must not only move beyond what he said, but equally beyond what was said by others of his age, and the trouble in all this is that we should have less and less evidence for drawing any firm conclusions about what he meant in some 'larger' sense. It is in this way that the search for assumptions, which are not clearly and logically tied to texts, takes us far afield, in fact into a bit of a swamp. The logic of a text, no doubt, is never all there is to it. But the question is, how much more is there, of a worthwhile and reasonably perspicuous sort, to which one can reliably turn one's mind. To investigate assumptions is doubtless an exciting sort of thing to do, but far from being *more* accurate, it is likely to give rise to the most extraordinary historical fantasy.

4. Conventions *qua* context

If a writer hopes to be comprehended, then she must express herself in a manner which is comprehensible. Given that she expresses herself at a given time, given too that she hopes to be comprehended at that time, then she must express herself in the idiom, or according to the conventions, which then obtain. Of course, a writer need not hope to be understood at the time at which she writes, as we are told frequently happens with architects, musicians and artists of every kind. But it remains that, if one seeks to be understood, one must at least express oneself in a manner that is somehow comprehensible. The problem presumably is to determine how to do this. If it is thought that one may be understood by conforming to the conventions of one's day, this in turn must suppose not only that these conventions exist, but that they are coherent. If they are incoherent, then of course one may happily proceed to do just what one likes, without 'violating' them in the least. If then we are told that, prior to understanding a philosophical or other text written at an earlier point in time (as is true by the way of any text whatever), we must grasp 'the conventions and limits acceptable' at that time, the problem is to determine how we would grasp these 'conventions and limits'.

Conventions must presumably be coherent if one is reliably to grasp them. Presumably, too, they are never fully coherent. One may reasonably suppose that a writer like Hobbes, Rousseau or Kant attempted to create a greater coherence than that which he observed about him. If this is so, it is difficult to see how, in focusing upon a circumstantial incoherence, a contextual confusion, one will be made better able to apprehend the quest for a higher understanding characteristic of major philosophical figures. In any event, conventions not being altogether coherent, it cannot really be possible to recover *them*. One recovers divergent views, outlooks, insights and commitments, but none of this adds up to '*the*' context or '*the*' conventions of the time. A philosopher who tries to understand a major philosophical argument by reference to 'the' context is perhaps like a record company seeking to capture the best of Charles Mingus in concert by scattering its microphones at the feet of a thumpingly appreciative audience. The 'context', the 'conventions', constitute in this sense background noise. But it remains what it is. To make a record of this background does not turn noise into music – nor context into philosophy. To recover the context is often to recoup nothing so much as gibberish – '*the*' context, which is always incoherent, does not exist.

Since the context, confused as it must be, at no point of itself implies Hobbes's (or anybody else's) solution or even formulation of a given problem, it is no use thinking to start with that context to reach and (in this central sense) to throw light on this or any other proposed solution. It cannot be 'a necessary condition' for communication at any given time 'that the form of S's utterance should fall within the conventions and limits acceptable' at that time, if it is the case that the conventions actually accepted do not cohere. Who can say, for example, what the 'conventions' are governing scientific discovery at the present time? The Popper–Kuhn(–Lakatos–Feyerabend) dispute clearly suggests that we can make no wholly confident and uniform statement on this matter. If we cannot do this for the near present, it cannot prove very much easier to do so for the more distant parts of the past. It is always major philosophical writers who take us furthest from the incoherence of ordinary discourse. Any ordinary context, taken as a whole, invariably reveals some significant incoherence, even dissonance. But it cannot be, if A at t_2 wishes to understand what it was that B at t_1 intended to communicate, that A, as a precondition, must, as Skinner (1970) requires, first grasp 'the (possibly very complex and wholly alien) conventions governing the methods regarded as acceptable at t_1' (pp. 135–6). This cannot be, for the reason that one is aware of no entirely coherent convention or method that is 'acceptable' in the sense of being 'accepted' at any given time. In short, there will be no one method or convention to grasp.

If it is the contradictions and confusions in the views obtaining at the earlier time (t_1) which are to be grasped, then in so far as they are contradictory and confused, presumably they cannot be 'grasped' in the relevant sense of rendering more intelligible the distinct analysis of an author H or R or K.

It is obviously impossible to grasp any convention which is 'wholly alien'. It is only and precisely those conventions which are *not* 'wholly alien' that we have any hope of comprehending. Thus while it is perfectly possible that we may mistakenly attribute to an earlier writer views which were not his – classic anachronism this – it does not follow that one can defend against this danger by 'first' recovering 'the whole range of conventions' that were 'acceptable' at the time that the author wrote; for what is tangled, confused and incoherent, unless we falsely construe it to be the reverse of all these things, is not readily 'grasped'. To understand the *whole* range of conventions acceptable at any given time, past or present, is obviously impossible. Perhaps such ambition may be entertained only on the basis of an unfortunate inductivism, supposing that by laying down granitic fact upon fact, one may build a high road to the heaven of truth. But as one cannot recover 'the whole range of conventions', the context as a whole, then it becomes pointless to enjoin that one should. If one retreats to the position that the 'whole' cannot be recovered, but only a part, it is automatically implied in this that the value of this part is partial, since the part recovered can never be more than a fraction of a 'whole' which we are compelled in turn to regard as infinite.

5. The Hobbesian context

Up to this point, we have reviewed Skinner's work on a more general level. Skinner (1974) himself provides a concrete test for the viability of the more abstract general position which he adopts. And it is to this test that we now turn. Skinner's general argument is that 'the recovery of the historical meaning of any given text is a necessary condition of understanding it' (p. 285). As a concrete test of this general principle, Skinner falls back upon the case of Thomas Hobbes, principally *Leviathan*, but also including Hobbes's other main political works. 'I agree that *Leviathan* is probably the most plausible candidate [for release from the Skinnerian contextual principle] but one of the main purposes of my historical articles about Hobbes has been to establish that even in this case' no exception can be made (p. 285). The implication is that, should Skinner fail to 'elucidate the precise character of [Hobbes's] theory of political obligation', together with Hobbes's epistemology, by exploring the 'prevailing conditions' (p. 286) of Hobbes's time, the general principle collapses.

The only way in which we can judge Skinner's effort in this matter is by reviewing a series of overlapping pieces on Hobbes, some extended, others very brief, stretching from 1964 onwards. These pieces, which include book reviews, reveal their author's minor shifts of orientation and emphasis over time. Despite the variability of the pieces under inspection, there is one main thread which runs through them, and this is essentially that Hobbes's political theory of obligation, as a *philosophical* argument, can be directly explicated in some significant way by an appreciation of his *historical* circumstances, meaning principally the climate of opinion in Hobbes's time, the nature and extent of his following, etc. It should be remarked that although several of Skinner's articles are of great historical interest, the present concern must exclusively centre upon the question of his success in attaining the chief end which he himself has set.

What appears to be Skinner's earliest published essay is on Hobbes and it happens for the most part to provide an exercise in textual analysis. Skinner (1964), in a review principally of *The Divine Politics of Thomas Hobbes* by F.C. Hood, seeks to undermine Hood's view that political obligation, for Hobbes, is 'grounded on a recognition that the Laws of Nature are not only the dictates of reason, but also the commands of God' (p. 321).

First, Skinner objects to Hood's concern to get at the meaning of *Leviathan* by looking beyond it to other texts. To do this, Skinner invokes Hobbes against Hood, in claiming that 'Hobbes regarded *Leviathan* as the last word' (p. 324). In fact, the actual citation used by Skinner does not bear out the latter's claim about Hobbes regarding *Leviathan* 'as the last word'. This claim, moreover, is inconsistent with Skinner's own procedure, a year later, in publishing an undated unpublished fragment of four paragraphs, not in Hobbes's hand, and placed perhaps two to three decades after *Leviathan*, and upon which Skinner places a surprising degree of stress to bear out his own gloss on Hobbes's views on political obligation. Skinner, in short, in later running to ground what he implicitly took to be 'the whole doctrine' of Hobbes, effectively followed much the same procedure as that which he had earlier identified and attacked in Hood.

Skinner's commentary, and the four-paragraph fragment which is its subject, are published together (Skinner, 1965b). But the length of the commentary exceeds that of the fragment tenfold. The few paragraphs attributed to Hobbes are qualified by Skinner himself as 'brief', 'short' and recognized to be marred by 'notably obscure observations'. But publication is effectively justified on the grounds of it being 'very remarkable to find Hobbes so patiently spelling out, as he does here, a crucial part of his political argument'. Hobbes engages in this patient spelling out in the space of half a printed page, while Skinner claims that the 'chief importance of the manuscript is undoubtedly for the new information which it adds about Hobbes's political views'. What this new information principally does, following Skinner's commentary, is simply to give point to Skinner's 'traditional' reading of *Leviathan*. The effect would be to undermine any reading of Hobbes as promoting a political theory of duty, to 'contradict any attempt at a deontological interpretation' of the Hobbesian theory of obligation. A reader might be excused for thinking that Skinner makes rather a lot out of little. But no matter; he is, in this, to be seen moving beyond a principal text to secure a purchase on its meaning. But he is also to be seen engaged in an elaborate and self-conscious piece of textual exegesis.

Second, Skinner (1964) objects to Hood's analysis of Hobbes's meaning by reference to 'Hobbes's own claim that his intention was to assimilate politics to psychology' (p. 323). Here Skinner's quotation is more apt, where Hobbes is shown to 'ground the Civil Right of Sovereigns, and both the Duty and Liberty of subjects, upon the known natural Inclinations of Mankind'. But again, all of Skinner's substantive arguments, in seeking to counter Hood, are derived from Hobbes's text. For Skinner, Hood's account rests 'on a failure to recognize the logical structure of *Leviathan*; Hood's account is built upon 'a sequence of *textual* misunderstanding' (p. 324); or it has 'no sufficient *textual* warrant'; 'Hobbes *himself* ... never uses the concept of artificial obligation' (p. 325); 'Hobbes did not *himself* conclude ...' (p. 326); 'Hobbes *himself* never makes any such division' (p. 327, all italics mine). Skinner consistently falls back upon quotation from Hobbes's text with a view to demonstrating that Hood is mistaken. And this is as it should be.

Skinner is an excellent historian of ideas. He is clearly less apt at exegesis. A part of the difficulty, in his discussion of Hobbes on political obligation, may perhaps stem from an overly generous reliance on the work of D.D. Raphael. Putting Hood's own analysis to one side – for although Hood correctly detects a genuine logical difficulty in Hobbes, he is mistaken in presenting his own as Hobbes's solution – we can see that Skinner does not really grasp the philosophical ambiguity involved in Hobbes's theory of political obligation. It is precisely this ambiguity which has given rise to so much post-war reflection on Hobbes's meaning, as most strikingly in the case of Warrender, but also in Taylor, Hood, NcNeilly, Gauthier, Watkins and several others. What Hood and some others have done is conclude that Hobbes presents us, as Skinner observes, with a political theory of duty. Skinner rejects this view, and adopts what may be called the 'traditional' position to the effect that Hobbes's political theory of obligation, in Skinner's words, is to be 'explained as the enlightened calculation of individual self-interest' (1964, p. 321).

Skinner justifies his rejection of the opposing gloss by reference to Hobbes's text, that for example which refers to the grounding of obligation in 'the known natural inclinations of mankind'. There are no doubt many such inclinations. But we have no difficulty in appreciating that, of these, Skinner views self-preservation as the most important or fundamental for Hobbes. This is clearly seen in a later essay by Skinner (1966a [revised in 1972d]) belonging to the same period. There he is largely concerned to show how widely accepted in Hobbes's own time was that reading of *Leviathan* – the 'traditional' view regarding Hobbes's true meaning. Skinner writes that all of Hobbes's followers 'were concerned to emphasize the obligation to obey any successfully constituted political power' as well as that 'the grounds and the necessity of this obligation lay in man's pre-eminent desire for self-preservation' (1966a, p. 314). This 'traditional' reading is that which Skinner himself accepts. He quotes Wilkins with apparent approval to the effect that Hobbes 'invented' the notion that 'self-preservation as the fundamental law of nature supersedes the obligation of all others' (p. 314).

Let us take it then that Skinner regards Hobbes's position as one which argues that civil obligation is based upon man's psychology or 'natural inclinations', conjoined with the assumption that the most fundamental of these is the urge towards self-preservation. To attempt to counter the argument (whether advanced by Warrender, Hood or anyone else) that Hobbes's theory of political obligation is a theory of duty, it will be seen that to quote Hobbes and/or his followers, as we noted Skinner to do above, is in no way to clear up the issue. And this is because what Hobbes wrote, or what his followers claimed that he meant, is on this point internally unstable. It is all very well to claim that Hobbes, together with those who both opposed and supported him, insisted that 'self-preservation is the fundamental law of nature'.

The trouble is that this self-preserving inclination may be regarded either as (1) an invariable physical law or (2) as an individually or collectively imposed social or behavioural rule. There is a logical ambiguity here which lies in Hobbes's own formulation; nor can it be seen as to how one might clear it up by a mere accumulation of contextual detail. If Hobbes means (1), then it is clear that not everyone – at wild moments in life, perhaps no one – is governed by such a physical law. And if this is so, then Hobbes's initial premise is shown to be defective. Alternatively, if Hobbes means (2), and if he only means madmen to be excepted from it, then there must presumably be some form of moral imperative involved. And if this is so, then the 'traditional' view of Hobbes (which precludes the presence of any ethic) is in turn shown to be defective. (For an extended review of this problem, see King, 1974, especially Appendix 5.)

It is probably fair to say that one interpretation of a text can only be countered by another interpretation of that text. The two questions which always arise – we need not shrink from calling them 'perennial' – are (1) whether the text is factually correct and (2) logically sound. One may be perfectly entitled to venture outside the text to enquire about the content of the author's letters, the demands on his purse, the source of his profits, the character of his love and of those who received it, the reception of his writing, whether with joy or pain, and so on. But at any time one does this, one must do so on the grounds, either that these matters hold out an independent interest and are not really material to the meaning of the text under review or on the grounds that the meaning of a specific text is not necessarily to be discerned only between the covers of some nominated tome. What one cannot coherently do is to object to looking at, say, a philosopher's work 'as a whole doctrine', while simultaneously rummaging about in his private correspondence to try to get some clue as to his meaning in some singular book, essay or letter. Where we move beyond the text in this way, we inevitably attribute to the author an attempt at coherence, as expressed in the text and beyond.

At all events, Skinner provides his own textual interpretation of Hobbes. He cites Brown, Krook and Raphael as presenting the sort of interpretation he favours, together with a great deal of commentary from Hobbes's time. He pulls out the Hobbesian texts, or portions of texts, which he thinks bear a plain meaning, and holds them out to his readers for inspection. I believe it is fair to say that Skinner's interpretation is thin. His excuse or reason for this is that he seeks to say nothing 'novel', adhering as he does to the 'traditional' view. What this approach reveals, however, is that Skinner does not detect the problems in the 'traditional' approach, problems which have prompted so many thinkers to attempt to pick their way round that approach.

Skinner (1964), although the bulk of the analysis is at this early stage textual, was not content to rest his case on this exercise alone. Skinner attempts to undermine Hood's analysis of Hobbes in a more roundabout fashion. Skinner's approach consists in assigning Hood to 'a particular tradition in the study of intellectual history, by which it is taken to consist (both necessarily and sufficiently) of a type of philosophical exercise'. What this means is that the student considers the work of a writer as a whole and attempts to construct from it 'the most coherent theory' he can (p. 322). 'The investigation proceeds', Skinner contends, 'exclusively by rationalizations of texts'. Skinner regards this as 'a type of study which is itself misconceived'. Skinner assimilates to this 'tradition' a variety of figures, including Hood of course, but most notably Warrender and Macpherson. All err in the same way, even if the severity of the offence is adjudged more 'acute' in some cases than in others. What is the nature of the misconception involved? Skinner explains that 'all interpretation, involving rationalizations of an author's own statements must depend in effect on textual suppressions' and that this 'allows the omission of alleged inconsistencies' (p. 323).

One difficulty for Skinner is that he admits Warrender's 'rationalizations' to be 'virtually self-justifying' and yet does not tackle the latter's work. If, in short, the strongest case of 'textual analysis' of the Hobbesian *oeuvre* available to Skinner was one which he knowingly side-stepped, he would have little basis for claiming all such approaches to be somehow 'misconceived' in principle.

A second difficulty for Skinner is that he at no point seriously attempts or demonstrably succeeds in pinning this abstract notion of a 'tradition' or method of approach upon his chief subject of review. Hood, in the preface to his book on Hobbes, welcomed 'Warrender's book on Hobbes's Theory of Obligation as opening a new era ... in which close examination of the relevant texts should yield increasing understanding'. Perfectly plausible. It is not a univeral claim. We are only entitled to infer that Hood favours textual analysis, as does everyone in some degree. Skinner's own practice in this regard, if less than stunning, can be cited in support. Hood, however, is unfairly saddled with the view, a view not expressed by him, not just that intellectual history is or ought to be, sometimes or mostly, an engagement in logical analysis, but that it is 'both necessarily and sufficiently ... a type of philosophical exercise'. In short, Skinner attributes to Hood a more ambitious aspiration than any he ever in fact espoused.

A third difficulty is that Skinner puts himself in a position where any attempt to give the benefit of the doubt to an author, by allowing the strongest possible rendering of his position, must reduce 'to rationalization'. As an extension of this, any interpretation at all must violate Skinner's criteria (1964) of acceptability, since every interpretation is selective and all selection, if one wishes to put it thus, 'must depend in effect on textual suppressions'.

The important point in all this is that Skinner's only telling points against Hood are based on textual analysis. Where Skinner seeks to say more – namely, that this 'type of study' *qua* type 'is itself misconceived' – he trips badly in the ways indicated. He falsely concludes of Hood that 'exegetical coherence is gained at the expense of any historical plausibility'. What Skinner comes closest to demonstrating (here textually) is that Hood's analysis simply does not sit comfortably with what Hobbes explicitly says, that Hood's coherence renders more acute the appearance of Hobbes's incoherence. It may well be the case, in short, while being in no way demonstrated by Skinner, that 'an historical dimension' is vital to achieving some understanding of the meaning 'of a classical text' (1964, p. 333).

The review by Skinner (1964) of Hood, unfortunately, apart from the comment on the fragment (1965b), is his first serious effort to unravel Hobbes's political theory of obligation. Skinner exhibits impressive control of historical detail. Perhaps the virtue becomes a fault. This, for the reason that so engaging a pursuit of detail may lead one to exaggerate its importance. Whatever the case, the crucial problem for Skinner must remain that of practically demonstrating a connection between deciphering the meaning of Hobbes's text and detailing as fully as may be the context out of which the text emerged.

Skinner (1965a), in his article on history and ideology in the English Revolution, does not carry this logical project any further forward. He provides a great deal of interesting detail on Hobbes's contemporaries. And he may be perfectly entitled to conclude, from the available evidence, that 'the conventional concentration of attention on Hobbes has caused his contribution to [the seventeenth-century discussion of conquest, sovereignty and by extension political obligation to be] overestimated'. But Skinner goes on to maintain that 'Hobbes did not even provide the most original or systematic formulation of the views at issue' and that he 'may to some extent have adopted his views from earlier discussions' (p. 170). This is a remarkable claim. One difficulty stems, however, from the fact that Skinner omits to advise us as to who, specifically, was *more* original or *more* systematic than Hobbes. Skinner is ready enough to refer to the work of Ascham, Nedham and others, but is never so rash as directly to make a claim of such amplitude for them. And though it is easy for commentators to 'exaggerate' the originality of a thinker like Hobbes, who could affect not to be surprised at the discovery, in Hobbes's time, of a dozen writers expounding, as in the days of Thrasymachus, some variation of a 'might makes right' thesis – that 'Fealty and Homage [should go] to him that hath possession *de facto*'? It is often enough said, without ceasing to be true because of the currency of the view, that a philosopher's originality is less to be found in the novelty of the parts, than in the manner in which they are made to combine. One is scarcely likely to be embarrassed by the claim that Hobbes's *Leviathan* – if one cavils at the expression 'unique' – is an extraordinarily distinctive work, made so by the imaginative and sustained acuity of the analysis.

In any event, while Skinner (1965a) never expressly retracts the statements he makes about Hobbes's supposed lack of originality, etc., the ensuing six years sober him to the point where he lets slip avowals whose effect is flatly to contradict the earlier position. Skinner (1972a) calls 'de facto theorists' all those who, like Hobbes, defended a title to rule as just where derived from conquest or effective control. He goes on to say that although 'all the lay defenders of "engagement" did explicitly state this new *de facto* theory of obligation none of them *argued for it in a very systematic way*', and so on (my italics, p. 93). Hobbes himself, from being a nothing, is allowed to swell a progress or two, and is suddenly elevated to the status of a 'genius', the 'only one' now allowed to be 'at large in the discussion' (1972, p. 94). From the position that Hobbes may have adopted his views 'from earlier discussions' (Skinner 1965a), we observe a retreat to higher ground, where Skinner (1972a) notes that the *de facto* theorists made claims similar to Hobbes's, not necessarily that either influenced the other, and that 'Hobbes ... articulated their own view of political obligation in a *uniquely systematic and comprehensive way*' (my italics, p. 94). It is difficult to imagine a more complete turnabout. One is required to call it unstable simply because the author nowhere acknowledges it.

The point is not that Skinner ever entirely abandons textual analysis. In his article on Hobbes and the engagement controversy, for example, we shall find Skinner (1972a) countering those who view Hobbes as a proponent of duty with quotations from Hobbes himself, quotations designed to set the record straight. But it is no longer the textual analysis, this being all the more exiguous, which claims our attention. For in the meantime, Skinner (1996a, 1972d) sets out what he takes to be the philosophical implications of his contextual commitment. Skinner (1966a) comes to the view that to sketch in Hobbes's ideological context 'will not only produce an historically more complete picture' but will also help to resolve substantive 'questions about the proper interpretation of Hobbes's views' (p. 287). What Skinner seeks concretely to establish is that 'the historical study of Hobbes's intellectual milieu can be used to help assess the philosophers' various interpretations of Hobbes's meaning' – the meaning of his book(s). Thus Skinner maintains that the exploration of the 'ideological context ... can be shown to carry analytical as well as historical implications' (p. 313). What a theory is, in terms of what it logically implies, cannot, claims Skinner, be divorced from the context out of which it emerges. Skinner (1972d) then purports to turn his back on the concern to determine directly, i.e. 'as a matter of textual exegesis' whether for example Warrender's kind of analytical approach 'offers the best account of Hobbes's meaning'. He takes it that 'the intellectual milieu' or the 'ideological context', where properly set out, can of itself establish or undermine the accuracy of a gloss on a text where this relates to its meaning or logical thrust. This then represents a radical twist in Skinner's argument. And this appears to be the point of his conclusion that 'the weight' of mid-seventeenth-century testimony 'is perhaps sufficient in itself' to discredit any present-day interpretation, like Warrender's, which imposes upon Hobbes a theory of duty (p. 137).

We have no difficulty in accepting Skinner's researches, on the historical level, as fruitful. But we shall be occasioned equally little difficulty in seeing that he comes to the point of exaggerating their value. Either the weight of exegetical opinion in a writer's age is itself adequate to discredit the interpretations of subsequent generations, or it is not. So we appear entitled to ignore Skinner's 'perhaps' to surmise that he thinks it is adequate. Otherwise, he would be saying nothing at all different from Pocock (1962a), for example, who maintains that history and philosophy are distinct and from which position Skinner (1964, p. 330, n.13) consciously seeks to distance himself. Skinner then expects historical context to validate or subvert readings of philosophical texts. Accordingly, he sets out to establish how Hobbes's contemporaries understood the latter's political theory of obligation. Skinner assumes that these contemporaries, sharing the linguistic and social conventions of Hobbes himself, are authoritatively placed to elicit a fellow contemporary's meaning. Hence Skinner's conclusion that an interpretation of Hobbes in our day, which does not jell with those views of Hobbes current when he was about, is automatically subverted. What we are dealing with here, however, is only a wobbly form of probabilism. One need only consider how easily any contemporary observer may be induced to think that he has seized a position, which the author may conclude has not been properly apprehended in any one or more of its several significant aspects. If Skinner were tempted for example to think this of the present interpretation, we might discover in the thought further support for our position.

Take the case of Clarendon. Let us accept that he believes Hobbes to be expounding, not 'a theory of duty', but the view, in Clarendon's words, that 'self-preservation is the fundamental law of nature and supersedes the obligation of all others' (Clarendon in Skinner, 1972d, p. 139). Even if *all* of Hobbes's contemporaries believed this, then that belief in no way helps to resolve the chronic logical instability, adverted to earlier, regarding the status of 'self-preservation' as a 'law of nature'. If, for example, self-preservation is ever made to imply more than just an overwhelming psychological 'drive', and instead or as well some principle to govern the behaviour of self-conscious beings, then the simple opposition between 'self-preservation' and 'a theory' or 'sense' of 'duty' cannot prove tenable. (And we know well enough that any individual who ceases to seek to preserve himself may, in other respects, prove perfectly 'normal'.) Here, we appear to get precisely nowhere, where we assume that understanding the historical context (i.e. Clarendon) explains the philosophical text (e.g. *Leviathan*). The difficulty of coming to grips with Hobbes's theory of political obligation has all the appearance of a logical problem that is internal to, and not external to, the text.

One cannot object if Skinner should seek to resolve the philosophical problem by endorsing, for example, present-day arguments for a 'prudential' Hobbesian morality. There are, as it happens, good reasons both for accepting and rejecting such an interpretation of Hobbes. But where we welcome such a gloss, we endorse an interpretation current in our own century, and one which takes us a little beyond the intellectual milieu of Hobbes's seventeenth-century contemporaries.

It is a help to us that Skinner (1966a) should pull together considerable evidence in support of the view 'that Hobbes came to be cited and accepted within his own lifetime ... as an authority on matters of political theory' (p. 297). But if we accept Skinner's account to be accurate, all that he effectively shows is that many of Hobbes's contemporaries held views similar to his own on obligation and that virtually all of them understood Hobbes to mean that 'a man became absolutely obliged to obey *any* government that could protect him' and that 'when a subject was not adequately protected his obligation must cease' (p. 315). Let us take this to be a fair thumb-nail summary of a significant aspect of Hobbes. One consideration is that it would remain so, even had Hobbes's contemporaries taken a different view.

We have already drawn attention to the intrinsic instability of the Hobbesian concept of self-preservation *qua* law of nature. But what matters is that a gloss accepted by one or even all of Hobbes's contemporaries, unless Hobbes somehow himself, directly or indirectly, sanctioned it, could not reliably or logically permit us to infer that this was Hobbes's view, as opposed to theirs. It can be instructive to piece together the way in which a writer was received. But the subject of a reception is still to be distinguished from the reception itself. It would be quite out of place to frown upon any scholar's pursuit of circumstantial detail in the attempt to enlarge our understanding of ideas. But Hobbes's historical context, researched with a view to establishing the character of contemporary opinion, remains circumstantial to Hobbes's logic, as embodied in his text. Skinner's thin textual analysis of Hobbes's theory of political obligation, conjoined with the more elaborate contextual analysis (of Hobbes's 'Intellectual Milieu'), while fascinating enough, does not appear to shed further light on that theory.

A large part of the difficulty is that Skinner simply misapprehends some of the implications of what he is doing. Skinner (1972d) may well be able to claim that Hobbes's theory of political obligation enjoyed a 'contemporary ideological relevance' (p. 130). But all that this undermines is the proposition that Hobbes's theory enjoyed no such relevance. To say, however, that Hobbes attracted a great deal of flak in his day (which is what Sterling Lamprecht presumably means when he maintains that there were 51 unfavourable published reactions to Hobbes during his life, and only one in favour), and that he in this sense stood alone, is not necessarily to say that Hobbes had no contemporary relevance. But even where Skinner aptly contradicts those who may mean that Hobbes was somehow obscure or unacknowledged or wholly devoid of influence, success in the matter, a success moreover to be applauded, brings one no nearer than before to affirming or controverting claims regarding the philosophical meaning of Hobbes's argument. If contemporaries were to claim that Hobbes was or was not an atheist, a materialist, a proponent of divine right, of *de facto* power or whatever, any conclusion that we might draw that he must be any of these things, on the simple grounds that these were the claims of his contemporaries, must obviously prove mistaken. Indeed, it would appear that none of Hobbes's contemporaries quite grasped the complexity of his system. We may say that Skinner himself fails to do so, if we take account of the false transparence which he projects for the Hobbesian principle of political obligation.

It is possible that no given method will yield consistently reliable results. To fall back principally upon one or a series of textual statements by the writer himself, in this case Hobbes, is an attractive proposal; and to treat such texts seriously and faithfully where we seek to elicit their meaning cannot prove an absurd rule of thumb; but it remains that an individual's claims about his own intentions are not always and necessarily either accurate or truthful. Besides, what a writer denies at one point may be admitted at another. It will not matter where one position replaces another, as long as the substitute view is itself coherent. But on occasion the contradiction is not of this simple temporal sort; it may assume the oppressive reality attributed to ghosts; the author cannot be sure that he has seen it, and may indeed be quite certain that it does not exist. The difficulty is that where contradiction is located, so too is whatever meaning or intention one chooses or is tempted to see. To fall back principally upon the reconstruction of a context to understand a text is to many a no less attractive proposal. But this is only so where one supposes that one already understands the text. If one cannot quite make sense of what Hobbes means by grounding the science of politics upon the known natural inclinations of mankind, then further exposure to contemporaries who detail similar claims is unlikely to help.

Skinner seeks to recover Hobbes's intentions in writing his main works by investigating his seventeenth-century context. One suspects in this a confusion between the different objects of intentions. An intention may relate to a psychological motive to achieve a social or political or physical effect, such as winning a war or winning over an adversary or working a quarry. But an intention may also quite distinctly refer to a philosophical engagement to explore the logic of one or a set of propositions. The difference is that, where an intention to do something (as in the first case) exists on only one level, the intention to think through a problem (as in the second case) exists on two. The logical problem is a level to itself. But the problem solved, when resolved, may possibly be used – this places it on another level – to serve some distinct, perhaps 'secondary' purpose. Hobbes took it that he had solved a problem in logic relating to political obligation. But it is also possible to see, whatever our personal feelings about his 'secondary' object (assume this to relate to the Engagement controversy), that the logic of his solution is inadequate. Skinner's mistake appears to consist in confounding Hobbes's specific historical intention, an intention to achieve an external end (whatever this may in fact have been), with a quite distinct philosophical intention, the concern to resolve a problem in logic. In this sense, to discover what Hobbes *intended* will not necessarily tell us what he *meant*.

In his paper on Hobbes and the engagement controversy, Skinner

(1972a, pp. 79, 81) argues that 'one of Hobbes's main aims in *Leviathan* was to contribute to [a particular] debate about the rights of *de facto* powers' at the climax of the English Revolution in the opening months of 1649. Skinner later extends this conclusion to apply to 'Hobbes's main political works' as a whole, which, he writes, make a 'highly important contribution to the lay defence of "engagement"' (p. 96). Skinner goes to considerable lengths to show that all of Hobbes's major work (which must include *De corpore politico* and *De cive*) was produced to serve one quite specific political purpose, without claiming that no other functions or purposes were served. The point would appear to be that Hobbes was not just abstractly concerned to argue 'that any political power with the capacity to protect its citizens is for that reason a justifiable political authority, and so is entitled to their obedience', but that this argument was directed to a particular audience and was prompted by a specific set of events in 1649. Skinner works on so broad a canvas that he never allowed himself to consider a critical but obvious flaw. *De corpore politico* and *De cive*, so very like *Leviathan*, were worked out before 1642, and well before Charles was executed, and thus much in advance of the engagement controversy. An argument which was worked out in its essentials *before* the event, could not have been worked out *for* the event. Even a critic so sympathetic to Skinner as Wiener (1974) is prompted to observe that 'Hobbes's political philosophy seems to have been worked out, not at all as a response to the engagement controversy, but much earlier, in the 1630s' (p. 256). It is interesting, too, that in Skinner's reply to Wiener, this critical riposte is nowhere touched upon (Skinner, 1974). The reason for this omission may have been occasioned by Wiener's sanguine conclusion, despite the difficulty noted, that Skinner's essays on Hobbes 'demonstrate that an exclusive reliance on textual analysis leads to a faulty understanding, particularly of Hobbes's theory of obligation' (p. 258). These essays on Hobbes, which are held to prove that the discussion of the latter's contemporaries (his context), elucidates the meaning of what Hobbes wrote (his text), precisely fail to achieve this object.

6

Hobbes: Texts and Contexts

1

Thomas Hobbes (1588–1679) was beyond doubt the first great English philosopher. He is, arguably, the greatest of all that followed. He stands out for at least four reasons: first, the sweep and coherence of his analysis; second, the energy and vividness with which he expressed his views; third, the detailed and inventive development of argument, without reverting to declamation; and fourth, simple, pellucid conclusions, thoroughly unsettling to both contemporaries and successors, and so virtually impossible to ignore. There is much contemporary argument to do with the extent of Hobbes's influence in his own time. It is a debate that is unlikely to be settled in any altogether satisfactory manner. What cannot be denied is that Hobbes's work has been paid more sustained critical attention in the twentieth than in any preceding century, with the possible exception of his own. It can scarcely be doubted, given the attention Hobbes commands, that he speaks to us, and proves, in various ways, significant and relevant to our concerns.

Even as we circumnavigate Hobbes, it is easy to see that the hubble-bubble emanating from his centre is rather unusual. He was more analytical than Machiavelli, more concise that Bodin, more historical than Descartes, more insightful than Spinoza, more coherent than Locke, and perhaps more 'modern' than any of them. He was able to argue powerfully on virtually any plane, scriptural, logical or historical. His claims were accordingly broader, the range of counter-argument with which he contended so much more extensive. He appeared never to shrink from debate, and was bold and inventive in the use of it. Though his posture was emphatic, it was not dogmatic, being informed by reasoned *pro et contra*, not rhetorical expostulation.

If Hobbes's 'greatness' is now universally agreed, the reasons informing the conclusion vary from one critic to the next. Most admire Hobbes professionally; like a good lawyer, he makes an impressive case. Some simply agree with the case he makes; people who have never heard of Hobbes may readily appropriate his language to identify nature, for example, as 'nasty, brutish and short'. Academics in disciplines ranging from anthropology (e.g. Marshall Sahlins) to international relations (e.g. Hedley Bull) look to Hobbes to supply a supposedly unanswerable case to the effect that we must choose between the state and anarchy, or to the effect that order precedes justice. Some observers simply take Hobbes to be significant, indicative or representative. For C.B. Macpherson, Hobbes reflected a new bourgeois market mentality. Leo Strauss, more broadly, saw Hobbes as a 'modern'. Lubienski took Hobbes to supply 'the first great effort' to turn ethics and politics into a science 'without the help of religion'.

Great writers are not retrieved entire, only in part. Even where we seek to apprehend them as a whole, we cannot do better than to treat with them from one or some of many possible perspectives. Even the idea of approaching an *oeuvre* 'as a whole' inevitably consists of nothing more than a particular perspective on it. Thus to understand an object is always to interpret it, not to replicate it. Interpretation or 'critical assessment' is the heart of all philosophical and scientific endeavour.

Still, where one interprets, where the critical faculty is invoked, it is to be assumed that some *thing* is being interpreted, that there is something which is the object of criticism. To critically assess Hobbes assumes (relativism to one side) that there is a Hobbes that can serve as the object of assessment. And yet, to understand this or any writer *in se*, outside the critical reconstructions which locate him, would appear an impossible task. We shall of course point to Hobbes's work. But we shall, unfortunately, have to do better than that. The work is too encompassing. As great as it is, it is far from being perfectly perspicuous. So we have no choice but to abbreviate, to select, to arrange and in all this to supply a perspective, not a palpable essence.

Perfectionists will complain. So will all those who assume that there is a self-evident Hobbes whose essence is beyond contention. But even these must argue their case. And to argue the case for an 'essential' Hobbes must reduce to advocating some particular gloss on Hobbes. To say what the position is, as one sees it, is to characterize it. It is to abridge, to abstract, to omit, and to make connections, connections which are not necessarily there. Thus does the perfectionist, in cobbling together a case regarding the identity of the real Hobbes, promptly fall into the same slough of abbreviated contention as the rest. The conclusion must be that a writer, doctrine, philosophy or ideology is understood via the rival reconstructions which are made of him or her or it, and that we cannot do better than this.

2

In discussing Hobbes, there is always the danger of losing sight of the man. Though his impact was unquestionably great, it is difficult to suppose that this made him, as an individual, any less of an isolate. He had no direct family, no wife, no progeny. Nor had his parents any standing in a country, in an era immensely conscious of 'class', or status. He was a bright boy whose work was furthered by powerful protectors, who made good use of him. He was a man in service to the Cavendishes. He was a tutor to their young. He was a dependant, with an intellect dazzlingly, but never proudly or pyrotechnically, independent. Hobbes was, in short, a loyal retainer. He theorized both equality and subjection, but was more familiar with the second than the first. His theory could be said to reflect his condition: he knew his worth, but he also knew his place. In this, we are to distinguish between social inequality and intellectual superiority. It was Hobbes's intellect, and that only, which made him sovereign.

Not enough of Hobbes's personality comes across to us. But we do know that he was orderly, efficient, quick, productive, restrained and curious, with an immense interest in science. Science is an established means of escaping class entanglements, or of reversing hierarchies of esteem. Hobbes's most important, if not his only, experience of class equality was among savants, where it was more the argument than the person that mattered. If Hobbes was ever, in his lifetime, in receipt of deference, it was among the well-placed who detected in him a spark of genius. Hobbes's arguments were convenient to the powerful, even while removing from these some of their lustre. On Hobbes's account, even if he was a servant – and he was – then so were those who were less than sovereign. Not only did Hobbes's intellect make him equal to his betters, but he employed his intelligence to illuminate the principle of equal subjection by all strata to *Leviathan*. The sovereign, following Hobbes, was not sovereign due to any special virtues attaching to him or her or them, but due to a rationally established need for someone or a few to assume the purple. No divinity doth hedge Hobbes's king, only a prudent and mutual need for common authority. Were Hobbes's tastes and sympathies more bourgeois, or more aristocratic? Among those prepared to supply an answer we may identify Macpherson and Wood.

Hobbes, as Skinner remarks, was most probably freest and happiest among friends and associates in France. Skinner may be perfectly correct in his explanation of Hobbes's exclusion, in England, from the Royal Society. At this later stage in his life, perhaps Hobbes was argumentative, magisterial and disparaging. But then, Hobbes was back from a not uncongenial exile in France. And there can be no question that there he had found himself among admirers. If he had been as unpleasant in France as he appears to have been in England, these admirers would presumably have been fewer and less earnest. Did Hobbes have admirers, was he shown deference in England? Opinion is divided. Skinner thinks so. Stephen State is full of doubt. Certainly, Hobbes was likely more of a grump – it is generally agreed that he was much more on his own – in England. But is this to be explained more by an arbitrary change in the man, or by a critical difference in his circumstances when relocated from the eastern to the western flank of the Channel?

Hobbes, of course, was not a free-standing 'intellectual'. On the contrary, he could scarcely have had much independent standing at all. In France, however, he served as an intermediary, who could speak to the foreign host, and on behalf of representatives of his war-torn nation. He could be treated and received as a friend among French notables, without bringing their own status into question. That could not quite be so at home. In England, he functioned as the dependant of a noble family. He voted with them, as required. He served them, as they saw fit. Hobbes's later irascibility may well have kept him out of the Royal Society. Equally, his irascibility may have been defensive. To argue was to play to his obvious strength, and largely to his only strength. If Hobbes, in England, was determined never to be proved wrong, perhaps it is that he could not afford to be proved wrong. What else, indeed, had Hobbes going for him, if not being right?

Hobbes's exclusion from the Society may significantly have signalled a more profound exclusion from society at large, at least as a social equal. Hobbes's exclusion, on class grounds, is all the more plausible, if we take the Royal Society as a microcosmic representation of society as a whole. If, indeed, Skinner is right, in characterizing the Royal Society as 'something much more like a gentleman's club', it will be obvious that Hobbes could not possibly *belong*. It is no more likely that Hobbes could have belonged in England than could Rousseau, a century later, in France. Except that, in Hobbes's case, we confront an intelligence espousing an absolutism which would impose an equal subjugation upon all.

3

Since to state summarily (or even *in extenso*) what Hobbes is about can never amount to more than a gloss, what follows will serve a minimal purpose only as long as readers do not assume these claims to be presented as somehow incontestable. The prefatory recall of Hobbes's position can do no more than supply scaffolding up and down which other minds will scamper in the construction of their own glosses. This species of *glasnost* and even *perestroika*, however, has nothing whatever to do with the fabrication of a relativist maze. The point is only that the real Hobbes, or the Hobbes that we hypothe- size, can only be accessed methodologically by the continuing criss- cross of argument on him, his background, his logic, his purpose and meaning. We have to follow the argument, in all its twist and turns, and not assume that any 'essential' Hobbes will be found (none at least that we can locate) on the other side of it. That the argument stops does not mean it is over.

It is as well to observe, too, that, if Hobbes belongs to the past, then the past is also present, etching its way into an evolving and remar- kably inventive future. As the argument moves, so does 'Hobbes', and this is the only Hobbes we can expect to 'catch'. On this understand- ing, Hobbes is as much a part of the future as of the past, unknowable in any ultimate sense because unabridgably and unpredictably open to both deconstruction and reconstruction. Any student who sup- poses that he or she can have 'the final word' on Hobbes need only attend a very limited time to discover the extent of their delusion. Witness my own work (King, 1974, p. 328, paragraph 2).

I shall begin by outlining what I take to be the bare essentials of Hobbes's argument. While this argument is encompassingly philo- sophical, its burden is archly political. Hobbes's universe, human and natural, is subject to uniform explanation. No item requiring explana- tion can receive this without being resolved into its component parts. The ultimate components of human society, for Hobbes, are indivi- duals. The ultimate components of the universe are atoms. And what governs these is motion. The individual moves and is moved, in the manner of one atom striking another. The individual, however, is moved not just physically, but also psychologically, i.e. by motives. Indeed, physical determination is largely a function of psychological direction. The chief motive which determines human action is that of self-preservation. Whether this is to be read as a mere factual datum, or as a moral principle, is subject to dispute. But self-preservation, for Hobbes, is the underlying desideratum.

Although human individuals, for Hobbes, may be solipsistic, or self-contained, they are not self-sufficient. Indeed, one of the major difficulties for Hobbes is to determine how solipsistic individuals overcome their solipsism sufficiently to be able to establish orderly social relations. Hobbes's view of self-preservation is far more complex than at first appears. He is more likely to mean, not that the individual's first and only concern is and ought to be to preserve the self, but that the individual is, as a matter of fact, governed by an underlying fear of premature death and that this fact is not to be regarded as inconsistent with a proper morality. Indeed, Hobbes hoped to show how self-preservation was consistent with a morally grounded submission to the state, or how fear of authority was consistent with a morally grounded obedience to it.

Just as Machiavelli distinguished between *fortuna* and *virtù*, so Hobbes distinguished between 'unguided' and 'regulated' trains of thought. For Hobbes, all trains of thought were caused, were determinate. But in some cases, the cause lay within, in other cases outside, the agent affected. 'Regulated' thought was that which obtained when the process was 'regulated by some desire, some design'. Humans, for Hobbes, enjoyed an enormous capacity for internalizing causes, which is to say for thinking in a highly 'regulated' or rational way. The first problem was not to establish human causal control over 'nature', but to set up regulated or rational communication among 'men'. This, for Hobbes, was the job of language.

Language was not a by-product, but a precondition, of human organization. For Hobbes, humans relate to one another, not so much by empathy, as Rousseau would later maintain, but by speech. It is by language, as Hobbes sees it, that we 'make known to others our wills and purposes'. Here, too, in discussing the reach of 'regulated' thought, there is room for debate. Either Hobbes showed that (1) all dispute can be resolved rationally, or that (2) public authority has to be blindly obeyed since there can be no such authority if every subject keeps his own counsel. The difficulty is that (2) sounds like a paradoxical variant of (1), which Hobbes was determined to refute.

Reason is a form of regulated thought available to humans. Reason is a form of language, and is not altogether independent of it. It is the instrument by which humans understand, and thus combine, one with another. Language has no preordained meaning or purpose but that which individuals individually give it. Hence the importance of human nature, of human will and of social contract. A society for Hobbes is a form of verbal order. It expresses a convergence of wills. Individuals are not just social creatures, but self-interested solipsists, who enter into society as part of an express or tacit desire for personal good and gain. Individuals accordingly do not exist for society, but society for individuals. For Hobbes, however, the ultimate achievement of human rationality is a firm recognition of the limits of rationality, and consequently of the need for authority. Rationality, for Hobbes, leads to the conclusion that order, which he assumes all humans to desire, can only be purchased at the cost of submission to some external authority. Here again there is much room for dispute as to how consistently authoritarian Hobbes's conclusion actually proves.

Hobbes's overall philosophy provides both an explanation and a justification for the emergence of the state, and for the consolidation and concentration of state power. It is in part because he does this so powerfully and coherently, and in the apparently neutral, scientific language of modernity, that Hobbes is rightly taken to be so great a figure. He establishes from the outset a continuity between natural and social science. He lights upon the biological and decisional autonomy of the individual. He insists upon individual difference, in the form of divergent perceptions and interests, even while insisting upon equality of human condition. It is indeed this very equality which for Hobbes supplies the ground for a legitimate and rational mutual fear. For Hobbes, it is this fear which contradicts prospects of social peace and simultaneously foreshadows the logic of its accomplishment.

Since there is no natural accord, and everyone cannot be sovereign, the security to which reason and speech point is submission to some individual (or group) among them. Thus does Hobbes take up from Bodin the logic of the idea of sovereignty – the logic of establishing an ultimate and all-powerful arbiter who cannot effectively be argued against. But again there are interpretive difficulties: what are the limits that Hobbes may or may not have intended to apply to sovereign authority? If the individual's own interest – self-preservation – is paramount, then how can this interest be meaningfully protected without legal constraints of any kind upon the sovereign? There is the inevitable problem about empowering a *Leviathan* to protect interests which he, at the same time, cannot be legally bound to respect. There is the puzzle as to how a sovereign with no legal obligation to subjects may be consistently viewed as the equal defender of the natural rights of each and every one of them.

4

Lubienski (1930) is one of those who argues that it is 'by the fierceness of the attacks of his adversaries' that Hobbes is to be judged. From the scale of the attack, Lubienski infers the magnitude of the accomplishment. The work of one so great as Hobbes, he assumes, is perennial. As to the substance of Hobbes's position, Lubienski sees him as a figure interested in religious liberty, but committed to the authority of the state as a means of avoiding the chaos which such liberty is disposed to produce. Lubienski sees the absolutism of Hobbes's sovereign as grounded in and limited by the law of nature. Hobbes, accordingly, is not seen as an absolutist in any enveloping sense. He becomes an advocate of parliamentary sovereignty, which Lubienski distinguishes from simple Diktat, and thus from simple absolutism so conceived.

As Lubienski reads him, Hobbes failed to establish a case for complete individual obedience. Such obedience is obstructed by the ultimate conflict between the sovereign will, on the one side, and the law of nature, on the other. Hobbes's commitment to the law of nature – specifically grounded as this is in individualist, self-preserving proclivities, and as illustrated in Hobbes's view that the individual may refuse armed service – significantly undercut for Lubienski the absolutist outcome. Where most observers readily concede the extent of Hobbes's authoritarianism, the present tendency to lay emphasis upon his modernism, and most especially his individualism, is directly signalled by Lubienski's approach. This writer is not altogether interested in Hobbes as the mere inventor of an abstract political doctrine of absolutism. He begins to detect in Hobbes less an argument to be quarrelled with, than intimations of a sovereign parliamentary democracy to come. For Lubienski, 'in questions of morals no absolute, universal and "objective" rule can be established' anyway – hence the hint of an inclination to shift the emphasis from 'truth' to questions of historical influence.

Lubienski's design was to retrieve the work of a great man, which he believed had fallen into neglect. Sterling Lamprecht (1940) – ten years on – developed a less general and more focused orientation. Lamprecht was less disposed to think that Hobbes was neglected, than that estimates of his influence were unreliable. Lamprecht takes much the same line as Lubienski regarding the bulk of the early literature on Hobbes: it is accounted indisputably hostile. Lamprecht concluded, for that very reason, that subsequent understandings of Hobbes got muddled, since virtually all of his interpreters belonged to the enemy camp(s). Lamprecht contends that Hobbes's bad press was, in effect, latent in the position which Hobbes himself had detailed, a position which attacked every major Reformation interest, including the Papacy, Presbyterians, the clergy in general, religion as such, the gentry, the royalists and the universities.

Lamprecht implies that had Hobbes been less well known for the more polemical *Leviathan*, and better known for the more moderate *De Cive*, the distorted perception of his purport, as passed down to later generations, would not have been so marked. Lamprecht believes that the cool reception which attended Hobbes's speculations on science (geometry and optics) was transferred to Hobbes's analysis of political behaviour, which Lamprecht views as independently derived. Thus the older view of Hobbes as a moral ogre, political absolutist, promoter of power *über alles*, Lamprecht would reject as overdrawn. For him, Hobbes did not conclude that 'the king can do no wrong'. Indeed, 'cruelty, iniquity, contumely and other like vices' in a ruler offended against a Hobbesian conception of the laws of nature. Perhaps Lamprecht himself began to overdraw the case. His reconstruction of Hobbes, in any event, hints more fully at the latter as a precursor of a proto-liberal position. Through Lamprecht's eyes, though Hobbes's absolutism remains, it takes on a much less threatening aspect than hitherto.

Curtis (1962) draws us back to Hobbes's attacks upon Oxford and Cambridge, institutions disseminating Greek and Roman philosophy, extolling the ancients, supposedly inculcating the promotion of 'popular government "by the glorious name of liberty"'. The Presbyterian ministers trained by these institutions, following Hobbes, encouraged a view of themselves as ambassadors of God. They attacked the monarchy as tyrannous and in this bred sedition. Curtis suggests that 'one would have to be as authoritarian as Hobbes himself' to adopt so unbalanced a perspective. For Curtis, the universities were not 'the core of rebellion'. Puritanism, moreover, 'led few if any men before 1646 to adopt republican views'. The explanation, argues Curtis, lay elsewhere – in the fact, simply, that the universities 'prepared too many men for too few places'. They gave young men a sense of destiny, of 'high calling' in the service of the monarch, hopes dashed in a real world of limited openings. The universities, in short, by overproducing, 'precipitated an insoluble group of alienated intellectuals who individually and collectively became troublemakers'.

Where Hobbes explains rebellion in terms of too free a market in ideas, or simply by reference to the courses of study on offer at Oxford and Cambridge, Curtis counterpoises more material considerations, earlier hit upon by Tocqueville, and subsequently referred to as 'revolutions of rising expectations'. It will be obvious that Curtis's purpose is not so much to explain Hobbes as to correct him. Curtis starts with Hobbes's text, and then assesses the restricted historical claim it contains against the recuperable historical background, or context. Curtis's procedure is simple and economically executed, supplying a good example of a truth-claim (perhaps historical, perhaps logical), whether emitted three or 300 years earlier, being subjected to a perspicuous form of contemporary testing (or validation). The intriguing question is whether one is entitled to test moral claims, universal claims about political obligation, in the same historical way.

Hobbes has been commonly located at the crossroads of an ongoing debate between liberals and authoritarians, only a trace of which survives in the essays by Lubienski and Lamprecht. Hobbes was commonly treated as the exemplar of a particular logical position relating to the deductively appropriate quantum of authority to be allocated to the state. In early commentaries, it was customary to contrast Hobbes the absolutist with John Locke, *homo liberalis*. The one was depicted as supporting an unlimited state authority, the other as calling for checks upon this authority in the name of inalienable human rights. The one would be invoked in time of crisis as a proponent of strong government, the other, perhaps in less troubled times, as an advocate of popular rights. This simple opposition has in many ways been increasingly called into question. First, a considerable analytical and historical effort was made to establish a closer alignment between the ideas of Hobbes and Locke on sovereignty. Second, Peter Laslett was able to show that Locke's *Second Treatise on Government* was not best understood, historically, as a reply to *Leviathan*. Third, the acclaim (or notoriety) of C.B. Macpherson, in particular, radically unsettled the hitherto mostly analytical character of this debate.

Macpherson (1962) was not concerned with whether Hobbes was more of an absolutist or liberal. He scrambled these concerns. He interpreted Hobbes as a child of his time, one reflecting powerful contemporary social forces. Macpherson read Hobbes's position, not as an abstractly logical claim about the theoretical relations between humans and society, but as a reflection of Hobbes's concrete commitment to or awareness of a newly emerging competitive order in which an earlier medieval corporatism had dissolved. Macpherson portrayed Hobbes's state of nature, not as a system of universally autonomous individuals, but as a new set of social relations instituted in seventeenth-century England. In this setting, following Macpherson, individuals were cut adrift from one another; each man had his price; each instantiated an animate calculus of self-interest; labour and skill had become commodities; and out-and-out competition required the vigorous imposition of state authority.

For Macpherson, the chief oversight of Hobbes lay in supposing that it would be more a powerful individual than a propertied class that would play the role of sovereign. In all this, Macpherson moved a confusingly great way from assessing Hobbes's position in straight-forwardly logical terms. He generated considerable turbulence from the attempt to make sense of a set of universal claims by reducing them to the contours of a specific historical context. Macpherson's approach was 'confusing' in the sense that he was a man of the left who none the less avoided a conventionally 'liberal' attack upon Hobbes; confusing too in that, while his politics were 'idealistic', his methodology was plainly 'materialist', even determinist.

There were many objections to Macpherson's claims. The lines of attack were basically two. First, there was the concern that the views Macpherson attributed to Hobbes were not in fact grounded in what Hobbes himself said. Second, there was the concern that the historical perception which Macpherson entertained of Hobbes's time was unreliable or illusory. Isaiah Berlin was one of the first to rehearse one or both of these claims.

The first complaint that Berlin (1964) lodges is precisely the claim that Macpherson paid insufficient attention to Hobbes's texts, to what Hobbes himself wrote. Berlin insists, against Macpherson, that 'a political theory stands or falls by what it says and omits to say'. It does not depend on the manner in which we may suppose a context to condition or occasion an author's errors or obscurities. For Berlin, those writers whom we consider great, and whom we research most voluminously, are the exceptional thinkers least engaged in merely mirroring their own conditions or crises. The idea then is that one cannot really come to grips with Hobbes merely by study of his background. More broadly, the 'vitality of the classics springs from some quality that transcends their times'. Berlin thus detects in Macpherson an historicist tendency, and objects to the idea that the logical coherence of an author should be made to turn round the supposed match between his or her views and the material conditions of the time.

The claim by Skinner (1964) that the logical meaning of a text cannot be divorced from the historical context in which it is lodged directly counters the independence of the text, as argued for by Berlin. Skinner has attracted considerable attention in virtue of his sustained effort to press this case. Hobbes's philosophy was long regarded as sufficiently comprehensive and coherent to warrant being attended to with primary (not exclusive) regard for what he himself wrote – his texts. Many important studies of Hobbes – by Taylor, Warrender, Strauss and Goldsmith *inter alia* – proceeded in this way. They projected it as their problem to establish the most credible reading of

Hobbes, less by reconstructing his background than by concentrating on his books. Such was the approach promoted by Berlin. When Skinner turned to Macpherson, the burden of the position seemed to be not so much that Macpherson read the texts in some given way, but that he placed too great store by reading texts as such.

The nature of Skinner's objection is first hinted at in his 1964 review of F.C. Hood's mostly textual analysis of *Leviathan*. Hood proposed, by means of 'a close examination of the relevant texts', to show that Hobbes was not a proponent of a utilitarian calculus, but rather of an abstract and universal duty, contained in natural law, as dictated by God and reason. Hood's proposal would represent the significant encroachment of an anti-traditional view, first broached by A.E. Taylor, on the thrust of Hobbes's ethical and political doctrine. And Skinner proved understandably unhappy with this agenda, as did many others who entertained no particular interest in an historical or contextual method.

Skinner, in countering Hood, contends that the latter's position does not logically derive from Hobbes's text, but from 'a sequence of textual misunderstandings' and even from 'a failure to recognize the logical structure of [Hobbes's] work'. What is of interest in Skinner's 1964 review of Hood is that there is nothing new to be remarked in the critical method resorted to, adhering as it does to a traditional, which is to say a mostly textual, approach. Nor does Skinner's substantive judgement jump the queue, representing a position behind which most scholars at the time would have lined up. What is distinctive is Skinner's intimation – and it is here little more than that – of an inclination to declare against textual analysis as such.

Hood's analysis of *Leviathan* falters basically on textual, not on contextual, grounds. Skinner, however, attributes the difficulty not merely to faulty interpretation, but also and possibly more importantly, to faulty method. He taxes Hood, in short, with the adoption of an insufficiently historical or contextual approach. Skinner (1964) does not fully argue the case, but he does broaden it. In accusing Hood of a necessarily faulty textualism, Skinner extends his opprobrium to Macpherson, although Macpherson, like Skinner, and as Berlin observed, is himself in essentials an historicist or materialist or contextualist. It follows that those whom Skinner accuses of adopting a textual approach are not necessarily distinguished by this proclivity. It is only safe to say they are marked off by their embrace of conclusions with which Skinner has found it difficult to concur.

In his more straightforward historical essays, Skinner (1965a) reveals, far more sympathetically than elsewhere, something of the concrete nature of his concern. The problem that he specifically locates is that of political ideologists concocting and espousing a particular theory about history which is entirely devoid of any historical foundation. Skinner's attention is caught by the 'Whig view' of history. It was a view universally accepted by parliamentarians and monarchists, because it suited the different purposes of both. Seventeenth-century parliamentarians could not acknowledge William's 1066 conquest of England as conquest, since this would imply for them that parliamentary 'sovereignty' was derived from the pleasure, and prior title, of the monarch. Nor could monarchists acknowledge 1066 as an act of conquest, since this would imply, for them, that the title of the monarch was grounded in usurpation (as by Cromwell).

The myth that flowed from all this was that William's eleventh-century conquest was no such thing, and that his authority derived from election. Here, then, to later observers, was a transparent attempt to bolster contentions for present rights by reference to past subjection, with the 'correct' contemporary ideology being made to depend upon a false set of historical 'facts'. Skinner's proper object was to point the way to the avoidance of such errors. What was not clear, and became subject to considerable debate, was whether there was any single simple method, 'historical' or otherwise, which would cause us to operate in a manner less 'ideological'.

Skinner (1965–66) again takes up a concrete historical problem. He seeks to show that claims relating to Hobbes's isolation, and which depict his influence as purely negative, are overdone. Skinner modifies the picture supplied by such antecedents as Lubienski and Lamprecht, to the effect that the early literature on Hobbes was essentially antipathetic. Following Skinner, Hobbes was an intellectual power in both France and England, a presence accordingly of continental proportions. Skinner makes an important case for Hobbes's continental impact. He accepts none the less that, in England, Hobbes was a distinctly isolated figure, both with regard to the volume of work produced and the quality of intellectual contacts sustained. Skinner's case for a more positive Hobbesian influence in England is met with a sharp rebuttal from Stephen State (1985).

Hans Maier (1968) is only superficially concerned with Hobbes's personal history. Influenced by F. Tönnies and Leo Strauss, he betrays only the slightest interest in reconstituting Hobbes's meaning by reference to the circumstances of his time. After a brief replay of background, there follows an intellectual portrait of Hobbes, less as an absolutist or totalitarian (consistent with Macpherson), than as a percipient theorist, indeed the first important theorist, of the modern state (consistent with Strauss). Hobbes is thus portrayed not so much as a theorist who belongs in the past but as one who exercises a continuing influence in the present. Where a figure such as Skinner stresses continuity with the seventeenth-century intellectual milieu, believing that too much may be made of Hobbes's originality and distinctiveness, Maier wishes to emphasize just these qualities to set Hobbes apart from contemporaries.

Skinner (1969b) takes up yet another specific, historical question. Here he seeks to establish why it is that Hobbes was excluded from the Royal Society. Skinner's conclusion is that Hobbes's exclusion followed from the fact that he proved dogmatic and opinionated in debate, was antipathetic to two members of the Society, and that the other members (even where they admired Hobbes) were not disposed to countenance his 'excessively "magisterial" and "disparaging" manner'. In this, Skinner seeks to counter two other assumptions: first, that the Royal Society bristled with Puritans whose collective urge was to have no truck with the atheistic materialism attributed to Hobbes; and second, that Hobbes was excluded 'because he was not a proper scientist at all'. Skinner's brisk dismissal of these claims is refreshing. But it is secured at the cost of detaching Hobbes from his structurally dependent status and converting him into an autonomous intelligence abstracted from the sharply hierarchical society of the time.

J.M. Wiener (1974) provides an account, a defence, and a criticism of Skinner on Hobbes, bringing Warrender, Hood and Mintz into the discussion. Wiener takes Skinner's position broadly to be that political philosophy must be executed contextually, on the grounds that concentration upon texts leads to 'historically absurd glosses on them'. For Wiener, Skinner's contextual approach is taken to be the proper one, for the reason that 'an exclusive reliance on textual analysis leads to a faulty understanding' of the very texts under study. This is not, however, a position which Wiener attempts to validate. What he actually recognizes Skinner concretely and systematically to do is simply to analyse Hobbes from the perspective of the latter's continuity with other writers of the time, generally excluding any consideration of his originality and distinctiveness *vis-à-vis* these others.

Given Wiener's sympathy for Skinner's contextual approach to the history of ideas, the type of criticism that he is able to bring against it is inescapably of an internal kind. One is almost able to say that Wiener's criticism of Skinner is implicit in the contextual approach itself. Wiener complains that Skinner supplies too thin, too insufficient an account of the context. Wiener insists that, if Hobbes forms 'part of a group of ideologues' driven by a particular programmatic imperative, than we need to know more about the members of this group. In claiming that Skinner's contextualism does not go far enough to establish his case, Wiener equally contends that Skinner, in concentrating upon *Leviathan*, 'puts [Hobbes's] political theory in too narrow a context'. This sort of criticism of a contextual approach is 'internal', being somehow created by the approach itself, in the sense that, or in as far as, there is no way of stipulating in advance how much and what sort of historical detail will suffice to explicate the thrust of the text(s) we seek to decode.

E.G. Jacoby (1974) displays a degree of understandable impatience with the inclination to interpret Hobbes from an almost exclusively political perspective. The inclination is generated in part, but only in part, by the contemporary emphasis upon contextual approaches. The preferred outcome of such an emphasis is the disposition to apprehend the writer more as a political agent than as a philosophical thinker. Contextualism stresses the *point* of an act, as opposed to the *logic* of an idea. In these circumstances, virtually anything that the writer *qua* agent thinks must be brought back to the political colour of his purpose. Jacoby is, then, moved by a concern to remind us that '*De Cive* presented itself as the third part of a system, in which natural philosophy was central'. He notes and favours 'recent discoveries' by 'French and Italian scholars whose work was less focused on an isolated political science context'.

Jacoby belongs to a doughty, if small, band of scholars whose inclination has been to see and to comprehend the Hobbesian *oeuvre* as an analytical whole. Work on Hobbes, initiated by Jean Jacquot and H.W. Jones at the publishers, J. Vrin, in Paris, is now being pursued by a substantial team of researchers. Under the general editorship of Yves-Charles Zarka, and with the sponsorship of the Centre National de Recherche Scientifique (CNRS), Vrin has begun to bring out a 17-volume French edition of Hobbes's work, freshly translated and annotated.

Zarka's is the sort of fully fledged project which one might have expected to see executed on English soil. Such a characteristic omission might be put down to the notoriously unphilosophic or even anti-philosophic character of the British, far preferring parliamentary to more abstruse forms of debate. The relevant explanation, however, may prove less grand. The dominant intellectual enthusiasm of educated Britain, after all, is history, tradition or even 'conversation' (as Oakeshott put it) and (more narrowly and professionally) the inspection of context. May this proclivity of itself necessarily devalue texts, and, *a fortiori*, any significant commitment to their retrieval, such as has been undertaken for Hobbes in France? Richard Tuck (1985) at least will not have it so.

Jacoby rightly signals the importance of the earlier biographical work of Arrigo Pacchi and Frithiof Brandt. This, it should be added, has been significantly supplemented by the bibliographical work of W. Sacksteder. Most importantly, the concern to view Hobbes's work less contextually or exclusively politically and more as a philosophic whole has been nurtured by figures like Brandt and J.W.N. Watkins. This comprehensive philosophic orientation, moreover, has been given a significant fillip by Zarka himself in the form of a major book on Hobbesian metaphysics. It remains that Hobbes's philosophy is one of the most important and certainly comprehensive political philosophical analyses of modern times. Whether his politics is best understood separately from, or as an extension of, his metaphysics is an issue explored, in different ways, by Ashcraft and Gray.

Mark Gavre (1974) takes a view of Hobbes as a transhistorical figure, a great writer, one who had an impact on his own times and upon subsequent generations. Gavre takes an historical approach, but of a more comprehensive kind, without intending his history to be overwhelming or exclusive or to dissolve the ultimate riddles of humanity and the universe. A great writer, Gavre suggests, is one who forges a new world view, a view that is satisfactory and comprehensive, appealing to different audiences in markedly different styles and ways, so that 'the theory remains interesting and challenging well after the political crisis that occasioned it is forgotten'. Hobbes accordingly becomes a singular figure.

Gavre finds Hobbes, in both *De Cive* and in *Leviathan*, a defender of royal power. For Gavre, Hobbes is (not 'was') a great theorist precisely because sufficiently acute to invent an unorthodox and non-sectarian way of servicing this defence. Hobbes spoke to the men of science, to the men of commerce and to the Puritans alike, but addressing each of these constituencies with different arguments which required to be mutually consistent. Gavre attends particularly to Hobbes's Calvinism, to his chronicle of pride, vanity, fear and power-seeking, to Hobbes's conclusion that fallen men require that the ruler be rendered as powerful as the fallen are conceded to be sinful. Gavre insists upon 'the same two alternatives' in Hobbes as in Calvin: 'a deadly, brutish, "fallen" condition of disorder versus an orderly, secure, moral community ruled by an absolute sovereign'.

Gavre's approach reduces to a distinct type of contextualism. Yet it is markedly more ecumenical than many. For it insists, not just upon knowledge of contemporary understandings which a writer like Hobbes would have been countering or confirming, but equally upon sensitivity to multiple audiences, to multiple arguments, to very different layers and styles of debate, thus serving to highlight rather than to obscure the singularity and enduring value, where applicable, of a given writer's contribution. Any approach which simply reduces an author to his background, as Berlin thinks Macpherson tends to do, or which merely insists upon those gross similarities which a figure shares with his contemporaries, which Wiener takes to be Skinner's inclination, must ride roughshod over these subtle but all-important nuances constitutive of philosophical genius. Although Gavre's 'broader, historical approach' is satisfying for its breadth and suppleness, it is still not demonstrated that the supply of greater historical detail in this way directly or logically assists in testing, e.g. any one of the possibly several Hobbesian 'justifications for political obedience'.

Warrender (1978) supplies a brief account of the Hobbes edition he was preparing (Clarendon Press, Oxford) prior to his death. This was to embrace five volumes as follows:

(I)   Hobbes's *Vitae* and *The Elements of Law*;
(II) and (III)   *De Cive* (Latin and English versions);
(IV) and (V)   *Leviathan* (Latin and English versions).

Warrender's approach to Hobbes was philosophical, analytical and textual. His book on Hobbes's political philosophy was the most important and tightly reasoned study of its subject in the three decades following World War II, attracting counter-argument from a variety of observers, among them Thomas Nagel, D.D. Raphael and Brian Barry. Warrender's analysis, splendid as it is, was not proof against attack: none is. What may be of greater interest and significance is that on the whole and in hindsight what really seemed to be under attack and on the skids was the analytical fashion itself, of which Warrender was a prime exemplar.

Following the surge of contextualism, and the declining favour of philosophy (in Britain), Warrender's work has been increasingly neglected, a development against which B.T. Trainor (a past student of Warrender's) justly complains. Warrender, *faute de mieux* or by choice, largely worked alone. The Clarendon Press edition of Hobbes's works which it was his responsibility to assemble was neither grandly conceived nor sumptuously subventioned, and it is to be presumed that there was a reverse causal connection between these two. The modesty of this halting operation, which did not even envisage an attempt to place the Hobbes correspondence before the public, is to be contrasted with the scale of planning and funding that has gone into the Zarka edition unfolding in Paris.

Richard Ashcraft (1978), in contrast to Jacoby, insists that 'Hobbes was, in the first instance, a political theorist'. Whether Hobbes was or was not primarily a political theorist may not be crucially relevant, if the question is really whether Hobbes's political conclusions derive from his metaphysics or, by contrast, rest upon an independent experiential ground. Ashcraft, like Skinner, Wiener and Gavre, is concerned generally with Hobbes's historical context, but more specifically with 'the political importance of Hobbes's thought to his contemporaries'. Ashcraft wishes to go beyond opaque claims (such as that of Plamenatz) to the effect that Hobbes's political thought was a 'product of civil war and strife', in order analytically to link context to text, 'the historical genesis of a theory and its substantive content'. The link, for Ashcraft is not between Hobbes's supposed commitment to geometry, on the one hand, and an emergent *Leviathan* on the other. It is not between Hobbes's metaphysics and his politics. It is between England's history of civil strife and Hobbes's resultant absolutism.

Ashcraft's specific project is lodged within a broader Skinnerian framework. Although Ashcraft is concerned to press a contextualist case, he, like Skinner, proves unable to do so without heavy reliance upon what Hobbes himself writes, i.e. without recourse to textual exegesis as a principal means of establishing Hobbes's purpose. Indeed, the second part of Ashcraft's essay is a matter exclusively of textual analysis. What this textual analysis confirms is the intimate methodological tie between *Leviathan* and *Behemoth* – not a source of any sustained argument among scholars – leading into the third and most helpful part of Ashcraft's paper.

Ashcraft nicely explores, extends and supplements our picture of what the English Civil War, as a concrete piece of history lived by Hobbes, will have meant for him. In the course of this, but without arguing the case, Ashcraft intends as well that history may somehow serve as a substitute for textual analysis. Ashcraft implies either that 'logic and scientific methodology' ought, at the extreme, to be excluded from the history of ideas or, less extreme, that they ought to be accorded secondary importance *vis-à-vis* contextual history. Ashcraft is sufficiently confident to admit to a methodologically 'trenchant' approach. And it is precisely this, separable from the concrete history he supplies, which will occasion doubt. It is consistent with Ashcraft's methodological trenchancy that he should endorse without qualification the connection between 'Hobbes's political thought' and 'the Engagement controversy of 1650–51', a connection 'convincingly demonstrated' by Skinner, but argued to be spurious by Wiener.

It is true that Skinner himself set a dismissive tone in some of his earlier essays. The style can be accounted understandable in the circumstances. In the 1950s and 1960s, analytical philosophy, putting the Popperian 'school' to one side, was in the ascendant. And much of the 'textual' analysis which Skinner opposed was that practised at Oxford among legions of linguistic analysts, even though Skinner himself was suspended from the Ariadne thread held out by J.L. Austin. Skinner's close association, however, with members of the Cambridge establishment like Peter Laslett, even when doing philosophy, would understandably tempt him to perform more as an historian than not. If Skinner was occasionally dismissive, this was consistent with a sharp new style, set most strikingly by Ernest Gellner in *Words and Things*. It is perhaps significant that Gellner, who began life at Oxford, who bit the philosophic hand that cradled him, and who wintered for many long years at the London School of Economics, later found himself ensconced at Cambridge, a colleague of Skinner.

Skinner, then, somewhat in the style of Gellner, was pushing against a firmly shut door. He had for this reason the better part of aptness on his side. Some of his essays were convolutedly analytical, as though mock imitations of the very professional disposition he seemed committed to overtake. The anachronism he criticized perhaps in the name of Cambridge and plain historical truth was anathematized paradoxically in the dry, hair-splitting, philosophic language linked by Gellner to the other institution. Skinner's concrete underlying proposals for the remedy of specific forms of anachronism were important without always being clearly formulated, the language becoming popularly identified with a commitment to displace textual analysis altogether, an aversion not consistently reflected in Skinner's practice and not conclusively sought by him.

Robert Gray (1978) represents an inclination to benefit from a conjunction of both textual and contextual approaches. He is concerned to project Hobbes as instancing what might be called a 'whole' doctrine, linking the politics and the metaphysics by a single logical thread. At the same time he seeks to inspect the Hobbesian context in order to determine whether the timing and sequence of the major works throw any light on Hobbes's probable intentions.

Taking account first of textual and philosophical integrity, Gray, more like Brandt and Watkins, less like Strauss and Warrender, is disposed to appreciate Hobbes from the comprehensive perspective of *The Elements* rather than from the more narrowly political perspective of *De Cive* and *Leviathan*. In this connection, Gray makes a series of points. To begin, the orientation shared by Hobbes with the Greeks was the belief that 'to know is to know by way of cause'. Next, Hobbes assumes knowledge to proceed deductively from generals to particulars. The latter accordingly cannot be known until all that which, by presupposition, they stand upon is known. Hobbes assumes that the original and most general of all causes lies in motion. Finally, '*The Elements of Philosophy*, consisting of three separately published works, *De Corpore*, *De Homine* and *De Cive*', reflects just such a scheme, attending most generally to the motions of bodies, then to the salient traits of human individuals, and finally to the laws governing human associations.

Turning more to context, while Gray accepts that Hobbes published *De Cive* before and independently of the other components of *The Elements*, he finds in this no reason for inflating *De Cive*'s significance, thus distorting what he takes to be Hobbes's overall purpose. Where the third part of Ashcraft (1978) seeks to derive *Leviathan* directly from the experience of civil war, Gray seeks to reverse this approach and to ground *Leviathan* and *De Cive* in the more general analysis, first, of *De Corpore* and secondly of *De Homine*.

As a part of this, much of Gray's discussion is taken up with Strauss, the central point of the dispute turning round the question whether Hobbes, on the basis of both textual and contextual evidence, achieved his mechanistic, 'scientific' awakening early or late. If early, then *De Cive* will have been affected by it. If late, the contrary inference applies. Gray contends that Hobbes's study of Aristotle only came after his 'philosophical awakening as a mechanistic philosopher', and that 'Hobbes's earliest concern with geometry, and, hence, with Euclid, was a consequence of his mechanistic view and not vice versa'. Gray provocatively concludes that 'Hobbes's early political views, at least his almost blind preference for monarchy ... represent a distortion of his later, systematically mechanistic ... views'.

Tricaud (1979) reminds us of the difficulty involved in establishing reliable texts for Hobbes's work, especially *Leviathan*, with its 'head', 'bear' and 'ornaments' editions, in descending order of dependability, but all dating from 1651, and all marked by numerous variations. The 'head' edition has been inspected most closely, and there are variations, if not significant ones, even within it, not to speak of the other editions, which have not been subject to such rigorous review. Tricaud believes that 'even the idea of a "good" text becomes problematic'. He concludes that the pre-eminence accorded the 'head' by Waller, Macpherson and himself (in Tricaud's French translation of *Leviathan*) is not justified.

Gary Seifert (1979) registers reservations about larger contextual claims and opines that 'there is still something to be said for more textual exegesis'. He says this against the backdrop of a wide range of inconsistent contemporary interpretations of Hobbes. We are reminded of the views on Hobbes as (1) a modernist (Strauss), (2) a proto-Marxist (Macpherson) and (3) a proponent of natural law

(Warrender). Seifert also signals what he calls (4) 'the traditional case' (regarding the system as consistently materialistic–mechanistic), (5) the natural law case (taking Hobbes to supply two unrelated scientific and ethical systems) and (6) contextual or 'individualistic' methods. The last, in Seifert's view, are occasioned by an attempt to transcend the clash between the 'traditional' and the 'natural law' approaches.

Having reviewed this range of debate, Seifert attends specifically to the textual reliability of the glosses supplied by Oakeshott and Watkins. In this connection, however, Seifert indirectly signals a difficulty that often attends analyses of a predominantly textual kind. Where a thinker makes a claim which the student finds implausible, it may be inferred (a) that the claim is itself unreliable, (b) that it is unreliable because attributable to someone else, e.g. an editor, (c) that it is unreliable even if attributable to the author because inconsistent with his or her views as overwhelmingly established elsewhere, or (d) that it is reliable but either empirically or analytically false. But then there is something else that might happen should (d) obtain. And this is for the student to confuse the invalid conclusion drawn by the author, on the one hand, with, on the other, a conclusion which 'he [the author] cannot have meant' (*because* of its invalidity).

Neal Wood (1980) takes it as axiomatic that Macpherson's portrayal of Hobbes is untenable. Wood is less disposed to disavow Macpherson's method, however, than its results. For Wood, as for Macpherson, Hobbes is allowed to be little more than a child of his times. The Hobbesian absolutist state, far from constituting 'a complex machine to prevent the self-destruction of bourgeois man', as in Macpherson's account, becomes rather 'a masterful project', as Wood would have it, to salvage the aristocracy. *Leviathan* was devised as a means of curbing, not the 'money-makers and merchants', but 'the English landed gentlemen in their frenetic pursuit of honours'. Wood's intriguing historical (historicist?) case then is that Hobbes 'generalized the outlook and conduct of that specific class into the *bellum omnium contra omnes* ..., he transmuted the crisis of the aristocracy into the universal condition of humanity'. The approach, the method, is exactly parallel to Macpherson's and is significant precisely because of the divergent conclusion which Wood is able to extract from it.

Noel Malcolm (1981) provides fascinating historical and biographical detail relating to Hobbes' involvement in the Virginia Company, where he loyally supported Cavendish interests. Malcolm does not simply supply an alternative historicist account of how it is that Hobbes's concrete historical circumstances caused him to write in the general and philosophical way that he did, a contextually deterministic account as appealingly arbitrary as any it might replace.

He does better; new material is actually appended to the record. The record is far from adequate. But the picture of Hobbes that here emerges is of a dependable vote, of an intelligent, literate and utterly reliable place-man. What is demonstrated is the perfect subordination of reason (Hobbes's) to interests (Cavendish's).

The primary economic concern of the Virginia Company was the importation of tobacco on a monopoly basis. It is demonstrated that Hobbes, if fully on behalf of his patrons, was (like Locke) very much involved in and knowledgeable about financial affairs. Against this backdrop of considerable contextual detail, Malcolm rightly notes how little echo of this involvement there is in all that Hobbes wrote. Malcolm also remains rightly circumspect, despite his success with this article, about the philosophical implications of his historical researches. As he sensibly concludes, although 'the evidence of Hobbes's part in the Virginia Company makes it possible to illuminate in some detail a period of his life which was hitherto obscure, the light which this in turn casts on the development of his ideas remains necessarily oblique'.

J.C. Carmichael (1983) argues that Macpherson's account of Hobbes as a possessive individualist is brilliant, original, lucid and meticulous, but nothing to do with Hobbes. Carmichael's complaint, like Berlin's, is that Macpherson's contextual assumptions simply do not accord with what Hobbes says. One unenunciated implication underlying this is that the deciphering of a context can prove every bit as thorny as the decoding of a text. Where the text is difficult, the context may prove equally or more so. It may indeed be that the context is nothing more than another sort of text, such that neither of these can be viewed as representing a 'final solution' to the other, with each in various ways replicating the problems of the other.

Where Skinner complained that Macpherson paid insufficient attention to Hobbes's context, Carmichael protests that Macpherson's difficulty derives from insufficient attention to the texts. Hence Carmichael's axiom: 'Hobbes's text is the basis on which Macpherson's interpretation must eventually be judged'. C.B. Macpherson (1983) in turn counters Carmichael textually, adjudges his claims to be hasty and ill founded, and concedes not the slightest bit of ground to his adversary. Carmichael's reply briefly replays the dominant themes of the original argument, to the effect that 'Macpherson's interpretation depends essentially upon reading into *Leviathan* postulates which it does not state explicitly'. Carmichael renews his plea that 'the text should be read more exactly, with greater respect for its precision'.

Just as Macpherson proposed to decipher Hobbes with reference to his context, so did Skinner. But the context which absorbed the

one differed radically from that which attracted the other. Where
Wood attacked Macpherson more for his result than for his method,
Skinner attacked him more for his (supposedly textual) method than
for his (historicist possessive–individualist) result. It is not that
Skinner agreed with this result. Rather, Macpherson and Skinner were
just working different rows of cotton. Where Macpherson was more
exasperatingly innovative, seeking to demonstrate that Hobbes was
really a 'possessive individualist', Skinner was complicatedly defensive, seeking to show by circumstantial means that Hobbes's theory
of political obligation was actually much the same as we had always
supposed it to be. Borrowing Seifert's language to describe another's
project, we could say that Skinner adopted a contextual or 'individualist' method to prove 'the traditional case', i.e. that Hobbes's theory
of political obligation was a consistent materialistic–mechanistic
system.

Stephen State (1985) is aware that Skinner wishes to have Hobbes's
theory of political obligation understood in its traditional guise. State
has Skinner understand Hobbes as a 'rationalist–utilitarian' whose
talk of a 'natural law duty to God' is mere 'window-dressing'. Skinner
is made to endorse Hobbes as a 'utilitarian' in order to dismiss claims
for him as a 'deontologist'. The chosen approach is not now, however,
from the vantage point of Hobbes's texts, but from that of his context,
engaging specifically the views entertained of Hobbes by his contemporaries, including, on Skinner's account, a host of 'disciples'.

The two contextual, historical accounts supplied by Skinner and
State are in constant counterpoint. Where Skinner claims to have
located 'an authentically Hobbist following', State responds that
'Skinner has misconstrued the evidence'. Those whom Skinner
identifies as Hobbists, State transmogrifies into 'these so-called
Hobbists'. For State, these men are so-called Hobbists because they
'are by no means agreed on ... Hobbes's position', 'are a motley crew'
and none of them ('with one possible exception') presents a 'rationalist–
utilitarian argument devoid of religious sanction'. So where Skinner
embraces a general commitment to resolve difficult problems of
textual exegesis by means of contextual reconstructions, State comes
to the conclusion that 'the interpretation of Hobbesian texts cannot
be resolved by Skinner's recourse to History'.

As to the detail, State claims that Skinner 'seriously distorts
Ascham's position', shows that Ascham was critical of Hobbes, and
also that Ascham had no altogether reliable understanding of what
Hobbes was actually about anyway. As for Nedham, State concludes
that 'Skinner has been less than candid in concealing [his] eclecticism',
suggesting that Nedham makes so many different and incompatible

claims that it is just as plausible to view him as a natural law deontologist as a rationalist–utilitarian, etc. In sum, 'The Hobbists do not
agree in their interpretation of Hobbes.' State goes on to claim – it is
an important insight – that 'the boundaries of genuine theistic natural
law theory' are indistinct. Thus is State able to fly at least a small kite
for Hobbes as a natural law man.

Richard Tuck (1985) reviews Warrender's Latin and English
editions of *De Cive* (volumes II and III, respectively). Volume II is
Hobbes's Latin rendering of 1642. The second is the English translation from the Latin originally published in 1651 as *Philosophical
Rudiments concerning Government and Society*. Tuck records it as 'an
extraordinary fact that there has been hitherto no proper modern
edition of the works of Thomas Hobbes', with 'many letters to him
and even some written by him' still unpublished. Tuck views this as
'testimony to the unhistorical character of so much philosophical
writing in England'. He omits to observe that the French are conventionally viewed as marked by a highly philosophical and unhistorical
bent, and yet manage to produce critical editions of major philosophical figures usually of a standard far higher than anything ever
even aimed at in Britain.

It seems open to question whether the small interest displayed in
England for critical editions of major texts is to be accounted for by
a preternaturally 'unhistorical' disposition. What is at least plausible,
in some broader sense, is that Britain is markedly anti-intellectual.
This approximate anti-intellectualism may appear in the form of the
undirected hair-splitting of many of those belonging to an earlier
generation of analytic philosophers, to be replaced by the equally
undirected minutiae-mongering of so many of the historicists/
contextualists of today. It is not the case that we are or were in either
case confronted with an unmitigated disaster. But it is the case that
we are confronted with a great deal of irrelevance. And it is this that
is to be deplored, which is less to do with an aversion to intellect than
with an impoverished sense of the best use to make of it.

Tuck's brief discussion is revealing. He takes the opportunity, in
the discussion of the Warrender edition of Hobbes, to supply a clear
and concrete example of one way in which a purely contextual reconstruction can apparently aid in deciphering the meaning of a text.
Two texts by the same author appear more or less simultaneously in
1651, one being the new *Leviathan*, the other a new version of *De
Cive*. These texts make different and opposing claims about the
role of the Church. One gives the sovereign greater power over it, the
other accords the sovereign less. The question arises, Was the author
confused? Or can one of these texts be conceded precedence over the

other? The substantive difficulty centres on the degree of absoluteness concretely accorded by Hobbes to the sovereign. Tuck mounts an excellent case, on the basis of external evidence, for according precedence to *Leviathan*.

In a case of the kind that Tuck offers, unless one text clearly repudiates the other, whether directly or indirectly, it is difficult to see how any purely internal reading of either or both can resolve the puzzle set. Of course, it does not follow, in the face of the internal difficulty, that the problem can be resolved by going outside the text. But to seek a possible contextual solution in the circumstances would certainly make sense. At the same time, it is relevant to observe in this case that no question is raised regarding the meaning or intent of either of the texts involved, not *De Cive* nor *Leviathan*. The problem is not one, strictly speaking, to do with textual meaning. It abuts only upon the rather narrower question to do with which of the texts we are entitled to believe was favoured by Hobbes at the material time.

There are probably several unspoken lessons to be derived from Tuck's example. First, a contextual reading may well help to elucidate an author's purpose. If we can establish on external grounds that Hobbes likely favoured the argument L over the argument DC, we are certainly eliciting his purpose (at least some part of this). Second, an author's 'purpose' is not to be collapsed into his 'meaning'. The distinct meanings Hobbes divulges in *Leviathan* and *De Cive* are clear but neither text of itself necessarily establishes what he 'purposed'. Third, Tuck's procedure does not, strictly speaking, solve any problem relating to the internal sense or logic or meaning of a text. Fourth, the idea of an author's purpose, though perfectly intelligible, remains a partly psychological reconstruction of personal motives, and thus is inherently difficult to authenticate in a way that the meaning of a text (assuming it to be coherent) is not. Fifth, since authors like Hobbes make different and at least marginally incompatible claims at different times, it behoves analysts to be particularly careful in the construction of 'whole doctrines' from their subjects of study. Finally (this will be taken up again in section 5), textual and contextual problems, inasfar as they are different, are complementary, without it being clear that to decipher the one directly resolves the other.

Perez Zagorin (1985) provides an account of Hobbes's background and development in relation to Clarendon. As a part of this, Zagorin contends that Tuck, who places Hobbes in the context of the Tew circle, 'seriously misrepresents this relationship'; that many of Tuck's claims are 'surprising and groundless'; and that Tuck's account of Hobbes as a follower of Selden is not 'even remotely plausible'. All the evidence, following Zagorin, points not to Tew's influence upon Hobbes, but to Hobbes's influence upon Tew. What we find then in Zagorin is an historical case, running counter to the sort of case made by Tuck and Skinner, for the distinctiveness and singularity of Hobbes in the English setting. For the rest, Zagorin is largely concerned to replay and to assess Clarendon's own highly critical estimate of Hobbes.

Brian Trainor (1988) performs a service in bringing together the two apparently inconsistent perspectives on Hobbes, textual and contextual, by Warrender and Skinner, respectively. As suggested earlier, Warrender's textual concern fixes upon the logical coherence of Hobbes's position, and argues for Hobbesian political obligation being grounded ultimately in natural law. Skinner's problem has been to adduce contextual evidence to demonstrate that Hobbesian duty is derived from a prudential calculation of self-interest. Trainor seeks to show that the mostly contextual criticism of the textual analysis is largely 'wide of the mark'. His attack on Skinner is similar to that of Carmichael on Macpherson; the charge in each case is that insufficient attention is paid to Hobbes's text.

Like State, Trainor contends that Skinner's characterization of Hobbes as a non-natural-law thinker is untenable. Trainor concludes that 'if we wish to discover the intellectual and ethical foundations of the Hobbesian doctrine ..., then with Warrender, we will seek full supporting arguments in Hobbes's published texts', for which Hobbes was 'fully responsible', rather than in 'the real historical world', implicitly awash in ambiguity, confusion and incomprehension, and which lay 'beyond Hobbes's control'. Quentin Skinner (1988), in a brief reply, acknowledges it to be Warrender's view that the laws of nature derive their obligatory force as or from 'the command of God'. But against this view he contends that 'Hobbes never advances this argument at any point in any of his political works'.

Skinner here defends himself both against Trainor and Warrender, not now by reference to the views of Hobbes's contemporaries, but by reference to 'Hobbes's own description of his theory'. He indicates an earlier concern to overcome a textual impasse by recourse to a contextual procedure but had 'always assumed that Warrender's interpretation must of course be judged basically in the light of Hobbes's texts'. Unhappily, Skinner remains silent about any possible change of view regarding the continuing force of his early contextual objections to textual approaches. Beyond this, and in parallel to Macpherson's defence against Carmichael, Skinner makes no concessions to his adversary.

Mark Whitaker (1988) is dissatisfied both with Macpherson's 'ahistorical model of seventeenth-century English society' and with Skinner's propensity to connect 'a great text of political philosophy

... to "real politics" only through the writings of its imitators and borrowers'. Whitaker takes it that, before 1649, Hobbes was concerned to explain civil war in general, but that the task of *Leviathan* in 1651 was to 'respond to the specific character of the English conflict'. The significant difference between *De Cive* and *Leviathan*, for Whitaker, lies in the latter's overwhelming concern with religion. Whitaker characterizes Hobbes's view of Reformation England as one wherein clergy and congregation 'were equal in that they had a common text in front of them', but remained 'unequal in that the minister, through his linguistic skill', could and did supply exegetical readings of a subversive bent.

Whitaker, in short, is less concerned with the logical complexity of Hobbes's argument than with the rhetorical and political purpose which inspired Hobbes to advance the argument as and when he did. Whitaker thus sees *Leviathan* 'not as an act of philosophical reflection on England's chaos, but as an *intervention* into English revolutionary politics'. Whitaker's essay can fairly be read as something of an extended development of the remarks supplied by Tuck on the same subject. The only difference is that Whitaker is clear that he is only concerned to supply a perspective, not a panacea, given that, methodologically, 'there *is* no revolution one can assume as a context for *Leviathan*' anyway.

If, indeed, *Leviathan* is/was a revolutionary act or engagement of some kind, it directly forms a part of the context, so that the distinction between text and context now necessarily becomes blurred. And if the text is the context, there can be no complaint about studying it on its own, since 'it' can never be said to be 'on its own': to study a text is always simultaneously (if indirectly) to study that by which it is occasioned and that to which it adverts. These references and connections must obviously, in significant degree, lie embedded within the text itself, and all the more so, the more elaborate, sophisticated, self-conscious and coherent the text happens to be. Indeed, in this sense, a text may be understood to supply its own context, such that the latter cannot be regarded as some species of inert externality.

5

Most of the articles discussed in section 4 above directly or indirectly advert to appropriate means of recovering what Hobbes said and could be understood to mean. In the course of this it can be seen that textual and contextual approaches are sometimes treated as though perfectly and firmly distinguishable. It has to be observed, in a general way, that they are not always so. The context itself, for most purposes, either is or can be read as a text, with the same problems of reliability and consistency which all other texts present. Lamprecht and Skinner, for example, where they seek to reconstruct Hobbes's 'context', understood as the way in which Hobbes was received by his contemporaries, are doing no more than sieving other seventeenth-century documents, i.e. they are scrolling other 'texts'. If we take this to be contextual research, it appears substantively identical with the textual variety.

If the context may be understood as nothing more than one or a series of texts, then text and context become much the same. In this case, it becomes awkward to insist that the one must be understood in advance of, and as a prior condition for, the understanding of the other. If the one is the other, the context cannot take one outside a text. It only spews one from the gut of one text into the innards of some other, some different, text(s). If one must understand the context in order to grasp the text, and if the context is just one or a set of different texts, then before one can understand the context of the text, one must have a prior grasp of the context of the context. And before this, one must seize the context of the context of the context, and so on. There looms the risk, accordingly, of an infinite regress where we insist upon grasping contexts in advance of texts.

Inasfar as contexts and texts are substantively the same, then a claim such as that of Wiener (1974), where he professes to agree with Skinner that 'an exclusive reliance on textual analysis leads to a faulty understanding' of these texts, courts the otiose. If texts have their own contexts, if a text of itself implies and adverts to a context, then there could not substantively be any such thing as 'exclusive reliance on textual analysis'. The text itself always fall short of being *sui generis*. It in some measure refers and responds to external events. Texts minimally consist of language; language is social, hence there can be no text which does not advert to and incorporate some social reality. Seen from the perspective of other events, the text itself becomes an external event. Texts may in this way be viewed as supplying the major content of what we call contexts. Assuming that contexts are largely constituted of texts and that a text at least in part generates its own context, no 'textual' approach can consistently prove to be exclusively textual, nor any 'contextual' approach to be exclusively contextual.

Contexts and texts are substantively the same. And yet there is good reason for insisting upon a difference. Where it is said that a context, at least in the history of ideas, is almost invariably some other sort of document or text, what is being signalled is a *substantive* identity. While we may accept that the substance of a context is essentially the same as the substance of a text, this need not stop us from distinguishing between context and text in *relational* terms. Thus:

> Though context and text are substantively the same, *the context* may be relationally viewed as some species of text which lies outside of or is external to another text; this 'other text', for whatever reason, is accorded greater importance or centrality; hence it is called *the text*.

Now on this relational understanding, though context and text are necessarily connected, they are not interchangeable. They are distinguished, by analogy, as is 'outside' from 'inside', or 'secondary' from 'primary', or 'last' from 'first'.

On this relational understanding, it at least becomes conceivable that we might (rather ambitiously) study a context before its text, or (more modestly) seek to elicit the point of a text by reference to its context. We might compositely label these procedures 'methodological contextualism'. While the first approach (study the context before the text) becomes conceivable, it is not automatically made sensible. One can for example study the history of the English Civil War before one reads *Leviathan*. But it is far from self-evident that (in principle) one should. After all, though the history is a part of the book, the book is equally a part of the history. 'The history', 'the context', only consists of another book (such as Clarendon's book on the war), or of a series of books, of letters, of despatches, etc. *Leviathan* is itself, of course, but another page in the record, and though we most commonly view it as 'the text', there is nothing to stop us turning it round, perhaps to serve Clarendon as 'the context'. And this is the point.

Simply because we declare 'the context' to be, say, Clarendon, there is no good reason to suppose that we absolutely ought not to read Hobbes before Clarendon. Either *can* be read before the other and most commonly one is read *rather* than the other, but there is no compelling reason for deferring the study of 'the text' just because we have chosen not to call it 'the context'. It is not persuasive to contend, simply because we light upon Hobbes's book as our 'text', that we ought in principle to read the text of someone else first, such as Clarendon or Ascham or Nedham, or Plucknett or Judson. And this is quite independent of the question how much study of the context, whether on a scale elaborately irrelevant or lamely exiguous, is to be allowed to count as 'study' in the first place.

At its most sensible and commonsensical, methodological contextualism emits a modest and cogent claim. And this is a rule of thumb which enjoins that we seek to elicit the purpose of an author, in writing a text, by reference to the context in which that author was located at the time of writing, at least where we have reason to do so, and on the understanding that we do not always have such a reason. If there are significantly different interpretations of a text, it may be that a better understanding of the context will throw light upon the matter. Yet it has to be confessed that we have as yet no significant examples of this. There are no contextual discussions of Warrender, for example, which refute his claims about Hobbesian political obligation. And we have no contextual refutations of Macpherson's textual claims, since Macpherson's principal and distinctive claims are themselves contextual.

Methodological contextualism will have achieved much of its present vogue by virtue of its legitimate concern to avoid distorting the meaning of texts in the way that often results from taking them 'out of context'. It is an idiom of the language that to take any proposition 'out of context' involves some form of falsification. Can the distortion that springs from omission be definitely squelched by plugging all gaps and plastering over every hiatus? The germ of disquiet whence this proclivity derives is not hard to detect. It is perfectly obvious as to the effect that leaving a word out here or there may have on the sense of a sentence. Judicious omission is a classic tactic for the tiring business of setting up and bowling out straw men. The shadowy atheist is widely reported to have *admitted*, 'there is a God'; but when the record is inspected what it reveals her to say is: 'I admit that most people *believe* there is a God'. Such distortion by omission can win virtually any debate and it is for this reason that we are commonly of a mind to stand up for 'the whole truth', with each jot and tittle in its rightful place.

We should note, however, that this idiom, which enjoins us not to take matters out of context, is not altogether reliable. It tends to imply that to leave something out is itself to distort. And yet we know too well that any account must leave something out. The general problem of distortion and falsification is encountered, not simplistically where we leave something out, this being inescapable in supplying any account, but where we leave those things out which, *being left out*, effectively distort the account we give. And 'methodological contextualism' in the history of ideas may be tarred by some such extension of meaning, from equating the virtue of not being 'out of context' with the impossibility of 'saying everything that might be said'. When we look past the idiom – 'out of context' – to the legitimate general concern underlying it – 'distortion' or 'falsification' – it becomes clear that we may as readily distort by saying too much as too little, by adding on as by taking away, by over-contextualizing as by under-contextualizing.

We may distort by cut-out (as with President Nixon and the Watergate tapes), but equally by overload; it is for example information overload that is distinctive of new forms of censorship. Democratic politicians do not distort by refusing to answer, but by faffing on, determinedly filling up the record with irrelevancies. A barbed point is often swathed in relentless banter. The ordinary person, blurting out her anger, dissimulates her intent by adding a smile, or a strategic change of subject. By adding on in this way, one distorts (undercuts) the significance, or confounds the sense, of the other elements that have already been entered into the record. Circumlocution is of course the classic stratagem deployed where the agent seeks to obscure or soften (and thus distort) his point by embalming it in a surfeit of data. The modern inflation of language in general is a part of this, as where we replace 'dustmen' with 'sanitary engineers'.

Shakespeare commits Antony to inflating the record to falsify intent. Antony's funeral speech is an exercise in irony, circumlocution and dissimulation, demonstrating as clearly as one might wish that subtracting from the record is far from being the only means of distorting it. What Antony intends is that Caesar was a great leader and patriot, that a pack of villains slew him, and that the murderers should be brought to book. But Antony dare not say what he means. He delays. He cries. He lies. There is a controlled padding out of the account: 'I come to bury Caesar, not to praise him'. 'Brutus is an honourable man.' 'So are they all honourable men.' 'I speak not to disprove what Brutus spoke.' Antony spins it all out, he adds and reiterates, all precisely with a view to concealing his purpose. Shakespeare knows all too well how to have him do this, to such a point that every schoolchild knows the passage. So again, distortion is not only secured by deletion, but also by accretion, by putting in as by taking away an excess of context.

Methodological contextualism almost certainly springs at least in part from this generalized concern to supply increased circumstantial detail. But the abstract failure to expand content, as understandable as the concern may be, no more argues against than for the soundness of scholarship. It is always possible to add more. But 'more', unfortunately, really does not equal 'better', nor necessarily apt or relevant or helpful. Even where more might be better, it is often just churlish to demand it, since the abstract demand is exasperatingly open-ended, being logically impossible of satisfaction. Usually, the fact that any good report or letter or book is not longer than it is, is obviously not an appropriate criticism of it. There could always be more, even of a good thing, but how long is a piece of string? The consideration that there could be more, rather than being returned as a criticism, might best be viewed as a celebration of the breathtakingly multifaceted perspectives implicit in all scholarship, especially in modern times.

Skinner's account of Hobbes and the Royal Society, for example, depicts Hobbes as a genuinely autonomous intellect, a materially unencumbered mind, one perfectly free to comment upon the most serious and sensitive matters of the day, *sans entrave aucune*. And yet Hobbes, even in his own words, must by implication be described as a 'servant', an attendant, a dependant, a travelling companion, tour guide, tutor, amanuensis, translator, hired man, a place-man – and yet no relevant account whatsoever is taken of this servitude. There is legitimately 'more' along these lines that Skinner could have done. And yet, is it not absurd to lodge or to take such an asseveration as a 'complaint'? To note the omission is to do no more than signal an appropriate direction for future work. It does no more than under-score another of the illimitable perspectives from which a life such as Hobbes's may be viewed.

It appears sometimes to be supposed that contexts are more reliable than texts, or that they serve as a court of last resort, that they are more factual or more authoritative. This is sometimes reflected in the preference for history over philosophy, the concrete over the abstract, the empirical over the rational. The pre-emptive and ideo-logical concern with imposing 'an historical approach', the fear of being 'unhistorical', reflects in part this proclivity. Ashcraft's apparent inclination to banish or subordinate 'logic and scientific method' seems consistent with this prejudice. In this connection, there are two points to be retained.

First, given that the context is usually reducible to some other sort of text, there is no authoritative reason for supposing that the one can be more reliable than the other. Second, given that every history, every era, every context, has or presupposes its own logic, reducing otherwise to sheer incoherence, there is no possible choice of history over logic. The history is subject to a firm logical structure or it is gibberish, i.e. more hysterical than historical. What we take to be history, what we construe as a context, is never self-evident or self-validating. The history, the context, these are themselves matters of logical construction and reconstruction.

Without in any way giving up on historical truth, reliability, testability and veracity, it remains that the products of any era or history or context can be packaged and repackaged in myriad ways. A context is a building that can be put up in as many different styles as there are architects to design it. The factual array available to the historian is immense. The overall picture consists of an infinity of parts. The whole with which we are presented does not impose itself, since the mind must reduce infinity to a 'story'. The mind invents stories; these are abstracted from and imposed upon an infinity; they do not and cannot replicate it. Infinity – the unwritten 'record', out there, which we hypothesize – is not accoutred with beginning and middle and end. It is our stories, histories, herstories, our eras, constructs and contexts that confer or impose these attributes.

A history can only be made coherent by patching together its divergent parts. And this patching is in the eye, not in the record scanned. The historian does not see 'the period' or 'the context' as such. He or she invents it by imposing upon the data an 'interstitial' logic that is the property of the observer, not the observed. It is this that explains the need, but also the inevitability, of 'the historical imagination'. Even the most boring of historians must possess in however minimal a degree some imaginative faculty. The job cannot otherwise be done. However much there may be in the record, it is never self-evident as to how the record holds together. However much there may be, the holes subsist, always bigger than the walls of information they enclose. It is in this way that the logic of an epoch, 'the spirit of the times', is larger than the record, is in fact just a way of construing the record, almost in the way that we may 'infer' (not syllogistically) a personality from a face.

There can be no doubt that Hobbes himself was perfectly well aware of this 'interstitial logic'. He knew well enough that history does not simply exist, that histories are inventions, that they are put together, that they have a point, that they tell a story, that they reflect choice, selection, order and judgement, that the good historian is both imaginative and accurate in adhering to the logic that enables and invites an audience to attend to what he or she has to say. This is surely Hobbes's point in commending Thucydides ('the most Politick Historiographer that ever writ') as he does: 'He filleth his Narrations with that choice of matter, and ordereth them with that Judgment, and with such perspicuity and efficacy expresseth himself that (as Plutarch saith) he maketh his Auditor a Spectator.' To do this, one must know not to say too little, but equally not to say too much.

7

Historical Contextualism: The New Historicism?

The career of Professor John Pocock is distinguished both by industry and insight. A new collection of essays, edited by Phillipson and Skinner (1993), has been produced in his honour. Two features mark this book, impose an unusual coherence and reflect the recipient's style and interests. First, virtually all of the essays are to do with seventeenth- to eighteenth-century thinkers and movements. Second, all are exercises in small-scale, historical reconstruction, being more concerned to describe than to exemplify political or philosophical discourse.

The book forms part of the Cambridge series 'Ideas in Context'. It is significant for bringing together two of the most important 'contextualist' writers at work today: Pocock himself, and Quentin Skinner. It provides an appropriate occasion for review of the tenability of the contextualist project generally. Two broad objections are to be considered. At its strongest, contextualism may appear to reduce to a *truism*. At its weakest, it may amount to an *impossibility*. Yet, much of the work done by those who think to apply this approach is of genuine interest. Can it be that good historical reconstruction emerges despite, rather than because of, the method of contextualism?

1. Truisms and tail-chasing

Take the idea of contextualism as truism. The charge stems from the consideration that a perception or perspective achieved by any observer, O, of any putatively independent datum, d, never leaves d alone, untainted, *in se*. Harvey could not map the circulation of the blood without dissecting bodies. We characteristically measure the temperature of liquids by intruding thermometers. I know that my soup is ready by tasting it. Any new novel that I read is automatically made sense of by, contextualized in and assaulted on that bed of data and disposition that constitutes my mind. I cannot handle any datum or text without somehow manipulating, affecting or adding something of myself to it. The observer makes sense of a datum or text by squaring it, putting it in the context of, everything else that s/he knows. Thus perception itself can be conceived as 'creating a context for' what is perceived. A context is automatically supplied by, since it consists in the mind of, the knower. To insist in the abstract that we place ideas in context must prove redundant; we have no need to demand what we cannot escape. The question, perhaps, is less whether ideas as such should be placed in *context*, but whether this idea or that has been placed in the context that is *most apt* for one's purposes: literary, economic, religious, historical, social or whatever.

Now take the idea of contextualism as *an impossible procedure*, as articulating a methodological demand that cannot be met. How can I meaningfully think to place every text that I employ in context? For a start, the text is just a set of claims or arguments. The context that I create for it only amounts to additional data – to supplementary claims and arguments. If I am *always* to contextualize, then the context itself (which is substantively reducible to one or more additional 'texts') must in turn be contextualized. Let us say that I place text t_1 in context by juxtaposing to it text t_2. I place this in context in turn by adding to it text t_3. But to contextualize this I must append text t_n. I cannot of course continue endlessly in this way. Am I being enjoined to do what I cannot do? If a necessary condition of my securing a reliable grasp of a statement, of a text, is that I be able to place it in context, then I shall never be able to accomplish this. For at the moment that I create the context, I only do so at the expense of leaving the latter out of context.

For present purposes, the *type* of context does not really matter, be it social, literary, political or whatever. Substantively, the context is equivalent to just another text or set of texts. Any 'framework' material – any context – offered to readers as a piece of historical reconstruction, must be reducible to one or a set of propositions. The context may be viewed as related to or derivable from 'raw' or primary evidence of some description. Yet the description, whatever it is, if communicable at all, takes the form of, or can be translated into, one or more propositions. Contexts *are*, effectively, propositions. And texts, equally, are effectively propositions. Contexts and texts therefore are much the same, taking account of their propositional character. The context relates to the text somewhat in the way that a musical variation relates to an underlying musical theme. Context and text, then, only differ relationally, not substantively. The text is merely that cluster of propositions that comes first, in time or emphasis. In this way, the text offers itself up as a potential subject, even sacrifice, to those subsequent and additional texts which seek to 'enframe' (i.e.

supply some framework for) it. Any such framework text we designate as 'context'.

The formal meaning of a 'context' can be fairly economically expressed, thus: 'one or more propositions, whose purpose is consciously to supply a framework for any antecedent proposition(s), denominated the text'. A text makes claims. But a context also makes claims, either about or relating to the text. Of course the text (it would be otiose 'in this context' to call the text 'original') is always itself replete with claims about *other* texts. For example, the text, '*L'Etat, c'est moi!*', presupposes an innumerable string of further texts, among them, these: 'There is, or at least I imagine there to be, an entity called the state'. 'I am a human being.' 'I have a distinct identity.' 'I am not a cat.' And so on, endlessly. In this way, one can see not only that the context consists of some claim about a text, but also that every text itself consists in claims about or relating to yet further texts. And this is to say no more than that even the 'text', any text, given an appropriate change of perspective, is open to reformulation as a 'context'.

So texts and contexts are complicatedly interconnective, and resist being distinguished substantively, as opposed to relationally. For example, the previous sentence *qua* text may be placed within the context of this paragraph, the text of this paragraph within the context of this section, this text in turn within the context of this chapter as a whole, the latter within the context of this book, these texts within the context of philosophical criticism generally, or of the past two years, or of the last 200 years and so on, illimitably and interminably. Thus texts are contextualized. Contexts, once formulated, become subject to the same process, i.e. they themselves become texts and will in turn be placed 'in context'.

There is nothing in the least self-limiting or self-evident or magically self-revealing or methodologically privileged about 'the' context. It supplies no miracle cures or instant restoratives. It only marks a *direction* in which one might explore, but not as such a methodologically preferable *type* of exploration. It advises *where* to look – outside the text – but not what to look for which would render the text more or less *valid*. This directional advice cannot be useful in regard to truth-claims, since the preference for context over text cannot distinguish between truth-claims, except in terms of precedence. In terms of truth-claims, contexts and texts are identical. They do not differ substantively or propositionally, but only relationally, where the one precedes the other and may serve it accordingly as a subject.

Substantively, contexts are resolvable into texts, and texts equally into contexts. We view Hobbes's *Leviathan* as a text. Every time we reflect on it, or write on it, we generate for it a context. To be able to deal with it at all is automatically to place it within the context of everything else that we know. This context can be logical (this is the context imposed by most of what we might call 'textual' analysis) or historical, cultural, social, etc. It cannot possibly be, for example, that to impose an *historical* context is necessarily more valid than to impose a *logical* context. In any event, a context is always imposed whenever we contemplate a text. Equally, a text like *Leviathan*, were we able to treat with 'it' exactly as did its author at the point of creating it, would no longer be a 'text', because the externality which marks our present relationship to it, would be dissolved. This text would no longer be that item on which we have a grip. Rather, it would dissolve into the swirling perceptions and engagements out of which the author devised it. The author's 'text' is not, for him, a text. It is the context, logical, historical and positional, which his own perception and engagement impose perforce upon *other* texts which serve him as subjects. The text, in short, for one who authoritatively inhabits it, is the context. And this is really what we mean when we speak of a text creating its own context. Whether a proposition *is* a text or a context depends merely upon the position of the observer.

What can be the purpose of an abstract insistence upon 'contextualization'? There will always be some context. And to cite context c_1 may prove more relevant than to cite context c_2. But as contexts are resolvable into texts, and as the only difference between them is one of position or perspective, can it persuasively be claimed that viewing events, e.g. from a distance is always preferable to seeing them up close, or vice versa? The object must surely be to clarify or somehow improve understanding. Does a dogmatic contextualizing procedure necessarily do this? It may well take one further from, rather than closer to, what one seeks to learn. If it is contended that all texts require contextualization, there is implicit in this the assumption that contexts, by contrast, somehow escape any such requirement. But what possible sense can it make to claim or imply that the study of a context will necessarily disclose more than will the study of a text? If texts and contexts are always complicatedly interconnected, if by the simplest change of perspective any text can be converted into a context, if both texts and contexts are accepted as always incomplete, taking account of what they tell us, then there can be no possible point in calling for contextualization in the first instance or in general or in the abstract as a solution to the difficulties we encounter in deciphering the meaning or validity of *texts* as such.

If one encounters a difficulty *in* a text, then it may be wise to look *elsewhere* for solutions to it. But if one has not looked closely enough at a text to determine the problems that it itself disgorges, then 'to look elsewhere' – call it context – is bound to be a bootless business. 'The context' after all is as large as life itself, and as unrelenting. Nor is it one; contexts are irresistibly plural. And if one has no sense of what the text is about, if one does not first take from it some sense of what is to be pursued, then the context in turn, unbounded as it is, neither will nor can reveal anything of relevance. The preference for context over texts only presumably makes sense on the misleading assumption that texts, as distinct from contexts, are necessarily unclear or incomplete. The trouble is, that if *all* texts *qua* propositions, require further explication, there is every good reason to conclude that contexts require this too. And this must make it impossible for us to claim that contextual reconstruction is somehow in itself sounder than textual analysis, or that it should precede it.

If all texts are necessarily unclear or incomplete, then contexts (i.e. the propositions we advance to embellish texts) must also be unclear and incomplete. If all texts necessarily require further explication, then so must contexts require such explication. If no proposition is entirely autonomous or self-explanatory, then no contextual proposition is autonomous or self-explanatory. If I must legitimate texts by placing them in context, then presumably I must equally legitimate contexts ... by placing them in context.

The trouble is that it is logically and physically impossible for any individual endlessly to contextualize the context of the context ... of the context. The problem here is that of Fido's tail: to chase and never to catch. The construction of a context is never conclusive, nor logically sounder, merely by virtue of it being a context. A 'context' is nothing more than a text which, by virtue of being last in place, has not yet been and cannot itself yet be contextualized. Abstractly to recommend contextualization is then to place an automatic value on subsequent propositional claims in preference to antecedent propositional claims. The effect is a *fuîte en avant*. Obviously, there will be an infinite variety of contexts. But if I privilege claims merely because they are contextual, then I privilege them only because of their position as the *last* claims that have been made. My demand for contextual claims is accordingly necessarily self-aborting. My contexts are only dubiously contextual, since I cannot myself confer upon the very last context I create *its* own context. My contexts, further, are doubly dubiously contextual since, so long as there are other and subsequent observers, their reflections and researches will convert my contexts into texts, which must underscore the lack of finality and the inconclusiveness of my contexts.

If the 'context' is the last claim advanced, then it is the context, at the conclusion of the proceedings, that is accorded 'the last word'. It is one thing to acknowledge this as a procedural matter of fact. It is an entirely different matter to attempt to constitute of it a methodological Golden Rule. There can be no reason, morally or methodologically, why what we call a 'context' should be accorded 'the last word'. There can be no sound reason to privilege 'contextual' above 'textual' assertions, nor to allow contexts a moral, hermeneutic or scientific precedence not allowed to texts.

In summary, the integrity of the doctrine of historical contextualism seems problematic. First, contextualization, taken as a simple act of perception, is automatic, so that any abstract demand for it must be superfluous.

Second, abstractly to demand contextualization, if it is not superfluous, seems to imply the superior purchase of contextual over textual claims. The position is untenable. Every textual claim, once made, is automatically the subject of further attention, which creates for the text a context. However, once contextual sallies are made, enveloping their subjects, they too become independent subjects of attention, which is to say that they too must be viewed as texts. If, in the truth stakes, contexts trump texts, then no context can be safe. For as soon as ever a context is formulated, and is in a position to be attended to as an independent claim, then the fact of considering it as such a claim, automatically demotes it from context to text. The distinction between text and context being positional, once the position of the context changes, once it itself becomes the subject of attention, it loses its locational character as context. To be a context, then, is not a position which any claim, once uttered, can sustain. Defence against automatic demotion from context to text is hopelessly circular. Thus any methodological demand which accords priority to contextualization in this prioritises an impossibility.

Third, the preference for contexts over texts merely reduces to a positional preference for later over earlier claims. 'The last word', as a matter of the sequential positioning of a claim, becomes equated with 'the last word', as a matter of the effective validation of a claim. But it is absurd to suppose that claims made last are those that are most reliable, and equally absurd to imagine that contexts *in se* are somehow more reliable than texts.

Properly to attend to texts need not be wantonly to worship them. Indeed, if their seriousness warrants it, there may be good reason for texts to be read 'over and over again'. Sustained attentiveness to serious argument in the form in which it actually appears can be no worse than insistently ignoring and reconstructing a text on the basis of what else may have been said like it or about it in 'the same' period. (There is usually a watery ambiguity attaching to what 'the same' here might mean.) Contexts, in short, may best be supplied only when and as needed, with reference to hermeneutic or explanatory problems that actually arise, not with reference to such incompleteness as may attend all empirical or logical propositions, which may never be overcome.

2. Omissions of the fathers

On the one hand, it is a truism that (a) every claim I make is contextual, in the sense that to perceive a datum or to inspect a text is always to add something to it. On the other hand, (b) it is logically impossible to prevent any contextual claim I may make or inspect from itself turning into a text. The boundary then between texts and contexts is porous. The problem with contexts (as with texts) is less whether or not to attend to them, but which to attend to, and how scrupulously. In the Cambridge series on 'Ideas in Context', many ideas, many texts are indeed placed in context. We can see that this must be trivially true, given that to apprehend anything is in some sense to 'contextualize' it. But the editors, Phillipson and Skinner, are saddled with a striking and, in this case, evitable contextual omission: they have declined to put the recipient himself in context. Here, 'context' would mean some species of summary overview and location of the recipient's text(s).

Given the force of (a) and (b), the relevant question is not generally whether there should or should not be some context. The question rather is why the editors of an 'ideas-in-context' series should omit to supply the most apt of contexts for a volume bearing on the work of Pocock. May they have regarded Pocock's procedures as so well-known or so ineffable as not to require, or to be incapable of, brisk formulation? The omission of any substantive editorial context kicks dust in the face of the essays that follow. It saddles Pocock's own concluding essay with the bucking, helter-skelter resolve somehow to round up the rest. The essays to be corralled are all sturdy, some spirited. But they canter along a road that is not clearly lit. Pocock's contextualism is less clearcut and emphatic than Skinner's. And to omit a clearly stipulated agenda for him fails to banish the disarray.

Pocock, in his essay on 'A Discourse of Sovereignty' (Phillipson and Skinner, 1993), does not clarify the position. He attempts to *précis*, to agree, to differ, to add to the other essays offered. He becomes trapped in a discursive quick-fire engagement which, while exciting, cannot be sure-fire. Being allowed twice the space of other contributors, Pocock is usually and understandably courteous to them. But the overall effect is to be reticent and sweeping, magisterial and evasive, to range widely, and to make some claims that are much too broad. The book, in this way, just borders on being cosy.

Take the question of broad claims. This tendency might usefully distinguish Pocock's contextualism from Skinner's, where the one is almost romantic in his sweep, the other usually more severe, more narrowly focused. Pocock states that absolute sovereignty, meaning (as he says) 'Bodinian legislative sovereignty[,] was a condition not a cause of the English Civil Wars; it existed already, everyone knew where it lay ...' (Phillipson and Skinner, 1993, p. 389). The claim is (1) sweeping and (2) unreliable, which is not to say that (2) derives from (1).

First, *a contrario*, there is strong evidence that Bodinian sovereignty is *not* limitedly 'legislative', certainly not in the English sense.[1] Second, if *everyone* in England in 1640 knew where sovereignty lay, there could not have been such stirring debate about whether or not, in time of crisis, the king alone had final say. The fact is that 'everyone' did not accept the king's word as final. Royalists like Ferne and Digges contended against Hunton and others that 'In England there is only one supreme authority, and that is the king'. Ferne and Digges and others like them believed Parliament had no rightful legal authority at all without the king. For them, in the end, the king was entitled to rule 'by the legal power he possesses in his own right' even if only 'until he and the two houses can agree'.[2] The fundamental dispute about who should have final say, in case of a stand-off between Crown and Parliament, meant precisely that *there was no Bodinian sovereign*, known and recognized by 'everyone' in England.

One may see that the basic structure of the Phillipson and Skinner volume is flawed. The book contains many good things, to which I shall return. What it does not contain is a clear statement of the Pocockian principles that are said significantly to have inspired it. I have already argued in general that the methodology of historical contextualism appears logically untenable. But does this hold in particular for the contextualism of Pocock? Pocock (1962a) accepts that 'there is no one set of assumptions from which alone it is proper to approach the history of political thought' (p. 184). Further, the same piece of thought may be viewed, simultaneously, 'as an act of political persuasion and as an incident in the pursuit of under-standing'. For Pocock (1962a), accordingly, the political thought of a given period 'will prove on inspection to exist on a number of differ-ent levels of abstraction' (p. 186). Skinner goes beyond such claims as these. Whereas Pocock appears to sanction the possibility of independent logical reconstruction of a text, Skinner (1964, p. 330) rules this out. For Skinner, the sense of the text cannot be deciphered independently of a reconstruction of the context.[3]

3. Lumpers and splitters

Because contexts are congruent with and can be extruded from any textual claims that we care to address, contexts are as various and encompassing as are propositions themselves. To be instructed to recuperate 'the' context is consistent with recruiting anything at all that is additional to the text. Logically, the context could be the recent past or the distant past, the near future or the distant future. One may reflect upon a text in the context of its past or present or future. Nor is there anything at all problematic about reflecting on a text in the context of its future. Indeed, we who reflect upon any text always and necessarily do so subsequent to its appearance, are associated with its future, and thus create for it a future context. 'The' context then is virtually all-encompassing. It extends front and back, chronologically speaking, of any designated text. And there is no field – science, architecture, social structure, economics, politics or philosophy – which can be excluded from it, in principle.

Those then who embrace so abstract a methodological project as contextualism must inevitably wander along many divergent paths. What binds proponents together is not the unravelling of any particular context, but context as such. Since contexts as such are virtually infinitely extensive, one student will always omit what is signalled by another. They may be disposed to assume that 'the' context means 'their' context. Thus the recovery of some new context will tend, usually mistakenly, to be viewed as defeating claims for some older or more familiar context. Most who seek to elucidate various contexts are historians, who simply and legitimately happen to be interested in such matters, without any methodological *parti pris*. Some however, are methodological ideologues, who insist that contextual reconstruction must always precede textual analysis. And it is these contextual methodologists who may be conveniently – but never finally – divided into lumpers and splitters.

Pocock's analysis is more ambiguous and less methodologically stringent than Skinner's. He nowhere goes as far as Skinner in the formal exclusion of textual exegesis. But much of what he says can be read in a manner consistent with Skinner's project. For example, Pocock (1962a) complains that the 'historian' who reconstructs a philosopher's thought is disposed 'not only to follow it, but actually to assist it' (p. 187). He means that the student 'has a constant tendency', not just to replay the philosopher's text, but also to improve on it, to endow the text 'with the highest attainable rational coherence' (p. 190). Pocock never develops this case as clearly and fully as he might. But the thrust of it is that to read a text 'on its own' encourages the student to make it more coherent and rational than it in fact is likely to be. The implication is that one must have recourse to the context to keep the text in balance and to make proper sense of it. Is this claim valid? If so, then only imperfectly.

For example, first-year students, reading Plato's *Republic*, very rarely give the author the benefit of the doubt, and find the text highly unpersuasive. The instructor resorts to contextual reconstructions to portray the text as more coherent than it can possibly appear to be (on the face of it) to the modern reader. This use of a context, however, is most dramatically appropriate, not when the text appears perfectly clear and sensible, but precisely when it does not. To contend that one can never take the meaning of a text as given, even where the text seems perfectly perspicuous, appears perverse. Of course, apparent clarity may mislead. But here the old saw applies: Hard cases make bad law. One best signals the danger without forging from it a rigid rule of procedure. In any event, the rule imposed by historical contextualism seems, as suggested, either superfluous or self-defeating.

Pocock (1962a) supposes texts are burdened by an 'indefinite rationality' (p. 186). This seems to imply that every text is somehow opaque or that no text *in se* discloses 'the whole' of its meaning. In as far as Pocock takes this view, he is brought much closer to Skinner. If Pocock intends that *all* texts have this 'indefinite rationality' then the difference between his position and Skinner's becomes difficult to discern. The claim that all texts are marked by an 'indefinite rationality', in the sense that their meaning is necessarily ambiguous, is either true or false. If this claim – that all texts are of necessity ambiguous – is valid, then it still will not follow that falling back upon contexts can, as such, alleviate the difficulty. This is because, as already argued, a context, substantively and propositionally, is no different from a text. The context gains no firmer purchase on truth merely because it positionally and temporally follows the text and supplies it with some given framework culled from an illimitable set of parallel possibilities. If the text is intrinsically ambiguous, requiring a context, then so must the context be ambiguous, itself requiring a context. If the audience of readers need texts to be interpreted first, before these texts are directly approached, they will also require the interpretations to be interpreted before they are directly approached, and so on, endlessly.

Thus, even were it true that all texts are of 'indefinite rationality', this would not strengthen the position of historical contextualism. In

•

any event, the claim is a highly doubtful one. It is not clear as to the sense in which such a claim as '2+2 = 4', or 'a+b = b+a', is 'indefinite'. The same applies to any strictly historical claim such as that 'Einstein claimed that E = mc^2', or that 'Hobbes believed there to be no conception in a person's mind which is not generated in whole or part by sense experience'. Any of these claims may prove untenable. But none is strikingly ambiguous. If they are ambiguous, then all claims are. If all are, we are no longer able to distinguish between what is clear and what is not. Thus the contextualist position must itself prove ambiguous. More significantly, it will merely prove to be trivial. The fact that some or even most texts are opaque should not lead us to the conclusion that all are so. Sabine, as Pocock contends, may well have forced upon Burke a greater coherence than the relevant texts warrant. But this would not imply that the rationality of Burke's text was 'indefinite'. It need imply no more than that Burke's texts are so full of omissions and inconsistencies that the doctrinal precision which interpreters sometimes wish upon them is delusory. Were the text more coherent, secondary commentary which attempts to repair the damage might be rather less necessary.

Along with the assumption that texts are marked by 'indefinite rationality', Pocock (1962a) supposes there to be some 'strictly historical task' involved in the assessment of the meanings of texts. This task he claims to consist in 'determining by investigation on what levels of abstraction thought did take place' (p. 186). But this either means that (a) historical investigation of contexts centrally determines the meaning of texts or that (b) such historical investigation merely circumstantially adds to what we know about texts. There is room for argument here. I suspect that the preponderant weight of Pocock's position points to (b). If that is right, then Pocock's position is sound, but not startling or innovative. He would be making no radical claims for history being, or becoming, but only of it circumstantially adding to, the understanding of philosophy. And that is more or less the traditional position, sometimes misleadingly conceived as a 'textualist' position. Not everyone, however, will accept this reading. As the earlier argument suggests, there are at the very least *elements* of a rigid methodological contextualism in Pocock's position. Nor is this more rigid position one which Pocock, as far as I am aware, anywhere expressly repudiates.

There is some evidence that Pocock, like Skinner, may view the context as a way of determining the meaning of the text, to the point of being at least a partial substitute for it. Colour is lent to this reading by the fact that Pocock gives firm preference to tradition (equals context) over text and (unlike Michael Oakeshott) effectively construes the tradition as a form of ideology. Pocock is at least partly influenced by Michael Oakeshott's idea of tradition.[4] Oakeshott (1962), as it happens, however, had no overwhelming problem with textual analysis. For him, it was 'the tradition' which proved 'a tricky thing to get to know' (p. 35). For Pocock, mastery of this trickiness became the special preserve of the historian. Whereas, for Oakeshott, ideology was an 'abridgement' of a tradition, for Pocock (1962a), the business 'of abstracting ideas from particular situations' (p. 194) itself constitutes 'the language of tradition' (p. 195). Where Oakeshott opposed ideological 'abridgement' on the grounds that it violated the integrity of tradition, Pocock embraced precisely such abridgement as the relevant unit of study. Where Oakeshott's 'particularist' position could be squared with the defence of texts, Pocock's defence of ideology would be consistent with the erosion of these defences. In this way, Pocock registers a significant interest in traditions *qua* ideologies. Thus, with Pocock the gap between tradition and ideology contracts. And the concern with recovering the gross ideology of a given period threatens to swamp any concern with the integrity of singular texts located there. The Pocockian dispositional *liking* for ideology over text, may give way to a firmly Skinnerian, methodological preference for ideology, as antecedent and superior to the text.

   Pocock likes spectacular vistas and places great emphasis upon continuities. Though Skinner takes ideology for granted, he is yet fearful of false connections, and places great emphasis upon discontinuities. Pocock is excited, like A.O. Lovejoy, by the sweep of great, integrative themes. Skinner is deeply suspicious of such romanticism. He will keep the integrative traditionalism, indeed the ideological panorama, but only for some local setting, in some distant past. If we take Skinner's most extended work, *The Foundations of Modern Political Thought* (1978a), he admits that he has 'tried not to concentrate so exclusively on the leading theorists' and has 'focused instead on the more general social matrix out of which their works arose' (p. x). He discusses texts only in the shadow of the social and intellectual gibbet from which they are deemed to hang. But this 'framework' or 'social base' to which Skinner refers is only erected out of such evidence as there is for it. And the bulk of this evidence consists pretty much exclusively of other (paper) texts, or inferences drawn from them. The 'intellectual context' to which Skinner refers is exactly the same, or rather even more of the same, viz. secondary (paper) texts, and inferences drawn from them. Skinner's aim then is always 'to construct a general framework within which the writings of the more prominent theorists can ... be situated' (p. xi). This could prove a pretty frail structure, unsuitable for hanging any weighty *corpus*.

As a matter of adding data to the record, there can be nothing wrong with this. But Skinner's position is more demanding. For he thinks that to focus upon the major texts themselves is of itself to defeat any prospect of 'genuine histories' of political ideas. His position is that we can achieve no genuine 'historical understanding' of political ideas if we 'focus our main attention on those who discussed the problems of political life at a level of abstraction and intelligence unmatched by any of their contemporaries'. So, for Skinner, to 'focus on the study of ideologies', to 'study the context of any major work of political philosophy, is not merely to gain additional information'; it is the method by which we penetrate 'its author's meaning'. Clearly, then, Skinner's context is not just an addition to, but a partial substitute for, the text. If we take Pocock's *The Machiavellian Moment*, by contrast, we note his emphasis upon the developmental links between Aristotle, Rome, Machiavelli and indeed the American Revolution. The substance of this link or tradition consists in the idealization of the citizen as an active agent who is formed by virtue of civic engagement, thereby keeping despotism and corruption at bay. If Pocock, like Skinner, prefers contexts to texts, he also prefers great, vertical shafts of time to Skinner's local, horizontal clearings of understanding. Pocock in short is a lumper; Skinner is a splitter.

4. Context: Holy Grail, white whale

Insistence upon context can be comprehensive or narrow. Either way, it must diminish, may distort, and sometimes demeans, the importance of the text. It is some such charge as this that V.B. Sullivan (1992) lays against Pocock. Her attack is of precisely the kind that a younger Skinner might have launched: Pocock 'merely presupposes, rather than establishes' the influence of Aristotle upon Machiavelli; he neglects 'salient elements of Machiavelli's thought'; he 'so emphasizes Machiavelli's context' that he imposes it (unjustifiably) upon Machiavelli's texts. Sullivan is not concerned to enquire whether or not there are traditions, nor whether 'civic humanism' is one of them. The question she raises is whether the tradition Pocock discerns is accurately reflected in the texts of the key figures to whom it is assigned.

Machiavelli's *The Prince*, as Pocock in part admits and Sullivan insists, reflects no Aristotelian Republicanism. As far as it goes, the text of *The Prince* offers no support for an ideal of civic republicanism.

The conventional view is that Machiavelli's republicanism is displayed in the *Discourses*. Pocock also takes this view. But the actual evidence of the *Discourses* does not bear him out. More relevantly, as Sullivan points out, Pocock in no way tries textually to demonstrate that it does. It is in this way we can see that Pocock's comprehensive contextualism, which broadly reconstructs the thought of Machiavelli's period, may overpower and thus falsify what Machiavelli himself actually says. Attention to the context always and necessarily deflects some attention from the text. But in this case, it also distorts and falsifies the text. If we give precedence to the exegete's contextualization, we may also allow him to colour and blunt our entry to primary documents. This is the danger of all contextualization. By reducing attention to the actual argument of a text, one may impute to it a provenance or character, which may well be abroad in the period, without being a part of the text under review. For Sullivan, Pocock's 'reliance on the context' is in the end unfounded: it is 'nothing more than a leap of faith' (1992, p. 317).

There is nothing wrong as such with the concern with context, taken as a disposition. The disposition only goes wrong where reinvented as a 'methodology'. There is nothing wrong with reconstructing, or even inventing a context, and every hypothesized context is necessarily in part an invention. What is wrong is to perceive it as a simple and superior matter of incontestable fact. 'Contextualism' can just as readily lead to over-interpretation as can 'textualism'. Its posture at the least is no sounder, nor more secure. Indeed, if 'contextual' and 'textual' approaches could be genuinely distinguished, then the latter would be sounder. Let us say that any 'approach' to a text is automatically contextual. Thus even a textual approach is contextual. Let us say that what distinguishes the 'textual' from other approaches is its concern with the *internal logic* of the text. Until this logical framework is in place, one cannot relevantly construct any *other* context for the text. To establish the propositional logic of the text *first* has to be the rule, else one can have no idea as to what relevant questions may be put to, and answers extracted from, an infinitely extensive and otherwise amorphous context. As for the deciphering of texts, it cannot be a matter of over-interpretation, but only of sound and fair procedure, to press the most logically coherent reading which the letter of the text allows. This is not to be confused with according to texts strengths they have not got. But it does defend against reducing texts to Rorschach tests, taking on the appearance, at the worst, of straw men.

In the end, no sustained distinction between 'textualism' and 'contextualism' is feasible other than as set out above. This is because the underlying distinction between 'text' and 'context' only operates relationally, and otherwise has no substance. For a start, the context always implies a text. If the logic of the text cannot be recuperated and somehow understood, there is no relevant sense in which any other context can be constructed for or deployed around it. It will be obvious that the priority if not the autonomy of the logic of the text is a primitive *sine qua non* for the creation of any other related context. It does not, however, follow, because the logic of the text must be accorded priority, that the text is autonomous. The text always implies a context, even if only that recuperable from the text itself.

As shown earlier, the text may always be viewed as adverting to yet another text; the text is one set of propositions relating to or commenting upon yet another set of propositions. Thus Plato's *Republic*, which advances one concept of justice, involves – as a part of this – commentary upon and rejection of certain other concepts of justice, such as that justice is the same as 'giving every man his due', or as promoting the interests of those who are most powerful in society. The logic of the text, then, if prior, is not autonomous. It does not merely *relate* to the world, it is a *part* of the world. It may be physically contained like the pages between the covers of a book. But its claims cannot be logically delimited. Each argument creates a context for some antecedent argument.

The distinction between texts and contexts being only relational, the logical prospects for any methodological contextualism must founder from the outset. It is too much to ask that the context be reconstructed *as such*. If, instead, we ask for (1) the reconstruction of a *relevant* context, then it cannot coherently be intended that this should be set out in advance of (2) establishing *the logic* of the text. For (1) is a function of (2). Historical contextualism fails because it is committed to reconstructing contexts generally, in advance of securing the internal logic of the texts to which these putative contexts would relate, a perfectly irrational procedure. There is, however, no fault to be found in what we might call a contextual *disposition*, where the predominant interest is less in the logic of the text than in the broad circumstances out of which the text somehow emerges.

The difficulty lies in the contextual *methodology*, which prioritizes context over text, and seeks either wholly to dissolve the logic of texts into their contexts, or partly to reduce the internal logic of an author's text to what is said by other authors in other texts. A contextual methodology, as distinct from a contextual disposition, either tempts or requires one who has it to impose context upon text, in the questionable sense of either allowing the context to override the text, as with Pocock on Machiavelli (following Sullivan), or allowing the context simply to take the place of the text, as with Skinner (1966a, p. 314) on Hobbes (following Chapter 5 above).

Where the danger of the contextual disposition is to under-interpret the text, that of the textual disposition may be to over-interpret it. The latter charge, however, as brought, e.g. against Warrender's (1957) *The Political Philosophy of Hobbes*, appears without foundation. For if Warrender was wrong, the corrective would appear to lie more in a closer reading of the text than in a better circumstantial grasp of the context. In any event, textual and contextual dispositions (*not* methodological commitments) will both bear fruit, but differently, depending upon the subject. The textual disposition is apt at seeking out the distinctiveness, even eccentricity, of an analysis. The contextual disposition, by contrast, best serves to detail the way in which an analysis merges with its background. Apart from this, there can be no abstract preference for one over the other. A textual emphasis works best for innovative figures, a contextual emphasis for the more pedestrian. To merge an ordinary writer with her/his period is appropriate. Not to mark off exceptional figures from their setting is inept. It is possible, all the same, for any writer to be treated from both perspectives.

Is contextualism, as an historical methodology, necessarily obfuscatory? Certainly the risks of truism and circularity earlier noted are not encouraging. Do contextualist premises prompt writers to be discursive, digressive, prolix and pointlessly technical? Such a passage as the following from Condren on Newcastle (Phillipson and Skinner, 1993) is not reassuring:

> This refinement of classical rhetoric ... provided a fairly coherent semantic organisation within political language and was used to suggest a powerful reductionist economy of priorities to which we metonymously attach Machiavelli's name as providing the supreme encapsulation of a discernible, if fluid, tradition (p. 165).

The style of Skinner's 1993 essay is polished and the substance of the argument has interest (pp. 67–93), but a structural obscurantism marks the piece from the outset. It springs from Skinner's claim that since (1) the seventeenth-century authors whose work he reviews are bilingual, it follows (2) that a sensitivity to (meaning the retrieval of) both languages 'can engender new insights into the character of even the most closely analysed texts'. Occasionally, no doubt; but where the principle is applied rigidly, we are rewarded less with insight than with loquaciousness. The reward we obtain for excessive sensitivity is essentially a repetitive, cluttered page. Rather than merely writing 'benefit', Skinner's method dictates that he also give us the Latin (*beneficium*); rather than 'reasoning', *ratio*; for 'socially valuable', *utilis*, etc. The project of supplying more and more detail, more 'context', merely spawns an overlong text.

Skinner can write perfectly interesting history. Why does he not stick to this? His methodology, where allowed to take over, is stultifying. Where does the substance of Skinner's account, in his 1993 essay (essentially on Hobbes) take us? It takes us on a tour round Hobbes's change of mind about rhetoric – between the 1640s and the 1650s. In logic, the problem is a minor one: Hobbes eventually comes to reverse himself, to the effect that argument, to be persuasive, must not only be sound, but also attractive. It is just that the contextual 'apparatus' deployed to make the point is mistaken (it is overstated) and intrusive, getting in the way of the valid, historical point to be made.

5. Carapace from flesh

To make a meal of the Phillipson and Skinner volume, the reader must remove the ill-fitting carapace of method that has been imposed on it. The 'flesh' is a set of small-scale essays in history. Burns' opening essay is dense but nicely judged, developing an account of the subversive role of Buchanan's teaching, showing how it penetrated the thought even of the monarchical absolutists themselves. Lamont plunges his sharp tongue into 'the false debate about Arminianism' and withdraws, savouring Richard Baxter as a species of 'heroic' individualist. Goldie's essay is thickly textured, but brisk, clear and subtle, supplying an excellent story of the anticlerical element that informed Whiggism and *pro tanto* the modern state itself. Schochet, more limitedly, supplies a straightforward description of the extreme nominalism, intolerance and absolutism of Samuel Parker. The essays by Schwoerer, Scott, Klein, Hont, even (especially) Phillipson, are all interesting exercises. They project no collective party spirit and range from the stolidly soothing (e.g. Phillipson) to the delightfully unsettling (e.g. Tully).

In general, then, the shell of theory which frames the Phillipson and Skinner volume is contextualist, with its opposed 'lumping' and 'splitting' proclivities, with splitters in the ascendant. But the overarching theory is not tenable, as has been demonstrated elsewhere (see Chapter 5 above). Pocock's 'lumpers' are possibly better grounded (perhaps for being more ambiguous) than Skinner's 'splitters'. If Pocock is mistaken, in the sense of overriding his text (e.g. *The Prince*), the mistake may not be systemic. If Skinner, however, is mistaken about the possibility of contextualism, then either his theory must cripple his practice (as in the first part of the 1993 essay), or his practice must constantly ignore his theory (as may be observed of the sub-stantive story he seeks to tell in the 1978 *Foundations*).

It may be due to the 'lumper/splitter' confusion that Phillipson and Skinner (1993) do not attempt to put Pocock 'in context'. Though both editors and recipient are contextualists, none on this occasion has anything much to say about what this contextualism comports. The editors write that the 1960s witnessed 'the beginning of a revolution in our ways of thinking about the history of political theory' and that 'John Pocock himself was one of the most important and active of the revolutionaries' (Phillipson and Skinner, 1993). But they are not long on the content of this revolution. The book is organized under a contextualist research programme, but is vague as to what the programme is. Where the programme is not vague, the essayists are not notably responsive to it.

One concludes that the Phillipson and Skinner volume achieves its success in spite of its methodological framework, not because of it. In this volume, in the end, it is left to James Tully (Phillipson and Skinner, 1993, p. 253ff) – incidentally in one of the most absorbing essays in the book – to supply a useful summary of one specific 'revolution', nothing wider, to do restrictively with the work done by Laslett, Pocock and others on Locke. Even here, in Tully's eight-point summary of the findings on Locke, important as we may agree these findings to be, none has anything to do with the intrinsic meaning of what Locke wrote, as opposed to identifying the target, and the audience, and the way in which what he wrote was received by, or impacted upon, his readers.

The bulk of the 17 essays supplied in Phillipson and Skinner (1993) are straightforward exercises in *history*, most by professional histor-ians, working from departments of history. Historians conventionally work to a small scale, and so here. It is in this sense only that they appear more like Skinner, than Pocock. They are little engaged in 'textual' analysis. Insofar as they are, their focus is upon secondary or minor figures. Each generally attempts to reconstitute a limited aspect of a limited period. The approach is overwhelmingly repor-torial. The contributors are disposed neither to argue with nor demur from what they describe. They appear to connect with what they describe as either a tradition or an ideology, but perhaps more the latter.

6. Definitional end-play

Every context ultimately reduces to some species of text and it is
basically with some text that study must begin.[5] To deal finally with
the theoretical problems of methodological contextualism, it is
essential to locate five key concepts. We need to distinguish between
(1) text, (2) context, (3) history, (4) contextualism and (5) historicism.
Having made these distinctions, we are better placed to note connections. A text is effectively the subject of all writing or research. A
context is data that one appends to texts. History is a narrative account
of text or context or both and is never substantively reducible to one
as opposed to the other. 'Contextualism' is a mistaken, methodological claim whose gravamen is that the only valid history is
predominantly or exclusively 'contextual'. Contextualism courts
historicism in its inclination to overrate the importance of the sometimes 'spectacular differences' between various historical periods
(Popper, 1960, p. 101), in its resistance to any form of social generalization over substantial units of chronological time, in a marked
concern to avoid moral judgement of the past, together with a sharp
disinclination to apply moral lessons from the past to the present.[6]

1. **Text**: A 'text' may be construed as (a) a specific artefact or
document (e.g. Piltdown Man or *The Prince*); or (b) as a collection
of artefacts or documents (as of bones and hand-axes at Olduvai
Gorge in Kenya or the collected writings of a particular author,
perhaps James Harrington). On this scheme, any specific event or
sequence of events, such as the English Civil War or the execution of
Charles I, can be taken as a 'text', in the sense of being resolved into
such documentary or other data as may attest to it. The text *qua* 'event'
is quite as thin or fat as we make it or take it; perhaps just a meagre
execution, but equally perhaps all of that rambunctious, revolutionary turmoil that led to this. The 'text' is conventionally construed
very safely, which is to say narrowly. It can also be construed very
broadly. But however much we broaden it, so long as we do not equate
it with totality, it can never expand to the point of escaping altogether
some prospect of being placed in 'context'.

The 'text', whatever its raw form (e.g. skeleton, potsherd, stylus,
papyrus, oral history, printed document), may be reduced to one or
a set of propositions. This process of reduction or interpretation or
translation is always taking place, at least so long as thought is taking
place. No text stands on its own, in the sense of being above or beyond
interpretation. The recuperation of texts, through interpretation, is
our only means of knowing them, of knowing anything at all. Interpretation of itself always constitutes some type of contextualization.

And there will be as many contexts *for* texts as there are interpretative angles *on* texts. In recuperating texts, therefore, the question cannot be to do with *the* context, but with *which* context.

2. **Context**: A 'context' always implies a 'text'. A context is merely data that is added to, in order somehow to throw light on, the 'text'. 'To place in context' merely means to locate some species of text within a wider, but related, set of data, so as to yield a new perspective on, and perhaps a deeper appreciation of, that text. A context *qua* context has no autonomy. It is by definition an adjunct, an embellishment. It presupposes that the text itself, in some way, in some degree, already exists, already makes some sense. Otherwise there would be no sense in which light could be thrown on it.

The sort of 'widening' that 'placing in context' involves has three distinct dimensions. The first is horizontal and covers the notion of contemporaneity. The second is vertical, covering the past. The third is also vertical, but covers the future. To supply a context, accordingly, is always to append data to a text on one or more of these planes.

The first, or horizontal, plane involves contemporary detail external to but affecting the text in its own time: the reception, the setting, parallel events, etc. The second or vertical plane is oriented to the past and involves data about the antecedent forces or influences which somehow occasioned or gave rise to the text. The third, equally vertical, plane is oriented to the future and involves details about the text's less immediate impact and more distant effects. (These distinctions between past, present and future require careful attention.)[7]

Though to impose a context is always to add to the text (hence '*con*' text), it is always and simultaneously to *shrink* the text. To view a house down below in the context of the valley from the height of the mountain above, is never to apprehend it in the detail ready to hand and eye from a seat on its veranda. This is to say that, although supplying a context always adds detail, it must in equal measure, and at the same time, sacrifice detail. Thus a context *vis-à-vis* its text always amounts to a specific and limited perspective. It does not necessarily or absolutely add to the data available, but only makes a different type of data available. By the same token, given the three different dimensions of contextual discourse (past, present and future), to contextualize on one level is always to relinquish or to ignore contextualization on some other level. There is no one context, but many. Changing contexts is like changing texts. Each context has its perspective and accompanying data, while excluding other perspectives and their accompanying data. 'Context' accordingly is far from supplying some species of 'magic bullet' capable of emphatic penetration of historical or other truth.

There is no way of recovering historical detail as such. Detail in principle is infinite. Intelligence is selective. It is said that no more than 5 to 10 percent of the stock of a large, average, university library is made use of in the course of any given year. It is also said that, though our senses transmit to the brain about 10,000 units of information every second, the brain is unable to do much better than somehow select and focus upon seven of these, ignoring the rest. The point is that there can be no question of recovering 'the' context or simply of supplying detail *per se*. The detail you run down is always outrun by those unnumbered other details you can never catch. 'The' context merely amounts to the plane on which you happen to be nesting, not those others to which your reach and imagination cannot simultaneously extend.

It is to be emphasized accordingly that an appeal to context is never without its costs. First, a context can never simply take the place of a text; were it thought, or *per impossibile* allowed, to do so, then this would merely defeat the purpose of contextualizing, which is to embellish. Second, to supply a context, even if it enhances, in the sense of throwing new light upon, a text, must also diminish it, in the sense of deflecting attention from it *in* its own terms, which is to say in terms of its own textual detail. Third, inasfar as the object of a context is abstractly to supply greater detail 'on' a text, then the intention is in some degree always and necessarily abortive. For what the agent gains from attending to external detail (*on* the text), must be balanced against what he loses by relinquishing internal detail (*in* the text).

3. **History**: This may be concerned to supply an account of an artefact or a document. But that is not enough. It may lean heavily upon detail, but neither will that suffice. It is pointless to say that history *should* focus upon the context. Whatever history focuses upon is by definition some species of 'text'. This text or these texts either constitute a story or they imply one. History, as it focuses upon texts via the simple selective application of perspective over the broken terrain of the past, of itself *constitutes* a context. But once the history is forged, it is also abandoned to become itself yet another text, telling yet another story, perceived from a distance by yet other minds, including the evolving mind that first conceived it. Not all texts are histories. But every abandoned history is a text. Every text supplies some sort of account. Every historical text tells, specifically, some sort of story. If there is no account to extract from the history of Herodotus or that of Thucydides, it is difficult to see what context we might relevantly or meaningfully erect around *it*.

A history, where complete and an object of attention, becomes *pro tanto* a text. But a history that is being forged, that is in the process of battening upon other texts as its subject, is (in this) perforce a context. It is nonsensical in consequence to demand that history be contextual rather than textual. What a history must do, narrowly or encompassingly, is to tell a story, whether of war and famine, or of philosophy and science. The sort of story the writer tells should be viewed as nobody's business but his, as long as the story is coherent, and consistent with the facts (as represented by texts).

History battens upon artefacts or documents only where conceived as the mute or open-mouthed embodiment of events or narrative. This last, to succeed, must be sustained by an overview. This, the story-line, is not the slave but the master of detail. History is argument and narrative and picks only on what it thinks it needs and binds the rest to silence. History is not 'nomothetic', since it does not seek to establish abstract general laws for indefinitely repeatable events. But neither is history 'ideographic', in the sense of being concerned only with what is supposedly unique or non-recurrent.[8] History is a 'story', it is narrative. It supplies an account of an aspect of what is reckoned to have happened, from a perspective embedded in the present. No history can aspire to cover all that has happened. And it is irrelevant whether it will have happened only once, or, like the winter migrations of birds, recur repeatedly in some well-established pattern.

History may take the form of a context. The text being given, observers may weave stories round it. But texts also tell their own story, i.e. they constitute their own contexts. To think to reduce history to context in the sense of subordinating or excluding the claims of texts is to forget that context and text are in substance the same. To think to reduce history to context is merely to dogmatize about who may tell stories, and which stories, and how. It is merely to license some narratives and to exclude others.

A history of political ideas, of ideas in general, of philosophy in particular, remains a *history*. A history of philosophy is more than a catalogue, it is a narrative, a story. It is automatically contextual, in that it feeds upon texts. But once it comes into being, it itself becomes a text. A history of philosophy is not mere chronology; it is substantive, event-full. It cannot merely attend to robotic externalities, but must register inner principles of action, of mind. A history of philosophy is not a matter of static, logical analysis, but tells a story that moves with purpose and feeling through time. History is not the same as the past. It is a selective account reconstituted from data embedded in the past. History consists of, but is not exhausted by, past materials. It equally consists of a perspective, of necessity a present perspective, together with the contemporary influences this comports. The perspective of the present is not optional; without it we could retrieve no past data, nor give stories direction, nor tell stories at all.

Sigmund Freud had a keen sense of 'story', and therefore of historicity. To tell a story requires a firm perspective from which events are recalled and judged. Sidney Lee's compendious 1898 *Life of Shakespeare*, as has been observed more than once, conveys little or no insight or understanding of its subject. Freud's modest *Leonardo*, on the basis of meagre detail, supplies a provocative study of the shape and direction of a mind. Freud presciently imagines a firm continuity between the biography of a person and the history of a society. 'Historical writing', he suggests, began by keeping 'a continuous record of the present', and only later 'cast a glance back to the past, gathered traditions and legends, interpreted the traces of antiquity that survived in customs and usages, and in this way created a history of the past.'[9] *A history of the past*, including the philosophical past, consists in a narrative, told from some distinct perspective, which may draw from, without being swamped by, an infinity of (past) data. It is of necessity that only the tiniest proportion of the actual past fails to be overlooked, compressed, suppressed or judiciously shredded.

There can be no such thing as 'the' history of philosophy. There are only *histories* of philosophy. There are unnumbered stories worth telling. History of philosophy is not just a combination of 'history' and 'philosophy'. Each history is a story with its beginning, intermediacy and end, fashioned from a palimpsest of distinct philosophies. Hegel at least (whatever his faults) saw this clearly (Hegel, 1968). He saw that 'the' history of philosophy is a story. What Hegel did not see, of course, is that it is *not* just *one* story.[10] What he equally did not see, just because the history of philosophy is important, is that philosophy without history is not straightaway an absurdity. To admit the purchase of historicity is not to deny the distinction between, say, ethics and a history of ethics, or logic and a history of logic, or physics and a history of physics, or mathematics and a history of mathematics. It is perfectly possible to supply an intelligible account of truth-tables, without supplying a history of thinking about truth-tables. One can supply an analytical account of the concept of equality, without telling a story about the evolution of thinking about equality. To say that history and philosophy are distinguishable is not to say they have no connection, no more than to say 'the son of Priam is a singular individual' denies the claim that 'Hector shares with Priam half his genes'. Analysis will always be marked by history, but is still intelligible without a prior historical account.

4. **Contextualism**: This is a piece of methodology which, were its range of application more comprehensive, might qualify as an

ideology. Its central injunction is: 'Recuperate the context'. The injunction might be unexceptional if accompanied by riders such as: 'Sometimes', or 'As and when you need to'. But these qualifications do not apply. Rather, the position is that the text, somehow in itself, is incomprehensible unless *first* 'taken in context'. This injunction, however, must imply (a) that it describes an action that is avoidable, and (b) an action that is possible.

Formally, in applying one's mind to any text, one always and necessarily generates a context by virtue of being located in the present, and from having, in the temporal sense, the perspective of that present. In this way, the generation of contexts for texts is not optional.

Furthermore, text and context are always tightly and logically interconnected, in that the presence of the one always implies the substantive presence of the other. Propositionally and substantively, one can only make sense of a context *as a text*. In this sense, accordingly, the charge that one must make sense of the context *before* one can decode the meaning of the text becomes a plain impossibility.

Finally, in any event, contexts are limitless. One may take the context as the text working backwards (the past context), or as the text working forwards (the future context), or as the text working sideways (the period contemporary with the text). These temporal divergencies (past, present and future) are nothing like as simple as contextualists appear to imagine.[11] Contexts diverge temporally in the tripartite fashion indicated. But inside these zones, they are infinitely capacious, endlessly branching into subject and sub-subject, to the point that 'the' context *in se* must be viewed as plainly irretrievable. *Which* is the context to be retrieved? How can there be meaningful talk of the context or of contexts *as such*, in abstraction from some (always partly) intelligible text? A context is itself intelligible only as a function of what it focuses upon: the text. If the text can be conceded no prior respect, is deemed to make no sense in itself, then neither can one meaningfully recuperate any relevant context for *it*. A context for *this* text is only intelligible on the grounds that the context demonstrably and logically relates to the text. So if we can assign no prior logic or meaning to a text, then neither can we assign to it any 'relevant' (in quotes because redundant) context. The texts putatively being contextualized must be accorded some prior integrity, or else the contexts assigned can have no purchase, have nothing to grapple with, and will fail to qualify as contexts. A 'context' which contextualizes nothing in particular is itself nothing in particular.

A context can be circumscribed very encompassingly or quite narrowly. If we take Pocock and Skinner, we may distinguish between method and practice. Pocock's method, in fact, appears rather permissive, although a dogmatic element can be retrieved should we insist on it. Skinner's method, however, is emphatic to the point that the dogmatism cannot be mistaken, even where we wish to ignore it. Formally, Pocock's method is more expansive than Skinner's, which is why it is appropriate to characterize the one as a lumper and the second as a splitter. Effectively, the narrower rule that Skinner sanctions might be put thus: Always recuperate the meaning of thinkers by reconstructing the material and intellectual circumstances of their time, the modes of thinking characteristic of their contemporaries, and not directly by reference to the apparently express logic of their own claims.[12]

The effect of such contextualism is consistently to displace the text and to have it dissolve into the context. This is the deliberate approach of Skinner in his *Foundations* (1978), and it is foreshadowed in earlier attempts at dissolving Hobbes into his background. In 1965, Skinner claimed that 'Hobbes did not even provide the most original or systematic formulation of the views at issue (1965a, pp. 151–78). In 1972 Skinner referred to Hobbes's theory as 'uniquely systematic and comprehensive', but only in the sense that 'his' position was one already held by the *de facto* theorists, and that Hobbes's distinction was to express an unoriginal view uniquely well (1972a, pp. 79–98). When I first wrote about this matter in 1983, I was clearly over-generous (i.e. mistaken) in attributing to Skinner withdrawal from the 1965 claim (King, 1983). On rereading the 1972 piece, Skinner seems genuinely emphatic that there is to be found in the argument of Hobbes 'nothing unusual or even particularly original' (1972a, pp. 79–98).

Inasfar as 'the' context is in fact many contexts, each of which is infinitely extensive, one is quite unable to recuperate 'the' context. That is why contextualists are bound ever and anon to squabble with one another about what it is – it must always be something – they have mutually left out of account. Working up the context, one student (C.B. Macpherson) will see Hobbes's text as supplying a defence for an emergent bourgeoisie. Sticking with the context, yet another student (Neal Wood) will see Hobbes's text as a stratagem for salvaging the aristocracy. These adversarial exercises are interesting enough. They are only misplaced in that, or as far as, they assume that the circumstantial data they retrieve somehow takes the place of the text and directly clarifies and determines its meaning. Any such approach, whatever the protestations of those bearing it, is reductionist; it must destroy the agency and autonomy of the text and of its author. If the contextualist rule assumes the restrictive Skinnerian form, it must blithely turn its back to the consideration that what my contemporaries do and think is not necessarily the best guide to what *I* do or think – especially where (or if) I have gone out of my way to affirm my difference.

Contextualist adepts have retrieved much useful data. There would be no quarrel with any of the contextualists where and if they self-consciously conceived their job merely to be to add to the store of knowledge recovered for the history of ideas. There is a quarrel precisely because they have put too great, exclusive and pre-emptive a value on what they are about. For many of the leading exponents do not see themselves as engaged in a 'value-added' procedure, but, on the contrary, as displacing and liquidating some other 'school', partly Straussian but mostly mythical, call it 'textualist'. It may be unsettling, in this connection, for Minogue to declare that Skinner 'is really a philosophical imperialist in historical disguise', but the charge is not unfair.[13] The appropriate objection, however, to contextualism, is not, abstractly (with Minogue), that there is little that can profitably be said about 'method', but only that the contextualist method in particular is untenable.

The contextualist is not distinctive merely in virtue of his or her concern to avoid anachronism. The hypothetical 'textualist' will be equally concerned to secure that the thought of past writers is recaptured in some degree in the way that they themselves would have done, 'to see things in their way', to recover their concepts, distinctions and chains of reasoning.[14] To exclude this concern is to overthrow the most elemental commitment to accuracy. A concept from the past many not match up to a straightforward parallel in the present. A word in current use may not mean what it appears to mean or used to mean. Machiavelli's *virtù* does not translate as 'virtue'. Hobbes's 'diffidence' means something other than 'shyness'. But there is nothing new in this. And the avoidance of anachronism is more a cautionary tale than a 'method'. The trouble only arises when those who are disposed to seek out what is different about the past, rather than what is relevant to us from it, contend both directly and indirectly that the concern with continuity and relevance is methodologically inept and 'historically' out of place.

It should be obvious that, if too great an insistence upon 'textual' analysis risks over-interpretation, then too great an insistence upon contextual reconstruction runs the risk of under-interpretation. To withdraw from texts some significant autonomy is equally to withdraw from authors any meaningful agency. To suggest, moreover, that authors 'from the past' have nothing to say to readers 'in the present' is based only on the most simplistic understanding of the inter-relationship between 'past' and 'present'. On the most elementary level, it will be plain that every item ever written (on the basis of one formulation of the distinction between past and present) belongs to the past (see Chapter 2 above, p. 28ff.). So if we have no access to, no dialogue with, the past of a century, a decade, a minute ago, we have also no prospect of any meaningful communication here and now among ourselves. What is genuinely 'past' is a matter to be proved. If 'past texts' are genuinely irrelevant to 'our times', then that too is a matter for proof; there can be nothing categorically privileged about the claim.

5. **Historicism**: To divorce oneself from any prospect of judging the past, because it is past, may lead into an unfortunate relativism. Thus does historicism prospectively enter the lists. If we take historicism to be a doctrine which claims that a proposition is either empirically or normatively valid as a function of the period in which it was enunciated, then contextualism may take on the appearance of a postmodern historicism. But it would presumably take the shape of a claim to this effect:

> Since I (the modern historian) can only truly understand the past on its own terms, and since by definition these terms differ from those of my present, then *I* (who belong to, have agency in, and can only act upon, my own time) am still unable to make any *relevant* judgment of any past time.

That sounds a highly relativistic and historicist position. Contextualism may perhaps be able to escape the charge. Skinner, certainly, protests that his contextualism firmly excludes any relativistic spin. I am not certain that it does. The risks, surely, are real. Dr A. Gabbey, for example, writing to members of the British Society for the History of Philosophy, is quite untroubled by the consequence: 'I cannot see what sense it makes to say that some philosophical doctrine, past or present, *is* true or false' (1987, pp. 20–1).

The methodological problem originally raised by historicism (e.g. the *Historismus* of Wilhelm Dilthey) focused upon a (or the) distinctive historical method – not a positivistic scientism – appropriate to the study of the humanities and the social sciences. This approach placed an emphasis upon constant historical evolution, the uniqueness of each successive historical moment, and the subjective and unpredictable play of human agency. Scientific knowledge might well be universal and abstract, but historical knowledge was adjudged always local and concrete. This was the force of the position advanced earlier by R.G. Collingwood (1939) and more recently by Peter Winch (1958, 1963). Winch agreed with Collingwood that all human history is 'the history of thought'. He takes it that 'social relations only exist in and through the ideas which are current in society'. Winch concludes that social relations must be an 'unsuitable subject for generalizations and theories of a scientific sort' (p. 133). Of course the most striking feature of Winch's claim is his own violation of it: the idea that we should not or cannot generalize is itself a generalization.

In one form or another this historicist proclivity is amazingly persistent. It reflects a disposition which appears to suppose that one can understand no other mind unless one's own is in every way commensurate with it, and that one can apprehend no contemporary claims without a prior grasp of how they originated. It always helps, no doubt, to know more and to know better, but these cannot be conditions for knowing as such, since the implication of this must be that none of us knows anything at all. In some fashion or other, we shall have not the slightest difficulty in establishing that no mind, no time, no group is commensurate with any other. But this can only suggest, correctly, that to come to grips with any mind, time or group necessarily depends upon something less than perfect identity with them. Of course we know too well that agents far too commonly display the most dogged and incompetent incomprehension of one another. Yet it is no less common to observe the remarkable failure of most agents even to discern their own motives, even to secure the most elementary self-knowledge, despite the fact that agents are at least identical with themselves.

No: understanding presupposes difference, not identity. It presupposes a capacity for standing apart, whether from oneself or from one's time, or from any other time or from any other self. A mind or society or period, which we might hypothesize to be completely absorbed *in* itself, could have no understanding *of* itself. Understanding implies difference; difference yields perspective. The error of Winch, and of many who think like him, stems from the supposition that, because logic, like language itself, arises from social life, i.e. from some *specific social setting*, it only makes sense, is 'only intelligible in the context' of, that specific setting, that way of living (p. 100). But this is like saying that, because Richard Wright wrote his novel, *Black Boy*, out of the pain of growing up poor and black in Mississippi, no one bereft of this experience could make sense of his novel. Or it is like saying that Euripides, being a man, could not write aptly and revealingly about Medea, because she is a woman, and that the play *Medea* (431 BC) can say nothing to us immediately and contemporaneously about the vengeful wrath of an abandoned wife (the conventions of a distant past being too egregiously different from our own). It is even more like saying that, because dreams only occur in sleep, they necessarily cease to be intelligible to one now in a waking state.

Historicism seems constantly to evolve into yet newer forms. Much work that impinges on it or directly gives expression to it may remain highly valuable. This is obviously true of Wittgenstein on language (*The Philosophical Investigations*), less true of Collingwood's method of question and answer (Collingwood, 1939), least true of Peter Winch on the social sciences (Winch, 1958, 1963). However much of striking interest remains to be salvaged from such dicta, there can be little question that Karl Popper (1960) is still right to insist that 'the historicist overrates the significance of the somewhat spectacular differences between various historical periods' (p. 100). Popper of course concludes in favour of transhistorical discourse and trans-historical claims.

The new 'historicism', however, if that is what it is, is not that attacked by Popper. Even David Easton's attack, directed at the history of political thought as practised in America in 1953, is not quite *à propos* of the new scene. Easton remarks that 'the contemporary historical approach is historicist solely because it believes that very little more can be said about values except that they are a product of certain historical conditions and that they have played a given role in the historical process'. Easton was troubled by the thought that political theory in America at the time amounted to nothing more than descriptive courses in the history of ideas which effectively 'managed to crush the life out of value theory' (1963, pp. 235–6). This attack was somewhat similar to that mounted by Bernard Crick (1959). Yet, the lack of 'value theory' today is not finished.

Contemporary historical contextualism sharply differentiates between past and present, as does every historicism, but largely with reference to linguistic usage. This is not the historicism of Marx, nor that excoriated by Popper, in the latter's repudiation of 'scientific' prediction of the future. Contemporary contextualism is averse, not only to moralizing abut the past, but equally to somehow using the past to moralize about the present. If this is not Easton's contextualism, there are recognizable family resemblances.

If historical contextualism has failed to keep normative theory in prison, it has nowhere helped to get it out. Contexualism, by morally neutering history, has helped to make the history of thought (appear) irrelevant to contemporary moral issues and crises. What historical contextualism indirectly underscores is the celerity of change in modern times. But it draws the wrong moral. The difficulty is not so much that the past is dead, and that we must turn our backs on it. The problem rather is the reverse: all of our past, as far as we know it, is and has to be *alive*. The dead can tell us nothing. We only hear those who speak, thus those whom we hear cannot be dead. As for what we have in hand, we must only discriminate a little; beauty from ugliness, helps from hurts, future from ruin. It is not possible to turn our backs on the past. But it is possible to heed more the sense than the nonsense in what the past has to say: we should not so fiercely oppose putting to one side that which merely clutters up the stories we seek to tell.

NOTES

1 I sought to demonstrate this long ago, in Appendix 3 of *The Ideology of Order* (1974, 1999).
2 Margaret Judson's ([1949], 1988) *Crisis of the Constitution* distils the research of a lifetime: I borrow these words from her [p. 393].
3 See Ch. 5 of this volume.
4 Cf. Pocock in King and Parekh (1968), *Politics and Experience*, pp. 209–37.
5 See Ch. 6 of this volume, sections 4 and (especially) 5.
6 For fuller treatment of the distinction between chronological and substantive time, see Ch. 2 of this volume.
7 *Ibid.*
8 Cf. E. Nagel (1961), *The Structure of Science*, on nomothetic and ideographic claims, at pp. 547 ff.
9 S. Freud (1910, 1957, 1963), *Ein Kindheitserrinerung des Leonardo da Vinci* reprinted in trans. as Vol. XI of *Complete Psychological Works*, and as *Leonardo* in Penguin, trans. Alan Tyson, p. 119.
10 Keith Ansell-Pearson claims, in parallel, that 'there cannot be the *one* history of philosophy' and firmly nudges me to attend properly to Heidegger's *Being and Time* (1927).
11 See Ch. 2 of this volume.
12 See Ch. 2 of this volume.
13 Kenneth Minogue in J. Tully (ed.) (1988), *Meaning & Content: Quentin Skinner and His Critics*, p. 180.
14 Skinner (1988), in Tully, *ibid.*, p. 252.

8

Historical Contextualism Revisited[1]

To deal with the methodological problems of historical contextualism, it is useful to distinguish between (1) text, (2) context, (3) history, (4) contextualism and (5) historicism. A text is by turn the outcome and object of all writing or research. A context is any perspective on a text, including the background data that one may append to it. History is a narrative, a story, which is focused upon a text or context – inasfar as the two are the same, viewed as propositions. 'Contextualism' is a methodological claim that valid history is only secured or demonstrated via the reconstruction of the context, especially where the latter is to do with a perspective on the background to a text. Historicism is disinclined either to extract present moral judgements from or apply them to the past; it resists more broadly any form of social generalization over extended units of chronological time; it thereby displays a liability to overrate the importance of the sometimes 'spectacular differences' (Popper, 1960, p. 101) between various historical periods. Historical contextualism may be construed as a new variety of historicism. The emphasis of the present account is more broadly upon the logical futility of historical contextualism in general and less upon its specifically historicist character.

1. Truism and impossibility

Methodological contextualism is a truism and an impossibility. This stems from the understanding that a perception of perspective achieved by any observer, O, of any putatively independent datum, d, never leaves d alone, untainted. Harvey could not map the circulation of the blood without dissecting bodies. We characteristically measure the temperature of liquids by intruding thermometers. I know that my soup is ready by tasting it. The new novel I read is automatically made sense of by the data and dispositions that constitute my mind. I cannot handle any datum without somehow adding something of myself to it. The observer makes sense of a text by squaring it, or putting it in the context of, everything else that s/he knows. This descriptive position, in effect that one can make no claim which is not somehow automatically 'contextual', we may call 'descriptive contextualism' (DC), and it is a truism.

If DC is converted into a methodological principle to the effect that we ought to place ideas in context, then we have something different, which we may call 'methodological contextualism' (MC). MC is the essence of historical contextualism. More than a truism, MC supplies us with an impossibility. MC is obviously redundant, in that we have no need to demand what we cannot escape. As we cannot avoid contextualizing, it is pointless to ask that we do. More, the demand that we contextualize presupposes that we can contextualize, which is to say that we can choose to do so or not. But since we have no such choice, the abstract demand that we choose the contextual methodology is a demand that it is simply impossible to meet. Nor is this the only sense in which historical contextualism is impossible.

Take the context to be a perspective on, including background to, a text. It is a matter of supplementary claims and arguments – related and/or additional to a text. The text is an initial set of claims or arguments. The context is just a subsequent set of such claims which take the text as its object. Now take historical contextualism to be a demand that I place every text I employ in context. If I am always to contextualize, then the context itself (which is substantively reducible to one or more additional propositions, i.e. 'texts') must in turn be contextualized. Let us say that I place text t_1 in context by juxtaposing to it text t_2. I place this in context in turn by adding to it text t_3. But to contextualize this I must append ... text t_n. I cannot of course continue endlessly in this way. Am I being enjoined to do what I cannot do?

If a necessary condition of my securing a reliable grasp of a statement, of a text, is that I am able to place it in context, then my contextual claim must itself be able to pass the same test. This means that my contextual claim cannot hold unless I can place it, too, in context. So where my contextual claim is itself left out of context, there can be no warrant for accepting it. But I cannot place everything I say in context. Such a demand is infinitely regressive. The buck must stop somewhere. The demand for contextualization, advanced as essential to getting at the truth, must then itself stop, even fall, short of the truth.

2. Identity and difference

Substantively, contexts and texts are identical. The text is a set of propositions, and so is the context a set of propositions. Contexts and texts are identical, taking account of their propositional character. The context, whatever it may be, if communicable at all, takes the form of, or can be translated into, one or more propositions. Any contextual material ('background' or 'framework') offered to the reader as a piece of historical reconstruction, must be reducible to propositional form. The validity of contextual claims must be judged on the same basis as textual claims. The one can be assigned no authority higher than, or intellectually superior to, the other.

Relationally, contexts and texts are different. The text comes first, in time or emphasis, followed by the (or some) context. They constitute a sequential relationship featuring the context as subsequent, and the text as prior. We designate contexts as subsequent propositions which erect a framework round initial propositions, which are designated as texts. We can only distinguish between contexts and texts relationally or positionally by holding constant the identity between them as propositions. Musically, we may fancy the relationship of context to text as that of a variation to an underlying theme.

Because of the interplay between identity and difference, the comportment of the context is always shiftily ephemeral. All study inescapably begins with some form of 'text' as its object (see Chapter 5). And any context, once become an object of study, equally takes the propositional form of a text. Once the context is born, once firm enough itself to serve as an object of study, it automatically transmutes into a text. Here the relationship of subject to object (context to text) is reversed, to become that of object to subject (text to context). The context, as a relational construct, proves too ephemeral to provide any foundation on which to build any solid methodological project. Substantively, the text is always privileged, since only it may be adjudged better/worse, true/false, probable/improbable. Relationally, the context is always subordinate, since it can only serve as a context on the grounds that it is relevant to, i.e. governed by, the text.

The movement between text and context can go either up or down. An illustration of upward movement from the text is as follows. This sentence *qua* text may be placed within the context of this paragraph, the text of this paragraph within the context of this section, the text of this section within the context of this chapter as a whole, the latter text within the context of this book, such texts as these within the context of philosophical criticism of the next 100 years, or 200 years, or as far forward as the record manages to stretch. Forward movement from the text is always a contextualizing movement, which sees later claims enveloping earlier claims – which equates with objects of attention being 'placed in context'.

An illustration of downward movement from the text is as follows. The text, '*L'Etat, c'est moi!*', presupposes an innumerable string of further texts, among them, such as that: 'There is, or at least I imagine there to be, an entity called the state'. 'Order is at risk where there is no clear chain of command.' 'There are very good reasons for obeying my orders.' 'I have a distinct identity and a special claim to power.' And so on. One can see that every text can itself be made sense of, by being resolved into, or at least related to, yet further texts, which are either consistent with or contradictory to it. So what is for us the 'text', can always be repositioned downwards, revealing its purchase upon still earlier texts.

Plato's *Republic*, which advances one concept of justice, involves commentary upon and rejection of certain other concepts of justice, such as that justice is the same as 'giving every man his due', or that it is the same as promoting the interests of the ruling element (the most powerful) in society. The logic of the text, once we adjust to its focus, is not autonomous. It not merely relates to the world, it is a part of the world. It may be physically contained, like the pages between the covers of a book, but its claims cannot be similarly delimited. The text which we inspect, once entered into, can be seen itself to supply a perspective on and background to still earlier texts, related concerns and antecedent arguments.

Hobbes's *Leviathan* is a classic text of modernity. Were we able to treat with the text exactly as did the author at the point he created it, what we would be treating is not the 'text' we now know. Our hypothetical relationship to 'this' text, like Hobbes's actual relationship to it, would be one of internality, not our present externality. That which we should have to treat with, rather than the present text, would be the swirling perceptions and engagements upon which the author had set to work but which only yielded up *Leviathan* when that labour was at an end. The author's text is not, while the author is engaged in generating it, a 'text'. It is the context, of whatever kind, that the author's perception, engagement and acuity impose upon other texts that serve as objects of attention. The text, for one who authoritatively inhabits it, is not a text. Only when completed, abandoned and allowed to make its own way in the world, does the authorial ego transmute from subject to object – from context to text.

So any text, like *Leviathan*, can be read, so to speak, 'up' or 'down'. To read it 'up' is to focus upon it within a wider framework. To read it 'down' is to focus upon it within a narrower framework. Both of these are contexts. And then there are further contexts within these contexts, which can be historical, cultural, social, logical (as in much of what we call 'textual' analysis), etc. It cannot be abstractly supposed that to impose an historical context is necessarily more valid than to impose a logical context. Nor can it be supposed that to study the text from the perspective of how it has been influenced is either better or worse than from the perspective of what this text in turn comes to influence. Nor can we say it is better to focus more on the views of the contemporaries of the author as opposed to the contemporaries of the commentator. It seems quite useless to advise anybody, in the abstract, that they should read, for example, Hobbes contextually, whether 'up', 'down' or otherwise.

3. Lumpers and splitters

Properly to attend to texts need not be wantonly to worship them. But should their seriousness warrant it, there may be good reason for texts to be read 'over and over again'. Sustained attentiveness to serious argument in the form in which it actually appears can be no worse than insistently ignoring and reconstructing a text on the basis of what else may have been said, like it or about it, in 'the same' period. (There is usually a watery ambiguity attaching to what 'the same' here might mean.) Contexts, in short, are always in place. To appeal to 'the context' is no more likely to get at the truth than to appeal to 'the text'. The two are connected, like 'heads' and 'tails' on a coin.

If historical contextualism (understood essentially as MC) is to make any sense at all, it must presumably always be converted into a less categorical and more contingent demand, such as that we impose some particular type of context, perhaps a context suitable to the observer's interests or purposes, whether literary, economic, religious, historical, social or other. The abstract appeal to context is unintelligible without specifying some particular sort of context, given that contexts are many and infinitely varied.

If to make any claim is straightaway to impose a context, then any contextualist is always such *malgré lui*. The interesting question will not be whether one imposes a context, but which context(s). Is the concern to inspect the logic of a specific text on its own? Will the focus be upon the entire *oeuvre* of a writer? Will interest settle upon the glutinous practices and assumptions of all this writer's contemporaries and competitors? Will the focus be more upon its emblematic role, popularity, integrity, future notoriety, actual influence? Will the reconstruction privilege historical reliability? Contextualism supplies no answer.

Phillipson and Skinner (1993) as editors of a book of essays honouring John Pocock, contribute to a series whose specific object is to set 'Ideas in Context'. Such a project provokes two considerations. First, inasfar as ideas, being part of the process of being apprehended, are necessarily placed in some context, the object of an ideas-in-context series can already be regarded as having been accomplished, on some general level, in advance of its initiation. Second, inasfar as the different contexts in which ideas can be placed are to be presumed without end, the demand for contextualization must prove meaningless, unless some limited type of context is plainly designated.

Skinner and Pocock are widely recognized as the most important of historical contextualists today. It cannot be enough to say that they laud 'contextualization' in general, since any claim automatically and necessarily establishes some context. The only question worth exploring is the sort(s) of context which this contextualist or that might be disposed to promote. In Phillipson and Skinner (1993), perhaps the most obvious type of context is omitted, viz. one supplying some summary overview and location of Pocock's own texts, in part or whole. To supply such a context would at least make it easier to determine the sorts of context that this 'ideas-in-context' series recommends.

What then are the forms of contextualization promoted by Pocock and Skinner? Broadly, where Pocock is excited, like A.O. Lovejoy, by the sweep of great, integrative themes, Skinner is deeply suspicious of any such ideological abandon, and seeks to confine panoramic effect to some local setting in some distant past. Where Pocock likes spectacular vistas and places great emphasis upon continuity, Skinner is fearful of false connections, and places great emphasis upon discontinuity. Where Pocock reaches for the telescope, Skinner clutches at the microscope. In sum, where Pocock lumps, Skinner splits.

If we take Pocock's *The Machiavellian Moment* (1975), we note his emphasis upon the developmental links between Aristotle, Rome, Machiavelli and indeed the American Revolution. The substance of this link or tradition consists in the idealization of the citizen as an active agent who forms himself by virtue of civic engagement, thereby keeping despotism and corruption at bay. If Pocock, like Skinner, prefers contexts to texts, he also prefers great, vertical shafts of time to Skinner's local, horizontal clearings of understanding.

If we take Skinner's most extended work, *The Foundations of Modern Political Thought* (1978a), we find he avows that he has 'tried not to concentrate so exclusively on the leading theorists' and has 'focused instead on the more general social matrix out of which their works arose' (p. x). He discusses texts only in regard to the social and intellectual 'framework' or 'social base' out of which they emerge.

This framework in which texts are set is itself devised from such evidence as there is for it – which is merely a matter of additional (paper) texts, and inferences drawn from them. Skinner's 'intellectual context', accordingly, is secondary, supplementary, background, 'noises off'. Skinner's aim is 'to construct a general framework within which the writings of the more prominent theorists can ... be situated' (p. xi). But this framework is also a gibbet, the object of which is to supply a final solution to what these theorists did or did not mean. Some profess to make out, fluttering above Skinner's architecture, the little ghost of reductionism.

Pocock (1962a, pp. 184, 186) appears to sanction the possibility of independent logical reconstruction of a text, even if that is not his primary interest. He allows that texts 'exist on a number of different levels of abstraction', so that those texts which, by implication, are sufficiently coherent and abstract, may supply, through their logic, their own context. If this is right, then Pocock's contextualism becomes more private preference than methodological imperative.

Skinner (1964, 1966a) seems concerned to close the door which Pocock leaves open. He seems to take the view that it is not tenable to suppose that the logic of any text can supply its own context. Skinner's reason is not that one can infer the context from the text (and so vice versa), but that 'the context' (which for him equals the assumptions and responses of those contemporaries for and to whom the author might have communicated) imposes a lid, an 'ultimate framework', on the range of conventional meanings that it was possible for an author to have entertained (see the second part of Chapter 5 above).

Skinner (1978a) argues that to focus upon the major texts themselves is of itself to defeat any prospect of 'genuine histories' of political ideas. His position is that we can achieve no genuine 'historical understanding' of political ideas if we 'focus our main attention on those who discussed the problems of political life at a level of abstraction and intelligence unmatched by any of their contemporaries'. So, for Skinner, to 'focus on the study of ideologies', to 'study the context of any major work of political philosophy, is not merely to gain additional information'. Rather it is the method by which we penetrate the 'author's meaning' (1978a, p. xiii). The plain suggestion of this would seem to be that Skinner's context is not only an addition to, but also some form of substitute for, the text.

It is odd, despite such apparently obvious differences, that Pocock and Skinner appear to take it that the business which they are about is much the same. All schools, of course, betray significant internal divergence. But the sharpness of divergence among contextualists may be more economically explained by the uncertain foundations on which their cathedrals of hope are raised.

'Contexts' are as various and encompassing as are any other propositions, including 'texts'. To be instructed to recover 'the' context is consistent with recruiting anything at all that is additional to the text. Logically, the context could be the recent past or the distant past, the near future or the distant future. One may reflect upon a text in the context of its past or present or future. Nor is there anything at all problematic about reflecting on a text in the context of its future. Indeed, we who reflect upon any text always and necessarily do so subsequent to its appearance, are associated with its future, and thus create for it a future context. 'The' context then is virtually all-encompassing. It extends front and back, chronologically speaking, of any designated text. There is no field – science, architecture, social structure, economics, politics or philosophy – which can be excluded from it in principle.

Those who embrace a methodological project so apparently redundant as contextualism presumably must be forced out along many different paths. What binds proponents together is less an ammoniac awakening to some specific context than the treacly embrace of context as such. Since contexts overall are infinitely extensive, one student is always liable to be glued to this perception, while her/his fellow student is stuck to that. The adept is disposed to assume that 'the' context means 'my' context. What excites Ego's attention, may repel Alter's. The construction of some new context will tend, usually mistakenly, to be viewed as burying claims for some older or more familiar context. Most who seek to elucidate 'contexts' are historians, genuinely interested in some particular patch of academic *terra incognita*, unburdened by the hunched back of an enlarged dogma. Those, however, who insist that direct textual analysis must only follow contextual reconstruction (which, in Skinner's case, equals an account of what contemporaries were about) are in a bind.

To contend that one can never take the meaning of a text as given, even where the text seems perfectly perspicuous, appears perverse. Of course, apparent clarity may mislead. But here the old saw applies: hard cases make bad law. One best signals the danger without forging from it a rigid rule of procedure. The use of context seems most appropriate, in the sense of an emphasis upon contemporary background, not where the text appears perfectly clear and sensible, but precisely where it does not. First-year students reading Plato's *Republic* seem rarely to give the author the benefit of the doubt, finding his text highly unpersuasive. It is in this circumstance, rarely otherwise, that the instructor rightly resorts to contextual reconstructions, so to portray the text as more coherent than it can possibly appear to be in the light of present-day understandings.

4. Indefinite rationality and historicism

In the end, it may be that even the lumper–splitter divergence assigned to Pocock–Skinner, is untenable. For Skinner, it is clear that every text is opaque, from which opacity his contextualism is designed to rescue us. Can a fair reading of a parallel sort be derived from Pocock? It would appear so. The claim by Pocock (1962, p. 186) that texts are burdened by an 'indefinite rationality' may be held to reverse the direction earlier established for his position. If Pocock intends by 'indefinite rationality' that every text is somehow opaque, that none *in se* discloses its meaning, then the difference between his position and Skinner's seems to dissolve.

So it is in order to consider two questions. The first is whether all texts are ambiguous. The second is whether the consequences would favour contextualism, even if they were. To the second question first.

As we have already observed, if the text is intrinsically ambiguous, requiring a context, then so must the context be ambiguous, itself requiring a context. If the audience of readers need texts to be interpreted first before these texts are directly approached, they will also require the interpretations to be interpreted first, before the interpretations are directly approached. Thus, even were it true to claim that all texts are of 'indefinite rationality', this would not strengthen the methodological pretensions of historical contextualism. Now to the first question.

The claim that all texts are 'indefinitely rational', is doubtful. And the fact that some or many or even most texts are opaque will not allow us to infer that all are. It is not clear as to the sense in which such a claim as '2+2 = 4', or 'a+b = b+a', is 'indefinite'. The same applies to any strictly historical claim, such as that 'Einstein claimed that $E = mc^2$', or that 'Hobbes believed there to be no conception in a person's mind which is not generated in whole or part by sense experience'. Any such claims may prove untenable. But none is strikingly opaque or ambiguous. If these are ambiguous, then all are ambiguous. If all are, we can no longer distinguish between what is clear and what is not. And if that is so, then the contextualist position will prove as ambiguous, trivial and self-defeating as any other.

Along with the assumption that texts are marked by an 'indefinite rationality', Pocock (1962a, p. 186) supposes there to be some 'strictly historical task' involved in the assessment of the meanings of texts. This task he claims to consist in 'determining by investigation on what

levels of abstraction thought did take place'. But this either means
that (1) historical investigation of contexts centrally determines the
meaning of texts or that (2) such historical investigation merely
circumstantially adds to what we know about texts. There is room for
argument. If the preponderant weight of Pocock's position points to
(2), then it is sound, but not startling or innovative. Pocock would be
making no radical claims for history being, or becoming, but only for
it circumstantially adding to, the understanding of philosophy. And
that is more or less the traditional position, sometimes misleadingly
called a 'textualist' position. On the other hand, there are, at the very
least, elements of a rigid methodological contextualism in Pocock.

So Pocock, like Skinner, may view the context as a way of determining the meaning of the text, to the point of being at least a partial
substitute for it. Further colour is lent to this reading by the fact that
Pocock gives firm preference to tradition (equals context) over text
and, unlike Michael Oakeshott, effectively construes the tradition as
a form of ideology. Though the contextualism of Pocock (1968,
pp. 209–37) is partly influenced by Oakeshott on tradition, Oakeshott
himself (1962, pp. 1–36) never evinced any particular problem with
'textual' analysis. For him, it was rather 'the tradition' which proved
'a tricky thing to get to know', and which might be violated by ideological forays of the sort apparently approved by Pocock.

For Pocock, mastery of the trickiness of tradition became the
special preserve of the historian. Where, for Oakeshott, ideology was
an 'abridgement' of tradition, for Pocock (1962a, pp. 194–5), the
business 'of abstracting ideas from particular situations' itself constituted 'the language of tradition'. Where Oakeshott opposed ideological 'abridgement' on the grounds that it violated the integrity of
tradition, Pocock seems to embrace such abridgement as the proper
unit of study. Where Oakeshott's 'particularist' position (Chapter 4
above) could be squared with the defence of texts, Pocock's defence
of ideology would be consistent with the erosion of these defences.
Pocock, registering an interest in traditions *qua* ideologies, risks
removing the insulation which, in Oakeshott, protects tradition from
ideology. The concern with recovering the gross ideology of a given
period threatens to undermine the integrity of singular texts located
there. Thus, Pocock's dispositional liking for ideology over text may
yet give way to Skinner's firm methodological preference for ideology,
for the framework, as superseding recourse to the text.

5. Methodology versus disposition

There can be no objection to the concern with context, taken as a disposition. The disposition only goes wrong where reinvented as a 'methodology'. There is nothing wrong with reconstructing, or even inventing, a context. Every hypothesized context is necessarily in part invention. What is wrong is to suppose that peripheral vision always trumps telescopic stare. 'Contextualism', as an approach, is as prone to mislead as is 'textualism', if not more so. Sappho's poetry seems, plainly and textually, to reveal elements of lesbian desire and longing. But some contextualist readings have simply reduced Sappho's texts to an ancient poetic genre which conventionally depicts the desire of adolescent girls for one another as preparation for hetero-sexual marriage (DuBois, 1991, p. 19). Shakespeare's *Love's Labour's Lost* is a light romantic comedy. But in the hands of one inventive contextualist, it implausibly becomes a serious attack on Queen Elizabeth's persecution of Catholics (Stocker, 1995).

Contextual or background readings, as such, cannot prove more reliable than textual or foreground readings. Indeed, were it substan-tively possible to distinguish 'contextual' from 'textual' approaches, the latter must prove sounder. If we ask for (a) the reconstruction of a context, this cannot coherently be set out in advance of (b) some sense or logic for the text to which the context relates. For (a) is a function of (b). If we cannot somehow recoup the sense of the text, then neither can we deploy any relevant context for it. Inasfar as we accept a later–earlier sequential relationship between context and text, then to attempt to establish the propositional logic of the text first would have to be the rule, or one could have no idea how to decide between the amorphous and infinitely extensive contextual claims that may pop up claiming inheritance.

The priority of the logic of the text is a primitive *sine qua non* for the creation of any related context. To accord the logic of the text formal priority is not to concede it autonomy. The text can always be resolved 'downwards' into those antecedent propositions or concerns out of which it later emerges. This downward movement buries the text in an inescapable spiral of antecedent or parallel texts, in parallel to the way the same text, looking 'upwards', subverts the autonomy of later commentary upon itself. So again, to plump for the priority of the logic of the text is not to plump for the autonomy of the text.

As for deciphering the argument of a text, it cannot be a matter of over-interpretation, but only of sound and fair procedure, to press the most logically coherent reading which the letter of the text allows. This is not to be confused with according to texts strengths they have not got. But it does defend against reducing texts to Rorschach tests, taking on the appearance, at the worst, of straw men. Historical contextualism would have to be considered an irrational procedure inasfar as it is committed to reconstructing contexts in advance of securing the internal logic of the texts to which they relate, and insofar as it opposes the most rational possible reconstructions of these texts *qua* texts.

No defect is to be found in a contextual disposition, where the predominant interest is less in the logic of the text than in the broad circumstances out of which the text emerges. The real difficulty is the contextual methodology, which prioritizes context over text and seeks either wholly or partly to dissolve the logic of texts into their contexts, into background, into the claims of contemporaries. A contextual methodology, as distinct from a contextual disposition, either tempts or requires him or her who has it to impose context upon text. This may take the form of either allowing the context (here equals 'background') to override the text, as with Pocock on Machiavelli (following Sullivan, 1992). Or it may take the form of allowing the context (here equals 'views of author's contemporaries') to determine the meaning of the text, as with Skinner (1966a, p. 314) on Hobbes (following the second part of Chapter 5 above).

6. Closing the circle

Historical contextualism, conceived as a methodological demand, seems hopelessly circular. The trouble is that it is logically and physically impossible for any observer endlessly to contextualize the context of the context ... of the context. A 'context' is nothing more than a text which, by virtue of being last in place, has not yet been – and cannot itself yet be – contextualized. Abstractly to recommend contextualization is then to place an automatic value on subsequent propositional claims in preference to previous propositional claims. The effect is a *fuîte en avant*. The construction of a context is never conclusive, nor logically sounder, by virtue of being a context. If I privilege claims merely because they are contextual, then I only privilege those claims last made. My contextual claims are only dubiously contextual anyway, since I cannot myself confer upon the very last context I create its own context. My contexts, further, are doubly dubiously contextual since, so long as there are other and subsequent observers, their reflections and researches will convert my contexts into texts, which must underscore the universally tenuous and ephemeral status of contexts.

If 'the context' is distinctive only by virtue of representing the last claim advanced, it cannot follow that it must be the soundest claim advanced. The context, at the conclusion of any proceedings, supplies 'the last word'. But this is no more than an elementary, procedural matter of fact, which does not stretch to a methodological Golden Rule, allowing us to equate 'the last word' with the right word or any form of sensible conclusion. There can be no reason why what we call a 'context' should be accorded any moral or methodological finality. There seems no sound reason to privilege 'contextual' above 'textual' assertions, nor to allow 'contexts' moral or hermeneutic or scientific precedence over 'texts'.

'The context' is not magically self-revealing or methodologically privileged. It supplies no miracle cures or instant restoratives. It may mark a direction (considered, e.g. as 'background') in which one might explore. But it ring-fences no methodologically preferable type of exploration. It may advise where to look – outside the text – but not how to render the text more or less valid. Contexts and texts are not distinguishable in terms of truth-claims. The preference for context over text is not the same as a preference for a valid over an invalid claim. The relational order of context to text (of subsequent to previous) does not correlate with any order of superior to inferior validity. It involves nothing more than a matter of logical sequence, where text is antecedent to context and may serve it accordingly as an object of attention.

If one encounters a difficulty in a text, then it may be wise to look elsewhere for solutions to it. But if one has not looked closely enough at a text to determine the problems that it itself disgorges, then 'to look elsewhere' – call it context – is bound to be a bootless business. 'The context' after all is as large as life itself, and as unrelenting. Nor is it just one: contexts are irresistibly plural. If one has no sense of what the text is about, if one does not first take from it some sense of what is to be pursued, then the context in turn, unbounded as it is, neither will nor can reveal anything of relevance. The preference for context over text only presumably makes sense on the misleading assumption that texts, as distinct from contexts, are necessarily unclear or incomplete, or on the assumption that more data always make for greater clarity.

The trouble is, that if all texts, *qua* propositions, are necessarily unclear or incomplete, then all contexts – the propositions we advance to explain or embellish texts – are equally unclear and incomplete. If all texts are defective, then so are all contexts defective. If all texts require further explication, then all contexts require such explication. If all texts require to be enhanced in order to make sense, then all contexts require to be enhanced in order to make sense. If no textual proposition is entirely autonomous, then no contextual proposition is entirely autonomous. If, to legitimate texts, I must place them in context, then to legitimate contexts ... so must I place them in context. More detail does not necessarily get us closer to the truth. Most detail is irrelevant to what we can or seek or need to learn. A contextualizing procedure, which perhaps asks us to inspect the views of Hobbes's contemporaries, rather than the text of *Leviathan*, may well take us further from, not closer to, what we can or seek or need to grasp.

What can be the purpose of an abstract insistence upon 'contextualization'? There will always be some context. Normally, to cite the logical context of Machiavelli's *Arte della Guerra* may prove more relevant than its military context, and the latter more relevant than its architectural context, etc. But which of these one has recourse to is appropriately a function of the purpose one seeks to realize. If one takes the logic for granted, or alternatively if it is ambiguous, then the study of the military setting may richly illustrate the logic, or even help to remove some of its ambiguity. If one takes the military setting for granted, or if it is ambiguous, then the study of the structure and emplacement of early sixteenth-century forts may underscore or clarify the significance of some of the strategies and tactics Machiavelli was concerned to promote.

The vital difference between text and context is to do with the position and purpose of the observer. As some context is always automatically in place, there is nothing intelligible about recommending context as such. The matter of relevance concerns the context to be chosen. As this is a function of the angle and purpose from which one happens or chooses to observe, the appropriate context to explore cannot be recommended in the abstract. Viewing events, e.g. up close, will not plausibly be shown always to be preferable to seeing them from a distance. A thorough grasp of detail will not always prove more valuable than a sense of perspective. Taking in the view *from* the Lincoln Memorial will not always prove more apt or valuable than peering directly *at* the Memorial.

Beyond the logical problems that dog historical contextualism, there is the oddity of its actual effect upon historical practice. Even where historical contextualism has not directly consigned normative theory to prison, it has nowhere helped to bail it out. Contextualism, in its historicist mode, by morally neutering history, has helped to make the history of thought (appear) irrelevant to contemporary moral issues and crises. Those few contextualists who seek to plot an escape from neutrality and indeterminacy seem lost in a maze (Dunn, 1979). To qualify contextualism as a species of historicism, however different from historical materialism, or social Darwinism or liberal progressivism, is still to identify it as a relativism. Only as a relativism is it like contemporary postmodernism. The latter commonly emits a bright anti-authoritarianism, as in Foucault. The colours of contextualist historicism, by contrast, fly at half-mast, and range from neutral to conservative.

What historical contextualism indirectly underscores, and perhaps rightly fears, is the celerity of change in modern times. Being intensely aware of change, it warns against anachronism with a renewed sense of urgency, and indeed against making connections of almost any kind. None the less, historical contextualism draws the wrong moral. The difficulty is not so much that the past is dead, and that we must turn our backs on it. Nor is it that we require to cocoon the past against the vulgar, probing eye of modernity in order to keep it as it was. The problem, on the contrary, is that all of our past, as far as we know it, is (and has to be) present to us and in us. Inasfar as we know the past, what we know is only by courtesy of a present perspective. The trick is not to make the past inaccessible, which we can only pretend to do, but to heed more the sense than the nonsense in what it has to say.

NOTE

1 This is a condensed and slightly divergent version of Ch. 7 in this volume.

9

Alasdair MacIntyre: Rationalism and Tradition

The idea that individualism in its various forms is incompatible with tradition as such is best abandoned. In turning directly to rationality or to rationalism, we find that the same conclusion holds: rationalism emerges out of history and is, thus far, historical; it emerges out of tradition, and is, for the same reason, traditional. This is not to claim that it is a nonsense in every sense to oppose 'reason', say, to 'the dead hand of tradition'; but when the philosopher, *qua* salient *provocateur*, promotes this sort of dust-up, the point of it can only be to have 'reason' cuff the proposition that an ageing idea is, by virtue of age, more valid. If respect for tradition, which we might fairly transmute into 'traditionalism', requires that I account any proposition or prac-tice valid merely because it has chanced to survive for some indeter-minate period, then we ought never to have got to the point of taking the earth to be round, or the sun to lie at the centre of the solar system, or authority (parental, governmental and other) to deserve or to demand questioning.

If most of what we say is mistaken, and little of what we say is new, then it is improbable that philosophical necromancy will provide reliable access to truth and justice. A proposition is no more privileged because it is old than because it is new, and vice versa. We daily employ propositions and can scarcely avoid the engagement. Since to say of propositions that they are new or old provides of itself no reliable guide as to their validity, one is required to seek reliability elsewhere; and if not elsewhere, then more carefully in the space to which we are confined. The seeking cannot itself be avoided. We are condemned to employ 'a' criterion of validity. It turns out of course that we employ 'criteria'. And it is in recognizing this that we attempt to reconcile these criteria, for fear of subsidence into a perfect irrationality.

We are boxed in by such notions as reason, rationality and rational-ism. It is no use to think categorically to overthrow them. An attack on rationalism, for example, unless it is mere incoherence, can only be taken to represent a slip of the mind or an exercise in irony. The opposition sometimes erected between reason and tradition may be read in this way. For an attack on reason to make any sense, it has to be read as an attack upon figures who claim their positions to be reasonable whereas in fact, as we may intend, they are not. Where we attack rationalism, we cannot intend that our attack is itself an essay in irrationalism. Nor can we mount any attack upon abstraction which can itself avoid being abstract. Every concept – 'human being' or 'love' or 'glass' (and 'concept' itself) – is an abstraction. This is a lesson taught long ago by Plato in *The Meno*. And we do not require to digest what Popper objected to as 'methodological essentialism' in order to assimilate Plato's lesson. Abstraction is the categorical price we pay for speech. It is not a cost we can avoid save through silence.

In this we are supplied at least with a clue regarding the meaning to be attached to the attacks we repeatedly observe being mounted, as by writers from Burke to Oakeshott, upon reason or rationality or rationalism in the name of tradition. In Alasdair MacIntyre's *Whose Justice? Which Rationality?* (1988) we encounter another, but far more self-conscious, example of this genre, despite the author's repeated expressions of disdain for Burke (he 'theorized shoddily') and studied silence on Oakeshott. MacIntyre's book presents us with a lengthy piece of string that loops back and forth, creating risks for himself and his readers. The story that he tells is challenging, if markedly underedited, raising the central question as to what makes it rational 'to act in one way rather than another'. But the answer, like that intimated by Eliot's *Prufrock*, is hard to decipher.

MacIntyre's argument proliferates into an excess of overwhelming questions to do with the nature of justice and rationality and the connections that may obtain between these; the self-evident status of first principles or their lack of such status; the history of philosophy and some philosophy of history; objectivity, relativism and historicism; tradition and context; abstract argument and validity; and the predicament of contemporary philosophy and of modernity generally. All of this is set out in a volume devised to explore the competing and/or incommensurable notions of justice and rationality that extend from Homer to Hume, and even beyond, since the author concludes with an abbreviated discussion of a very encompassing notion of liberalism.

What MacIntyre is most perturbed by is the presumption of an Enlightenment project in which 'reason would displace authority and tradition'. He is stunned by the thought that predecessors could have supposed either that they themselves were possessed of 'principles undeniable by any rational person' or that such principles, whether humanly possessed or not, somehow existed, independently and universally. MacIntyre takes it as a serious objection to this

Enlightenment project that the *Encyclopédistes* and Rousseau and
Kant and Bentham (*inter alia*) all flew distinct flags which unfurled
different and conflicting signals regarding which principles were in
fact universally valid independently of 'particular times and places'.
The fact that there were such differences, the fact that they persist, is
somehow taken by MacIntyre to prove that a universally agreed
rational justification of any such principle is 'impossible to attain',
that our culture is unable to do this (p. 6). But of course as we have
noted, reason never displaces tradition; at best, traditionalism may
become another way of reasoning.

We have no choice but to suppose that there is a true and a false,
or else we can say nothing at all. And in action we are also committed
by implication to a better and worse. And if I claim that p is true, a
part of what I mean is that it is true unconditionally, and this could
be construed to mean universally. When I say that this action is right
or just I may also mean it unconditionally or universally, at least in
the sense that I intend it as a statement concerning something more
than my simple interests or wishes or preferences in the matter. To
speak of universals in such contexts can obviously prove misleading,
since to make a valid claim for truth or justice in one context will not
necessarily guarantee its validity in another. What is important is to
be able to make this point without having it confounded with an attack
upon reason or rationality as such.

For example, should an individual today make the factual claim
that she, as a matter of fact, is 18 years old, this is not a claim which
she can consistently make 365 days hence. What is verbally and
factually the same claim will not necessarily retain its validity
irrespective of the circumstances in which the claim is made. Similarly
with moral claims. It may be perfectly right that the child should
divulge the whereabouts of a parent, but not perhaps if it is the Nazis
who are enquiring. We may see by means of such examples that the
'universality' that we may attribute to truth or justice is less transparent than sometimes it at first appears. But to make such a qualification is in no way to surrender to subjectivism or irrationalism. And
we are right to persist in our assumption that truth, rationality and
justice are not consistently to be dismissed as merely whimsical and
arbitrary creatures of our invention, despite the egregious errors into
which we are fated repeatedly and no doubt unendingly to fall.

We have little choice, then, but to conceive of rationality as a
lapidary given, however varied the shapes in which it is rendered, and
however mistaken we may be in assuming that we have achieved some
grip on the thing. It smacks of a rack to whose independent form we
are bent. It is not to be conceived as a fanciful item of clothing into

which we may slip or not, at will. But if rationality conveys this granitically independent character, the trouble is to square this definiteness, which we must hypothesize, with the extraordinary delusions by which we suppose everyone else (and occasionally ourselves) to have been flattened. It is a notorious commonplace for many who think themselves to be in the right to do so without the slightest inkling of doubt, to think not merely that there is a truth that is absolute, universal and timeless (which might be accounted bad enough), but moreover that they themselves are directly or indirectly in possession of it.

There are men and women who confidently claim not only for example that there is a God who is omnipotent and omniscient, but that they, narrow and constricted mortals, are none the less privileged to know what this unbounded being wishes and even commands. The message of Jahveh is conveniently supplied to the resourceful Moses on tablets of stone. Joseph Smith proved himself no less agile, by means of a casual jerk, in lifting into view one of the divinity's most recent imprints, the Book of Mormon. According to the mortal, Mohammed, the word that he transmitted came from the Archangel. The Ayatollah Khomeini was accustomed to characterize his fatwas as applications of the obviously transhistorical truths of the Qu'ran. Philosophers such as Hobbes, Spinoza and Kant were less disposed to argue a case in terms of divine revelation, but they were equally clear that they had discerned universal laws, and that they were not offering up a record of merely personal proclivities.

This human disposition to believe that one has proved so blessed as to receive or conceive some transcendental truth was evoked by Nietzsche with withering contempt. In *Jenseits von Gut und Böse* (1886) he wrote:

> What provokes one to look at all philosophers half suspiciously, half mockingly, is not ... how innocent they are ... but that they are not honest enough in their work, although they make a lot of virtuous noise when the problem of truthfulness is even remotely touched upon. They all pose as if they had discovered ... their real opinions through the self-development of a cold, pure, divinely unconcerned dialectic ...; while at bottom it is ... a desire of the heart that has been filtered and made abstract, which they defend with reasons they have sought after the fact. They are all advocates who resent the name, and for the most part are wily spokesmen for their prejudices which they baptize 'truths', and are very far from having the courage of conscience that admits this .... (pp. 202–3, Kaufmann trans.)

It is an attack which met with considerable sympathy in figures such as Husserl and Heidegger.

The difficulty that we normally encounter in this sort of circumstance is that of the 'universal' demonstrating itself to be rather more *prétendu* than real. The cry, quite naturally, seems to go up: 'If the Universally Rational (call it Ur) is present, will it please stand up?' Any supposed Ur that dares do so is eventually rendered the worse for wear. Ideas that claim to encapsulate 'the truth, the whole truth and nothing but the truth' have a way of going down for the count. And how can we, imperfect creatures that we are, utter formulae untainted by our own imperfection? And yet, what are we to do? If our own utterances are imperfect, does this mean that this admission of imperfection is itself imperfect, which is to say that some prospect of perfected utterance, i.e. some dependably rational formulation of truth and of justice, yet lies open to us? And what is the alternative?

It would be unreasonable, whatever a colleague of MacIntyre's standing may on occasion say, to take a serious philosopher to intend that no universally rational principle is attainable. For if no universally rational principle is attainable, then this very principle, although negative, is no less universal, and by the standard which it itself sets must fail. In any event, by taking us back into a distant past, MacIntyre certainly, by his own admission, seeks to reveal to us 'a conception of rational enquiry ... according to which the standards of rational justification themselves emerge from and are part of a history in which they are vindicated'. Moreover, he does aspire, with whatever fear and trembling, to take us forward to a time when 'conviction' and 'rational enquiry' will be 'reunited'. So although a philosopher may be understandably rattled by folk talking about and professing these universally rational first principles, we have no cause to conclude that the face of such a one has been set against rationality.

The question can only be to do with the sort of rationality that one is trying to disengage. MacIntyre basically appears to be saying two different things. The first of these is that conflict about justice and rationality in the modern world is endemic. The second is that, when folk maintain that there is, or that they have secured possession of, some transhistorical truth, we shall find that this supposed truth has identifiable historical roots. Of course we should note that it does not logically follow from the existence of conflict that this conflict is insurmountable. Nor is it demonstrated, merely because we can trace the historical origins of a concept or proposition, that this concept or proposition cannot be universally valid. For example, the salience of the claim in ballistics that 'exit wounds are larger than entry wounds' (because the bullet tumbles after impact) derives specifically and historically from the recent origin of firearms. But from the fact that we can in this way 'historicize' the concept of an exit wound, advancing key historical propositions about it, it does not follow that the claim, 'exit wounds are larger than entry wounds', would somehow prove less true in the tenth than in the twentieth century, or more true now than ten decades later.

It is MacIntyre's view that the ligament connecting convictions about justice to their 'rational justification' has been ruptured. That we are witness to a vivid display of 'conflicting convictions' is obvious enough. But is it the case that these conflicts are necessarily grounded in 'incompatible sets of premises'? Contemporary concepts of justice clearly vary as between such doctrines as focus alternately upon 'dessert', 'human rights', 'utility' and 'social contract'. MacIntyre does not believe it possible to adjudicate between 'these rival and incompatible' notions of justice by recourse to some independent and superior rationality, since he takes our views of rationality to be just as distinct and incompatible. Again, it is clear enough that we do entertain different notions regarding what makes for rationality, whether calculating and promoting an individual self-interest, or aspiring to a position of neutrality *vis-à-vis* all interests (including one's own), or promoting some ultimate good that is hypothesized to hold for all humans as such. These differences are obvious enough. The question is, what we are to mean and how far we are to go in qualifying them as 'fundamental'?

To even begin to try to clear up this sort of problem, I suspect that we must return to base. In this context, 'base' consists in recognizing (1) that we cannot advance any propositions about the world without implicitly committing ourselves to some notion of an objective truth, and (2) that we cannot live in a society or community of any kind without implicitly committing ourselves to some notion of justice. How we fill out the blanks that correspond to (1) and (2) is a distinct matter, but the implicit commitment to these blanks is, I believe, fairly plain. At the same time, life in any community, at any point in time, whether in a Nuer village along the Nile or in a presidential mansion along the Potomac, is always marked by some degree of cognitive and volitional dissonance. That there is such dissonance is not unduly remarkable. What is to be attended to is/are the means by which we go about resolving such differences. In this connection, two caveats must be entered. The first is that, in characterizing the means we adopt to resolve differences, we must leave open the prospect that this will include means that may not previously have been employed. The second is that we cannot account a problem resolved 'merely' because most or even all of those involved agree that it is.

Now if we are to insist on maintaining that disputes are fundamental and incommensurable, we can adopt what I shall call the 'basement paradigm'. In this case we entertain a conventional picture of disputes starting with surface conflicts. The idea is that we try to drown these by descending to lower levels of common accord. Protagonists then proceed in a downward spiral from specific to more basic contentions until they hit the cemented basement of mutually opposed first principles, a shattering conclusion which terminates with extreme prejudice any possible resumption or extension of the argument. The idea involved here is that once we have sunk so low, we can sink argumentatively no further. And the problem with this paradigm is that it just confuses *de facto* shock with the impossibility in principle of going deeper.

Given dissatisfaction with the basement paradigm, we can try upending it, yielding what one might call the 'hole-in-the-roof paradigm'. It, too, maintains that disputes are fundamental and incommensurable, but following of course a different trajectory. Suppose we have to do with two individual thinkers, locked in argument. We note not only that they are distinct thinkers, but also that they entertain distinct and opposed claims. Each thinker provides a rational justification for her central thesis. Suppose these thinkers to appeal to divergent higher principles (one perhaps to liberty, the other to equality) to resolve some lower level dispute (e.g. as to whether Tertia is entitled or not to an abortion) and suppose them to appeal to still higher principles (perhaps contractual or utilitarian concepts of justice) to resolve the dispute over the intermediate principles (and so on *ad infinitum*). It is of course this unfortunate *ad infinitum* that accounts for the hole in the roof.

It is important to remember that the hole-in-the-roof paradigm is no less pessimistic than its twin. In neither case is there any reason whatever to suppose that differences between disputants will ever be resolved. The only difference is that one imposes a limit on the number of principles allowed (in the basement, no more than one per contestant) while the other says: the sky is the limit. Of course it may be supposed that, if we can always reach out to some higher principle to break a particular deadlock, this has got to give greater scope to prospects of a solution. And that may well be so. But not in the hole-in-the-roof case. Let us postpone temporarily any discussion of the reason for this.

Let us assume for the moment that, as between A and B, locked in argument, each always reaches for a higher explanatory or justificatory principle which diverges from that elicited by the other, and that there is, accordingly, no particular reason why they should ever end up in agreement. We might try to resolve the issue by setting up, in a Lockean way, a common judge between them. But if this judge, to be called C, is basically similar to A and B, there can be no obvious reason for supposing C to be miraculously apprised of a still higher principle that has somehow eluded A and B themselves. In other words, if A and B cannot locate a higher principle of accord, there is no particular reason to suppose that some species of 'known and indifferent judge' will be better placed to find one for them.

Now the reason for being pessimistic about ever finding any solution to disputes of whatever kind as between A and B, even where we place no arbitrary limit on the range of higher principles to which they can appeal, is that we have implicitly built into our conceptions of A and B a solipsistic assumption. This is exactly what Hobbes did. If A and B are regarded as individually self-enclosed, if each is merely an animate solipsis, then each can only judge in her own terms. Hence there is no reason to suppose that they will ever be able to resolve their disputes. If we conceive of any supposedly independent judge in these same terms, then again we shall guarantee the same results. Even if some judge, C, were actually somehow able to reconcile A and B, we should still have to view the winning principle as an arbitrary one, accidentally hit upon by C.

The implication of the above is merely that, if all thinkers are ultimately regarded as rationally self-enclosed, solipsistic creatures, then we must conclude that there is no means by which any who dispute should ever resolve their differences by purely rational means. By the same token, there can be no perfectly independent or neutral authority, neither of an individual or a group, that is capable of making up this rational deficiency. If it is the case, as MacIntyre (1988) claims, that 'disputed questions concerning justice and practical rationality ... are treated in the public realm, not as a matter for rational enquiry, but rather for the assertion and counterassertion of alternative and incompatible sets of premises' (p. 6), I can see no particular virtue in looking further afield for an explanation. The fact that 'academic philosophy' or the universities or 'partisan sub-cultures' have been and continue in dispute among themselves ante-dates the Enlightenment by many a century, whether we look to ancient India, China, Greece, Rome or Medieval Christendom, and the fact that such dispute has accelerated among ourselves cannot of itself render our predicament more dire than theirs.

One way forward must certainly lie in the abandonment of the basement paradigm, and of the solipsistic assumptions attaching to its twin. Rather than viewing individual thinkers, at their various points of conflict, as rational solipsists, perhaps the more useful approach lies in hypothesizing common ground which thus far has not been spotted, or indeed which may even require to be shovelled

into being. Because we *create* common ground does not make it any
the less real once we have put it in place. Such indeed is the normal
procedure to which we resort. It is not possible consistently to
hypothesize just solutions and at the same time to attribute incom-
mensurability to opposed thinkers, or indeed to 'ultimately' opposed
commitments. It is not possible to hypothesize true propositions while
simultaneously assuming there to be no rational means of either
reconciling or deciding between mutually contradictory versions of
the facts.

There is no reason to suppose that debate *qua* debate should ever
come to a close. For a given participant to withdraw can never of itself
signal the close of argument, even of 'the' argument. Each thinker
may be required to respond to bodily calls upon her time, up to and
inclusive of the Grim Reaper's own categorical imperative. There is
no reason why we should be so thoroughly disturbed by the claims
some will have made, either now or 400 years ago, that we may settle
disputes among us by 'appeal to principles undeniable to any rational
person' (MacIntyre, 1988, p. 6). The fact that we do not 'agree as to
what precisely those principles were' or are, does not for a start entail
that we cannot. Moreover, even assuming that we never agree such
principles, it does not follow that there are none that might ever be
contrived. The fact that we are displeased (some of us) that the
concrete principles that we formulate do not serve us as unassailable
renderings of truth and justice in no way logically diminishes our
implicit commitment to both.

We have little scope in all of this. The problem is to avoid the quick
fix, simply because we are desperate for some more obvious and
popular solution – one, that is, which transcends our fairly obvious
limitations. It is plain that many of our predecessors will have supposed that the problems imposed upon us by the elusiveness of truth
and justice could be easily resolved by having recourse to self-evident
first principles, undeniable to any rational being. Because we reject
this, it makes little sense that we should adopt the other extreme in
promoting historicity, indeed historicism, context, tradition and
traditionalism, since these solutions are equally untenable. If we insist
that the truth or rationality or justice of a proposition is to be gleaned
only in context, it is plain that such claims merely lead to an infinite
regress. If the proposition, 'a proposition is only valid in context' (call
it p), is valid, then the proposition, 'p is valid', is only valid in context.
And so on, world without end. Establishing 'the context' in any
satisfactory way is not just difficult, it is impossible.

We have no difficulty in accepting that, in conceptualizing the
world, we presuppose rationality. We equally accept that, in social

action, we presuppose principles of justice. We are forever exploring beneath and above the surface of our thinking and acting, seeking to expose the deeper or higher unenunciated principles of justice and of rationality upon which we may suppose our thinking and acting to rest. In this, we cannot be convicted of irrationalism simply because we leave it open as to how and whether rationality and justice are logically connected. Nor can we be condemned simply because we decline to submit forever to a rendering of truth or justice that we may chance to have favoured on an earlier occasion. Nor are we to be accounted wise because we mistakenly infer from (1) the fact that we are repeatedly cast into the pit of error, and from (2) the principle of 'procedural scepticism' to which we reluctantly resort as an imperfect defence against (1), the conclusion (3) that there can be no rationality or justice. There is no good reason why any individual should be immobilized by this train of thought. But should we encounter so unfortunate a case, we are probably right to assume that the problem lies more in the psychology of the individual than in the logic of the position.

In exploring the underside and topside of our thinking and acting, we are commonly distressed by the recovery of distinct principles which we find it hard to reconcile, taking them to be rival principles even if they are not. After submerging or emplaning to capture some phantom principle that we assume to overlay or underlie our thinking, we may land again or resurface with the conventional clutch or catch of competing principles or metanotions of truth, variously labelled, perhaps, 'coherence' or 'correspondence' or 'testability', etc. In parallel, seeking to disclose the principles of justice that we take somehow to be implicit in our social and political activity, we continue to effect re-entry with imperative specimens that either enjoin or explain, e.g. 'Give every man his due', or 'Do unto others as you would be done by' or 'Treat every person as a means and not an end', etc.

The trouble with these formulae, when we have wrenched them from the sea or rescued them from outer space, is that they are readily corroded by the new environment into which they are necessarily introduced for analysis. On fuller consideration – which means to say subject to further probing, testing, questioning and counterargument – one is unaware of any concrete principle of truth or justice which our predecessors or contemporaries have recovered which has been perfectly able to sustain such investigation without evident strain. This is plain, irrespective of whether we say that these principles of truth and justice for which we grope are universal and self-evident, that they are intuitively detectable by all who are rational and of a disposition to see; or whether we claim by contrast that these principles are artificially concocted, the fruit of compromise and self-interested contractual invention and thus varied, but each quite correct or right or well-judged or apt in its own peculiar context, its own unique time and place.

The only significant difference is this: we cannot demonstrate a negative. We cannot show, simply because we have produced no workable universal standard in fact, that there can be none in principle, or that there is none somehow implicit (if undetected) in our practice. Whereas, on the other side, we can show that the claim that there are no universally valid propositions is self-defeating, since it is itself universal. And we can show that claims that propositions are only true or right in context are vitiated by an infinite regress.

What clearly remains is that, in reflecting and acting, we think and we are bound by an implicit commitment to truth and to justice, even when we remain unhappy that the clumsy principles that we concretely succeed in formulating are not unassailable renderings of the truth and justice to which the logic of our condition commits us. The sooner we recognize (1) that the inadequacy of our concrete formulae does not cancel our implicit commitment to truth and justice as such, and (2) that this historical inadequacy does not and cannot invalidate the existential claim that there is a universal truth and justice, and (3) that metaphysical counter-claims to the effect that there cannot be any universal truth and justice do not in any way advance the discussion, then so much the sooner may we approach (4) some genuine prospect of eluding the lurid – and enduring? – temptations of historicism as the most pervasive of contemporary subjectivisms.

What is particularly attractive about a figure like MacIntyre is that, despite his obvious historicist tendencies, he is still clearly and earnestly resolved – so much cannot be said of important figures like Oakeshott, Feyerabend and Richard Rorty – to try in every way to avoid a subjectivist outcome. The trouble is that he commits too many of his troops to pointlessly turning the existential flank of the contention that there are universally self-evident first principles. He pushes so hard against this monumentally irrelevant enemy that in the heat of the engagement he scarcely notices that the historicist 'ally' he has summoned to his side is infinitely more threatening (to his anti-relativist convictions) than is the irrelevance he so delights in cudgelling. MacIntyre apparently thinks it impossible to fight a cognitive and volitional absolutism other than by consorting with and lending encouragement to the dissolute historicist claims (1) that truth or falsity is dependent upon historical origin and (2) that the history of ideas has nothing to do with the putatively timeless questions of truth and falsity.

There can be no question but that MacIntyre's myrmidons find the terrain here immensely difficult. On the one hand: 'Doctrines, theses and arguments all have to be understood in terms of historical context'. On the other hand: the 'same' doctrine or the 'same' argument may 'reappear in different contexts'. On the one hand, there is an implicitly uncompromising attack on the whole notion of a 'timeless' or 'universal' rationality or justice: 'rationality itself ... is a concept with a history'; 'there are ... rationalities rather than rationality'; 'there are justices rather than justice'; 'the concept of timelessness is itself a concept with a history'. But on the other hand, there may be timeless truths after all, i.e. 'Nor does it follow that claims to timeless truths are not being made' (by MacIntyre). The admission is painfully lame (1988, pp. 8–9).

However clumsily MacIntyre may cope with this problem, it cannot ever be said that he is altogether happy about combining with the forces of relativism. Unlike Rorty, he has a conscience in the matter. He does mount a vigorous if belated attack on relativism and on what he chooses to call 'perspectivism'. It remains that the chief object of his attack is what might be described as a 'pure rationalism', 'the Enlightenment project', the whole preposterous idea of sovereignly unencumbered individuals presiding in isolation over their fate. He accordingly comes to adopt the tactic – it has a somewhat formalistic appearance about it – of regarding rationalism and subjectivism as enemies of equal standing. He qualifies the latter moreover as 'the negative counterpart' of the former, as its 'inverted mirror image' (1988, p. 353). He almost appears to believe that by disposing of these two problems of rationalism and relativism, he will find some species of salvation in between, indeed a 'dialectic' of sorts which will allow for a pacific outcome to all this *Sturm und Drang*.

It is usual for attacks upon rationalism to be accepted as leading directly into relativism. It is this fate that MacIntyre seeks to avoid by eventually mounting a frontal attack also upon relativism and 'perspectivism' so as to preclude their survival as alternatives. Whatever may now be said about relativism, it cannot be clear, should one eliminate 'rationalism', as to what is left. MacIntyre's aim in *Whose Justice? Which Rationality?* was to provide what was omitted from *After Virtue* (1985) – an account, namely, of what makes morality rational. The direction in which he has continued to move to reach this answer is towards context, history, tradition. But the difficulty that anyone in this position encounters was indirectly hinted at by MacIntyre himself years earlier.

In *A Short History of Ethics* (1967), MacIntyre wrote in the following terms: 'Each society has its own standards and its own forms of justification.' Hence, he continued, 'every form of justification which attempts to provide norms of a supracultural kind is bound to fail'. MacIntyre found that the difficulty with Montesquieu was that he 'combined with his relativism a belief in certain eternal norms'. Thus MacIntyre's query: 'How can Montesquieu believe both that every society has its own standards and that, nonetheless, there are eternal norms by means of which such standards can be criticized?' (1967, pp. 179–80). MacIntyre, as it happens, has no difficulty with the idea that every society has its own standards and modes of justification. But he genuinely appears at points to think to escape Montesquieu's quandary by simply burning off the shaggy belief in universal norms.

By sending the eternal up in smoke, MacIntyre would vaporize the prospect of the ephemeral being judged by any standard other than itself. The troublesome question is not only whether torching the eternal may not prove logically *inàpropos* for this particular writer, but whether such measures may not directly regenerate the growth of relativism. Whatever may be said in general about this question, it can only be regretted that MacIntyre's formulation is not more coherent. For while at one point he would despatch eternal norms, at another he would allow entry to timeless truth. MacIntyre, for example, is grudgingly clear that for 'Doctrines, theses, and arguments … to be understood in historical context' does not logically imply the exclusion of 'claims to timeless truth' (1988, p. 9), as pointed out above.

MacIntyre, like Montesquieu, respects the propriety of local standards. But he, no less than Montesquieu, is in the end also induced to admit 'claims to timeless truth'. The quandary attributed to Montesquieu is not one which MacIntyre himself can be said safely to have escaped. In sum, it is very difficult to maintain (1) that every society has some standards of judgement relativistically peculiar to itself, and at the same time (2) that there is some 'objective' – or 'enduring' or 'timeless' – means of judging these standards, which does not, that is to say, merely endorse them.

If we inspect the performance of any writer who claims that there are no transhistorical standards by which we may judge or assess the standards of a given period, what we shall discover is that such a writer always instantiates that which is said to be evitable or impossible. For if I am to judge (fairly) between two children in a dispute over the ownership of a coin, it is not at the same time possible for me to be a 'party' to this dispute': I am required to stand apart from or outside it in the relevant sense. More abstrusely, if I am to judge a standard, as perhaps of 'fairness', where this means something other than merely agreeing with it, then I must in some sense stand apart from or outside the standard judged. If I am to reconstruct a history, and am to do this coherently, there must be a definite perspective from which I do so which is somehow external to what is being reconstructed.

I cannot conceive how it might be possible *for me* to paint a history which was purely and literally *about it – wie es eigentlich gewesen.* I do not see how I could reproduce anybody else's point of view without benefit of a selective framework provided by my own point of view. And if all of this is true, then it would appear to follow that 'judging', by its nature, somehow involves applying 'external' to 'internal' standards. It is not just that we apply our 'own' standards, but that we seem never to have a perfectly clear picture of what 'our' standards are, or (for the matter of that) of what 'our' tradition or 'our' religion or 'our' culture actually and fully amounts to.

If we inspect the work of MacIntyre, although his rational, trans-historical perspective could be plainer, we shall find that its basic outlines are not obscure. He is committed to the idea that moral concepts cannot and should not be understood abstractly or time-lessly or universally and he dispenses praise and blame up and down the corridors of history depending on whether or not his subjects of study recognize the truth of this idea. The classical Greek world tends to receive higher marks because of its more rooted or tribal conception of itself. By contrast, the Stoics and Epicureans of Hellenistic and Roman times get short shrift, since they are burdened by a univer-salism that is of a piece with the extinction of local ties brought on by the emergence of vast kingdoms and empires. MacIntyre's attack upon the Enlightenment is of a piece with this approach. So, too, with his attack upon what he calls 'liberal individualism', which is impressively ecumenical, to the point of encompassing just about everything modern – from liberalism, to socialism, to conservatism.

A common view has it that the individual of large views, of a universalist, as opposed to parochial, disposition, enjoys resources which warrant admiration. For MacIntyre, by contrast, the figure who thinks in universalist terms is rather impoverished. In *A Short History of Ethics* (1967), MacIntyre puts the case as follows:

> The individual who enquires, What do I desire as a man, apart from all social ties, in the frame of the universe? is necessarily working with a meager stock of description, with an impoverished view of his own nature, for he has had to strip away from himself all the attributes that belong to his social existence. (p. 100)

If the Stoic or Epicurean or Renaissance prodigy is to be charged with an impoverished view of 'his' nature, then this charge has to be strung from some standard which is external to, and which swings trans-historically across, the standard held to by the prodigy in question. MacIntyre's judgement is obviously suspended above, and cuts across, the swathe of history which he judges – and I cannot see that this could be otherwise. It is difficult to see how anyone should be able to judge of what an impoverished social existence might be without some implicit standard relating to a social existence that is not impoverished.

In saying all of this, one should be, certainly in MacIntyre's case, pushing against an open door. In *After Virtue* (1985), his admission of the difficulty could not be more manly: 'as I was affirming the variety and heterogeneity of moral beliefs, practices and concepts, it became clear that I was committing myself to evaluations of different particular beliefs, practices and concepts'. MacIntyre goes on to remark that 'it was as clear to others as it ought to have been to me that my historical and sociological accounts were, and could not but be, informed by a distinctive evaluative standpoint' (p. ix). But the conclusion which MacIntyre professes to reach in *After Virtue* – namely that 'nothing less than a rejection of a large part' of what he calls 'the ethos of the distinctively modern and modernizing world' will put the human world back together again, i.e. 'will provide us with a rationally and morally defensible standpoint from which to judge and to act' – is already implicit in his earlier history of ethics. What MacIntyre distinctively seeks to show in *Whose Justice? What Rationality?* is that the standard by which one values values, or judges standards, is somehow caught up in the historical record itself, in 'our' tradition. But as powerful and attractive as I find MacIntyre's intellect, I expect that it will not prove impossible to show that his hopes for tradition are misplaced – very likely being circularly valid.

10

History via Hypothesis

It would be far better if history were seen, more self-consciously, for what it always is, viz. an attempt, selectively, to tell a limited story, never mind how long or brief the account may be. History thus conceived firmly rules out both the ambition to capture the presumed infinity of 'reality' (*'wie es eigentlich gewesen'*), as also to divagate in an inconsequentially scholarly way, shorn of any obligation to get to 'the' (or at least to some) point. And this must mean, despite the relevant danger of anachronism, that the past (and 'past history', to speak redundantly) is in a crucial sense a creature of the present. The present forges the hooks which we trail to bait the past and to land it. Where historical particularism and methodological contextualism sunder past from present, or where they pretend that historical process is in some large sense irrational and inconsequential, then it is time to put them behind us. Overall, the essays in this volume do not genuflect to these tired idols. But though they are sensible in selecting an important and straightforward theme, they are not as bold as they might have been in sorting more sharply the sea-forms being trawled.

To adopt the theme of the individual in political theory and practice, with specific reference to Europe over the thirteenth to eighteenth centuries, is straightaway to embrace a contemporary and selective perspective. This leaves little room for the contextualist project, conceived as a methodological imperative, other than in some trivial sense. What, after all, is a 'context' if not some species of perspective? And how can there be any 'understanding' divorced from 'perspective'? Understanding is always a 'getting in perspective' or a 'putting in context'. And may this not approximate to Molière's *bourgeois gentilhomme* being instructed that it is 'prose' he has spoken all his life? It is hard to see how the contextualist project, construed as a methodological demand that we spy out 'the' context, as such, may swell any progress, assuming the only relevant sort of question

Note: This chapter is a review of Janet Coleman (ed.), *The Individual in Political Theory and Practice* (European Science Foundation, Oxford, Clarendon Press, 1996).

to be: Which context? Background? Foreground? Future? Present? Past? Logical? Historical? And very much more. The promotion of context as such falls short of a useful answer.

In this volume, Hans Guggisburg's treatment of 'the historical context of the Reformation' instantiates this redundancy, since his sub-theme means nothing more than 'background to the Reformation' or 'overview of the Reformation'. He is not so much setting out '*the* historical context' (an impossibility) as he is briefly sketching a particular sort of context (a background or overview) about the broad relationship of state to church. His sub-theme, as it happens, actually omits to specify what he is doing in particular, presumably because he assumes that to speak of '*the* (historical) context' somehow of itself serves as an adequate label for the brisk background claims he is prompted to make about church and state.

The selective burden of these historical essays is said to be to 'overcome the long-established historiographical tendency to regard states mainly from the viewpoint of their twentieth-century borders'. The project was funded by the European Science Foundation (ESF) and devised so that the 'analysis could not be in terms of geographical borders'. If this is not quite true, in that the analysis in fact *is* in terms of geographical borders, it is true that the idea is to transcend the limitations imposed by the frontiers of the *nation-state*. These essays are framed by the geographical logic of what are perceived as the present-day borders of Europe as a whole, consistent with the project of constructing a European Union. One problem of course is that Europe has no clear-cut boundaries 'as a whole'. Is the defining criterion racial or geographical or religious or cultural? This project implicitly excludes (on what grounds?) the lands 20 miles south of Gibraltar, sites like the former Carthage, and such cities as Alexandria, Bethlehem and Jerusalem. But it presumably includes (on what grounds?) such entities as Albania, Bulgaria, Romania, indeed Turkey. The European states given significant mention (apart from quick-fire references to the likes of Transylvania and Poland) are basically West European, mostly Atlantic, viz. England, France, Germany, Holland, Spain. There is a grand European theme underlying the professed plan of these essays, but it is not nearly so clear as it might be as to how 'Europe' is being constituted, especially since the plan is to reach beyond the frontiers of existing nation-states.

The editor certainly reflects a piece of selective imprinting in her understanding of historical process. She insists that the fall-out from Western European history between c.1300 and c.1800 is to be understood as 'unintended consequences', as 'not [being] the products of long-term rational construction', as 'utilitarian responses to contingencies', as 'without teleological assumptions', as 'unintended, but none the less progressive ... secularisation', etc. For her, it would appear, what marks historical process over these five centuries, and perhaps history as such, is that any given upshot is always 'unintended'. It is one of those large and fashionable claims that ritualistically kills off historical inevitability and predictability, rightly enough, but equally kills off any form of responsibility and therefore agency.

The editor wishes to say how we have got where we are, with our perhaps dry-as-dust individualism, but the essential gravamen of the claim is that we did not get here rationally, intentionally, purposefully. Hence the tension between an attempt at rational historical reconstruction, and the rejection of the notion that what has come about is/was in any way *intended* to come about. Is there no *via media* then between 'the Real *is* the Rational' and, as we might say, 'the Real is the *Irrational*'? Must we conclude – due to 'unintended consequences' or to the 'veil of ignorance' thrown over us by cumulative individual choices in the market, or because few if any members of the whole can perfectly foretell the upshot of the vote – that there is no rationality, intentionality or purpose? If the editor is right, then we should equally be entitled to conclude that all legislation in the Congress or Parliament is unintended or irrational or non-rational, for the reason that not every, possibly not any, member wills the whole of any given piece of legislation that eventually succeeds. If there is any coherence at all in social evolution, then there is to be presumed some moral or consensual common ground among those who are the agents of this evolution. And agency encompasses both rationality and intentionality. The selective emphasis which axiomatizes 'unintentionality' is surely due rethinking. It would do, for a start, just to omit these eerie incantations to do with the non-contributory effect of agents upon the institutions which evolve from their agency.

Are these claims regarding unintentionality and inconsequentialism actually justified by the essays that follow? If so, then surely not in any perfectly obvious way. The opening Coleman essay is brisk, clear, fresh, touching on many figures – from Aristotle through Bartolus – and its only emphatic conclusion is that the thirteenth-century individual is not the 'liberated' individual of the nineteenth-century 'modern state'. Coleman brings on site her various building blocks – Christian theology, feudalism, Roman law, etc. – and constructs an edifice whose summit is denominated 'modern individualism'. But it is uncertain, despite the flagging of private property as a check on emerging state power, as to which combination of these historical *explicanda* are holding the coping aloft. Bagge's concern is

more limitedly historiographical and he appears ambivalent as to
whether modern individuality owes more to the fact of increasing
social mobility or more to a supposedly Christian ideology of
'individual personality'.

Jacques Verger, by contrast, attending to the universities, is a plain
man and baldly informs us that 'the individual as a political subject
asserted himself in Europe from the thirteenth century onwards'. On
the one side, the recognition of the 'intellectual as an individual' is
claimed, at the end of the Middle Ages, to be 'an established fact' (p.
77); on the other – in view of the Inquisition, etc. – we are advised of
the 'loss of confidence in the positive values of debate and free expression' (p. 70). Where Coleman gives much play to the influence of ideas
on events, Guggisberg explains the emergence of religious tolerance
more materially 'as a consequence of external factors, such as economic or political pressures' (p. 98). Dupont-Bouchat sinks into an
ambiguity or perhaps subtlety which may well appall Verger. On the
one hand, she contends that the 'generalisation of the inquisitorial
procedure' somehow brought to centre stage 'the character of the
accused', thus promoting 'the individualisation of guilt' (p. 130); on
the other hand, she maintains that this same process had the effect of
undermining 'freedom of conscience' (p. 147). Weber records an only
slightly different undulation: absolutism contributed to individuali-
zation, while 'individualisation contributed significantly to the down-
fall of absolutism' (p. 214). Black is altogether less clear that there is
any direct, progressive trajectory: 'it can be argued that the sense of
individuality was as clear in the twelfth century as it was in the
eighteenth' (p. 330). Nor is he clear that individualism accounts for
Western modernity: 'Islam was not strikingly different from
Christianity' as regards the individual's (a) relationship with God and
(b) moral responsibility (p. 338).

Many of the essays may be ambivalent or perhaps *nuancé*, but the
writers seem to wish to make the most of rational historical reconstruction. For a start, even if modern individuality is the result of
'utilitarian' decision-procedures, these are still purposive and rational.
Moreover, all of the writers reflect commitment to some form of
rational explanation of the move, if and as they see it, from the pre-
modern to the modern individual. They may pitch upon theology,
philosophy, university education, private property, personal mobility
or political absolutism, etc., or some fuzzy combination of these, but
none of the particular essays seems to assume that there is no coherent
or truthful or useful account that can be given, even if the particular
author is uncertain which account to promote. So the book seems less
concerned to demonstrate non-rationality and inconsequentialism,

than to supply a series of overlapping surveys, each with its own interest, which together tell a broken-backed story about the emergence/persistence of individuality in/into modernity. What they sometimes allude to, and arguably do not make enough of, is the loss of individuality in modernity (as in Dupont-Bouchat's lament on the loss of freedom of conscience). One may conclude that this stocky volume happily does not really fit the toyish, unintentional, non-rational, utilitarian raiment that has been cut for it.

To theorize more openly, even boldly, however, in such a collection would be a virtue. Far from being alien to history, it would make for better history. Martin van Gelderen for example, is principally concerned with liberty and the Dutch Republic in the sixteenth century. He writes well and persuasively, yet never appears consciously to ask himself which concept of liberty it is that he is tracking. Liberty can refer to for example (1) the independent and sovereign power of one's state (race, tribe, clan), (2) majority rule, (3) defence of civil liberties (various kinds), (4) protection of traditional practices (perhaps primogeniture or cliterodectomy or the right to bear arms), etc. These can be combined in different ways. But each is distinct and each can contradict the rest. To do the history more coherently, you have to say more plainly which history it is that you propose to do. Thus van Gelderen does a history which is unsatisfactory only in the sense that we are never quite clear which of these stories he is telling. We accept that the Dutch loved 'liberty', but better to be clearer at the outset about the sort of liberty(ies) they loved and to say which major sort of liberty controls the present assemblage of data. The reader can of course figure most of it out. But the impression given is that the matter has not been considered: liberty is a doubtfully self-consistent concept.

Comparato's insightful account is almost entirely to do with theory, as opposed to practice. Balibar covers more familiar terrain, again entirely theoretical, in a dense and sparkling effort which along the way makes a refreshing case for (1) Locke as the first, the decisive 'initiator of modernity', by virtue of inventing 'the key philosophical notions ... in use today when dealing with individual rights' (p. 233); and for (2) 'a return to the original texts' in order to 'throw some light' on confrontations between current paradigms of the 'subject', the 'individual' and the 'citizen' (p. 239). One may endorse the good sense of Schmale's concern (consistent indeed with the title of the book) to deal as much with political practice as with political theorists without finding his encompassing definition of liberty (p. 173) at all helpful. Hampsher-Monk deals with Britain in the seventeenth to eighteenth centuries. Dilcher follows with a more wide-ranging piece. Stourzh implicitly raises the question whether 'equal rights' may not supply a more precise focus than 'individuality' for a study of the emergence of modernity.

Taking everything together, it seems fair to say that this collection, solid as it is, is undertheorized. It has a philosophical theme: individuality. It has a geographical locale: Europe as a whole. But it has no apparently consistent way of theorizing the theme and no fetching formula for historicizing the locale. It supplies an insufficiently concrete and integrating framework, as in the form of some consistent integrating hypothesis, to do with its subject. In the end, what is striking about this volume is that it focuses upon Europe as a self-contained cultural and social unit over a period when Europe can be least well explained in such terms. After all, Europe and modernity go hand in hand. And Western Europe in modernity is largely what it is by dint of the role it has come to play as a complex of dominant entities on a new and global stage. To think to explain Europe as an isolate is to miss a fundamental and also exciting desideratum.

There are of course always at least two sides to such discussions. On the one hand, there are historians like Norman Davies (*Europe: A History*, 1996) who seriously consider Europe to be a peculiarly self-contained and persistent cultural and geographical entity, which no 'Iron Curtain' either did or could rend asunder. On the other hand, historians like J.M. Roberts (*A History of Europe*, 1996) and even non-historians, like the world systems' theorists generally, deny Europe clear boundaries, geographical or cultural, seeing the overwhelming distinctiveness of European modernity to derive precisely from the global dominance achieved by the North Atlantic rim after 1492.

The key point is not that one or the other side is right, but that there is a position to be argued out. It is not enough merely to take for granted, as this book on the whole appears to do, some peculiarly homogeneous and distinctive spatial and social character for its subject. The conceptual hare that is being chased by this impressive pack of contributors might plausibly have benefited from slightly tougher, more elaborate engineering.

11

An Ideological Fallacy

1. Ideology: the word

For words are wise men's counters, they do but reckon by them;
but they are the money of fools ...

Hobbes (*Leviathan*, 1, 4)

The word 'ideology' was coined towards the end of the eighteenth century by the French philosopher Destutt de Tracy. He meant by it undistorted truth. Napoleon, however, imposed upon the expression a negative intent when he denounced as '*idéologues*' those philosophical speculators whose lucubrations he assumed to be subversive of the order enshrined in his person. This contrast reflects the indeterminate meaning of the term. For 'ideology' openly converses in terms of conscious purpose, scientific guidance, objective decisions and progressive advance, while simultaneously brooding over (and possibly presupposing) the reality of irrational commitment, partial interests and subversive inclinations.

Marx's use of 'ideology' is ambivalent. On the one hand, he condemns ideologies as distortions; at the same time, he implicitly supports ideology, if it is the right sort. Marx, of course, was very far from rejecting the negative connotation put upon the term by Napoleon. For, with Marx, an 'ideology' was very often a mask, or a reflection or even perhaps a reification of partial material interests, and to the extent that it meant this, it inevitably implied a falsity, the alienation of truth.

'Ideology', for academics in general, has tended to acquire a negative connotation, while, for political activists, the expression tends to be used in a highly favourable sense. Various scholars, taking up the matter where Marx the scholar left it, have tended to use the word in such a way as to suggest an inherent limitation upon, or alienation of, the truth. Karl Mannheim (1954), for example, drew attention to Bacon's warning against the deceptions of the *idola*: they

Note: Footnotes marked by an asterisk denote 1999 edition comments on the original 1969 edition.

were phantoms and preconceptions, 'sources of error derived some-times from human nature itself, sometimes from particular indivi-duals', 'obstacles in the path of true knowledge' (p. 55).

Mannheim, Sombart, Troeltsch, Weber and many others have been especially interested in the character of ideology. Mannheim accepted that interests affect the elaboration of systems of belief, although he supported the view that intellectuals as a group are freer from this sort of prejudice than other classes. Weber drew attention to the fact of ideology as a heuristic tool: it was important to study the manner in which interests have historically determined or conditioned patterns of belief. This was the primary interest reflected in his *Die protestantische Ethik und der Geist des Kapitalismus* (1904–5) as well as in such related studies as Tawney's *Religion and the Rise of Capitalism* (1922), studies attempting to relate patterns of thought to material interests and economic conditions. Such work was primarily influenced by the academic Marx, and later by Freud and most of it today is referred to as the 'sociology of knowledge'.

It is possible to argue, of course, that research into the sociology of knowledge completely by-passes any concern with bestowing praise or blame upon ideology, but this is not true. The sociology of knowledge is generally regarded in at least two ways: as an *alternative* to ideology, and as an objective means of *studying* ideology. In either case, there is a suggestion of the inadequacy of ideology, and the implication of some form of censure upon it. In fact, with most academics, this censure is applied quite openly. Werner Stark (1958), for example, believes it best to allow 'ideology' to imply distortion while substituting 'sociology of knowledge' where what is intended is merely a general outlook, inevitably dependent in some degree upon one's condition and position (pp. 48 ff.). What is implied in this sort of formulation is either the distinction between an acceptable and an unacceptable general outlook, or the distinction between an accept-able way of looking at (or investigating) a general outlook, and the unacceptability (or distortion) of the general outlook investigated. In the case of either of these distinctions, ideology is indicated as the diseased valve, and the sociology of knowledge as either a satisfactory cure or substitute. In fact, what one generally finds is that anyone today in search of 'truth' tends to be suspicious of 'ideologies'. It is typically for the academic, viewing ideology as an obstacle to truth (because assumed to be intrinsically distorted), that the expression retains its negative significance.

It is usually for the activist, by contrast, that the word ideology loses its negative significance. Whereas the academic's primary objec-tive is the determination of truth, the activist's is the realization of a particular aim. Thus, an ideology may obstruct the academic in his work, while it may be essential to the activist in his. The practice of politics requires an understanding of circumstances, conjoined with a programme of action and an ideology will contain both of these things. In a settled political order elaborate programmes of action are not so necessary, because what is to be done, and what is accepted as having to be done, are largely ingrained in the habits of a people, in the legal system which engirdles them, in the tacit relations of deference and command which may relate one class to another. In an unsettled political order, very little may be taken for granted; in a polity in crisis, there are few publicly recognized guidelines that can be followed; and it is typically in such circumstances that political leaders worry that they have no adequate overall understanding of the situation and no truly appropriate programme of action; and so they demand an ideology, or regret the absence of one, and *possibly* with reason in either case.

It is necessary to insist upon the difference in standpoint between the academic and the activist, but to insist also that in practice any particular individual, like Marx, may in fact prove to be both. It would be absurd to insist, moreover, that an academic ought not to be an activist; equally, that an activist cannot be an academic. To do this is to compartmentalize human capabilities in too crude a fashion. From this, however, the major point to be retained is that it is not particularly helpful to regard an ideology as being in itself either good or bad. It will be one or the other, depending upon one's perspective; and given that one's perspective is rarely unilinear, it may well be both. An ideology tends to be regarded as negative when it obstructs the attainment of truth. It tends to be regarded as positive when it assists in the implementation of programmes of social and political action. Thus ideologies will be regarded as erroneous and as bases of distortion which must be guarded against. They will equally be regarded in certain circumstances as providing a necessary framework for the conduct of political life and thus as deserving to be promoted. In short, a very important area of disagreement about ideology relates not merely to what it means, but to whether it is good or bad.

None the less, one reason why people disagree about the merits of ideology is because they do not impress upon it an identical meaning. Although it is inevitable that one should discuss the merits of definitions provided by others, it is equally necessary that such disputatiousness should not be too prolonged and that it culminates in and be abridged by some statement of what it is that the writer has in mind as forming the factual substance of his concern, as opposed to what he conceives to be the essentially correct meaning of a term.

It is necessary to deal first with some conventional meanings ascribed to the term because so many of them are short-sighted. 'Ideology' is usually regarded as a recent phenomenon, but the basic political reality referred to is by no means so. It is usually regarded as a secular phenomenon, but secular ideologies constitute a recent development, and even now do not hold the field alone. It is usually regarded as being, or as pretending to be, scientific. But it may simply be the case that 'science' is generally what we contemporaneously conceive to be objective or correct, which in a previous age would quite as acceptably have been labelled 'theology'. M reover, viewi g ideology literally, in terms of the 'logic of an idea', there is no reason why a 'scientific' political view should be considered intrinsically more ideological than one that is 'theological'. An ideology is generally regarded as being revolutionary or reformist. But Marx and Engels did not regard the 'German Ideology' as revolutionary, nor have we any particularly good reason for assuming that an ideology cannot be conservative or reactionary.

Reinhard Bendix (1964) sees ideology as a scientific and non-theological development. Following Carl Becker, he sees the major break between a pre-ideological and an ideological world as emerging somewhere between the thirteenth and eighteenth centuries. The pre-ideological, for him, is characterized by belief 'in the supreme deity'. The ideological he sees as characterized by a view of nature (human and otherwise) which conceives it as ultimately reducible to comprehensible and 'discoverable laws' (p. 295). It is of course useful to distinguish between the Middle Ages and the Renaissance, as well as between theology and science, but it is another matter to suggest that the distinction between the ideological and the pre-ideological can best be distinguished by reference to these differences If ideology is not in fact scientific, at least in the way that, say, physics is, then it is no more impossible for an ideology to borrow from the philosophical and practical trappings of theology than it is for it to borrow from those of science. If we say tentatively that the business of ideology is to provide an integrated understanding of the world, together with a programme of social and political action, it is clear that the acceptability of any particular ideology will vary with time and place; and, as its primary objective is the organization of a society, the variety of its intellectual accoutrement (whether scientific, theological or otherwise) must be imputed a purely secondary and inessential significance.

Hannah Arendt (1958), too, tends to see the development of ideology as a recent phenomenon, in fact 'as a very recent phenomenon' (p. 468). But the actual content which she assigns ideologies does not impress one as being particularly recent. She writes, for instance, that ideologies 'explain everything and every occurrence by deducing it from a single premise': but it is far easier to reduce Christianity to a single premise (the existence of God) than it is to perform similarly radical surgery upon Marx. Arendt (1958, p. 469) explains that an ideology

> is quite literally what its name indicates: it is the logic of an idea. Its subject matter is history, to which the 'idea' is applied; the result of this application is not a body of statements about something that *is*, but the unfolding of a process which is in constant change. The ideology treats the course of events as though it followed the same 'law' as the logical exposition of its 'idea'. Ideologies pretend to know the mysteries of the whole historical process – the secrets of the past, the intricacies of the present, the uncertainties of the future – because of the logic inherent in their respective ideas.

Much of this may be plain hyperbole; it is certainly exaggerated. The passage which avers that ideologies pretend to know the mysteries of the whole historical process is probably more applicable to Judaism, Christianity and Islam than it is to Marxism and racialism. The passage which insists upon the extreme *logical* coherence of ideology is also slightly exaggerated. It is possibly because Arendt insists upon the novelty and explicit coherence of ideologies that she can find so few of them, all of recent vintage. In effect, she reduces the field to two; she does not say that there are no others, but merely that racialism and Marxism are the most important (1958, p. 159). But liberalism is probably equally important, and as ideological, although there may be less awareness of it as an ideology because it is found more acceptable. Also, racialism is not very coherent at all, as compared for example with liberalism. (The point here is not to make a moral judgement.) Moreover, whether or not Marxism, socialism, racialism and liberalism are deducible from a single logical premise, they are certainly committed to gaining or protecting single political goals: as, for example, the dictatorship of the proletariat, improvement in the conditions of life of working people, the supremacy of one race over others, or an 'open society'. It is at least as much the commitment to an exclusive goal, as the deduction from a single logical premise, which leads into the distortions with which ideologies are usually associated.

Arendt (1958) is aware of Christianity as offering 'the most powerful and all-inclusive legendary explanation of human destiny'

(p. 208). But she promptly dismisses it from the court of her concern: 'Legends', she explains, 'are not ideologies'. Thus she toes the line drawn by writers like Bendix. Of course it is true that legends by themselves are not ideologies. But in what sense would it be true to say that Christianity is nothing more than a legend? It is for too many people a way of life, a basis of organization and a hope for the future, and all of this can, as in some countries it does, have great political significance. The point about a legend is that it is really supposed to have no significance, certainly not comtemporaneously, not politically. A legend is merely *legenda*, what is written, and, perhaps, forgotten; what is legendary is suggestive of what is ancient, mythical and, probably, historically untrue; a legend is certainly not a mode of organization, suffused with a directive purpose and associated with a concrete view of the way in which the world works and is structured. The conclusion to be drawn from this is that Arendt is mistaken; Christianity cannot be dismissed as a 'legend'; and it cannot be discounted as non-ideological. It has had far greater significance ideologically than racialism, for example, could ever pretend to have. And this is supported by the fact that so many racialists, as in South Africa and the southern United States, are inveterate theologists as well, who demonstrate the correctness of *apartheid* and segregation by reference to biblical passages which demonstrate that the sons of Ham were intended by God to be hewers of wood and drawers of water. The point of all this is that a commitment to religiosity may be ideological just as a commitment to ethnicity may be; and that the two may be combined to constitute a composite religio–ethnic ideology, as has happened in the Dutch Reform Church, among the Mormons, and elsewhere.

C.J. Friedrich and Z.K. Brzezinski (1956) tend to see ideology as a secular and reformist phenomenon. They define an ideology to be 'a reasonably coherent body of ideas concerning practical means of how to change and reform a society, based upon a more or less elaborate criticism of what is wrong with the existing, or antecedent, society' (p. 74). This sort of statement is generally satisfactory, although attended by marginal difficulties. For example, an ideology might well involve an elaborate argument *against* change; for where an established mode of life is challenged by a rigorous, systematic and ideological formula, the response may be to lift the concern with that mode of life from the mere level of behaviour onto the level of systematic and ideological reflection, so that, in this form, it constitutes a viable counter-argument to its challenger. Thus it is necessary to weaken the stress that tends to be placed upon ideology as a means of effecting change and reform exclusively, so that it becomes meaningful (that is, neither contradictory nor redundant) to speak of a 'conservative' ideology and of a 'reformist' ideology. Thus, if it is possible to call Marx an ideologist, it becomes equally possible to say the same of Hegel. The central element is present in both: a concern with total explanation, and an attempt to relate it to certain essential types of political and ethical behaviour.

From one important standpoint, there is in any case no great difference between attack and defence, reform and conservation. The central question, ethically, is, what is one to do? Either to attack or to defend is to act, and systematic reflection may at any time become relevant to the act, whether it be conservative or reformist. Certainly it is easier not to reflect if one decides to do nothing than it is to avoid reflection if one decides upon aggressive measures. But this scarcely warrants the conclusion that the radical is intrinsically more likely to become an ideologist than the reactionary. For the most radical of activists, the anarchist, is intellectually among the least systematic, and, in this sense, among the least reflective. In regard to systematic reflection, the De Maistres of this world will always win hands down over the Kropotkins and Bakunins. So one returns to the view that 'reform' should not be considered intrinsic to the meaning of ideology, but merely as one variant form of ideology.

Friedrich and Brzezinski, as already noted, tend to attribute to ideology a purely secular character. But if we return to their basic definition it is clear that the element of reform it indicates is in no way contradictory to religion: Christianity and Islam, from the very beginning, were reformist in the extreme. And as for the question of the extent of change that ideologies demand, certainly no more apocalyptic change could be imagined than that prefigured in the second coming. In short, Christianity, as one religion, easily fits into their basic and original definition of an ideology: it is quite coherent; it wishes to change society, although primarily by improving upon the morality of its members; and, as in St Augustine, it contains an elaborate criticism of the antecedent society. The only significant difference here is that Christianity holds out some promise of reward (for moral reform) in another life; whereas communism, for example, does not. The question is whether the presence of an other-worldly element on the one side and its absence on the other is sufficiently significant a consideration to warrant the differential classification of communism as ideological and of Christianity as non-ideological. It is difficult to think that it would. Early Christianity was primarily concerned with utilizing the instruments of church and state to save, or contribute to the salvation of, souls, and force (when Christianity became a state religion) was in no way excluded as a means of achieving this end. The communistic salvation of individuals must be read in a more materialistic fashion, since it has utilized the state as a means of increasing economic production and eliminating class oppression without in any way excluding force as a means to this end. The tentative implication that forms the point of all this is that the term 'ideology' cannot be usefully restricted to imply 'recent' or 'secular'.

Friedrich and Brzezinski, like Arendt, in discussing ideology in general are in fact more concerned with certain recent historical phenomena – namely, communism and fascism – rather than with anything else. They tend not so much to begin with ideology conceived as a central and *continuing* political experience, as with ideology conceived as a unique and *limited* political experience; they begin, in fact, with recent historical experience, from which they extract an ideological essence which is assumed to be recent and unique, although it is not. It is from this mistakenly foreshortened perspective that some writers have anticipated the end of ideology.

To cope with this confusion it is essential that we distinguish between forms of political organization and types of political belief-system. From this it follows that the recognition of novelty among the former will not necessarily entail an equal novelty among the latter. A new form of political organization, such as federation, can easily make do with an older type of political belief-system such as liberalism. Similarly, a totalitarian form of government could quite easily, in principle, make do with any one of a number of belief-systems, such as Calvinism (including innumerable other variant Christianities), Islam, Judaism and so on.

Friedrich and Brzezinski are actually more concerned with the concept of a totalitarian ideology than with that of ideology *per se*. They see a totalitarian ideology as one which is concerned with total destruction and total reconstruction, involving typically an acceptance of violence as the only practicable means of achieving these ends. It is, they write, 'a reasonably coherent body of ideas concerning practical means of how totally to change and reconstruct a society by force, or violence, based upon an all-inclusive or total criticism of what is wrong with an existing or antecedent society'. This concern with *totalitarian* ideologies should not, in principle, detain us, except for the question it raises as to whether in this case it is the ideology that is different or the totalitarianism. Most probably it is the latter. Totalitarianism does not so much seem to be made possible by novel ideas or idea-systems, however much it may be accompanied by these, but by radical advances in technique as regards communications, transport, production and weaponry. These not only make it easier to supply the wants of vast populations, but also to control, persuade and manipulate these populations.

At this stage we may omit further comment on the various meanings ascribed to ideology in the current literature. The writers so briefly discussed are reasonably representative. But from all this two primary areas of disagreement emerge. The first relates to the question whether ideology is good or bad. The second relates to the question as to what it actually means. All that has been established, in a preliminary way, is (a) that ideology may reasonably be considered both good and bad and (b) that the meanings attributed to it, however contradictory among themselves, and however arbitrary they must ultimately and necessarily be, tend on the whole to be too restricted to provide a proper understanding of the phenomenon to which they relate. The rest of this chapter is primarily concerned to broaden the meaning of ideology and to suggest one sense in which it involves (from an academic perspective) an error which it were better to avoid.

2. Ideology: the fact

Excelling all whose sweet delight disputes
In heavenly matters of theology;
Til swoln with cunning, of a self-conceit,
His waxen wings did mount above his reach ...
Marlowe (*Doctor Faustus*)

If we distinguish between systems of political organization and systems of political thought, it is clear than an 'ideology' is usually classified under the latter. At the same time, however, it is clear that we do not mean the same thing by political thought, or political philosophy, as we mean by ideology. If we take ideology literally and intend by it 'the logic of an idea', this meaning will not prove sufficient to distinguish it from any form of systematic political reflection. In all such cases we are confronted with ideas, and with the logic of these ideas. The difference between a political philosophy and an ideology does not relate to any quality logically intrinsic to either. Both relate to politics in a comprehensive manner and attempt to explain and even to direct it. Arguments which attempt to demonstrate why one should obey the state in general, or that certain types of state are best, obviously relate to politics in a directive manner, and these represent one typical sort of argument (although not the only kind of argument) advanced by political philosophers. Despite all this, one still tends to regard political philosophy as somewhat more objective than ideology. The reason lies not so much in differences of logical structure as

in the different uses to which they are put. It may be that Marx has
been viewed as an ideologist while Hegel has not, because Marx's
ideas rather than Hegel's have been utilized by parties and governments to explain, justify and direct their activities. Marx himself of
course helped to make this possible, since he deliberately intended his
ideas to be used as weapons: the point was not merely to understand
the world, but to change it. It is generally at this point, where ideas
are used to conserve and change the world, that they become capable
of assuming an ideological character.

An ideology, therefore, is not understood here as a system of
political thought, but not as a system of political organization either.
It involves a system of political thought as systematically and coherently applied by and to a particular group, whether the latter is the
government of a state, or a subordinate group, class or estate within
it. The notion of a system of political thought being 'applied' (to a
group) is intended to carry the sense of its providing a framework
within which, and a set of principles by which, the activities of the
group (or the decisions of its representatives) are explained, justified
and directed. No one will dispute the assertion that an ideology is not
a system of government. It is more difficult to slip past unchallenged
with the suggestion that it is not a mere system of political ideas
either.

Ideologies are generally accepted as systems of thought. The
reason, however, why this acceptance is unsatisfactory is because we
generally view a political philosophy as a system of political ideas,
and yet find that ideology and political philosophy are in some sense
mutually repugnant. Without immediately elaborating upon this
'repugnance', which we might refer to more neutrally as a 'difference',
attention may simply be drawn to the fact that an 'ideology' is usually
conceived as an idea in action or as an idea that seeks to be activated;
the fabric of a 'political philosophy', by contrast, is less inclined to
wear in this way. 'Ideology' is more likely to imply commitment and
action; 'political philosophy' evokes reflection and understanding.
While commitment and action are as important as reflection and
understanding, it is as well to record the difference and, indeed, the
mutual repugnance. This does not so much lie in logical structure as
in intended or actual application. Accordingly we must recognize that
ideology involves more than the conception of a system of ideas; it
is a conception of a system of ideas in action. Although it is true that
'ideology' is often used to indicate a system of political ideas, it is
equally true that it is used to indicate a coherent programme of
political action. In this chapter it will be used to imply a combination
of the two.

In order to accommodate the ordinary usage of those who intend ideology to convey nothing more than a system of political ideas, a distinction may be drawn between 'ideology by purpose' and 'ideology by function'. By the former may be understood a system of ideas which has not been organizationally activated (or 'applied' in the sense previously intimated) but which is either designed for this purpose or which is conceived (by anyone) as a potential means of fulfilling it. By the latter may be understood a system of ideas which has been organizationally activated. An ideology by purpose, then, is a system of ideas which is *intended* (by its author or by certain of its admirers) to serve as an ideology. An ideology by function is a system of ideas which actually serves this purpose. To conform to an important aspect of ordinary usage, and at the same time to abbreviate, an ideology by purpose could simply be called an 'ideology'. An ideology by function could simply be called an 'ideological system', an ideology as 'applied' to a system of government. In either of these senses ideology will carry the suggestion of application as either an existent application or as an intended application.

An ideology, then, will either involve the *actual* application of a coherent system of political ideas to a political system in such a way as to direct its activities, or it will involve the serious *intention* of making this application. Ideology is ordinarily used to convey both the notions of intended and of actual application. One may speak of 'the' or 'a' Marxist ideology when merely intending reference to a theoretical system. One may speak of the Soviet ideology when intending the actual application of such a system to the government of a particular state. Application, intended or actual, is involved in both cases. So the word 'ideology' may be used to cover both. It happens occasionally, however, that one wishes to keep the distinction in mind. When that is intended, the term 'ideological system' will be used in the sense previously indicated. 'Ideology' itself will inevitably be used in both ways.

Given that an ideology involves the actual or intended application of a coherent system of ideas to a system of government, in both an explanatory and a directive (or normative) sense, it will follow that an ideology will not merely be a political point of view or outlook (*Weltanschauung*) or philosophy or metaphysics. A political point of view may not be integrated or coherent; it may only relate to a particular issue and not constitute a general outlook. A political outlook, although more coherent than a point of view, may nevertheless fail to transcend a purely declaratory (more degenerately, a 'declamatory') stage and so remain unreasoning. A political philosophy, although more coherent than a political *Weltanschauung* and although thoroughly reasoned, may not be applied and may not be so intended *vis-à-vis* the direction of a group's activities. Whereas the absence of such an intention and application is possible in the case of a political philosophy, their absence is probable in the case of a political metaphysics, since the concern of this category of reflection is not only not to recommend, but altogether to escape concern with recommendation as a category.

The operations of every government involve some concept of right and wrong, of rules to be obeyed, of law; and laws are ideas which can be regarded as being both explanatory and directive. It is possible to argue that a system of law, like an ideology, can hold a society together. But it is equally possible to argue that the unity of a society otherwise held together can be reflected in a system of law, or rationalized in an ideology. A system of law, like an ideology, can be conceived abstractly as only being intended for application, or concretely as an actual procedure or practice. A law can be conceived as a rule written in a book or as a recurrent type of behaviour of which no one (who actually instances such behaviour) is consciously aware. Law, since it need imply nothing more than a recurrent mode of behaviour, may involve the recurrence of any type of behaviour and so may be good or bad. Just as law may diminish social tensions by drawing attention away from them, so it may exacerbate these tensions by drawing attention to them. An ideology is more encompassing than a system of law, but the latter can certainly be treated ideologically. Attention could be drawn to its assumptions, these collated, possibly reduced to a single assumption, premise or ground, and this then presented as an object of faith as well as a type of logical axiom whence the activities of a government are intended, or made, to unfold. In the same way that a system of law can protect or promote the partial interests of a social group, so may an ideology. In the same way that some laws may promote the interests of some groups within a society more than others, so may some ideologies. Although there will be only one system of law, there may be a variety of conflicting ideologies. The system of law as a whole may basically reflect the interests of a dominant group. The ideology of the government, if the government has one, may equally reflect those interests. But there may be other groups whose interests are violated by the law and obfuscated by the governmental 'ideology', and so they may concoct rival ideologies *vis-à-vis* one another as well as the government with a view to promoting their interests by incorporating them into the present or a projected system of law. Thus, within any society, governmental and any other groups may wield ideologies. It should be noted, however, that we have not asserted that ideologies are mere refractions of group interests. Nor has it been suggested that all governments and interest groups have ideologies.

That this is so, however, must turn upon an ultimately arbitrary distinction. An ideology, according to what has been said above, involves the application of a coherent system of ideas to political activity in order both to explain and direct it. Thus, whether or not we are actually confronted with an ideology in any particular case will depend upon how coherent we insist that an applied system of political ideas must be before it is magically reconstituted as an ideology. In pre-1989 Russia and China, for example, systems of political thought were applied much more thoroughly and coherently than, say, in France or England. The question is how precisely this line can be drawn.

All governments, parties and other such organizations have some point of view; but this will merely mean that they will have a point of view about something, and not necessarily about everything or even most things. Thus not every political organization, however superior or inferior, need be expected to have a systematic outlook upon all those matters which potentially fall within its range of concern, enabling it to utilize that outlook as a framework within which to explain and direct all of its activities. Some political organizations, like some individuals, will conceive of their activities much more coherently than others. (Although the question cannot be discussed at this stage, it is probably a mistake to regard the attempt at a coherent approach to political decision-making as bad. What is bad is when one assumes one is being systematic while being in fact merely circular.)

One would not say that an ideology was a 'truth'. It contains some conception of truth, but it also contains, beyond that, some conception of right. What is true and what is right are not necessarily compatible categories. If it is right to save the life of A, then it may be wrong not to lie in respect to A's whereabouts. An ideology contains an inherent tension between a conception of right and of truth, and cannot be reduced to either. An 'ideologist' who sees himself to be concerned exclusively with the 'truth' can no longer be described as an ideologist; nor can one be so described if exclusively concerned with right. For an ideology involves a conjoint picture of truth and right. A complete devotion to truth renders one at best a scientist, at worst a vegetable, and in either case divorces one from the universe of moral discourse. A complete devotion to right renders one at best a politician, at worst an aerated utopist, and in either case divorces one from the universe of factual inquiry. Of course it may be thought that the commitment to truth is somehow superior to the commitment

to right. But such a thought is mistaken. It is no more the case that
to establish truth necessarily advances right than that an established
right necessarily advances truth. Any outlook is composed of
tensions, and so is any political ideology. The tension between truth
and right is one of these.

An ideology involves both some manner of deduction from an
overriding principle and some sort of commitment to an exclusive
goal. It may involve more of one than the other, but more of either
one, rather than of any one in particular. It involves deduction as part
of a philosophical process. It involves commitment as part of a
political process. It is not necessary that we should attempt to establish
the manner in which an ideology is assembled. It is not likely that we
would discover anything more novel by pursuing this line of inquiry
than we would if we were concerned with the history of ideas in
general or, more narrowly, with the sociology of knowledge. Insofar
as an ideology attempts to marshal a group to attain a particular aim,
its adoption necessarily represents a commitment by the group
sharing it. The word (aim) may be quite rigidly confined, to mean
more a projection than a reality; but, if it is so confined, it should not
be overlooked that the *preservation* of a reality may equally be
projected, and thus become the object of an ideology. The point of
all this, however, is that an ideology does not possess an exclusively
logical or philosophical character. It possesses equally a political
character, without which it cannot be ideological.

Still, the sort of political commitment revealed in an ideology
usually assumes a specifically logical character. This consists in the
translation of the ideology into one or a few basic principles, whence
one may deduce not only what is correct in the objective mathematical
sense, but also what is correct in the subjective ethical sense. It is this
procedure which, as we shall later see, creates some difficulty. It is
impossible to characterize as fallacious in general any commitment
to an exclusive goal; such a commitment might be perfectly right in
the circumstances of the moment. But the assumption, by contrast,
that certain types of true logical deduction are necessarily politically
right will not stand up to inspection. (But this is a question which
cannot be further discussed at this stage.)

An ideology not only provides an understanding of a condition of
fact together with a recommendation of action, but it also provides
a focus for the general loyalties of an individual. One's understanding
of reality, since the latter constantly changes, must constantly be
reinterpreted. Agreement upon a broad objective may be too broad
to cover the innumerable intermediate decisions that must be taken
to achieve, and to avoid aborting, that objective. Thus, within an

institutional context, there stands the need for some sort of arbiter between the individual, on the one hand, and the correctness of their grasp of the ideology and its goals on the other. Since an ideology is a coherent system of ideas applied to a group, the ideology will be the focus of the individual's loyalty within that group. But since a coherent system of ideas does not altogether apply *itself* to the group, it is important to see one way in which this is done by human agents.

The formal loyalty demanded by an ideology is not, in the first instance, to an individual, nor is it to a set of individuals. It is, instead, to an idea or a principle such as freedom, equality, justice or salvation. These are ideas, but they are also goals; they can be aimed at, one can seek to achieve them. The difficulty is, that they are intrinsically abstract goals – and this is not affected if we say they are generalizations from experience, or abbreviations of experiences or if we say that they are rationalizations of selfish economic interests, or that what ought to be done can be deduced from them, or that they reflect a pursuit of intimations. As abstract goals, whatever the historical process through which they have become established as goals, they require a more concrete form if they are to hold a group together. Thus there must be priests, scribes, intellectuals, even lawyers, who manipulate these ideas in such a way as to demonstrate that the concrete practices of the group or its concrete aspirations are consistent with the general conceptions and abstract aspirations embodied in its ideology. And this is one of the factors that accounts for the highly intellectual character of an ideology; its official interpreters must explain the appropriateness of concrete aims by reference to abstract goals, and not by reference to the simple demands, commands or directions of some whimsical individual.

Devotion to an ideology is slightly different from mere devotion to a group or to a person, though it may begin within the context of such devotion. One may be devoted to a group or to a person merely because this expression of loyalty is mutually profitable. Within the context of American politics, the acceptability of loyalty in terms of a mutually profitable arrangement is often called 'log-rolling'. (More universally the invitation, 'you scratch my back, I'll scratch yours', reveals its nature.) Loyalties can be traditional, materialistic or merely based upon familiarity with associates. There are by contrast ideological loyalties, where one's commitment to the group is expressed in terms of one's commitment to the *ideas* which are conceived (in receiving the loyalties of all other group members) to bind the group together, to make it a whole.

Devotion to an idea can begin, however, in the form of devotion to a group. If one is American or English or Russian, it is quite possible for one to begin as a nationalist, out of simple familiarity with one's country, or for other reasons and then, on reflection, to extract some element which one thinks is peculiar to the particular national temperament of one's country, so that the loyalty which was originally and directly bestowed upon the group is now transferred to the distinctive idea or virtue with which the group becomes identified. One might still be called a nationalist, but then one's nationalism would have assumed a more pristine ideological form, as expressed in terms of one's devotion to the ideal of freedom embodied in the Constitution, or devotion to the concept of inflexible, undogmatic moderation embodied in the commitment to muddling through, or devotion to the construction of a communist society as originally projected in the works of Marx and Engels and furthered by the Revolution of 1917. But just as it is possible to move from commitment to the familiar to commitment to an ideology, so it is possible to reverse this process. For many people deserted their own lands to settle in the United States, in the United Kingdom and in the former Union of Soviet Socialist Republics because they thought they would find it possible to institutionalize and objectify their own otherwise abstract loyalties to such ideals as 'freedom', 'moderation' and 'communism'.

Ideologies are not necessarily restricted to governments. For a government is merely one type of social group, however distinctive its character. Ideologies may be wielded by any group or sub-group within a society. It is possible that a government might always adopt an ideological style; it is conceivable that it might never do so. It is possible that a government might or might not wield an ideology, permitting other inferior groups the same latitude. It is possible that a government might or might not wield an ideology, while refusing other, inferior groups the right to wield an ideology contrary to that held by the government, or to wield any ideology at all. All of this is possible. The distinction between an ideology as held by a government, and as held by other subordinate groups, is not for our purposes of any immediate importance. It is only important insofar as a government will, at least formally, possess more power than any other group internal to the same society. Thus, again formally, it will be able to impose its will upon these groups and so be able to permit or refuse them the right to operate in an ideological manner (however the government itself may operate).

An ideology as applied by a sub-group or a government is not necessarily tyrannical, although it may be. An ideology is tyrannical when it stipulates that some particular person or body has the exclusive authority to declare its implications in all or most cases.

When that happens, even though the ideology itself places greater emphasis upon loyalty to itself than upon any interpreters of its meaning, the point is nevertheless reached where the interpreters are *de facto* supplied with the loyalty of members so that it is they personally who are obeyed. In this case the form of politics remains ideological, but the content is personal. What is personally determined cannot be questioned but it is justified by the proponent as ultimately stemming, not from self, as it does, but directly from the ideology.

An ideology is not tyrannical when there are no serious limitations placed upon the rights of its adherents to discuss freely its implications and possible applications. This may happen within a one-party state which wields a particular ideology, as seemed to be the case in Tanzania under Nyerere, for example. And it may happen even more obviously in a situation where the government either has no determinate ideology or applies what it has sporadically (as in the United States). Of course, governmental groups may wield ideologies with varying degrees of deliberation, inflexibility and coherence.

Ideological parties, like ideological governments, can be organized around the principle of open debate as well as by reference to a structure of quasi-military command. It is not true of course that parties and governments structured by reference to open debate and deliberative accord will necessarily prove unequal to those structured by reference to command and obedience. For although quick and firm decisions may be obstructed through tedious debate, sure and convinced support may be alienated through arbitrary commands. Of course it will happen that individuals as well as governments who know what they want, when confronted with others who do not, will necessarily be better placed (*ceteris paribus*) to succeed. But it is the easiest thing in the world for a group to know, politically, what it wants, without being 'ideologically' oriented to its achievement. It is not necessary to have a systematic understanding of the world in order to want to conquer it (perhaps one may refer to Alexander or to Genghis Khan), or develop or destroy or control it, or (as perhaps with Switzerland) to profit from the world while keeping it at a distance. 'Single-mindedness', in short, is not a part of the meaning of 'ideological politics', since it will not always be found in an ideological system and will frequently be found in non-ideological systems.

One factor which needs to be considered is the deliberate smoke-screen effect so often encountered in ideological systems when they claim to embody the loyalties of group members while in fact they do not. An ideology is not likely to involve the smoke-screen effect when members' adherence to the group which the ideology engirdles is truly voluntary. But governments are often most hysterical in their manipulation of ideologies, not when the states they control are cohesive, but when they are or become fissiparous, so that often the ideological formulae, ubiquitous as they are, do not so much represent a unity, as a tenuous and final effort to constitute a unity. Put to such use, ideology achieves a smoke-screen effect. And behind the smoke-screen one may find little more than an estranged membership on the one side, with corrupt and bickering politicians on the other. There need be no single-mindedness at all as regards the implementation of policy, however well concealed the actual programmatic incoherence may be beneath an extraordinarily lucid, but irrelevant, flow of words.

Typically, tyrannical ideological systems are those applied to groups, but openly or tacitly rejected by them, and where the possibility of elaborating alternative ideologies is suppressed. It is also typically in these circumstances that an ideology becomes a smoke-screen and the political consciousness it embodies becomes 'false'. Here the 'official' ideology does not accurately reflect the outlook and commitments of the group members (the citizens or subjects) and therefore the official consciousness becomes a 'false' consciousness. It is clear that this may happen within any ideological system, whether communist, socialist, capitalist or otherwise. The official democratic ideology in the United States, for example, is still regarded by many African Americans as embodying, for them, a false consciousness. Similarly, the official socialist ideology of Ghana under Nkrumah was regarded by many Ghanaians as embodying, for them, a false consciousness. A 'false' consciousness may be so insofar as it does not reflect the outlook and commitment of the community or sub-communities towards whom it is beamed. But it may also be false insofar as it is simply and vigorously rejected by the national community or by certain of its sub-communities.

As we have seen, an ideological system is not merely an outlook, but a commitment, and not merely the idea of a commitment, but its practice. Thus the rejection of an ideological system is not just the rejection of an idea, nor of a practice, but of an idea as practised, or of a practice as idealised. So the rejection of 'socialism' in Ghana cannot be read as the rejection of a noble idea wrongly abused, but of a particular ideological system, in form and content, as it stood. The partial rejection of 'democracy' in America by figures like Farrakhan cannot be read as the rejection of a noble idea shamefully despised but of a concrete ideological system, both in form and content, as it stands. In these circumstances, the most extreme form which the repudiation of a 'false' ideology can take is its violent rejection. Ideological politics, especially open, permit sophisticated stratagems and superb argumentative subterfuges. But once it is assumed that this system of argument is really closed, then one may withdraw altogether and subject it to physical attack.

Short of physical attack, a great deal of argument can take place within any ideological system. The reason for this is not too difficult to see. First, however, it will be necessary to remark that the type of ideological system presently assumed is that of an 'official' kind – expressing or embodying the cohesiveness, outlook and purpose of a governmental group. This does not prejudice the applicability of the general conclusions of this discussion to all ideological systems; it merely advises that our immediate concern and examples will relate to governmental ideologies.

A governmental group, with its member-citizens, may operate as an ideological system. If this is to mean anything at all it must imply that there are governments (as suggested earlier) which do not wield ideologies. Such governments exist. However, as between all governments, it may be well to draw attention to one common factor (there are of course several others): decision-making. The difference between ideological and non-ideological systems very much hangs on a difference in the character of decision-making. The point of this, however, is not to suggest that non-ideological decision-making is of one type (no more than non-human forms of life are of one type).

In taking a decision for any group the decision may be explained or justified by reference to a common end that is supposed to bind the group together. A head of state may do this, no less than the head of a corporation or union or cultural society. He may explain or justify what he has done by reference to a common end which is supposed to express the shared purpose of all members. In the case of voluntary associations, this operation is usually easy to execute. That is because these associations are almost always of the sort where their purpose is actually spelt out in a charter or contract or constitution and thus the officers generally know quite concretely what aims they are to pursue and the members know by what yardstick their performance may be measured. In the case of associations where membership is involuntary, as with governments, explanation and justification by reference to a common purpose is rather more difficult to achieve (for various reasons which I do not wish immediately to touch upon). None the less this is often done, typically by governments which themselves have constitutions.

Now the difference between ideological and non-ideological decision-making is a difference of kind and yet it is a difference that must be measured in degrees. For example, in an ideological system the common purpose stated cannot be restricted to a particular time and place; it must be unending and its application illimitable. Also, it cannot be shared among individuals or groups who have conflicting understandings of the actual nature of the world and of history; the specific purpose cannot be divorced from the general outlook. Thus 'democracy' is an ideology, but 'home-rule' is not; 'peace' can be promoted ideologically, but a Korean (or Vietnamese) truce cannot be. These examples suggest differences of kind, and yet, at the same time, they reflect differences of degree. For the political abstraction is always burdened with institutional encrustations. (Why else do we speak of a given country as being, for example, the 'birth-place' of parliamentarism or the 'home' of the free?) And the concrete political aim can always be viewed as a particular expression of an enduring purpose (such as 'self-determination for all peoples'). Communism and capitalism, democracy and aristocracy can be viewed as ideological systems, by contrast with personal autocracy or enlightened despotism, which are basically non-ideological.

But even here, the quarrel between differences of degree and differences of kind re-emerges. If democracy and aristocracy can be admitted as ideological systems, then why not monarchy? And if monarchy, why not personal autocracy? And if this, why not any other system at all? This argument is not convincing, but it is plausible; what it really reveals is the continuity in degree between all systems of government. Of course a monarchy could be ideological if it invoked a highly coherent world-view conjoined with a commitment to a highly general and exclusive goal. It just so happens that most monarchies do not. Monarchy is usually just another name for hereditary one-man rule. And although it could in principle be turned into a sophisticated ideological system, it usually is not. There may of course be a reason for this that is intrinsic to the nature of monarchy, that it is simply too personal. We have already seen that an ideological system may indeed reduce to personal rule *de facto*; but that it can only do so to the extent that the ruler (refusing to justify himself *qua* himself) poses as an intermediary between the citizens and the achievement of their common goal. It is more difficult to alter this relationship in such a way that the ideology is made to consist of, as opposed to merely camouflaging, personal rule. Still, despite the difficulty, such an alteration remains possible.

Any particular group may be transformed into an ideological system or deflated into one that is not. Any given government can project an abstract goal for the society as a whole – such as freedom – and justify, or attempt to justify, all of its activities as following from the pursuit thereof, not only in domestic policy but in foreign as well. Foreign wars may be consistently justified and explained as an attempt to protect or extend liberty both at home and abroad. The refusal to establish a public health system, to provide more government scholarships, to initiate slum clearance schemes, can all be justified and explained as an attempt to protect the liberty of physicians in their practices, of universities and scholars in their researches, and the liberty of all individuals to buy, sell, build and destroy their own homes as and when they wish. There is no limit that can be placed upon the ways in which an abstract goal can be utilized by a government to justify and explain the unending series of concrete decisions which it must take. What becomes ideological about this is the way in which an abstract idea is consistently and coherently used to justify and explain to a group the directing decisions which impose upon it its apparent and active character *qua* group.

Now, it is clear that this ideological activity may be engaged upon more or less coherently, consistently, unyieldingly, extensively and consciously. That is why it becomes so difficult to point to any particular *government* or society or group organization, and say (except in extreme cases and even then for only limited periods of time) that it operates entirely as an ideological system. That is why it is difficult to maintain that democracy is an ideological system and monarchy is not or that 'communism' is and 'democracy' is not. Thus we must stop looking for easy examples of ideological systems and ask, instead, *when* it is that a system is operating ideologically. This assumes, then, that any system can do so and, further, that virtually no system does so all the time. Our criterion of an ideology thus becomes more dynamic and less static, and more similar to our disposition to ask, let us say, when it is that someone is behaving badly, rather than how we determine that someone is evil.

So much has been said about communism and socialism as ideologies that there is no need to rehearse these arguments here. It may be more interesting to explore, however briefly, the way in which a society not conceived to be ideological can and does operate in an ideological manner. When a government operates in an ideological manner, it justifies or explains itself by reference to general principles or abstract goals which it assumes that all citizens share and which are supposed to be continuous and overriding. Either the government can operate in this way, or other groups can do so, while attempting to impress their outlook upon the government itself.

Take a situation where a government operates in theory according to a constitution. The latter can be said to embody the ideals, purposes and procedures of the state. Whatever the government does that is right is 'constitutional'; whatever it does that is wrong is 'unconstitutional'. The constitution of the state comes to be viewed as the axiomatic ground of its organization and activities. Thus it cannot be questioned, except in ways which it itself permits, and it must be regarded as being politically sacrosanct. When one becomes a subject of a monarchy, one swears axiomatic allegiance to the monarch. When one becomes a citizen of such a constitutional state as has been described, one swears allegiance to the constitution, declaring thereby one's intention to uphold and support it. The constitution, like the scriptures and political philosophies, is interpreted, but it is interpreted by judges, rather than by priests and intellectuals. Further, these interpreters do not declare, or do not intend to declare, their will but merely that of the directing document whose meaning they do no more than elicit. A constitution can therefore be treated as the framework of an ideological system. 'Life, liberty and the pursuit of happiness' might well be its abstractly intended goal.

Now of course it is true that under most constitutional systems the general assumption is merely that the constitution provides a framework for governmental activity, not a directive clearly stipulating what must be done. And a framework of this kind cannot be ideological in that it is clear from the start that it is not so much intended to tell the government *what* to do, but *how* to do it; not as an axiom that will bear the weight of deductions, but as a mere launching pad, solid and unsinkable, whence any number and variety of group initiatives may be fired. The point is, however, that all depends here upon how the constitution is regarded. And for many segments of the community it will not be regarded as a mere framework, but as in fact stipulating what must be done, however abstractly, and as embracing an entire range of assumptions thought to inhere in the document itself. If the constitution in its relation to governmental decisions is regarded as an axiomatic principle, which fairly precisely determines all governmental initiatives as opposed to a stable pad whence various and even contradictory initiatives may be launched, then one is confronted with an ideological outlook; and if that outlook is adopted by a group, then that group becomes an ideological system; and where the government is that group, then it too becomes an ideological system. But the important point is this: it is only *to the extent* that a government adopts this outlook, and explains and justifies itself in the appropriate manner, that it becomes an ideological system. Thus it becomes reasonable to say of a government that is not ordinarily thought to be an ideological system that it becomes one to the extent that and for as long as it operates like one.*

---

* Were this essay being written anew in 1999, more attention would need to be paid to the operational 'closure' of the global liberal system, one far more rigid and unresponsive to rational debate than may first appear.

Within any group there will be certain tensions, within all states certain conflicts of interest. Typically, under an ideological system what will be posited is a common, if abstract, goal. The attempt to resolve tensions and to settle conflicts – where this attempt is made argumentatively – primarily consists in stating an overriding principle or common purpose whence may be deduced a correct settlement. Typically, under a non-ideological system, no such attempt is made. But this leaves open several possibilities, and this implies that, in fact, there is no 'typical' non-ideological method of resolving basic social tensions or conflicts of interest. Competing groups may simply attempt to get as much as they can before others stop them. Others may operate on a *quid pro quo* basis in the sense of making a concession for every concession made. Others may frankly assume that there is no common purpose or principle and that the only way to advance or protect one's interests is by forcibly removing or restraining those who happen to get in the way. And others still may simply have no idea whatever as to what common principles they should adopt, or whether it is possible meaningfully to adopt any at all.

Now a constitutional system begins to operate as an ideological system when it is no longer treated as a mere changeable framework, but as an object of belief and devotion. The constitution, formally the framework of action, becomes instead the distilled, guiding principle of action. It does not matter that a mere constitution cannot effectively guide a state over the shifting sands of foreign and domestic policy. It is only necessary to recognize that the actual conduct of a government can always be 'explained' or rationalized or commended by reference to what is supposed to be the spirit of the constitution or the intentions of those who initially devised it. The ideologist who wishes to convert a constitutional into an ideological system typically commences by insisting that all or certain classes of citizens formally swear allegiance to the flag or to the country or to the document which broadly stipulates how that country's government operates.

One instance of this sort of activity comes from New York State in the form of an act called the Feinberg Law. The purpose of this law was, according to its supporters, to guard against the subversion of the state constitution. This the law attempted to do by making it mandatory that all teachers and lecturers in the schools and universities of the state sign a loyalty oath. One of the interesting aspects of this sort of approach is the importance that is attributed to a generalized statement of intent and the sorts of consequences that can be deduced from it. Every state, of course, recognizes treason as a crime, and disloyalty towards the state, when translated into legal terms, would basically mean treason. New York State, however, at the time the Feinberg Law was passed, was not bereft of a law of treason. Thus the Feinberg Law did not add anything, in this respect, which was not already there. This reinforces the sense of redundancy attaching to the law. However varied the reasons may in fact have been for passing it, one of them, certainly, was to protect the community's 'right of self-preservation', as one US Supreme Court Justice put it. How was the community to protect itself? Not simply by punishing those who, in law, betrayed it, but by insisting upon a declaration by a certain class of community members that in effect they would never betray it. This approach is typical of the ideological style and in this we have one instance of it as it emerged within a particular constitutional system. There is a conflation of moral duty with legal duty. There is an initial insistence upon the word, rather than the deed. There is involved an excessive kind of moral abstractness without reference to time, place or propriety.

Ideological systems can be particularly pernicious (especially in an authoritarian tradition) because of their moral abstractness, which does not in fact permit the kind of precision in application that is expressly intended to be imposed by such systems. In January 1967 the US Supreme Court held the Feinberg Law to be 'unconstitutional' (which is what the law aimed to prevent everyone else from being) precisely because of its rigidity of form on the one hand, and vagueness of content on the other. For anyone who swore an oath of loyalty and then violated that oath would quite clearly become vulnerable to prosecution, thus the formal rigidity of the law. But at the same time, since the law did not adequately stipulate what loyalty consisted in, this automatically became subject to endlessly varying interpretations, thus the law's vagueness of content (and therefore the illimitable range of its applicability). Consequently, one could violate one's oath of loyalty by doing anything which one's superiors might consider disloyal, as perhaps by undressing publicly or (the actual example presented to the Supreme Court) by displaying publicly a copy of the *Communist Manifesto*.

But in the same way that an ideological system can be legally pernicious, so it can be logically vacuous. The latter, in fact, is the ground of the former; but it is also its trapdoor and escape hatch. For if an ideology can be manipulated by those in power so as to lead to such conclusions as they desire, it can also be amended by those who are out of power to lead another way. If a government claims a commitment to liberty, and enters upon foreign wars to extend it and internal censorship to protect it, there will always be those to argue that liberty cannot be imposed and that censorship defeats and routs it. If a government claims a commitment to socialism, and enters upon foreign wars to extend it and internal censorship to protect it, there will similarly be those to argue that socialism cannot be imposed and that censorship stifles and destroys it. Even a government which invokes the superiority of one race as a justification for trampling others underfoot will be met with the objection that the genius of the race was not to destroy, but to build, not to dispossess the weak, but to make them secure. Any ideological system is subject to such manoeuvring, for and against, since there is always an unintended gap between the general goal, principle or belief which it stipulates and the variety of specific causes the ideology can be made to serve.

As we have seen, a great deal of argument can take place within an ideological system. To shut off such argument these systems can become closed; but they may also be open; they can, in short, vary in the degree of tolerance or authoritarianism that they permit or require. But despite the degree of debate that can be permitted within an ideology, one essential feature of such systems is a demand for some form of belief. In much the same way that geometry demands axioms, an ideology demands a belief. The political application of a coherent system of ideas to a group is really nothing more than the elaboration of a commitment – a commitment of that group to the particular system of ideas. One is 'committed' to an idea, basically, when one cannot demonstrate its validity, or simply when one is inclined to accept it without such demonstration. Within a deductive system of argument, of course, one always reaches some fundamental position which cannot be demonstrated. The fundamental position, the axiom, must then simply be accepted. But usually it is accepted simply because it is believed to be 'obvious' or 'self-evident'. In short it is believed to be true, but it is not believed that its truth can be demonstrated. In this sort of case one must treat the fundamental position as an object of faith, of belief, or one must circularly attempt to demonstrate its truth by reference to all the other propositions which it has already presupposed.

An ideology, therefore, when 'applied' to a group, formally commits them to it in the form of a belief (its validity could not be *logically* demonstrated). The ideological system *as a whole* is not an object of belief. (If it were, there could be no argument within it.) But certain of its quintessential elements are those such as liberty, equality, self-realization, majority rule or the people's will, and so on. Any one of these can be advanced as a fundamental principle, out of which the logic of the system may be held to unfold, imposing a 'necessary' connection between the general principle(s) and the most important of a government's (or a group's leaders') particular decisions.

The area of commitment demanded by an ideology locates the

fundamental belief(s) required of its adherents. Beliefs, of course, are of different sorts and involve commitment to different perspectives and goals. Different ideologies will invoke different fundamental beliefs. But (as previously indicated) not all systems of government are ideological and, therefore, not all systems of government operate by reference to the holding of some fundamental, explanatory, justifying and directing belief. Some governments operate by reference to openly and recognizably contradictory 'beliefs', which may be invoked at will in any manner found suitable at the time. This sort of procedure will only be called ideological to the extent that the different 'beliefs' involved are treated as fundamental and exclusive when invoked. But it is not necessary that they be so treated, since it is quite possible to regard them not as guides, but as brisk summations of what in the circumstances it was thought the government might best do.

If, for example, a government explains and justifies itself by reference to the principle 'unity is strength', it may not really mean this universally, as a principle whence it deduces the need to merge its own administration with that of another state. It might simultaneously and quite consistently demand, and posit as its goal, 'Freedom now!', implying the end of its administrative absorption into another polity (as under colonial rule, for example). If it were merely positing in the present the principle of unity, whereas in the past it had supported the principle (in effect) of disunity, then it would clearly be operating contradictorily. But what is more probable is that the general 'belief', 'principle' or 'universal aim' is not so much that as a formula which does no more than briefly summarize the highly particular reasons for taking a certain decision at a given time. So to repeat: governments often operate by reference to openly contradictory 'beliefs' – but this is not necessarily to operate ideologically, since the 'belief' may not really be regarded as such by anyone, but merely as an essay in instant communication (a summarization of a much more involved and detailed argument whose conclusion was not apparent at the outset). In short, what appear to be contradictory 'beliefs' may be nothing more than slogans and maxims to be invoked at will. Such an approach is not ideological.

Not all systems of government are ideological, and thus not all societies are tied together by reference to a common belief system. An imperial polity, for example, is not so much tied together by belief as it is by conquest or force. (To obey a government because one fears it is not the same as obeying it because one shares its outlook and aims.) Under such circumstances rule does not tend to be legitimated by reference to values held in common between conquered and conqueror, but (insofar as they are held at all) by reference to values or beliefs restricted to the conqueror. In the same way that one group may conquer another without a discernible belief system operating commonly between them (and thus legitimating for both the act of conquest), so is it possible to make of several units (e.g. conqueror and conquered) one group (certainly administratively) without any common belief system uniting them. Insofar as a system of government can be non-ideological, this must mean that a society can be tied together without reference to any common belief system.

A non-ideological system must either be characterized by the total absence of belief systems or by the presence of more or less equal and competing belief systems. The presence in societies of competing belief systems is a historical commonplace; the absence from societies of all belief systems seems merely conjectural, nothing more than a logical and futuristic possibility. (But by 'belief system' is not intended any particular belief about any particular matter, but about a belief system in the sense of an 'ideological system', or a general and directive system of ideas that embraces some general conception both of what is and what ought to be as applied either to a sovereign or sub-sovereign group. Such a system can be conceived to flow from one or a limited set of principles or axioms, which then become objects of belief.) 'The absence from societies of all *belief systems*' is not intended to imply 'the absence of all *beliefs*'. For one may believe that one's redeemer liveth, or that one could have defeated Botvinik had one really tried, without in any way being able to prove either proposition, while divorcing both entirely from any political purpose, goal or consideration. What is intended is a *political* belief system (naturally a religion is capable of supplying this) or, in other words, the ideological direction and organization of a social group, whether the latter be sovereign or voluntary.

A group, however, that has many belief systems is in the same position as one that has no belief system from the perspective of its highest or sovereign point of organization. It follows as a matter of course that a society without a common belief system, which is so in the sense that it either has *none* at all or *diverse* belief systems, cannot be directed by reference to a single ideology. Where there is no consciousness of, nor an ability to refer to, a single belief system, no one can pretend to deduce (at least the governing or directing agency cannot deduce) what ought to be done from some prior and exclusive principle which is regarded as transcending all others. In these circumstances, of course, a government might make much ado about 'the common good'. If it approached such a good as a fundamental reality impervious to all considerations of fact, then 'the common good' would have been transformed into an *a priori* principle, an article of faith, and therefore into the basis of an ideological system. The position would be otherwise if it merely accepted that there *might* be a common good, which it could seek to elicit as a basis of general agreement. The hypothetical society which is entirely free of all ideological groups and movements must, so long as it remains in this state, equally remain free of all prospect of the government reverting to or assuming an ideological style. The society which contains diverse ideological groups and movements, however, can always entertain the prospect of its governing agency assimilating such a style (either by imitating an inferior group or by an inferior ideological group becoming the government).

A fundamental political belief, forming the spearhead of an ideological system, is not the same as a political programme. It is possible for a government to have no ideology, and yet to have a programme. The latter may be more or less rigorously pursued, realistic, realizable or consistent. But it need not imply commitment to any specific metaphysics nor need it be abstract. It is possible to test the extent to which a concrete programme has been implemented, and not by reference to an exclusive and fundamental principle. *The* programme will change, since the degree of its realization eliminates *pro tanto* as a goal its projections, and *the* programme, in historical retrospect, can always be regarded as *a* programme, which was only relevant to a particular time and place.

An ideology is often viewed as repugnant to a political programme. But insofar as an ideology stipulates as a part of its meaning the relating of a system of ideas to a programme of political action, some form of programme is always subjoined to an ideology. The point about this subjunction, however, is that it is always treated as dependent, not otherwise, because flowing somehow logically from initial premises. It is in this sense that an ideology and a programme can be viewed as mutually repugnant, in the situation where either is regarded as prior, or where both are regarded as independent. A political ideology turns a political programme into the consequence of a premise. A political programme turns a political ideology into either an 'abbreviation' of an experience or into a rationalization of a commitment. It is in this way that the two become mutually repugnant, although they may share a very similar defect, labelled in an ideology 'doctrinairism' (impracticality and rationalization) and in a programme 'dogmatism' (rigidity or inflexibility). All the same, whereas an ideology is intrinsically doctrinaire, a programme is not necessarily dogmatic.

Dogmatism tends to assume the form of mere stupidity. A doctrinaire stance, by contrast, is infinitely more subtle and intellectual.

Dogmatism posits belief, but basically an unreasoning belief. The doctrinaire position posits belief, but of the type conceded to the initial phases of a mathematical proof. But we are here concerned with political ideologies, not with political programmes. Within an ideological system, what is *politically* required of members is commitment to the stipulated if abstract goals of the group. Similarly, what is *logically* required is belief in the basic premise or premises of the ideology (or the general system of ideas). Belief in these premises will not only afford to the government (or directing agency of a group) the means whereby, and the framework within which, it explains, justifies and generally pursues its activities. It will also serve as a criterion by which is at least partially determined the status of members, and possibly even whether they are regarded as members at all.

We have seen that, where the organization of a group is translated into an ideological system, there is posited and presupposed some fundamental agreement upon an abstract goal, which takes the political form of commitment and the logical form of belief. It is clear that the presence or absence of this belief can be viewed as the distinguishing characteristic of a group member. And where someone can be recognized as a member of a group by virtue of their belief, so can they in fact become a member by accepting the condition that they believe. Not all groups or systems of government accept or reject potential members by reference to belief, however. Nor do all ideological systems do so *exclusively* on this basis. Members (whether of an ideological or non-ideological system) might be rejected, accepted and promoted by reference to other criteria, such as consanguinity (as in tribalism and racialism), accomplishment (as in a meritocracy) and location (as, theoretically, in most nationalisms), not merely by reference to belief (as often in Christianity, Islam and communism).

The more an ideological system universalizes its principles, and permits belief in them alone to stand as an earnest of one's adherence, the more pristine it becomes. For this reason, racialism does not provide an entirely satisfactory example of an ideology. Apart from the fact that there is no very coherent system upon which it can depend (as some ideologies do upon figures like St Augustine and Marx), racialism is accompanied by a limiting condition. Adherents of a racial ideology must not only meet the condition of believing in the superiority of a certain group, they must also be biologically affiliated to it. Adherents of a nationalist ideology must not only believe in the superior virtue, etc., of a national group, but they must also be located within it, either by birth or residence. It is for this reason that racialism and nationalism are not as good examples as can be offered of ideologies; it is difficult to be a racialist or a nationalist without somehow belonging to the race or nation one vaunts. For this reason the possibility of adherence to these types of ideology is more complicated than in other cases (such as communism, socialism and liberalism), for what is required is not merely commitment to some abstract goal and the acceptance of some fundamental belief, but the possession, too, of some characteristic feature which neither belief nor disbelief – of whatever kind – will affect. Such additional criteria of community inclusion lessen the force of an ideology. They deprive it of a purely logical character, and focus as much attention upon an individual's condition (race, location and function) as upon belief.

Elaborate ideologies of a racialist or nationalist kind are little more than half-way houses between tribalism and true ideology. For this reason I believe it mistaken to lump communism and fascism together indiscriminately, as most recent writers are inclined to do. Too much attention has been directed to the brutality of which both systems are extraordinarily capable: of brutality all systems are capable. What it is important to draw attention to here is the ideological difference, or the degree thereof: communism is far more *ideo*-logical than nationalism or racialism. It will not do merely to argue that communism's primary concern is class, while racialism's is with race (although this is true). For within a communist system it is possible for an adherent to shed class identity; indeed, one of the basic goals posited is the shedding of all class identities. But within a racialist system it is impossible for just anyone to become assimilated to the group in this way; without the necessary genetic qualifications his beliefs will count for little; and thus the logic of this system, as a device designed to assimilate membership by reference only to a fundamental belief or principle, is inhibited. It will not do to conflate the ideological character of communism with that of racialism; *qua* ideology, the latter is more primitive and less developed than the former. Communism is a much purer example of ideology.

In the application of a system of ideas to a group, where the system is intended to convince by the strength of its consistency, and to secure as substantial support for government policy as is possible, and in this sense to unite a group in as complete a fashion as can be, there can be no doubt that one whom the system designates as an enemy must be treated as essentially assimilable in order to add to the strength of the system. The ideological system which does not do this automatically weakens itself, since, although it is designed to convince, it becomes intrinsically restricted to the possibility of only convincing some. An ideology is designed to convince, but if it posits conditions for affiliation which transcend conviction itself, it automatically limits itself to a particular audience. Ideology in its pristine form does not do this. Its appeal transcends all particularities. Thus it invites affiliation on the basis of belief alone. And this must mean that whoever opposes it will be regarded as a potential convert (not merely as an enduring enemy). Such is the character of its logic and, so conceived, the potential breadth of its appeal becomes universal. The logic of the idea expands outward without obstruction. Where the enemies of the system cannot be absorbed, then the logic of the system cannot embrace them. Where the logic of the system cannot embrace them, its political energy *qua* ideology is exhausted. It would be foolish to conclude from what has been said, however, that socialist governments, for example, are more powerful than Nazi or fascist governments. All that is intended is that their *logic* is more powerful, because the range of their potential application is greater.

There are religious ideologies and secular ideologies, totalitarian ideologies and piecemeal ideologies, authoritarian, materialistic and aesthetic ideologies, ideologies that appeal to blood, ideologies that appeal to class, ideologies that appeal to territoriality and ideologies – the most pristine of all – that appeal exclusively to belief. Ideologies are not just systems of government and they are not merely sets of ideas. An ideological system may exist for a moment, it may exist for years. When it exists, it exists in the form of a particular relation between a coherent system of ideas and a system of government (or of any sort of organized group); it exists as a coherent set of ideas, both normative and factual, which gives shape, or which is assumed to and is presented as giving shape, to the activities of a government. It is not merely a programme set in motion; for this may not be, and may not be presented as being, a deduction from a principle. It is not merely a principle, since a principle need not, while an ideology must, yield a programme of action. It requires of those who embrace it not just a belief, but a political belief, and not just any kind of political belief, but one that is fundamental. Since ideologies do not exist in books, no writer may be called an ideologist who may not also reject this label. Marx is, and Marx is not. Hegel is, and Hegel is not. Aquinas is, and he, too, is not. It will depend on how they are interpreted and the uses to which they are put. Perhaps every writer who is comprehensive enough, and who is actually read, could both accept and discard this tag.

Hobbes and Hegel, for example, usually are not utilized, and therefore are not understood, ideologically. It is often said of course that every government has an ideology and that every political philosopher is an ideologist. (Such assertions are usually intended to convey nothing more than that (1) every government has a general outlook or policy and (2) that no political philosopher altogether escapes the activity of recommending.) But this is not in fact so. The works of every political philosopher are not adopted by sovereign or sub-sovereign groups to explain and direct their activities. Political philosophers are ideologized only rarely – as in the case of Marx or (possibly) Aquinas. Also, not every ideology has a political philosopher (as with racialism), although this lack may tend to weaken the coherence of the ideology. And further, not every group has an ideology (whether elaborated by a single political philosopher or not), since many groups (whether sovereign or not) have very limited objectives (like most families and, indeed, most states). Also, an abstract objective (like justice) is not necessarily associated with any coherent world view at all.

Following on this discussion of ideology, the following is offered as a general definition:

> a coherent system of ideas of whatever kind, involving some understanding of man and the world, and which attempts to relate this understanding to a programme of political action, so that the understanding does not remain abstract but is (or is intended to be) applied, and is not (or is not intended to be) simply applied to an individual but to a group, and is so applied as to lead towards the achievement of an exclusive goal, but a goal formulated in a very general way.

Ideology, if it is a discernible fact, must have a discernible history. It will not merely be a history of ideas, nor will it be a mere history of institutions. (Let us not here debate the question whether institutions are reducible to ideas.) It will be a history of ideas in a particular relation to organized, institutional activities. The history need not be 'continuous'; there may be gaps. It need not be inevitable; there is much room for accident. The history provided in the following section will be potted, yet smooth enough, it is hoped, to convey the reader to the particular conceptual destination the writer intends. History is necessary to lengthen perspective, and that is the aim of the next section. Christianity may be taken as the first and most pristine form of ideology to emerge in the West. It is very much aware of itself as a dramatically new beginning. It is in fact obvious that our own methods of dating reflect the importance which we ourselves attribute to it as a new beginning. We may accept as appropriate the line of demarcation which it itself describes between past and present. Of course all such lines involve a geometry of myth. With this in mind, one may be allowed to ape the Christian division, very much due to the attraction of its neatness, thereby separating the ideological from the pre-ideological at the year zero.

3. Ideology: a history

There is neither Greek, nor Jew, circumcision, nor incircumcision, Barbarian, or Scythian, bond, or free, but Christ is all, and in all.

Acts x. 34

The year zero effectively demarcates because, as the name suggests, it marks the absence of something. This something is almost literally a 'logical' formula for the recognition, and therefore the inclusion and exclusion, of community members. Among the early Greeks and Romans the basic principle of inclusion was kinship. The emergence of Epicureanism and Stoicism resulted in the diminished importance of ties of kin, partly due to their displacement by the new concept of Humanity, of the brotherhood of all men.

Kinship can serve as the basis of an ideology, but only with difficulty, its criterion of recognition and acceptance is not sufficiently logical. It is true that a kinship system can always be hypostatized. Adoption is an example of this process. Where an individual does not meet certain basic biological demands for assimilation and internal status, the system's demands can always be disregarded in their strict, literal sense and stretched (indeed, abstracted) so as to allow one who is not in fact a son or whatever to be designated 'son', etc. Thus, 'son', 'father', 'mother' and other such terms can acquire a legal, rather than a biological, sense. A *complete* change of front along these lines, however, is a difficult feat to achieve. But where it is achieved, the kinship system has really become ideological. The identity of the kin has been transferred from a biological to a principled basis.*

One's brother may become such because he is *recognized* as a brother. There need be no particular reason for this recognition. It may simply be that he works well or is helpful or likeable or has no family of his own. To treat a stranger like a brother means no more than to treat him well, but within a system where it tends to be assumed that the necessary qualification for receiving such treatment is actual brotherhood, or kinship; so that when a person is shown friendship, this will not merely be described as friendliness, but as 'brotherly' love, or something of the sort. This idea of kinship as a uniting factor can be pushed so far that prospective friends may even feel that no genuine

---

*Over the 1970s especially, I taught myself a great deal about kinship systems, or at least enough to see that this opposition is too rigid. If kinship systems are established *with reference* to biology, they are never in *themselves* biological. Thus kinship systems may be viewed as those types of ideological construct most appropriate to small-scale, intra-breeding, pre-industrial subsistence or semi-subsistence societies. (See King, *Book of Identities*, forthcoming.)

fellowship and loyalty exists between them unless their wrists have been slashed and their blood has actually mingled. But where one reaches the stage that a 'brother' can become such by recognition, it is possible to move on to the point of completely locating brotherhood as a function of a shared principle, belief or faith, rather than as a function of a biological relationship. This movement is not inevitable; we need only remark that it has frequently occurred. Where this transpires, one's kinsmen become, perhaps, all good men, or all honest men, or all moderate men, or all freedom-loving peoples everywhere. When the transformation is as complete as this, it is clear that the kinship system remains no longer in any way intact. It has tended to become purely ideological. The focus of identity is no longer a biological relationship, but either the attainment of a general belief, or some other qualification. The sharing of the belief or quality can relate one to others, and at the same time assume the form of a goal to be attained. The goal is of a kind, however, that cannot be precisely defined, which must mean also that it can never be exactly or definitely reached.

Christianity incorporated the concept of universal brotherhood, and in fact employed it as a basis for conversion irrespective of condition, kin or location. This transition, for simplicity's sake, can be dated from the death of Aristotle (322 BC) to the conversion of Constantine (AD 312). This places an arbitrary line between the Antiquity of Kinship and the Modernity of Belief at the Year Zero. This date theoretically coincides with the birth of Christ as well as being intermediate between the eclipse of official paganism and the official sanctioning of Christian thought.

Ideological politics, in short, noticeably began with Christianity. The latter offered a mythological vision of the past, of the advent of the future and of a community of believers united in their acceptance of this vision, which was essentially untestable and irrefutable. Theoretically, condition, kin and location were irrelevant. But belief was not. Wealth, intelligence and skill were important, but secondary. What was immediately essential was not being a good *person*, but a good *Christian*, i.e. one who thoroughly and unquestioningly accepted the historical and futuristic vision of the truth as enshrined in Christian doctrine.

Of course it will be remarked that Christians are and were as much concerned with practising and living up to their beliefs as with accepting them. But this is only partly true. Christians were not equally concerned with these matters at the same time and in the same way. What was always asserted was the absolute necessity of belief for salvation. The qualification that only *some* believers would be saved followed after. The attainment of salvation depended, then, upon the individual meeting several conditions. But all of these were in principle possible for anyone, and the first of these was belief in Christ. If only practice were necessary, then it would become possible to lead a completely satisfactory life without declaring any faith at all. But in the same way that Christians have commonly assumed that a world without God must be immoral, so have they commonly assumed that an individual devoid of belief in God must be sinful. The initial belief is the foundation stone of (what is explicitly designated) The Faith, or The True Faith.[1]

It is true that many Christians have been greatly and almost exclusively concerned with practice. But it is equally true that many have tended seriously and immediately to insist upon faith alone. When this happens, the formal pronouncement of ideological allegiance may be made within a context where competing allegiances are possible, and possibly less dangerous. The formal pronouncement becomes a first and essential step; for the adherent, it may possibly be an act of bravery. Merely to *declare* (quite apart from considerations of practice) that one is a Christian (in Rome) or a Jew (in medieval Christendom) or a capitalist (in the former USSR or China) or a communist (in the United States) could be positively dangerous. This was why the famous disciple, after all, denied his lord, despite the crowing cock and the scornful judgement of succeeding generations. At such a stage, the basic demand is not that one practise one's preaching, but that one declare one's faith.

'I will tell them how to show their true faith: let them act according to their words.' So wrote Seneca. But this protest is more appropriate to a settled order. The declaration of belief, where it creates no dangers, and generates no consequences, becomes trivial. One form of this gulf between belief and practice is encompassed by the expression 'hypocrisy'. The term describes it and condemns it. But the condemnation tends to run in two directions: towards the notion that one should cease to camouflage one's actual behaviour, and towards the other notion that practice should be amended in the direction of the ideal. The trouble with this condemnation of hypocrisy, where intended to imply that one should ape the ideal, is that there may be no concrete or logical or otherwise ascertainable path leading thereto. The ideal (which is the principle or belief or faith when conceived as a goal) may simply be vacuous or inapplicable. From it may be adduced completely contrary activities, so serving to indicate its bankruptcy. Not only may ideals be too vague to lead logically to any concrete activity, but, even where they do, it may be wrong to follow them there. The gulf between belief and practice tends to become inevitable where the former reaches its apogee of abstractness and universality. When this happens, criticism which intends practical reform becomes logically pointless. The ideal itself can provide no guide. And, indeed, the continued acceptance of a vacuous, inapplicable or irrelevant belief may make the hypocrisy inevitable.

Our immediate concern, however, as well as being a logically prior concern, is not with the hypocrisy predicament, as sketched in the preceding paragraph, but with the belief predicament, where one feels forced or inclined to choose between rival ideologies. The representatives of an established order, whether ideological or non-ideological, may suppose that they can protect that order either by inducing individuals to abjure their beliefs or to accede to new ones. Early Christianity, as a non-sovereign ideology, was threatened and tested in this way; later, as an official or state ideology, it similarly threatened and tested others. What all of this was designed to produce was the voicing of fundamental principles and pieties, together with a display of icons and meditative gestures.

The fundamental belief essential to adherence to Christianity related of course to the divinity of Christ: 'but Christ is all, and in all'. This belief can be viewed as involving little more than absolute loyalty to a particular individual, combined with an inclination to accept as true whatever pronouncements he or she might make. In this there is nothing ideological. But as Christianity evolves, Christ is stripped of such irrelevant appurtenances as his whims, tastes, fantasies and body. He reaches a level of hypostasis where he no longer exists as a man at all but only as his 'essential' self, which is a principle. Thus, belief in Christ is translated from loyalty to an individual to loyalty to a set of principles, such as love, non-violence, etc., which have been fixed within a doctrinal mould. To declare a belief in Christ then would not merely involve an acceptance of these principles individually, but their acceptance within a particular, interrelated pattern, and capped by a special metaphysic and science, as regards, for example, the notion that the universe is controlled by a godhead, and that the latter is benevolent, and that he devised the world in a certain way and according to a particular time-schedule.

A community united in fundamental acceptance of such a system of ideas could be called Christian, and its doctrine Christianity or Christism or even Christianism (like Buddhism from Buddha and Calvinism from Calvin and Lutheranism from Luther and Marxism from Marx). This doctrine might acquire sufficient logical coherence, basic simplicity, explanatory sweep and political relevance to qualify as an ideology. And it might be classified as a *religious* ideology, not because it is non-political but because of its particular metaphysic which posits the existence of a controlling godhead, etc.

A community of believers implies the existence of non-believers. Some non-believers may not have been blessed with the opportunity of learning, but others may have first embraced and then rejected the true faith. In the first category would fit, for the Roman Church, such groups as Muslims, heathens and Jews. Into the second would fit heretics and apostates. For these, pardon was impossible since they, knowing the truth, evilly refused the grace of inclusion which the acceptance of this truth would entail. It was the opinion of so wise and mild a Catholic as Aquinas that such persons should not only be excommunicated but executed as well.

This same writer, in *De Regimine Judaeorum*, accepted that the Jews were to be excluded from ordinary concourse with Christians because of their sin, which, of course, was unalterably connected with their disbelief. Aquinas, addressing himself to the Duchess of Brabant, wrote:

> whether it is correct that all Jews in your realm should be obliged to wear some special sign to distinguish them from Christians. To this the answer is easy and in conformity with the decision given by the General Council. Jews of both sexes and in all Christian lands should on all occasions be distinguished from other people by some particular dress.

Christianity opposed particularism in every regard except that of belief. This was the basis of its universalism, its proselytizing zeal, its optimism, and its well-intentioned terrorism.

The emergence of the modern nation-state set the stage for a transition away from Christianity as the dominant ideology. Basic to this secular development was the late medieval rediscovery of Aristotle, which made possible the revival of the classical conception of the state. The Aristotelian ideal of the *polis* entailed an autonomous and autarchic state based on kin. This formula was consonant with the political and economic developments of the late Middle Ages, involving the overthrow of verbal adherence to the mystical *Imperium Mundi*, the diminution or rejection of the belief in *unus populus christianus* and the displacement of the power of the *corpus mysticum Ecclesiae*.

The modern nation-state disrupted the medieval synthesis. We need not, however, be concerned to refute the contention that this much vaunted synthesis was no more than a myth. We know that the Holy Roman Empire was neither holy, nor Roman, nor an empire. But it must be said that a myth, for all that, is not necessarily devoid of power. Ideologies as a whole are largely little more than myth. When,

therefore, we speak of a medieval synthesis, we are not to be understood to speak of an actual unity, whether economic, legal or political.
The medieval synthesis referred to here is basically ideological,
nothing more. What this means is that the literate European of the
Middle Ages probably thought himself to be a member of a universal
body of Christian people, that this body was subject to the political
control of the Holy Roman Emperor, that the Emperor was a member
of the holy body of the church, and that this entire structure was
spiritually supervised by the incumbent of the Holy See. Explanation
and justification of political acts would presuppose the existence of
God, and would take the form of a proof that what was done flowed
from or was permitted by His will. Disputes between emperor and
pope, and later between monarchs and popes, would primarily be
directed towards demonstrating that they really had received their
authority from God, and thus that their political acts, whether supervisory over or independent of the other power, were legitimate.
Whether or not God actually existed would not even matter. It was
assumed, of course, that He did. But this was posited as a matter of
faith, and need not have been argued within the system at all (although
occasionally it was), since the real argument related to the train of
deductions that could be made to follow from this initial axiom. So
many of the extraordinary political arguments advanced by writers
like John of Salisbury and Dante were only intended to prove who it
was that God intended should exercise authority.

No ideological synthesis is ever complete – which is to say, lacking
in a certain degree of incoherence. This is true of the medieval synthesis. When we speak of the 'breakdown' of such a synthesis, we only
refer to such a convincing demonstration of an area of incoherence
that it becomes impossible to continue to regard the given ideological
framework as viable; the consequence being that it is eventually
deserted. The emergence of the nation-state, however, is not coinci-
dent with the desertion of Christian ideology. The nation-state, after
all, was not at first inclined to justify itself outside a Christian framework, but merely to claim, within that framework and against the
pretensions of the Papacy, a divine right of rule by kings, independent of papal interference. But the nation-state, in winning its argument for independence from papal control, contributed at the same
time to the trivialization and dismissal of the ideological structure
within which it sought its justification. How could one take seriously
an argument from divine right, when it could be made to demonstrate,
equally convincingly, the justice of papal supervisory authority, and
the justice of monarchical independence from such supervision? One
could not obey both Henry VIII and the Pope. One could not be both

Protestant and Catholic. And yet it was necessary to choose. Was this choice not, perhaps, somewhat arbitrary, when set against the background of a belief in Christ and God, which was shared by both Catholic and Protestant? The reply of a Hobbes is yes. The percipience of such an observer leads him to regard Christian belief, and arguments leading from this, as basically trivial, insofar as they relate to the determination of the locus of legitimate authority. This is not to say that he attacks the belief, but that he begins to ignore it. But of course, Machiavelli had already ignored it and this would define the almost inevitable trend of the future. The emergence of the modern nation-state particularized Christian ideology. It did not displace it. But this particularization constituted an essential step towards its elimination since it trivialized the entire ideological framework of Christian belief.

There is no intrinsic incompatibility between a national and a religious ideology. National ideologies are often religious. Typically, under a religious ideology, it is assumed *either* that enemy states have not the same god, and that the weakness (or strength) of these states is a function of the weakness (or strength) of their god(s), *or* that you share a common god, and that the opposition (as in war) of the other state to one's own (or vice versa) is a function of error, a miscalculation regarding the intentions of the divine will. In the first case there is assumed a plurality of divine wills; in the second, that there is only one such will. Where it is assumed that there is only one divine will, this becomes a common will, and logically legitimates purely rational disputes between nations relating to the determinations of this will, particularly in respect of the rights and wrongs of conflicting national causes. But, as already suggested, where everyone invokes the same god to justify wildly divergent aims and policies, it may eventually happen that sophisticated persons will no longer find the basic axioms, principles or beliefs particularly useful in explaining or justifying the propriety of their actions especially to opponents who invoke the same initial beliefs. Thus, consciously or unconsciously, they may tend to discard them (as a basis of political argument). They might begin instead, for example, from the principle of natural right, rather than from that of divine will. Or they might begin from the axiomatic assumption that they must promote the specific interests and common good (materially defined) of the nation. But when that happens the ideological framework begins to shift radically.

As new types of fundamental social axioms and modes of argument attain the ascendancy, the reigning Christian ideology (*qua* ideology, not outlook) is either displaced or replaced (an ideology can be displaced without being replaced). In early and medieval

Christianity, it is not so much total disbelief that is feared, but a disbelief in Christianity assuming the form of a belief in something else (such as paganism, Manichaeism, Arianism, Pelagianism, Judaism, Islam and so on). But from about the sixteenth century, the danger no longer stemmed merely from the possible adherence to rival beliefs, but equally from the serious possibility of an atheistic denial of belief altogether. It is often precisely at that point in time where an ideology is least tenable, i.e. in greatest danger of eclipse, that the most strenuous efforts, involving considerable logical acumen, may be expended to save it. We witness such an effort in *le pari de* Pascal (1623–62), where the brilliant and devout mathematician is even prepared to resort to an argument from probability in order to place faith on a sound footing.[2] The interesting aspect of such an attempt is the fact that it indicates a new awareness of the intrinsic weaknesses of Christian ideology. It is precisely because important writers simply began to ignore a fundamental tenet of Christianity (the existence of God) that such exemplary attempts were made to reaffirm its central position, but without success. Christianity as a religion was not dead. But Christianity as an official ideology was dying. The demise of the ideology would go hand in hand with the rise of Protestantism, the tendency to regard religion as a private indulgence, the increase in tolerance and individualism and the resistance to ideological formulae in political argument (as, notably, in Machiavelli, Hobbes and Locke).

Protestantism and the Catholic Counter-Reformation represent a sort of ideological interregnum. Either no dominant ideology exists, or it has assumed no precise and recognizable form. Luther opposed the Pope, and supported the power of the local princes. Machiavelli opposed the Papacy and supported the vision of a unified Italy. The nationalistic slogan 'My country right or wrong' would suit neither of them. There is less of an overall ideological consensus. The safe shores of belief are in sight, but they are rival beliefs, and so actors set themselves a certain direction without collectively attaining the security of land. The nation-state, subsequently and increasingly, becomes the important focal point of decision-making. But although the framework within which states explain and justify their activities loses much of its former coherence, what remains a commonplace right up to the eighteenth century is the assumption that a universal moral principle of right political conduct is possible.

Despite Hume and Montesquieu and the modifications allowed by Kant, this view was even to persist into the nineteenth century. The existence or continuation of a belief in universal moral principles is essential to the existence or continuation of ideologies. In a theological age such principles may be declared to flow, more or less self-evidently, from the supposed nature or will of God. In a more secular age, they may be said to stem more or less directly from Nature itself – so that we increasingly confront the concept of natural, rather than divine, law. In a more technological age, discussion of what we ought to do may simply be regarded as a science. The nineteenth century produced no end of treatises on 'moral science', much ethico-political writing being influenced of course by Social Darwinism. (Later, one was even to hear of *Christian* Science). Of course, scepticism about the validity of universal moral principles goes as far back as Thrasymachus. But where such scepticism exists, ideologies are not likely to do so as well.

Probably the most important ideological force to succeed political Christianity was nationalism. *Nationality* is not the same as this. Nationality is a fact, a condition. Nationalism is a belief, a guide. One is a national by birth, by law. One is a nationalist by conviction or faith. The growth of nationality as an identity is intimately associated with the growth of the nation-state as an entity. Nationality generally involves an overlapping of kinship and territorial ties. Nationalism evolves when this identity becomes an exclusive object of pride. As such, it binds together all classes, it provides a common outlook, it establishes an object of veneration; and this incorporates the interests of the state, projected as a goal, to which commitment is invited, unquestioning, like a faith.

It takes a considerable time for nationalism to emerge as a full-blown ideology. Elie Kedourie (1961), perhaps too precisely, describes it as 'a doctrine invented in Europe at the beginning of the nineteenth century' (p. 9). Its many forms project various elements, such as racial identity, territorial identity, historical destiny and so on. We have already noted, however, the way in which a political system becomes decreasingly ideological in the degree that it projects an increasing number of discrete elements, seen either as axioms or as objects of faith, since this increases the difficulty of reasoning from a single abstract premise to a particular practical decision. In this respect, nationalism is not as purely ideological as, say, Christianity (conceived in a theocratic mould and not merely as a 'private' faith) or socialism or communism. Even in its purest forms nationalism projects more discrete items of belief than the latter; and it places extraneous limitations upon the assimilation of membership, and therefore upon the doctrine's persuasiveness, which the other doctrines do not. This is one reason why nationalism is usually more popular than Christian theocracy or socialism or communism: all the latter are considerably more rigorous, intellectually, than the former.

Nationalism, however, was from the start, unlike Christianity, in some degree regarded as an expedient, as a means of promoting the

cohesion and interests of a particular group. This was particularly
true of the German version. As F.O. Hertz (1944) writes:

> In no other country has such a vast literature on the national character
> been produced as in Germany, and its aim has mainly been to exhort
> the German race and mould the national character to a model
> purporting to be the only true one. (p. 46)

The quantity of this material must be viewed (1) in direct relation
to the extreme national disunity which obtained in Germany until
well into the nineteenth century and (2) in relation to the conscious
insistence upon the need for a German ideology. From this use of
belief to achieve a goal flows the imperviousness of nationalisms to
logic and the evidence of experience. In this regard, it will generally
become impossible to argue with convinced nationalists insofar as
they will usually refuse to consider or reflect on any fact that tends
to run in a direction contrary to their initial ideological presuppositions. Nationalist ideologies, therefore, seen in terms of their instru-
mentalist function, do not merely reflect a national or racial character,
dogmatically conceived. More importantly, they attempt to persuade
that this character exists and provides a basis for unity or a focal point
of group loyalty. An important assumption of nationalist theory
is in fact the *diversity* of member nationals. It might be *said* that
they were all one, but this was largely in order to make them so and
diminish feelings of separateness. Indeed, the fact of diversity, which
is to say, the popular and psychological perception of barriers between
peoples within the state, often increases the felt need for an ideological
identity.

Nationalism was necessarily self-conscious because its primary
purpose was to achieve a particular type or degree of social cohesion;
ideas were intended entirely to serve this purpose and so assumed a
subsidiary function. National ideologies offered a glorified vision of
the nation, of both its being and becoming, and usually not as an
aggressor but as a victim, or as an inoffensive – but virtuous – power,
always mindful of justice or, at the very least, almost always right,
demanding the citizens' sympathy and belonging, urging upon them
the suspension of judgement. In the case of nationalist ideologies,
what is important is service to one's county. As Christianity's ideal
adherent was not a good person, but a faithful believer, so nationalism's ideal was not justice, but patriotism, not good folk, but loyal
patriots.

The nineteenth and twentieth centuries especially have witnessed
a multiplicity of ideologies competing for favour. One need only
refer to liberalism, socialism, communism, racialism, nationalism,

anarchism, syndicalism, corporatism, existentialism and conservatism to bear this out. The fact that there are so many is itself witness to the difficulty of any one of them becoming dominant. Even the two that we might be inclined to label 'dominant' seem to show signs of disintegrating: here I refer to socialism and communism.

Of course it might be argued that nationalism is really the dominant ideology of our century. Although this is largely true of the nineteenth century, it would be difficult to maintain that it is so today. It must be remembered that nationalism is not the same as promoting the interests of the persons embraced within a particular territorial area, otherwise referred to as a nation. It involves this, but is not exhausted by it. An ideology is not defined simply in terms of the interests which it promotes, but in terms of the argumentative framework within which these interests are explained and justified. Thus, the Soviets and the Chinese, for example, had distinct and conflicting national interests, of which they were inevitably aware. But the disputes between them were not conducted by reference to these interests, but by reference to the deviation of the one or the other from communist principles. Thus their ideology was communist, not nationalist. There is no overt parallel with the American nineteenth-century concept of a nationalistic Manifest Destiny or anything of that kind. The Sino-Soviets, in *Novy Mir* and *The Peking Review*, couched their debates neither in terms of national interest nor even in terms of what was right or appropriate as such. Instead, they argued in terms either of who was (or was not) a *true* Marxist–Leninist or in terms of who conformed most (or least) closely to the spirit of Marxism–Leninism. It is not necessary here to explore the question whether the ideology involved was an opiate or smoke-screen or superstructure, or whatever, but merely to note what the ideology was.

An ideology may very well have an effect upon practice, in a predictable way, for what one does may well be affected by the way in which one discusses it. But the more a particular ideology is invoked to explain incompatible activities by separate and even opposed groups, the more likely it is that it will either die out or be superseded by a different ideology. The ideological force of Christianity is spent when Catholics can take Protestants seriously and see the reasonableness of their position. Here one recognizes the arbitrariness of one's own, and not only of the other's belief. Similarly, the ideological force of communism is spent when one party's line has to be accepted as more or less equal to another's. The overall doctrine no longer seems to produce any particular, predictable type of action in practice. Thus, if the doctrine is retained at all, it has to be superseded, for otherwise it simply ceases to be taken seriously.

Ideology emerged in Europe most dramatically with the birth of Christianity. This doctrine offered a criterion of community exclusion and inclusion on the basis of belief. There is no doubt that Christians thought their God the only true God and that there was no limitation upon anyone's admission to His temple of belief, apart from the requirement of belief itself. Early Christians, however, were not consciously aware that their belief was ideological.

With the emergence of nationalism, however, theocratic Christianity was definitely eclipsed and the new dominant ideology became, albeit in a glass darkly, remarkably conscious of itself as such. Christian apologists, however, had already begun to set the example. No surer evidence of the muddied waters of Christian belief – of a new, awkward, artificial self-consciousness of the form of belief demanded – can be provided than that of Pascal's wager.[3]

Here a primitive acceptance of Christian truth had been routed. In its stead the self-conscious probabilism of probability. The argument suggests that even doubt affecting the *central* assumption of religious belief – viz. the existence of God – should be dismissed, not so much because unfounded, but because prejudicial to the possible attainment or protection of one's future interests. This in no way suggests that Pascal was in the slightest degree atheistic, but that he had to tailor his recommendations to suit the increasingly materialistic outlook of his times. In doing so, it became possible to view Christian belief as a function of material interests, and not merely as a function of truth. In this way belief takes the place of truth, self-consciously, and the essential matter becomes that of accepting, not questioning, or of accepting as beyond question, an ideology or set of assertions, the acceptance of which involves some notion of utilitarian advantage, one such advantage being immediate admission into a *corps de croyants*. In Pascal, therefore, the precursor of contemporary Christian existentialism, we have some evidence of the fact that a waning theocratic Christianity, too, tended to become *self-consciously* ideological.

Consciousness, however, comes in degrees. There is very little or no self-consciousness about early Christian ideology. This is a claim which nationalist ideology cannot quite make. And in the modern age we are confronted with what one might call 'the Sorelian crisis', where beliefs may in no wise be viewed as embodying truth, but, instead, may be consciously manipulated in order to marshal the activities of people to achieve a frankly unquestioned goal. Ideologies often have a genuine strength when accepted as actually true. They lose this strength when consciously conceived as tools, or instruments of control (at least for those persons who consciously view them as such).

The status of ideology reaches a peculiar impasse with Marxist socialism. For, on the one hand, Marx condemned ideologies as distortions. And, at the same time, he implicitly supported ideology if it was the right sort. The materialist conception of history, for Marx, served the purpose of unmasking sinister interests lurking behind the effulgence of flowery words. And, at the same time – according to Engels's 1883 preface to the German edition of the *Manifesto* – he believed that a time would be reached when the displacement of a class interest (the bourgeoisie's) would lead into the emancipation of the whole of society from partial interests, when (in short) ideology would be at an end.

Marx, of course, never fully clarified his position and this has produced difficulties. Nevertheless, the position he advanced need only be regarded as self-contradictory if one insists that he was a strict historical materialist. Engels denied that either of them was. However that may be, if Marx were a strict materialist, then it would clearly prove contradictory to view one ideology as a distortion and another as somehow 'legitimate', 'just' or 'true'; to insist on the one hand that all thought is determined by interest and, on the other, that this would eventually cease to be so.

In any case, there remains in Marx this vagueness, this lack of clarity. Full blown, his might be called the Sorelian crisis. Georges Sorel (1847–1922) assumed the thoroughgoing truth of historical materialism (combined with the facile pragmatism of William James). And he believed that the triumph of a particular (i.e. the proletarian) interest would constitute the generalized triumph of justice. Sorel viewed ideologies (seen as the intellectual refractions of interest) as myths. They were not 'true' ('truth' being somehow irrelevant) but only 'real' or existent. Sorel's point was not that they were false, either. In regard to ideologies, truth and falsity were both irrelevant. Myths or ideologies he regarded as impervious to truth.

Sorel sought to propagate an ideology for the trade-union movement in Europe. He set out an apocalyptic vision of the development and triumph of a group. He consciously and deliberately insisted upon the prior importance of belief itself, and argued that the holding of the belief, quite apart from criticism, inspection, probing, probability or validity, was the only essential factor in the assurance of this belief's triumph. This belief related to the triumph of a working-class order, through adherence to the myth of the general strike which formed a vision of the action to be taken by this class, unthinkingly, unquestioningly, grouping its members in absolute distinction from the members of the opposed class.

In Sorel, ideology attained the full flower of self-consciousness.

Ideology, as has been suggested, may be seen to involve the acceptance of an unquestioned belief as the criterion for affiliation to a body of believers. Questions such as: *Is* Jones a socialist?, or *is* Jones *really* a liberal?; and assertions such as: Smith is a *true* Christian or communist, etc., usually reflect an ideological bias. The test of what Jones *is* or of what Smith *is*, is what each believes. One may fail, or one may not live up to, one's beliefs, but the important thing in determining the ideological orientation of a person is the doctrine s/he professes. From this one supposedly deduces how one will or (at least) how one wishes to live.

For Sorel (1907, 1912), all major social movements effected reform only by representing 'their future action in the form of battle images assuring the triumph of their cause'. A myth cannot be refuted since 'it is ... identical with the convictions of a group', since it is the expression of these convictions in terms of movement and since, consequently, it cannot be broken into parts. The myth of the general strike would form in the workers' minds a battle image which would assure 'the triumph of their cause' (pp. 32, 46 and 168). Sorel, therefore, became the first political writer to place his entire emphasis (as opposed, e.g. to a Platonic aside) upon the need for consciously elaborating a doctrine which is deliberately distorted in order to secure widespread popular adherence.

Given the feeling that people must believe in something, a bridge of quite narrow span suffices to convey us to the notion that any belief at all will do. Sorel's theory provides the basis for our crossing over into the twentieth century of indiscriminate belief in belief, and commitment for its own sake, irrationally conceived. Sorel is our bridge to Nazism and to Fascism, to voluntarism and to existentialism in politics. But he is also a bridge which may help to take us beyond these beliefs and, possibly, in some sense, beyond ideology itself.

One of the essential maladies of our time springs from the desire to promote belief even when it cannot be believed; from the desire to trumpet faith even when it is indifferent to truth. One reason why the desire is so strong upon us to promote belief is because we feel that society will collapse without it. But belief we always have, assumptions we cannot escape; yet to be critical of our beliefs, though this may constitute a danger, entails as well as this a ground for hope. Because we *do* believe, it is not necessary to infer that we *should* believe.

4. Ideology: a fallacy

The point is that the rules of morality are not of the nature of
eternal truths, immutable in their authority – but only rough
statements of what in ordinary cases is man's duty.

J.N. Figgis ([1907], 1931, p. 92)

Figgis was only mistaken in supposing that Christian ethics, to the
exclusion of other types, was possessed of this flexibility. Any moral
rule can be handled both flexibly and rigidly. There is nothing
intrinsic to the nature of any rule which will in practice enable us to
predict whether it will be applied in one way or another. In the case
of Christianity, there is of course ample evidence of strictness of
application. What it is necessary to realise, however, is that looseness
of application becomes a function of scepticism towards the absolute
legitimacy or appropriate applicability of the rule applied. The danger
is that any moral rule will be applied strictly where it is assumed to
be possessed of a universal rightness.

Now there are at least two problems that may arise in the application of a rule: one is that it may be applied too strictly (e.g. 'never
steal') and the other is that it may be too vague to entail any specific
application at all (as perhaps, 'be moderate in all things'). Most of
the Ten Commandments, for example, are capable of strict, and overly
strict, application. But the Categorical Imperative, The Golden Mean
and the Golden Rule may be very difficult to apply in any determinate
way whatever. This presupposes that the latter type of statement is
intended as a guide to conduct, of course. Naturally, it might not be
so intended. It is possible that Aristotle's conception of the mean was
not meant as a guide to judgement but as a statement of what good
or bad conduct consists of. It is equally possible that Kant's concept
of the Categorical Imperative was not intended to tell us how to
behave but to indicate what good behaviour consists of. But this is
improbable, judging from the texts, and certainly does not conform
to the prescriptive reading generally placed upon these texts.

Now such moral items as those contained in the Ten Commandments tend to be discrete and reflect no logical coherence. The
argumentative moral systems of an Augustine, however, and more
especially of an Aquinas, entirely transcend such a purely declaratory
phase. The latter in short become more purely ideological, which is
to say, more argumentative, more coherent and more capable of being
applied in a deductive fashion in the explanation and justification of
political activity, thus tending to acquire more the guise of a science
than a dogma. This sort of reflective activity takes us well along the
way to reducing discrete principles to some one in particular whence

all the rest may be deduced. Typical examples of this reduction in ethics are those general principles already mentioned: the Golden Rule, the Golden Mean or the Categorical Imperative, each of which may be viewed as containing the whole of morality, reduced to a particular formula. The point about these formulae, however, is that they cannot really tell one how to behave; they can be seen as varieties of an ethical Rorschach test, permitting the agent to read into them whatever behaviour he favours. How one applies the Golden Rule depends upon how one expects to be done by. And the intermediate point between one principle and another (such as anarchy and tyranny) is rarely clear or determinable.

There are several aspects of what I shall refer to as an ideological fallacy. One is the tendency to assume that there is always a rule to cover every particular case. Another is the tendency to believe that every given rule, where it can be indisputably applied, should be. And a third is a tendency to believe that a universal principle relating to moral conduct can be applied in any specific case.* The first, however, is more characteristic of the pettifogger, the second of the bureaucrat, and the third, more particularly, of the ideologist. The ideologist is really a kind of refined pettifogger. His general attitude is that there is or ought to be a rule, or that we must act as if there were one, which can and ought always to be abided by. But when we return to the conclusion that no rule, nor any set of rules, is broad or precise enough to cover all contingencies, it is clear that anyone who insists that there must be a rule (or indeed a 'line' to be deduced from a system) is forced to regard any specific injunction or decision as being necessarily entailed by a universal proposition. This sort of mentality, when transplanted to the centre of political decision-making, reveals itself as being basically ideological, if coherent enough, and a merely pettifogging if 'consistently' *ad hoc*.

Now it is clear that an ideology is not merely a system of ethics, as we saw earlier. Thus the fallacy to which one refers cannot merely relate to a deficiency in ethical reasoning. It contains such a deficiency, but primarily as related to a political context. When dealing with this context, we are broadly concerned with two sub-categories: political science and political philosophy. These categories are not opposites. They are mutually dependent and in some sense presuppose one another. The difference between them, however, is not that the one is

---

* I always disagreed with Oakeshott's attack on 'rationalism'. But the three tendencies noted here lay at the heart of his just animus. Imre Lakatos was puzzled by my interest in Oakeshott. 'But he's an irrationalist, isn't he?' My answer to Lakatos was, in brief, 'yes, and no'. The 'no' was significant.

descriptive and the other recommendatory. Political philosophers recommend, but they also describe. Political scientists describe, but they also recommend. The value/fact disjunction does not quite catch the philosophy/science disjunction. Perhaps it would be better to think in terms of logical considerations as distinct from descriptive considerations.

Both political science and political philosophy are explanatory, but they involve different *types* of explanation or different *areas* of explanation. The question then to be considered is this: what arguments can be levelled against the supposition that the primary and distinguishing characteristic of political philosophy is its concern with logic (assumptions, implications, contradictions, deductions, etc.)? If this supposition can avoid being punctured, then we can say that the political philosophy/political science distinction should be viewed in terms of the distinction between a primary emphasis upon logical analysis as against an emphasis upon descriptive analysis. This does not automatically exclude 'ought' from either category. But it does leave us with three possibilities *vis-à-vis* the normative aspect. (1) It has nothing to do with either category. (2) It overlaps both categories. (3) It exclusively overlaps with the 'science' category, the descriptive, the practical. (The fourth possibility – roughly, that philosophy is recommendatory to the exclusion of science – is probably not worth considering.)

Let us say that one cannot ascend from a purely factual statement to a recommendation. To do so affords an example of the naturalistic fallacy. Let us also say that one cannot descend from a purely logical proposition to a recommendation. To do so probably affords – in its purest outline – an example of an ideological fallacy. None of this is to imply that prescription is completely autonomous *vis-à-vis* logical and descriptive statements or analyses; that implication would be erroneous. But it does suggest that prescription, as opposed to explanation (whether logical or descriptive), involves a different procedure, approach, emphasis or concern. A prescription, when *recommendatory* in form (it could be hortatory, imperative, etc.), can fall back upon logic and description in support of itself; but no piece of logic or description can, in itself, entail a recommendation.

Now one might deduce from the above that the political philosopher or scientist, *qua* philosopher or scientist, cannot recommend (i.e. the first of the three possibilities mentioned two paragraphs above). But this would be mistaken. Given that recommendatory argument depends upon (i.e. has to fall back upon) a knowledge of both facts and logic and assuming that the philosopher and scientist are better equipped with this knowledge than others, then it follows (certainly) that they are in a better position to *assess* recommendations than others and (less certainly) that they are in a better *position* to recommend than others. From this it does not follow that philosophers and scientists are simply and legitimately in a position to *tell* people what to do; it only follows that (*qua* philosophers and scientists) they are in a better position to argue with people regarding what might best be done; this, of course, usually only relates to the public rather than to the private sphere, since a philosopher or scientist need not be expected to know the psychology, disposition, mood, interests, ambitions, aspirations, etc., of any particular person whom they happen to encounter (while all such considerations are presumably relevant to what any particular individual 'ought' to do).

Tentatively, therefore, one is inclined to opt for the second possibility mentioned three paragraphs above, i.e. that as a matter of fact and as a matter of appropriateness, normative discussion insinuates itself both into scientific and philosophical discourse; it is only important to be clear about when we are recommending and when we are explaining (or at least that we try to be clear). If an incisive argument cannot be marshalled against this position, then normative discussion could be said to overlap both philosophical and scientific analysis. In drawing attention to an ideological fallacy, one would only be ruling out the particular procedure to which it refers as a legitimately recommendatory one. Thus, it would not entail any statement about how we may or might or should proceed, but only one regarding a procedure to be avoided. It is difficult to say anything in general about how we *should* proceed (except in a negative sense), if to do so implies that an ethical criterion of truth is available to us.

Political science and political philosophy one can primarily distinguish by reference to the distinction between logical and empirical analysis. Both of the latter are involved in any discussion of what is and of what ought to be. Descriptive and logical thinking primarily involve, in political science, correspondence with the facts, and, in political philosophy, the internal coherence of an argument. These two elements can never really be divorced from one another. A political philosophy achieves whatever relevance it has from refusing to be entirely divorced from matters of fact. And the initial condition of a political science is that it should not accommodate logical inconsistency. As for the discussion of matters of fact and the testing of argumentative consistency, these activities can be conducted in an entirely non-recommendatory framework, although the question of whether and when that framework is non-recommendatory is difficult and perhaps ultimately impossible to determine. One can say, however, that insofar as there is a distinction to be made between explanation and recommendation, it is essential to see that the offer of an explanation is not the same as the offer of a recommendation. For when we 'recommend' an explanation we are not, in the ordinary sense, recommending anything at all, but are instead merely indicating what we think to be true.*

Recommendation, although not necessarily a part of political analysis, whether scientific or philosophical, does necessarily entail, when it obtains, the utilization of both of these categories. Although they may possibly exist without it, it cannot exist with them. But although theory can be divorced from recommendation, practice cannot. The need of recommendation for theoretical analysis is not reciprocated by the latter's need for it. The mutual necessity, therefore, does not obtain between recommendation and theory, but between recommendation and practice. Action without recommendation is impossible. Recommendation not intended to be acted upon is futile.

Ideologies, as we have already seen, are not merely intended as theories, but as guides to action. Therefore we must consider them as a species of recommendation, and therefore of ethical thinking – but, again, not within the private, but within the public, the political sphere. This ideological fallacy, therefore, will relate to an analytical error involved in the marshalling of a political recommendation. Although a political philosophy, conceived in terms of its predominantly logical emphasis, is not necessarily ideological, an ideology *is* necessarily political philosophy, conceived from this same logical perspective. For the ideology falls back upon philosophy (or logic) and science (or facts) in marshalling its recommendations. The fallacy that I am here concerned with, however, is more logical or philosophical than scientific or factual.

A particular recommendation may be described as right or wrong, as worthwhile or useless, etc. What we must seek to do is to improve our understanding within this category. And one of the means of doing this consists in saying that procedure x is erroneous, even though we may not be able to say that any other procedure is absolutely valid. A major contribution of the Greeks and Romans was to indicate a certain range of avoidable errors which, when kept in mind, would permit one to escape the more obvious risks of intellectual adventure. When we espy verbal floats and buoys which read *non sequitur, petitio principii*, and the like, we know to steer clear. Our collection of these devices constantly expands in size to include, for example, Moore's comparatively recent definition of the naturalistic fallacy.

---

*This expression of the position I develop more adequately in a work in progress entitled *Political Philosophy: Ideology v. Judgment*.

This ideological fallacy merely accounts for one instance wherein general recommendatory activity comes to grief and must be rejected. The matter of importance is not the word, though 'ideology' seems most apt, but the condition or error referred to. One may refer to an 'ideological' fallacy because the term ideology has never, since Napoleon's use of it, lost its negative character, not did it do so in Marx (or especially not in Marx) and not even in Sorel. 'Ideology' has usually suggested the distortion of an assumed truth, and the most important reason why people have come to express a need for it in principle is because they deny the possibility of truth, while nevertheless demanding a directional belief to synthesize an ordered, progressive and non-ritualistic society; and because they view ideology as advertisement, as deliberate propaganda, as a necessary cheapening of intellectual coin in order to secure the unquestioning support of the masses for a particular cause.

We may now approach ideology more directly. The acceptance of it creates an identity, and is intended to promote action. It is prescriptive or recommendatory. Yet there is an important distinction to note between prescription, in the strictest sense, and recommendation. 'Prescription' is more suggestive of dictation and command, and the least argumentative way in which information can be communicated is by propaganda; this, too, may be seen as one of the more sophisticated forms that a prescription can assume. Dictation, commands and propaganda may all be needed at times, but it is clear that there is a difference between these and recommendations. The difference is, that where recommendations require justification, reasons, submission to proof and refutability, the character of a prescription, in the strictest sense, rules out the possibility of it being brought into question. Ideology, insofar as it rules out the possibility of such disputes, arguments and questions as would put its *basic* tenets to some form of (what one might call) objective or rational test, neither explains nor recommends (insofar as this requires and implies argument) anything at all. The condition for an ideology actually serving as a guide to conduct is that it is in effect hortatory and prescriptive. If it is not, then it does not in fact *guide* conduct, but merely provides an innocuously formal framework, which is not actually deductive, within which guidance is executed, but upon which the latter does not distinctly depend.

Every recommendation of a political move assumes the possible choice of distinctly alternative moves. Since possibility inheres in what is given, informed recommendation must depend on informed acquaintance with the latter. Because, if we do not know what a given situation involves, we cannot know what possibilities it contains, and the degree of defect in our knowledge on this head is simply a corollary of our ignorance of what we are choosing between. To say that a particular choice is to be recommended is to say that it is good. The logic of argument here is based on comparisons between the alternative possibilities. Any recommendation which is universal is non-rational, or illogical. Because rational argument about choice depends upon the assessment of alternatives, assessment depends upon a knowledge of the alternatives, and the latter depend upon the specific situation. This always changes with time and thus alters the ground upon which all arguments for and against any recommendation must depend. But a recommendation which is universal rules out the possibility of particular circumstances making it inapplicable, while it does not rule out the fact that circumstances change. It therefore claims to be true irrespective of any context, which valid arguments for recommendation, however, must necessarily depend upon. Its claim, then, is *a priori*, analytical, arbitrary. And its logical form becomes not at all that of a recommendation, but that of command: its very nature proscribes discussion. Its truth can only then be psychological, i.e. emotional, intuitive, based perhaps upon a 'moral sense'.

We must not insist upon an *identity* between ideology and soap-box oratory or propaganda. There is a difference of tone and mode. What is distinctive about an ideology, as opposed to a straightforward command, is that it does not claim to be propounding an order but a truth. And here resides its inherent illogic, that it claims some universal recommendation (e.g. 'Stealing is [always] wrong', 'Irrespective of circumstances one should never steal') is right, *a priori*, in any context, whereas the 'rightness' of any choice logically depends upon the comparison of specific alternatives which a changing situation throws up.

So that to 'recommend' liberty, class stratification, equality, centralization, decentralization, etc., *universally*, as divorced from a context, is not to *recommend* at all, but to express a preference or pronounce a command. *Recommendation* we may agree to have a built-in demand for supporting reasons. And any recommendation, which of itself implies no particular context, eliminates the very possibility of there being such reasons. For these depend upon a context, in terms of the specific possibilities which it provides. In the degree that one specifically rules out an accounting for possibilities, to that degree one rules out the possibility of a recommendation being in any sense *rational*. Thus it becomes contradictory to assume that any recommendation is capable of truth when one eliminates the very grounds which are necessary to make it rational (i.e. capable of truth).

We may define this Ideological Fallacy as consisting in *a universal, non-contextual recommendation which claims to be true, but the possibility of whose truth is eliminated by virtue of its claim being non-contextual, both in space and time.*[4]

For many people the question arises as to whether there is any alternative to ideologies. In short, there is the question whether there can be assertions of truth within the category of recommendation. If there can be no truth, then there are only alternative visions which, though 'distorted', constitute the only 'truths' available. It is this question which I now wish briefly to discuss. And by way of preface it should be noted that truth, for the writer, subsumes two sub-categories of objective statement: characterizations of assertions as 'true' and 'false' and as 'right' and 'wrong'.

Some people say that truth is absolute; others say that it is relative. But to say what truth is – whether absolute or relative – seems to be quite impossible, and this because of entirely logical considerations.

If one says, for example, the first, one will and rightly be asked for examples. And the difficulty in such an event, is that so many assumed truths of past years have been found to be inadequate later on, that the universal propositions of today, even though not *proved* inadequate, are only accepted as provisional, particularly in the field of science.

However, if one says the second – that truth is relative – the statement traps, perhaps condemns, its maker. For if the truth of all statements *is* relative, then this very statement must also be relative, which is to say that it cannot be entirely true.

Now, there is a commonplace variant on the idea that the truth of all statements is relative. This is the idea that all statements, or systems of statements, for example, 'ideologies', are 'determined' by the environments whence they emerge.

The trouble with the assertion that systems of ideas are socially determined is that it says too much and too little. Determined in what *way*? Plato and Aristotle, for example, were contemporaries. Yet one urged the benefits of monarchy, the other the benefits of aristocracy, while both lived under a system of government which was in form more nearly democratic than anything else.

The notion that social and economic conditions determine ideas is imprecise. But even if it were assumed to be precise and valid, it would again be necessary to test the logic of this assertion against itself. In which case the necessary conclusion would be that the very assertion that ideas are socially determined, or conditioned, is itself socially determined or conditioned. But this conclusion only re-inforces the impression of imprecision attaching to the concept of social determinism. Determined in what *way*?

The reason why the notion p (that ideas are socially determined) constitutes a variation on the notion q (that the truth of all ideas is relative) derives from the following fact. Both suggest that no assertion can possess a universal validity. And, again, we may see that this assertion is vitiated by the necessarily entailed implication that it, itself, can contain no such validity.

We may note one last relevant variation on the notion that truth is relative. This is the belief that all ideas are *reflections* of a social order or that they *spring from* the same. Such a formulation suggests that material conditions are, in some sense, 'prior', and that ideas are derivative or 'secondary'. Apart from the fact that this may not mean very much, it is, to the extent that anything is, certainly false. There is no more reason to believe that facts produce ideas than that ideas produce facts. We only know that the world, for us, does not exist apart from ideas, or consciousness. This neither entails that ideas or facts are either prior or derivative. The two categories are simply inseparable from the dual process of knowing and being known.

The notion that 'ideas merely reflect a given social order' may be considered a variation on the notion that 'the truth of all assertions is relative' because the former implies that *no* assertion can be universally true.

We thus return to the apparent logical impossibility of characterizing truth – as either absolute or relative (whether determined, reflective or otherwise). Truth and falsity are categories *within*, not *above* which, we operate.

If we say that truth is absolute and then take any particular assertion as evidence of such absolutism, it is always possible to step back from the assertion, to re-examine it, and, in short, to ask whether it *really* is true. The fact that such a procedure is never considered self-contradictory (though it may reveal stubbornness) suggests that no universal assertion about the world is ever self-evident, whereas self-evidence is an essential characteristic of what we mean by 'absolute truth' (in the sense that a thing is so totally, obviously and self-evidently true that its truth cannot even be doubted).

If we say that all truth is relative, as we have already shown, this very formulation must be applied to itself, producing the result that even it cannot be quite true. Thus, again, the discussion of the nature, or basic character, of truth is necessarily left open.

Not only does it seem impossible to say that truth is absolute or that truth is relative. Equally, it is impossible to say that there is no truth. One cannot say what it is, or describe it, as a whole, as a category, as such; *and* one cannot deny it, as such, as a category, as a whole. For the very assertion that there is no truth, as Aquinas as shown, presupposes its own validity, and thus contradicts what it assumes.

It is because we cannot say that truth is absolute or relative or impossible that we must accept it as an inescapable category. We cannot get above it. We cannot get out of it. It is simply the category within which we must conduct our affairs when we try to see, to assess and to report upon the world as it is or as we think it is and ought to be. Since we have at hand no certain means by which we can ever say *what* is true, and since we cannot affirm, without self-contradiction, that there is no truth, the logic of our predicament imposes upon us a certain humility.

The definition of an ideological fallacy neither presupposes that truth is absolute or relative. It only presupposes it as the ultimately indefinable category of assertion within which we must conduct our affairs, and from which we only really escape in death. We cannot avoid assertions of true and false, nor of right and wrong. As long as we are concerned with the nature of the world, and as long as we remain alive and conscious to operate within it, we unceasingly weigh facts and assess or judge acts. This stipulation of a fallacy fundamentally presupposes nothing more. What it expressly designates is an error in political argument. But it cannot be ignored that what is an error for many will, for some, constitute an intentional act of stealth and cunning. We cannot judge the propriety of ideology universally. That sort of judgement we have already seen to be an error characteristic of ideologies themselves. We can only do what we have done, and that is to take note of a logical fault.

NOTES

1 Cf. J.N. Figgis, *From Gerson to Grotius* (Cambridge [1907], 1931), p. 20: 'The Holy Roman Empire ... did indeed attempt to realize the ideal of an all-powerful State, but that state was the Church ... It has been said that there was no Austinian sovereign in the medieval State. That is true of the individual kingdoms. It is not true of the Church ... Baptism was a necessary element in true citizenship in the Middle Ages, and excommunication was its antithesis.'

2 Pascal notes that there are two ways by which we are persuaded of the truth of religion: by reason and by authority. He remarks that no one utilizes the latter any more, which he thinks a mistake: '*on dit qu'il faut croire par telle et telle raison, qui sont des faibles arguments, la raison étant flexible à tout.*' In a sense he was right: reason can prove anything. But if one is stuck with a system which insists upon a connection between certain fundamental principles and an illimitable string of specific political decisions, then one is stuck with a system of rationalization – within which anything can be proved. Cf. Blaise Pascal, *Oeuvres* (ed. 1926–27), t. 3, p. 56.

3 Pascal, *op. cit.*, t. 4, pp. 39 ff. William James provides an excellent summary account in *The Will to Believe*.

4. One reason for my severity with 'historical contextualism' and 'historical particularism' lies in my concern to segregate the amorality of these notions from what Popper and others have referred to as the (moral) 'logic of the situation'.

12

Ideology as Politics

Is it unfair to remark that this long-awaited book somehow dredges up the fantasy of an elephant giving chase to a fly? Professor Seliger hopes to demonstrate the disadvantages of what he refers to as a 'restrictive' or 'dual' concept of ideology. This concept affirms that some thought-systems are ideological and others are not. This tradition (of usage) takes its origins in the work of Marx and Engels, for they always asserted, despite deviations, that, in societies divided by class, all social thought is conditioned and rendered false by such division. The problem was that they believed that communist theory somehow escaped such conditioning and distortion. One could go on about this but all it really means is that Marx and Engels thought they were right and that their opponents were wrong. This is scarcely unusual. They espied, however, the logical and systematic character of the opposition's position, and also saw a tie between the play of certain abstract, heartwarming ideals, on the one hand, and certain real but infrequently mentioned material interests, on the other. In the twentieth century, of course, the systemic character of Marxist thought was also grasped, together with certain of its irrational features. In the same way that bourgeois thought was caricatured by Marxists, so too did liberal democrats come to caricature Marxist thought – as a sort of reflex action, no better than a religious creed, and requiring at least as much in the way of faith. As we all know, the same word came to be used: those whom Marx called 'ideologists' threw the very word back at his adherents. And, of course, many folk, on whatever side, would proclaim the need for an ideology, meaning some form of coherent belief system, if even in the form of an entirely irrational commitment.

Clearly, we are all irrational, but also (whether often or rarely) rational; incoherent, but also lucid; mistaken, and yet correct; full of beliefs, while often being led by apprehensions of a more solid kind. We may speak of another person or system as ideological where we

Note: This chapter was originally published as a review of Martin Seliger, *Ideology and Politics* (London, George Allen & Unwin, 1976).

intend the description as praise, but that is rare. Normally, the purpose is to descry that distinct system as somehow distorted or mistaken. Of course, it probably is, in some degree, whatever the system be. By the same token, similar assertions at various points can probably be made about one's own – whatever it is. In this sense it is perfectly understandable that two things should happen more or less at once: (1) that we or what we identify with shall prove at some point partisanly 'ideological' and (2) that this is a condition which we and others should struggle to break away from where it is concretely brought to our attention. *Contra* Professor Seliger, there is nothing necessarily wrong about using 'ideology' in this potentially confusing fashion. But if we allow ourselves to think loosely, then of course we can always be needlessly confused. It is important to emphasize that the concern with ideology has most importantly and substantively to do with problems of truth and falsity; it concerns methodology, scientific and otherwise.

The author is not clear about his central terms, nor, more importantly, about his central problems. He speaks of ideology in a 'dual', 'restrictive' and 'inclusive' sense. The 'dual' notion would involve, for example, using the concept to cover one's own doctrine while regarding all others as 'distortions of reality' (p. 26). The restrictive concept confines 'the term to specific political belief systems' (p. 14). The inclusive concept stipulates 'the applicability of the term "ideology" to all political belief systems'. From these definitions it is not clear as to the sense in which the 'dual' concept could be distinguished from either the 'restrictive' or the 'inclusive'. Does the 'dual concept restrict the use of 'ideology' to apply to one's own? Does it presuppose that all political belief systems are 'ideological'? Or does it merely mean that all such systems can be *called* ideological but that one's own is 'correct'? This is, so far, a minor semantic problem.

Seliger argues that we should not (indeed that it is *mistaken* to) use the concept 'ideology' to refer to any form of partisanship, distortion, extremism or whatever. The question that we must ask is whether he supposes for a moment that there should be no term or terms to cover these notions. If he is proposing to legislate these concepts out of current usage, as opposed to merely changing the name of the game, then he will be faced with a stupendous problem, both philosophical and political (or practical). If he proposes to supply us with new symbols or words to cover these concepts, then he should do so (which he does not) as well as give us some good reason for revising present nomenclature. Seliger appears to be saddled with an unfortunate view of philosophical/political history which captures an evolutionary movement from a 'restrictive' (or 'dual'?) to an 'inclusive' (or 'dual'?) use of 'ideology'. And he generously distributes various degrees of blame to different writers depending on the extent to which they approximate to Seliger's own 'inclusive' usage. What never appears to occur to Seliger is: (1) that there is in fact no such evolutionary semantic movement to be espied; and (2) that such a movement, on a substantive, philosophical level, cannot even occur.

How can we reach the point of regarding all political philosophies, belief systems, ideologies (or whatever one wishes to call them) as equal – where they are all equally extreme, distorted, or partisan or whatever? Seliger will no doubt complain straightaway that he does not mean this. He will direct us to his 'reconstruction of the left–right continuum', which would permit us to make just these distinctions – as between the extreme, the moderate, etc. But what he will not see, despite baroque protestations, is that he is merely putting old wine into new bottles by insisting that we use 'ideology' in *his* (confused) way rather than in the older (confused) fashion to which we are accustomed. Whether we call political thought 'ideological' or a thousand and one other things, the important matter is to distinguish between truth and falsity, mere commitment (on the one hand) and openness to argument (on the other).

Seliger provides us with little help here. He does not even enjoy the advantage of advancing a really clear and coherent argument of a partisan kind. He wants us to call everything ideology. And still he wants to distinguish between open and closed and presumably between good and bad ideologies. This is surely the substantive problem with which he started, to the extent that he started with one at all. Admittedly, he believes that truth can spring from a clash of 'ideologies', but this is nowhere clearly elaborated upon. It is not his virtue, unfortunately, to tell us or to help us to find out *how* such clashes advance our knowledge.

However unsatisfactory the distinctions which Seliger wishes to establish between 'dual', 'restrictive' and 'inclusive' views of ideology, he does advance some very firm propositions about ideology *per se*. Such propositions are basically definitional, as suggested. According to Seliger, 'no generally accepted definition of the term exists'. He thinks it both a desirable and a necessary task that social scientists should 'establish a generally acceptable definition of ideology'. He quotes approvingly Birnbaum's lament about 'the continuing problem of an adequate definition of ideology'. All of this predictably suggests that the level of Seliger's concern is terminological. He notes that ideology is used to cover (1) only *some* belief systems, and (2) all belief systems whatever. In effect, Seliger wishes to impose the second usage. Seliger obviously feels uncomfortable about this; he repeatedly soothes himself with the thought that he is 'proving', 'demonstrating', etc., that the second is a better usage than the first. Such proof, demonstration and the like, are understandably difficult to supply. Very often, when Seliger wishes to 'demonstrate' a point, he merely employs some other inoffensive writer as a shield. In this case, S. Hampshire is recruited to 'remind' us that 'language ... is itself a kind of behaviour interwoven with other kinds'. Hence Seliger reinforces the suggestion that he simply wants to shift usages, possibly on the grounds that, since language is somehow caught up with the real world, by altering language, one will (in some undefined sense) alter reality.

Thus, all that Professor Seliger really does is to *start* with his inclusive definition of ideology, from which he deduces that the other/others is/are 'untenable'. For what he insists upon is that 'there is no politics without ideology' (p. 99). Any concept of ideology which projects it as partial, partisan, etc., is for him necessarily wrong because, by definition (for Seliger) all politics is ideological. The rest of his book merely provides us with various types of elaboration upon this view.

Seliger is, however, very ready with criticism of other work, criticism which sometimes applies all the more strikingly to his own. He seeks to compel Bernard Crick, for example, to withdraw from the 'semantic upheaval' caused by the latter's demand that 'politics' be restricted to exclude a species of committed partisanship often referred to as 'ideology'. But Seliger finds himself in precisely the same sort of vehicle, only proceeding in reverse: Crick would be entitled to maintain (given Seliger procedures) that Seliger himself engenders 'semantic upheaval' by expanding the use of 'ideology' to cover any form of 'political belief system'. The author can no more 'demonstrate' that Crick's usage is mistaken than that his own is exclusively 'tenable'. What does it really matter how Crick or others wish to use the word 'politics', as long as it is clear that we understand what is meant? By the same token, it cannot really matter much how Seliger himself decides to use the word 'ideology'. But it would have helped for him to clearly recognize and state what he was doing so as to spare us at least a hundred pages of mostly pointless complaints about other writers' definitions. Even his review of the literature is defective because he gets crucial points wrong. He repeatedly quotes a 1967 essay of the present reviewer, for example, as '*The* Ideological Fallacy', when the whole point of the essay, as embodied in its correct title, was to elaborate upon '*An* Ideological Fallacy'.

Given that Seliger starts from the proposition that 'politics is inseparable from ideology', that 'all politics is ideological', that 'there is no politics without ideology', etc., it is plain that much must turn round what he means by ideology. His definition of ideology, however, is only provided after we have persevered through more than a third of the book (pp. 119–20). Unfortunately, as this 'definition' stretches for more than an entire page (over 400 words) it cannot be quoted; nor can it be recommended for either brevity or clarity. One need only comment that Seliger's definition is *exclusive* in the sense that it only includes what he earlier referred to as the 'inclusive' version. And what he says about this 'inclusive' definition at the beginning of the book is somewhat simpler: 'It covers sets of ideas by which men posit, explain and justify ends and means of organized social action, and specifically political action.' Such a definition is not in fact very different from one which the present reviewer offered eight years earlier: 'a coherent system of ideas of whatever kind, involving some understanding of man and the world, and which attempts to relate this understanding to a programme of political action', etc. So much for common ground. It goes without saying (or should do) that such a definition does not 'prove' or 'demonstrate' anything. It merely draws a circle round an area of concern. Subsequent discussion would be designed presumably to draw out the implications caught up in such a starting point, or to deal with substantive problems which impinge upon it.

Insofar as Professor Seliger is suggesting that it is not particularly helpful to regard an ideology (for example, Marxism or liberalism) as in itself 'good' or 'bad', one would consider it a reasonable point to make. But this position, which I share, cannot be allowed to obscure the fact that there are fundamental problems connected with partisanship (or whatever we want to call it) in politics. Perhaps the most important problem is to do with how we can be committed to certain political beliefs while simultaneously remaining open to some species of genuinely rational argument. A certain kind of dogmatism, circularity, etc., might well constitute *a* fallacy (not so much *the* fallacy) which would prove deleterious to the continuation or initiation of a reasonably peaceful and rational political process. And there is nothing necessarily absurd about calling such a fallacy 'ideological' – although nothing is won by insisting upon what one conceives to be the essentially correct meaning of a term.

I commented earlier about the ambiguity which attaches to Seliger's use of 'dual', 'restrictive' and 'inclusive' definitions of ideology. The difficulty does not end there, for Seliger also fails to provide a clear statement about the relationship between political philosophy and political ideology. It is not inescapable that there should be a distinction. Anyone who, like Seliger, says that ideology covers ideas by which people explain and justify socio-political action, could as easily be talking about political philosophy. I should have thought this was a perfectly acceptable procedure, at least as long as room is left to cover certain types of error or distortion, which might be regarded as either occasional or endemic in ideology (or political philosophy). But, contrary to what one might expect, Seliger rejects the suggestion that political philosophy and ideology are the same. He speaks of ideologies as being 'buttressed ... by the teachings of a number of political philosophers' (pp. 96–7). He speaks further of a distinction which runs 'from political philosophy down to party ideology'. But whatever the variation in speech, the message is the same: that 'political philosophy' and 'ideology' label quite distinct phenomena (as on pp. 112ff.).

Seliger states that political philosophy and ideology possess the same 'formal content'. But the reader will want to know, given the author's definition of ideology, what it is that distinguishes them. All that Seliger says, rather vaguely, is that 'political philosophy should be judged to occupy a dimension altogether above ideology'. 'Above', in this context, is scarcely clear. He could perhaps mean of course that political philosophy is somehow error-free, or *more* error-free. But that interpretation would leave 'ideology' occupying the same position of obloquy in which we first found it. In this context it should be remembered that the whole thrust of Seliger's argument was to maintain that all politics is permeated, penetrated, coloured by ideology. He notes in the course of his discussion that a distinction within ideologies is always to be made as between fundamental principles and the divergent ways in which these are actually applied (the so-called 'operative' ideology). Thus one would have expected Seliger to make no distinction between political philosophy and political ideology. As we have said, and contrary to what one would expect, he does. He says there is a 'divide'. But he does not tell us what sort of divide. Is political philosophy that part of ideology which consists of fundamental principles? If not, how is it distinct from these? We are given no answers. The problem Seliger is up against is clear. If political philosophy in any way guides politics, then (on his definition of ideology) it must be ideology. And if political philosophy does not in any way guide politics, then it must be wholly irrelevant to the political process. Seliger thus thoroughly boxes himself in. On the one hand, he says that all politics is ideological. On the other hand, he claims that political philosophy (cut off from ideology by that 'fluid' divide) is *not* ideological.

From insisting upon his fluid divide between ideology and political philosophy, the author lurches back towards the notion that there is none at all. At one point, for example, he waxes warm about the superior virtues of political philosophy. The 'authentic' variety thereof, we are told, enjoys an aspect of 'openness', is not 'utopian' nor 'hopelessly dogmatic' nor unaware of 'the need for temporary or permanent deviation from their envisaged organizational embodiment' [*sic*] (p. 115). From this great noise made about its superiority, one would have imagined 'political philosophy' to embody some sounder or loftier procedure. But in the next breath Seliger tells us that 'openness graces only a very few' political philosophies while 'there are ideologies which are open ... and leave room for the reconsideration of fundamentals'. From this one would conclude that, within these two zones, one is permitted to transact precisely the same business. For Seliger, the relationship between ideology and political philosophy is crucial. His encompassing definition of ideology, taken together with his stipulation that *no* politics is un-ideological, make this unavoidable. But he leaves the reader breathless as he busily pushes directly past the problem. He will enlighten us, he seems to think, by sprinkling a name or two in his path (a relevant Mr Barry in the company of the late Mr Jaspers). Yet there are no discernible footsteps. And names and brisk quotations are no substitute for an argument which the author himself never makes.

Seliger confronts, without resolving, an entire series of conceptual problems. First, as regards the relationship he intends between ideology and political philosophy. There is the further problem to do with the relationship intended between the 'dual' and other ways of conceiving ideology. There is a problem to do with the relationship within ideology between what he calls its 'fundamental' and its 'operative' dimensions. There is yet another problem to do with the relationship between the so-called fundamental dimensions of an ideology and political philosophy. Apart from all this, it must be said that Seliger insists upon distinguishing 'ideology from merely practised belief systems' (p. 107). He repeatedly asserts, of course, that *all* politics is affected by ideology. If that is true, can what he calls a 'practised belief system' possibly exclude 'ideology'? There is a great deal of confusion here. And whether the answer to this last question is 'yes' or 'no', there remains the more specific question as to whether Seliger can possibly conceive of a distinction between 'practised belief systems' and 'operative ideologies' anyway. Seliger advances such an improbable distinction without troubling himself in the least to defend it.

By entirely withdrawing from 'ideology' that distinctive definitional feature which has usually in some fashion or other characterized the use of the term – as suggesting something partial, partisan, distorted and so on – Professor Seliger only switches a label. He believes that partisanship, extremism, etc., exist; he only insists that we not label them 'ideology' or 'ideological'. This heavy assault upon an entire literature is startling, at points useful, but basically incoherent. He articulates no clear-cut substantive problems and so fails to carry us forward towards some more significant understanding of 'ideology' – whether 'dual', 'restrictive' or 'inclusive'.

Journal Abbreviations

Amer Pol Sci Rev	American Political Science Review
Canad J Pol Sci	Canadian Journal of Political Science
Comp Studs Soc Hist	Comparative Studies in Society and History
Govt and Opp	Government and Opposition
Hist J	Historical Journal
Hist Pol Thought	History of Political Thought
Hist Theor	History and Theory
J Eur Stud	Journal of European Studies
J Hist Ideas	Journal of the History of Ideas
J Phil	Journal of Philosophy
J. Polit	Journal of Politics
Midwest J Pol Sci	Midwest Journal of Political Science
New Lit Hist	New Literary History
Past Pres	Past and Present
Phil Phenomenol Res	Philosophy and Phenomenological Research
Phil Quart	Philosophical Quarterly
Phil Rev	The Philosophical Review
Pol Sci Quart	Political Science Quarterly
Pol Sci Rev	Political Science Review
Pol Stud	Political Studies
Polit Theory	Political Theory
Pop Sci Month	Popular Science Monthly
Proc Aris Soc	Proceedings of the Aristotelian Society
Rev Metaph	Review of Metaphysics
Sci Month	Scientific Monthly
Soc Res	Social Research

Bibliography

Acton, H.B. (1952) 'Tradition and Some Other Forms of Order', *Proc Aris Soc, 53,* 1–29.

Almond, G.A. (1966) 'Political Theory and Political Science', *Amer Pol Sci Rev, 60:4,* 869–79.

Arendt, H. (1958) *The Origins of Totalitarianism,* London, Meridian Books.

Arnhart, L. (1979) 'On Wood's Social History of Political Theory', *Polit Theory, 7:2,* 281–2.

Ashcraft, R. (1975) 'On the Problem of Methodology and the Nature of Political Theory', *Polit Theory, 3:1,* 5–26.

—— (1978) 'Ideology and Class in Hobbes's Political Theory', *Polit Theory, 6:1,* 27–62.

Auspitz, J.L. (1976) 'Individuality, Civility, and Theory: the Philosophical Imagination of Michael Oakeshott', *Polit Theory, 4:3,* 261–94 (A Symposium on Michael Oakeshott).

Austin, J.L. (1961) *Philosophical Papers,* Oxford, Oxford University Press.

—— (1962) *How To Do Things with Words,* Oxford, Oxford University Press.

Bateson, F.W. (1953) 'The Function of Criticism at the Present Time', *Essays in Criticism, 3:1,* 1–27.

Bendix, R. (1964) 'The Age of Ideology: Persistent and Changing', in D. Apter (ed.), *Ideology and Discontent,* Glencoe, IL, Free Press.

Berdyaev, N. (1936) *The Meaning of History,* trans. G. Reavey, London.

Berki, R.N. (1977) *The History of Political Thought: A Short Introduction,* London, Dent.

Berlin, I. (1954) *Historical Inevitability,* Oxford, Oxford University Press.

—— (1961) 'History and Theory: The Concept of Scientific History', *Hist Theor, 1:1,* 1–31.

—— (1964) 'Hobbes, Locke and Professor Macpherson', *Political Quarterly, 35,* 444–68.

—— (1976) *Vico and Herder: Two Studies in the History of Ideas,* London, Hogarth Press.

—— (1979) *Against the Current: Essays in the History of Ideas*, bibliography Henry Hardy (ed.), London, Hogarth Press.

Bernheim, E. (1908) *Lehrbuch der Historischen Methode*, 2 vols, Leipzig.

Birch, A.H. (1969) 'Historical Explanation and the Study of Politics', *Govt and Opp, 4:2*, 215–30.

Black, A. (1980) 'Skinner on the Foundations of Modern Political Thought', *Pol Stud, 28:3*, 451–7.

Blackburn, S. (1973) *Reason and Prediction*, Cambridge, Cambridge University Press.

Bloch, M. (1955) *Reflections on the Historian's Craft*, Manchester, Manchester University Press.

Boas, G. (1947) 'Review of Bertrand Russell's *History of Western Philosophy*', *J Hist Ideas, 8:1*, 117–23.

—— (1948) 'A.O. Lovejoy as Historian of Philosophy', *J Hist Ideas, 9:4*, 404–11.

—— (ed.) (1953a) *Studies in Intellectual History*, New York, Greenwood Press.

—— (1953b) 'Some Problems of Intellectual History', in Boas, 1953a, pp. 3–21.

—— (1964) 'Bias and the History of Ideas: The Romantic Syndrome: by W.T. Jones', *J Hist Ideas, 25:3*, 451–7.

—— (1969) *The History of Ideas*, New York, Scribner's.

Boucher, D.E.G. (1980) 'On Shklar's and Franklin's Review of Q. Skinner, *The Foundations of Modern Political Thought*', *Polit Theory, 8:3*, 403–6.

Braybrooke, D. (1971) 'A Review of Gordon Leff's, *History and Social Theory*', *Hist Theor, 10:1*, 122–34.

Brown, K.C. (ed.) (1965) *Hobbes Studies*, Oxford.

Bury, J.B. (1932) *The Idea of Progress*, New York, Dover Publications.

Calogero, G. (1963) 'On the So-Called Identity of History and Philosophy', in Kilbansky and Paton (eds) (1963).

Carmichael, J.C. (1983) 'C.B. Macpherson's "Hobbes": A Critique', *Canad J Pol Sci, 16*, 61–80 (March).

Carr, E.H. (1964) *What is History?*, Harmondsworth, Middlesex, Penguin.

Cherniss, H. (1953) 'The History of Ideas and Ancient Greek Philosophy' in Boas (ed.) (1953a), pp. 22–47.

Cobban, A. (1953) 'The Decline of Political Theory', *Pol Sci Quart, 68:3*, 321–37.

Cohen, G.A. (1978) *Karl Marx's Theory of History*, Oxford, Clarendon Press.

Cohen, L.J. (1953) 'Do Illocutionary Forces Exist?', *Essays in*

Criticism, vol. 3, 119–37.

Cohen, M.R. (1961) *The Meaning of Human History*, La Salle, IL, Open Court.

Coker, R.W. (1934) *Recent Political Thought*, New York, Appleton-Century.

Coleman, J. (ed.) (1996) *The Individual in Political Theory and Practice*, Oxford, Clarendon Press.

Collingwood, R.G. (1916) *Religion and Philosophy*, London.

—— (1924) *Speculum Mentis: or The Map of Knowledge*, Oxford, Clarendon Press.

—— (1933) *An Essay on Philosophical Method*, Oxford, Clarendon Press.

—— (1936) 'Human Nature and Human History', *Proc Brit Acad*, vol. 22. (Reprinted in R.G. Collingwood, *The Idea of History*, Oxford, Clarendon Press.)

—— (1937) *Roman Britain and the English Settlements*, by R.G. Collingwood and J.N.L. Myres, Oxford, Clarendon Press.

—— (1938a) *The Principles of Art*, Oxford, Clarendon Press.

—— (1938b) 'On the So-Called Idea of Causation', *Proc Aris Soc*, vol. 38, 85–113.

—— (1939) *An Autobiography*, London, Oxford University Press.

—— (1940) *An Essay on Metaphysics*, Oxford, Clarendon Press.

—— (1942) *The New Leviathan: or Men, Society, Civilisation and Barbarism*, Oxford, Clarendon Press.

—— (1945) *The Idea of Nature*, T.M. Knox (ed.), Oxford, Clarendon Press.

—— (1946) *The Idea of History*, T.M. Knox (ed.), Oxford, Clarendon Press.

—— (1966) *Essays in the Philosophy of History*, with introduction by W. Debbins (ed.), New York, McGraw-Hill.

—— (1970) 'Oakeshott and the Modes of Experience', review of *Experience and Its Modes* in E. Homberger *et al.* (eds), *The Cambridge Mind: Ninety Years of the Cambridge Review, 1879–1969*, Boston and London.

Colodny, R.G. (ed.) (1962) *Frontiers of Science and Philosophy*, Pittsburgh, PA, University of Pittsburgh Press.

Condren, C. (1979) *Three Aspects of Political Theory*, Melbourne, Macmillan.

Crick, B. (1959) *The American Science of Politics*, London, Routledge.

—— (1967) 'Philosophy, Theory and Thought', *Pol Stud*, *15:1*, 49–55.

Croce, B. (1919) (1921) (1960) *History: Its Theory and Practice*, trans. D. Ainslee, New York.

Cropsey, J. (1964) *Ancients and Moderns: Essays on the Tradition of Political Philosophy in Honor of Leo Strauss*, New York, Basic Books.

Curtis, M.H. (1962) 'The Alienated Intellectuals of Early Stuart England', *Past and Present, 23*, 25–43 (Nov.).

Danto, A. (1965) *Analytical Philosophy of History*, Cambridge, Cambridge University Press.

Donagan, A. (1956) 'The Verification of Historical Theses', *Phil Quart, 6:24*, 193–208.

—— (1957) 'Historical Explanation', *Mind, 66:262*, 145–64.

—— (1962) *The Later Philosophy of R.G. Collingwood*, Oxford, Oxford University Press.

Dray, W. (1957) *Laws and Explanation in History*, New York, Harper & Row.

—— (ed.) (1966) *Philosophical Analysis and History*, New York, Harper & Row.

—— (1971) 'On the Nature and Role of Narrative in Historiography', *Hist Theor, 10:2*, 153–71.

DuBois, P. (1991) in P. Roche (trans.), *The Love Songs of Sappho*, Bergenfield, NJ, Signet.

Dummett, M. (1964) 'Bringing about the Past', *Phil Rev, 73:3*, 338–59.

Dunn, J. (1968) 'The Identity of the History of Ideas', *Philosophy, 43:164*, 85–104. (Also published in *Philosophy, Politics and Society*, Laslett, Runciman and Skinner (eds) [1972].)

—— (1969) *The Political Thought of John Locke: An Historical Account of the Argument of the 'Two Treatises of Government'*, Cambridge, Cambridge University Press.

—— (1979), *Western Political Theory in the Face of the Future*, Cambridge, Cambridge University Press.

—— (1980) *Political Obligation in Its Historical Context: Essays in Political Theory*, Cambridge, Cambridge University Press.

Easton, D. (1963) *The Political System: An Enquiry into the State of Political Science*, New York, Knopf.

—— (1966) *Varieties of Political Theory*, Englewood Cliffs, NJ, Prentice-Hall.

Edel, A. (1946) 'Levels of Meaning and the History of Ideas', *J Hist Ideas, 7:3*, 355–60.

Elton, G.R. (1969) *The Practice of History*, London, Glasgow and Sydney, Fontana.

—— (1970) *Political History: Principles and Practice*, London, Allen Lane, The Penguin Press.

Ely, R.G. (1969) 'Mandelbaum on Historical Narrative', by R.G. Ely, R. Gruner and W. Dray, *Hist Theor, 8:2*, 275–94.

Eulau, H. (1962) 'Comparative Political Analysis: A Methodological Analysis', *Midwest J Pol Sci, 6:4*, 397–407.

Fain, H. (1970) *Between Philosophy and History*, Princeton, NJ, Princeton University Press.

Femia, J.V. (1979) 'An Historicist Critique of Revisionist Methods for Studying the History of Ideas', Proceedings of the International Political Science Association, Moscow (August).

Field, G.C. (1953) 'What is Political Theory?', *Proc Aris Soc, 54*, 145–67.

—— (1956) *Political Theory*, London, Methuen.

Figgis, J.N. ([1907] 1931) *From Gerson to Grotius*, Cambridge, Cambridge University Press.

Finberg, H.P. (ed.) (1962) *Approaches to History*, London, Routledge & Kegan Paul.

Fischer, D.H. (1970) *Historians' Fallacies: Toward a Logic of Historical Thought*, London, Routledge & Kegan Paul.

Fling, F.M. (1920) *The Writing of History: An Introduction to Historical Method*, New Haven, CT, Yale University Press.

Friedrich, C.J. and Z.K. Brzezinski (1956) *Totalitarian Dictatorship and Autocracy*, Cambridge, MA, Harvard University Press.

Gabbey, A. (1987) 'On Listening to the Ungrateful Dead', *Newsletter*, British Society for the History of Philosophy, *I: 2*, pp. 20–1.

Gallie, W.B. (1964) *Philosophy and the Historical Understanding*, New York and London, Chatto & Windus.

—— (1972) Review of *Fact and Relevance: Essays on Historical Method*, by M.M. Postan and *Political History, Principles and Practice*, by G.R. Elton, *Amer Pol Sci Rev, 66:4*, 1342–3.

Galtung, J. (1967) *Theory and Methods of Social Research*, New York, Columbia University Press.

Gardiner, P. (1952) *The Nature of Historical Explanation*, Oxford, Oxford University Press.

—— (ed.) (1959) *Theories of History*, Glencoe, IL, Free Press.

Gavre, M. (1974) 'Hobbes and His Audience: The Dynamics of Theorizing', *Amer Pol Sci Rev, 68*, 1542–56.

Gellner, E. (1959) *Words and Things*, London, Victor Gollancz.

Geyl, P. (1962) *Debates with Historians*, London, Fontana.

Gottschalk, L.R. (1950) *Understanding History: a Primer of Historical Method*, New York, Knopf.

—— (1964) *Generalisation in History*, Chicago, Chicago University Press.

Gracia, J.J.E. (1975) 'The History of Ideas in Latin America', *J Hist Ideas, 36:1*, 177–84.

Graham, G. (1982) 'Can There Be History of Philosophy?' *Hist Theor,*

22:1, 37–52.

Graubard, S.R. (1974) Review of Melvin Richter (ed.), *Essays in Theory and History: An Approach to the Social Sciences, Hist Theor, 13:3*, 335–42.

Gray, R. (1978) 'Hobbes' System and His Early Philosophical Views', *J Hist Ideas, 39*, 199–215.

Greene, J.C. (1957/8) 'Objectives and Methods in Intellectual History', *Mississippi Valley Historical Review, 44:1*, 58–74.

Greenleaf, W.H. (1964) *Order Empiricism and Politics, Two Traditions of English Political Thought*, Oxford, Oxford University Press.

—— (1966) *Oakeshott's Philosophical Politics*, London, Longmans.

Greenstein, F.I. (1967) 'Art and Science in the Political Life History', *Politics, 2:2*, 176–80.

Gunnell, J.G. (1978) 'The Myth of the Tradition', *Amer Pol Sci Rev, 72:1*, 122–34.

—— (1979) *Political Theory: Tradition and Interpretation*, Cambridge, MA, Winthrop Publishers.

—— (1982) 'Interpretation and the History of Political Theory: Apology and Epistemology', *Amer Pol Sci Rev, 76:2*, 317–27.

Haddock, B.A. (1974) 'The History of Ideas and the Study of Politics', *Polit Theory, 2:4*, 420–31.

Hallowell, J.H. (1954) 'Review of Leo Strauss *Natural Right and History*', *Amer Pol Sci Rev, 48:2*, 538–41.

Harrison, W. (1955) 'Texts in Political Theory', *Pol Stud, 3:1*, 28–44.

Hartman, R.S. (1953) *Reason in History*, New York, Bobbs-Merrill.

Hegel, G.W.F. (1968) *Lectures on the History of Philosophy*, 3 vols, trans. E.S. Haldane and F.H. Simpson, London, Routledge.

Heinam, R. (1975) Review of J.G.A. Pocock's *Politics, Language and Time: Essays on Political Thought and History, Amer Pol Sci Rev, 69:1*, 254–5.

Hempel, C.G. (1942) 'The Function of General Laws in History', reprinted in Gardiner (1959). Also in Hempel (1965).

—— (1965) *Aspects of Scientific Explanation*, New York, Free Press.

Hertz, F.O. (1944) *Nationality in History and Politics*, London, Kegan Paul.

Himmelfarb, G. (1975) 'The Conservative Imagination: Michael Oakeshott', *The American Scholar, 44:3*, 405–20.

Hirsh, E.D. (1967) *Validity in Interpretation*, New Haven, CT, Yale University Press.

Holmes, S.T. (1979) Review of Quentin Skinner's *Foundations of Modern Political Thought, Amer Pol Sci Rev, 73:4*, 1133–5.

Huizinga, J. (1959) *Men and Ideas*, New York.

Jacoby, E.G. (1974) 'Thomas Hobbes in Europe', *J Eur Stud*, *4*, 57–65.

Joynt, C.B. and N. Rescher (1961) 'The Problem of Uniqueness in History', *Hist Theor*, *1:2*, 150–62.

Johnson, A.H. (1946) 'Whitehead's Philosophy of History', *J Hist Ideas*, *8:2*, 234–49.

Jones, W.T. (1961) *The Romantic Syndrome: Towards a New Method in Cultural Anthropology and History of Ideas*, The Hague, Martinus Nijhoff.

Judson, M. (1988 [1949]) *Crisis of the Constitution*, New Brunswick, NJ, Rutgers University Press.

Kaplan, A. (1964) *The Conduct of Inquiry*, San Francisco, Chandler Publishing Co.

Kaufman, H. (1964) 'Organization Theory and Political Theory', *Amer Pol Sci Rev*, *58:1*, 5–14.

Kaufman, W.A. (1949) 'Goethe and the History of Ideas', *J Hist Ideas*, *10:4*, 503–16.

Kelley, D.R. (1979) Review of Skinner's *Foundations of Modern Political Thought*, *J Hist Ideas*, *40:4*, 663–88.

Kelly, G.A. (1975) Review of Maurice Maudelbaum's *History, Man and Reason: A Study in Nineteenth-Century Thought*, *Amer Pol Sci Rev*, *69:1*, 247–9.

Kedourie, E. (1961) *Nationalism*, London, Hutchinson.

Kilbansky, R. and H.J. Paton (eds) (1963) *Philosophy and History*, New York, Harper & Row.

King, P. (1974, 1999) *The Ideology of Order: Comparative Analysis of Jean Bodin and Thomas Hobbes*, London, Frank Cass.

—— (1976, 1998) *Toleration*, London, Frank Cass.

—— (1983) *The History of Ideas: An Introduction to Method*, London, Croom Helm.

—— (1993) *Thomas Hobbes: Critical Assessments*, 4 vols, London, Routledge.

—— (1995) 'Historical Contextualism: The New Historicism?', *History of European Ideas*, *21:2* (March), 209–33.

King, P. and B.C. Parekh (eds) (1968) *Politics and Experience: Essays Presented to Michael Oakeshott*, Cambridge, Cambridge University Press.

Knox, T.M. (1946) Editor's Preface to Collingwood (1946).

Kohn, H. (1964) 'Political Theory and the History of Ideas', *J Hist Ideas*, *25:2*, 303–8.

Kracaver, S. (1969) *History: The Last Things Before the Last*, Oxford, New York, Oxford University Press.

Kramnick, I. (1981) Review of Isaiah Berlin's *Against the Current: Essays in the History of Ideas*, *Amer Pol Sci Rev*, *75:2*, 472–3.

Krausz, M. (1972) *Critical Essays on the Philosophy of R. G. Colling-wood*, Oxford, Clarendon Press.

Kristeller, P.O. (1946) 'The Philosophical Significance of the History of Thought, *J. Hist Ideas, 7:3*, 360–6.

Kuhn, T.S. (1970) *The Structure of Scientific Revolutions*, Chicago, University of Chicago Press.

Kvastad, N.B. (1977) 'Semantics in the Methodology of the History of Ideas', *J Hist Ideas, 38:1*, 157–74.

Lamprecht, S.P. (1940) 'Hobbes and Hobbism', *Amer Pol Sci Rev, 34*, 31–53.

Laslett, P. and W.G. Runciman (eds) (1956) *Philosophy, Politics and Society*, *Series II*, Oxford, Blackwell.

Leavis, F.R. (1953) 'The Responsible Critic: Or the Function of Criticism at Any Time', *Scrutiny, 19:3*, 162–83.

Leff, G. (1969) *History and Social Theory*, London, Merlin Press.

Leslie, M. (1970) 'In Defence of Anachronism', *Pol Stud, 18:4* (Dec.), 433–47.

—— (1973) 'What Makes a Classic in Political Theory?', *Pol Sci Quart, 88:3* (Sept.), 462–74.

Lewis, E. (1956) 'The Contribution of Medieval Thought to the American Political Tradition', *Amer Pol Sci Rev, 50:2*, 462–74.

Lockyer, A. (1979) '"Traditions" as Context in the History of Theory', *Pol Stud, 27:2*, 201–18.

Lovejoy, A.O. (1920) 'Pragmatism Versus the Pragmatist' in D. Drake *et al., Essays in Critical Realism*, New York and London, Gordian Press.

—— (1930) *The Revolt Against Dualism: an Inquiry Concerning the Existence of Ideas*, London and New York, Open Court.

Lovejoy, A.O. (1936) *The Great Chain of Being: A Study of the History of an Idea*, Cambridge, MA, Harvard University Press.

—— (1938) 'The Historiography of Ideas', *Proceedings of the American Philosophical Society*, reprinted in Lovejoy (1948).

—— (1939) 'Present Standpoints and Past History', reprinted in H. Meyerhoff (ed.), *The Philosophy of History in Our Time* (1959) New York.

—— (1940) 'Reflections on the History of Ideas', *J Hist Ideas, 1:1* (Jan.), 3–23.

—— (1948) *Essays in the History of Ideas*, Baltimore, MD, Johns Hopkins University Press.

—— (1961a) *Reflections on Human Nature*, Baltimore, MD, Johns Hopkins University Press.

—— 1961b) *The Reason, the Understanding, and Time*, Baltimore, MD, Johns Hopkins University Press.

—— (1963) *The Thirteen Pragmatisms and Other Essays*, Baltimore, MD, Johns Hopkins University Press.

Lovejoy, A.O. and G. Boas (eds) (1935) *Primitivism and Related Ideas in Antiquity*, New York, Octogon Books.

Lubienski, Z. (1930) 'Hobbes' Philosophy and Its Historical Background', *J Phil Stud, 5*, 175–90.

Mackie, J.L. (1974) *The Cement of the Universe: A Study of Causation*, Oxford, Oxford University Press.

Mandelbaum, M. (1938) *The Problem of Historical Knowledge: An Answer to Relativism*, New York, Harper.

—— (1948) 'Arthur O. Lovejoy and the Theory of Historiography', *J Hist Ideas, 9:4*, 412–23.

—— (1955a) (1969) *The Phenomenology of Moral Experience*, Baltimore, Johns Hopkins University Press.

—— (1955b) 'Concerning Recent Trends in the Theory of Historiography', *J Hist Ideas, 16:4*, 506–17.

—— (1955c) (1959) 'Societal Facts' in Gardiner (1959). Originally in *British Journal of Sociology*.

—— (1961) 'Historical Explanation: the Problem of Covering Laws', *Hist Theor, 1:3*, 229–42.

—— (1965) 'The History of Ideas, Intellectual History and the History of Philosophy', *Hist Theor, 4:3*, 33–66.

—— (1967) 'A Note on History as Narrative', *Hist Theor, 6:3*, 413–19.

—— (1971) *History, Man, and Reason: A Study in Nineteenth-Century Thought*, Baltimore, MD, Johns Hopkins University Press.

—— (1977) *The Anatomy of Historical Knowledge*, Baltimore, MD.

Mannheim, K. (1954) *Ideology and Utopia*, trans. Wirth and Shils, London, Routledge & Kegan Paul.

Masu, R.G. (1952) 'William Dilthey and the History of Ideas', *J Hist Ideas, 13:1*, 94–107.

Mazzeo, J.A. (1972) 'Some Interpretations of the History of Ideas', *J Hist Ideas, 33:3*, 379–94.

McCallum, R.B. (1943) See *Proceedings of British Academy*, vol. 29, 463–8.

McIlwain, C.H. (1932) *The Growth of Political Thought in the West*, New York, Macmillan.

MacIntyre, A. (1967) *A Short History of Ethics*, London, Duckworth.

—— (1985) *After Virtue*, London, Duckworth.

—— (1988) *Whose Justice? Which Rationality?*, London, Duckworth.

Macpherson, C.B. (1962) *The Political Theory of Possessive Individualism: Hobbes to Locke*. Oxford, Oxford University Press.

—— (1983) 'Leviathan Restored: A Reply to Carmichael', *Canad J*

Pol Sci, 16, 795–805 (Dec.).

Maier, H. (1968) 'Thomas Hobbes und der Moderne Staat', *Stimmen Der Zeit, 181,* 88–106.

Malcolm, N. (1981) 'Hobbes, Sandys and the Virginia Company', *Hist J, 24:2,* 297–321.

Meehan, E. (1968) *Explanation in the Social Sciences: A System Paradigm,* Homewood, IL.

Meyerhoff, H. (ed.) (1959) *The Philosophy of History in Our Time,* New York, Garden City.

Mink, L.O. (1966) 'The Autonomy of Historical Understanding', *Hist Theor, 5:1,* 24–47, reprinted in Dray (1966).

—— (1968) 'Collingwood's Dialectic of History', *Hist Theor, 2:1,* 3–38.

—— (1971) Review of David Hackett Fischer's *Historian's Fallacies: Toward a Logic of Historical Thought, Hist. Theor, 10:1,* 107–22.

—— (1978) Review of Maurice Mandelbaum's *The Anatomy of Historical Knowledge, Hist Theor, 17:2,* 211–23.

Minogue, K.R. (1975) 'Oakeshott and the Idea of Freedom', *Quadrant, 19:7,* 77–83.

Montefiore, A. (1975) *Neutrality and Impartiality: The University and Political Commitment,* Cambridge, Cambridge University Press.

Mulligan, L. (1979) 'Intentions and Conventions: A Critique of Quentin Skinner's Method for the Study of the History of Ideas' by L. Mulligan, J. Richards and J. Graham, *Pol Stud, 27:1,* 84–98.

Murphy, G.G.S. (1965) 'Sir Isaiah Berlin on "The Concept of Scientific History": A Comment', *Hist Theor, 4:2,* 234–43.

Nagel, E. (1961) *The Structure of Science,* New York and London, Routledge & Kegan Paul.

Newman, F.D. (1968) *Explanation by Description, An Essay on Historical Methodology,* The Hague, Mouton.

Nisbet, R.A. (1969) *Social Change and History,* New York, Oxford University Press.

Nowell-Smith, P.H. (1957) 'Are Historical Events Unique?', *Proc Aris Soc, 56,* 107–60.

Oakeshott, M. (1933) *Experience and Its Modes,* Cambridge, Cambridge University Press.

—— (1955) 'The Activity of Being an Historian', republished in *Rationalism in Politics* (1962).

—— (1959) *The Voice of Poetry in the Conversation of Mankind,* London, republished in *Rationalism in Politics* (1962).

—— (1962) *Rationalism in Politics and Other Essays,* London and New York, Methuen.

—— (1975a) *Hobbes on Civil Association,* Oxford, Blackwell.

—— (1975b) *On Human Conduct*, Oxford, Clarendon Press.

—— (1983) *On History and Other Essays*, Oxford, Blackwell.

Olafoon, F.A. (1969) 'Human Action and Historical Explanation', in J. Edie (ed.), *New Essays in Phenomenology*, Chicago.

Parekh, B. and Berki, R.N. (1973) 'The History of Political Ideas: A Critique of Q. Skinner's Methodology', *J Hist Ideas*, *34:2*, 163–84.

Passmore, J.A. (1958) 'The Objectivity of History', *Philosophy*, *33:125*, 97–111.

—— (1965) 'The Historiography of the History of Philosophy', *Hist Theor*, *4:3*, 1–32.

Paton, H.J. (1936) *Philosophy and History*, New York, Harper & Row.

Phillipson, N. and Skinner, Q. (eds) (1993) *Political Discourse in Early Modern Britain*, Cambridge, Cambridge University Press.

Pocock, J.G.A. (1962a) 'The History of Political Thought: A Methodological Enquiry', in Laslett and Runciman (1962), *Philosophy, Politics and Society*, Oxford, Blackwell, 183–202.

—— (1962b) 'The Origins of Study of the Past: A Comparative Approach', *Comp Studs Soc Hist*, *4:2*, 209–46.

—— (1967) 'The Dimension of Time in Systems of Political Thought', delivered in 1967 to *Amer Pol Sci Asso* (MS).

—— (1968) 'Time, Institutions and Actions: An Essay on Traditions and Their Understanding', in P. King and B. Parekh (eds), *Politics and Experience*, Cambridge, Cambridge University Press, 209–37.

—— (1975) *The Machiavellian Moment*, Princeton, University Press.

—— (1970) 'Working on Ideas in Time', in L.P. Curtis Jnr (ed.) *The Historian's Workshop*, New York, Alfred A. Knopf.

—— (1971) *Politics, Language and Time: Essays on Political Thought and History*, New York, Atheneum.

Popper, K.R. (1945) *The Open Society and Its Enemies*, London, Routledge & Kegan Paul.

—— (1959a) 'Prediction and Prophecy in the Social Sciences' in Gardiner (1959).

—— (1959b) *The Logic of Scientific Discovery*, London, Hutchinson.

—— (1960) *The Poverty of Historicism*, London, Routledge.

Porter, D.H. (1975) 'History as a Process', *Hist Theor*, *14:3*, 297–313.

Postan, M.M. (1971) *Fact and Relevance: Essays on Historical Method*, Cambridge, Cambridge University Press.

Proceedings of British Academy (1943) Obituary Notice on R.G. Collingwood, *29*, 463–85.

Rees, J.C. (1957) 'Review of G.C. Field's *Political Theory*', *Pol Stud*, *5:1*, 106–7.

Richter, M. (Ed.) (1970) *Essays in Theory and History: An Approach to the Social Sciences*, Cambridge, MA, Harvard University Press.

Rotenstreich, N. (1976) *Philosophy, History and Politics: Studies in Contemporary English Philosophy of History*, The Hague, Nijhoff.

Rubinoff, L.(1970) *Collingwood and the Reform of Metaphysics: A Study in the Philosophy of Mind*, Toronto, University of Toronto Press.

Russell, B. (1945) *History of Western Philosophy*, New York, Simon & Schuster.

Sabine, G.H. (1937) *A History of Political Theory*, New York, 3rd edn, Holt Rinehart & Winston.

Schaar, J.H. (1963) 'Essays on the Scientific Study of Politics', *Amer Pol Sci Rev, 57:1*, 125–60.

Schochet, G.J. (1974) 'Quentin Skinner's Method', *Polit Theory, 12:3*, 261–75.

Scriven, M. (1959) 'Truisms as the Ground for Historical Explanation', in Gardiner (1959).

Seifert, G.F. (1979) 'The Philosophy of Hobbes: Text and Context and the Problem of Sedimentation', *The Personalist, 60*, 177–85.

Sellars, R.W. *et al.* (1949) *Philosophy for the Future: The Quest of Modern Materialism*, New York, Macmillan.

Shklar, J. (1979) 'Skinner: The Foundations of Modern Political Thought', *Polit Theory, 7:4*, 549–59.

Siedentop, L.A. (1977) 'Whither Political Theory', *Pol Stud, 25:4*, 588–93.

Skinner, Q. (1964) 'Hobbes's *Leviathan*', *Hist J, 7:2*, 321–33.

—— (1965–66) 'Thomas Hobbes and His Disciples in France and England', *Comp Studs Soc Hist, 8*, 153–67.

—— (1965a) 'History and Ideology in the English Revolution', *Hist J, 8:2*, 151–78.

—— (1965b) 'Hobbes on Sovereignty: An Unknown Discussion', *Pol Stud, 13:2*, 213–18.

—— (1966a) 'The Ideological Context of Hobbes's Political Thought', *Hist J, 9:3*, 286–317.

—— (1966b) 'The Limits of Historical Explanations, *Philosophy, 41:157*, 199–215.

—— (1966c) 'Thomas Hobbes and His Disciples in France and England', *Soc Hist, 8:2*, 153–67.

—— (1966d) 'On Two Traditions of English Political Thought', *Hist J, 9:1*, 136–9.

—— (1967) 'More's *Utopia*', *Past Pres*, no. 38, 153–68.

—— (1969a) 'Meaning and Understanding in the History of Ideas', *Hist Theor, 8:1*, 3–53.

—— (1969b) 'Thomas Hobbes and the Nature of the Early Royal Society', *Hist J, 12:2*, 217–39.

—— (1970) 'Conventions and the Understanding of Speech Acts', *Phil Quart, 20:78*, 118–38.

—— (1971) 'On Performing and Explaining Linguistic Actions', *Phil Quart, 21:82*, 1–21.

—— (1972a) 'Conquest and Consent: Thomas Hobbes and the Engagement Controversy', in G.E. Aylmer (ed.), *The Interregnum: The Quest for Settlement*, London, Macmillan, 79–98.

—— (1972b) 'Motives, Intentions and the Interpretation of Texts', *New Lit Hist, 3:2*, 393–408.

—— (1972c) '"Social Meaning" and the Explanation of Social Action', in P. Laslett, W.G. Runciman and Q. Skinner (eds), *Philosophy, Politics and Society*, Oxford, Blackwell, 136–57.

—— (1972d) 'The Context of Hobbes's Theory of Political Obligation', in M.W. Cranston and R.S. Peters (eds), *Hobbes and Rousseau*, Garden City, New York, Anchor Books, 109–42. A revised version of Skinner (1966a).

—— (1973) 'The Empirical Theorists of Democracy and their Critics', *Polit Theory, 1:3*, 287–305.

—— (1974) 'Some Problems in the Analysis of Political Thought and Action', *Polit Theory, 2:3*, 277–303.

—— (1978a) *The Foundations of Modern Political Thought: vol. I, The Renaissance: vol. II, The Age of Reformation*, Cambridge, Cambridge University Press.

—— (1978b) 'Action and Context', *The Aristotelian Society*, supplementary vol., *52*, 55–69.

—— (1979) 'The Idea of a Cultural Lexicon', *Essays in Criticism, 29*, 205–23.

—— (1988) 'Warrender and Skinner on Hobbes: A Reply', *Pol Stud, 36*, 692–5.

Skotheim, R.A. (1964) 'The Writing of American Histories of Ideas: Two Traditions in the Twentieth Century', *J Hist Ideas, 25:2*, 257–78.

Sorel, G. (1907) (1912) *Réflexions sur la violence*, Paris, Rivière.

Spencer, T. (1948) 'Lovejoy's Essays in the History of Ideas', *J Hist Ideas, 9:4*, 439–46.

Spitzer, L. (1941) 'History of Ideas Versus Reading of Poetry', *South Rev, 6:3*, 586–604.

Stark, W. (1958) *The Sociology of Knowledge*, New York, Routledge & Kegan Paul.

State, S.A. (1985) 'Text and Context: Skinner, Hobbes and Theistic Natural Law', *Hist J, 28:1*, 27–50.

Staughton, L. (1969) 'Historical Past and Existential Present', in T. Roszak (ed.), *The Dissenting Academy*, London, Chatto & Windus,

92–11.

Stern, F. (1960) *Varieties of History*, London, Thames & Hudson (New York, 1956).

Stocker, M. (1995) in *Shakespeare Yearbook*, VI.

Stolnitz, J. (1961) 'Beauty: Some Stages in the History of an Idea', *J Hist Ideas, 22:2*, 185–204.

Storing, H.J. (1962) *Essays on the Scientific Study of Politics*, New York, Holt, Rinehart & Winston.

Strauss, L. (1936) (1952c) *The Political Philosophy of Hobbes: Its Basis and Its Genesis*, trans. E.M. Sinclair, Oxford (1st edn), Chicago (2nd edn).

—— (1945) 'On Classical Political Philosophy', *Soc Res, 12:1*, 98–117, reprinted in Strauss (1959).

—— (1948) *On Tyranny: An Interpretation of Xenophon's 'Hiero'*, New York, Free Press.

—— (1949) 'Political Philosophy and History', *J Hist Ideas, 10:1*, 30–50, reprinted in Strauss (1959a).

—— (1950) 'Natural Right and the Historical Approach', *Review of Politics, 12:4*, 422–42, reprinted in Strauss (1953).

—— (1952a) *Persecution and the Art of Writing*, Glencoe, IL, Free Press.

—— (1952b) 'On Collingwood's Philosophy of History', *Rev Metaph, 5:4*, 559–86.

—— (1952c) See 1936.

—— (1953) *Natural Right and History*, Chicago, Chicago University Press.

—— (1957) 'What is Political Philosophy?', *J Polit, 19:1*, 343–68. Extended form in Strauss (1959a).

—— (1958) *Thoughts on Machiavelli*, Glencoe, IL, Free Press.

—— (1959a) *What is Political Philosophy? and Other Studies*, New York, Free Press.

—— (1959b) 'The Liberalism of Classical Political Philosophy', *Rev Metaph, 12:3*, 390–439, reprinted in Strauss (1968).

—— (1964a) *The City and Man*, Chicago, Rand McNally.

—— (1964b) 'The Crisis of Our Time' and 'The Crisis of Political Philosophy' in H.J. Spaeth (ed.), *The Predicament of Modern Politics*, Detroit.

—— (1965) *Spinoza's Critique of Religion*, trans. E.M. Sinclair, New York, Shocken Books.

—— (1966) *Socrates and Aristophanes*, New York, Basic Books.

—— (1968) *Liberalism, Ancient and Modern*, New York, Basic Books.

—— (1970) *Xenophon's Socratic Discourse: An Interpretation of the*

Oeconomicus, with a new literal translation of the *Oeconomicus* by Carnes Lord, Ithaca, Cornell University Press.

—— (1975a) *The Argument and the Action of Plato's Laws*, Chicago, University of Chicago Press.

—— (1975b) *Political Philosophy*, New York, Pegasus.

Strauss, L. and J. Cropsey (eds) (1963) *History of Political Philosophy*, Chicago, Rand McNally.

Sullivan, V.B. (1992) 'Machiavelli's Momentary "Machiavellian Moment": A Reconsideration of Pocock's Treatment of *The Discourses*', *Polit Theory, 20:2*, 309–18.

Tarlton, C.D. (1973) 'Historicity, Meaning and Revisionism in the Study of Political Thought', *Hist Theor, 22:3*, 307–28.

Teggart, F.J. (1960) *Theory and Processes of History*, Berkeley.

Thomas, K. (1965) 'The Social Origins of Hobbes's Political Thought', in Brown (1965).

Toynbee, A. (1945) *A Study of History*, 3d edn, New York, Oxford University Press.

Trainor, B.T. (1988) 'Warrender and Skinner on Hobbes', *Pol Stud, 36*, 680–91.

Trevor-Roper, H.R. (1967) *Religion, the Reformation and Social Change*, London, Macmillan.

Tricaud, F. (1979) 'Quelques éléments sur la question de l'accès aux textes dans les études hobbiennes', *Revue Internationale de Philosophie, 129*, 393–414.

Tuck , R. (1985) 'Warrender's *De Cive*', *Pol Stud, 33*, 308–15.

Tully, J. (1988) *Meaning and Content: Quentin Skinner and His Critics*, Cambridge, Polity.

Von Wright, G.H. (1971) *Explanation and Understanding*, Ithaca, NY, Routledge & Kegan Paul.

Walsh, W.H. (1942) 'The Intelligibility of History', *Philosophy, 17:4*, 128–43.

—— (1951) *Introduction to the Philosophy of History*, London.

—— (1975) 'The Causation of Ideas', *Hist Theor, 14:1*, 186–99.

—— (1978) Review of Isaiah Berlin's *Two Studies in the History of Ideas, MIND, 87:2*, 284–5.

Warrender, H. (1978) 'Thomas Hobbes: The Collected Works, and a Note on a New Critical Edition', *Rivista Critica di Storia Della Filosofia, 33*, 242–46.

Watkins, F.M. (1964) *The Age of Ideology, Political Thought, 1750 to the Present*, Englewood Cliffs, NJ.

Watkins, J.W.N. (1955) 'Review of Perez Zagorin's *A History of Political Thought in the English Revolution*', *Pol Stud, 3:1*, 79–80.

Wellmer, A. (1979) Review of Richard Bernstein's *The Restructuring of Social and Political Theory*, *Hist Theor, 18:1*, 84–103.

Whitaker, M. (1988) 'Hobbes's View of the Reformation', *Hist Pol Thought, 9:1*, 45–58 (spring).

White, M. (1965) *The Foundations of Historical Knowledge*, New York.

Whitehead, A.N. (1925) *Science and the Modern World*, London.

—— (1933) *Adventures of Ideas*, Cambridge, Cambridge University Press.

Wiener, J.M. (1974) 'Quentin Skinner's Hobbes', *Polit Theory, 2:3*, 251–60 (Aug.).

Wiener, P.P. (1946) 'Logical Significance of the History of Thought', *J Hist Ideas, 7:3*, 366–74.

—— (1961) 'Some Problems and Methods in the History of Ideas', *J Hist Ideas, 22:4*, 531–49.

Wilkins, B.P. (1978) *Has History any Meaning?*, Hassocks, Sussex, Harvester Press.

Wilson, F.G. (1949) Review of John Bowles, *Western Political Thought: An Historical Introduction from the Origins to Rousseau*, *Amer Pol Sci Rev, 43:3*, 606–7.

—— (1953) Review of Eric Voegelin, *The New Science of Politics, An Introductory Essay*, *Amer Pol Sci Rev, 47:2*, 542–3.

Winch, P. (1958, 1963) *The Idea of A Social Science*, London, Routledge.

Wolin, S.S. (1961) *Politics and Vision: Continuity and Innovation in Western Political Thought*, London, Allen & Unwin.

—— (1963) 'Essays on the Scientific Study of Politics', *Amer Pol Sci Rev, 57:1*, 125–60.

—— (1969) 'Political Theory as a Vocation', *Amer Pol Sci Rev, 58:4*, 1062–82.

Wood, N. (1973) Review of L. Strauss and J. Cropsey, *History of Political Philosophy, Polit Theory, 1:3*, 341–3.

—— (1978) 'The Social History of Political Theory', *Polit Theory, 6:3*, 345–69.

—— (1980) 'Thomas Hobbes and the Crisis of the English Aristocracy', *Hist Pol Thought, 1:3*, 437–52 (Dec.).

Zagorin, P. (1985) 'Clarendon and Hobbes', *J Mod Hist, 57*, 593–616 (Dec.).

Index